Tantra
The Cult of the Feminine

Tantra

The Cult of the Feminine

André Van Lysebeth

WEISER BOOKS
San Francisco, CA / Newburyport, MA

First published in English in 1995 by
Red Wheel/Weiser, LLC
York Beach, ME
With offices at:
500 Third Street, Suite 230
San Francisco, CA 94107
www.redwheelweiser.com

Library of Congress Cataloging-in-Publication Data
Lysebeth, André van.
    [Culte de la féminité. English]
    Tantra : the cult of the feminine / André van Lysebeth.
        p.   cm.
    Includes bibliographical references and index.
    1. Tantrism. 2. Sex—Religious aspects—Tantrism. 3. Shaktism.
    I. Title
    BL 1283.842.C8513 1995
    294.5'514—dc20   95-17217
                                                          CIP
ISBN 0-87728-845-3

Translated by André Van Lysebeth and Lore Dobler.

Cover art is a pastel on paper titled "Mistress of the Floating Grove" by Richard
Stodart. Copyright © 1995 Richard Stodart. Used by permission.

Typeset in 10 point Palatino.

Printed in the United States of America
EB

10 09 08 07 06
8   7   6   5   4   3

The paper used in this publicarion meets all the minimum requirements of the
American National Standard for Information Sciences—Permanence of Paper for
Printed Library Materials Z39.48-1992 (R1997).

Table of Contents

Part 2—Human Sexuality: The Other View

Part 3—Myths and Symbols

Part 4—The Tantric Ritual

Part 5—Sexual Control

Part 6—Tantra for Our World

Introduction

Human beings originated, according to modern anthropology, somewhere in Africa. But, being hunter gatherers, humans migrated north and first of all settled around the Mediterranean. Some tribes started populating Spain, France, etc. while other tribes wandered to the Middle East. As hunter-gatherers, humans lived on the food they found in their environment. This went on for hundreds of thousands of years. Then came the neolithic revolution: humans started to *produce* food. In the Middle East, agriculture had been developed—and as we are told through the anthropologists—by women. Becoming agriculturists meant to become, at least, semi-settlers. The invention of farming had a great influence on the position of women in the tribal society. They embodied the mystery of life, since they gave birth, thus allowing the tribe not only to survive, but to grow, and when women started producing more food through farming, their status still rose. Women became the object of a cult and the innumerable statuettes representing women found in Europe and everywhere proves this. Society became matriarchal and the Great Mother-Goddess is humanity's first religion.

But some other tribes, too, made their neolithic revolution; i.e., started to produce their own food. Being hunters, they went northward to follow the herds, and invented cattle-raising, which made plenty of food available. Being hunters, they had to devise arms not only to kill the game (horses, stags, wild boars), but dangerous animals as well, like bears, and eventually human beings; the hunters became warriors. For raising cattle they had to move in order to find more pastureland. From the cold, high north, they had to migrate southward, and met other cattle-raising tribes. To steal other tribe's cattle was fun and profit, but meant war. They killed the enemy warriors, enslaving the women, whom they shared as parts of the loot. Soon the cattle-raisers found out that by having fifty ewes but no ram, nothing happened, but as soon as they added even one ram, soon they could see results. This fact gave the male priority over the female. Society became centered on the warrior and the male: the organization became patriarchal and pyramidal. Their gods were deified heroes. Those tribal men were strong, brave, but reckless warriors, with the chief of the tribe at their head. Today our social organizations are the very copy of this plan.

Meanwhile, the farming tribes slowly migrated peacefully from their Mediterranean and Middle-East homes to the Indus Valley. Migrating, they mixed with local tribes and people, and in India, they mixed with aboriginals who already had started creating cities and ports. Mixing the migrating farming tribes with the aboriginal ones made the Dravidian race, who developed around 3000 B.C., the Indus Valley civilization, which became an empire with hundreds of cities, some having a population of thirty to forty thousand souls. They became highly civilized. Their cities were very comfortable. Practically each house had its own well and bathroom. Unlike, for instance, the ancient Egyptians, they did not raise huge buildings, like temples, palaces, or pyramids, but had a clever sewage system. Remember, 18th-century Paris had no sewage system. Their cities were plagued by the floods of the Indus, and each time they rebuilt the houses on the old foundations. They built the harbor of Lothal which could handle up to fifty ships. They were bold sailors, and, for instance, traded with Ancient Egypt, Syria, Sumer, and many other countries.

On the other hand, the barbaric patriarchal tribes, the Aryans, invaded India from the north, in order to find pastures for their huge herds. They started to conquer the Indus Empire, which was vast— 1,500 miles square. It took a couple of centuries to conquer the Indus Valley people. When the conquest was over, the Aryans imposed their patriarchal organization. The population became divided into four classes: first, the Brahmins or priests, followed by the Kshattrias or warrior-class, their chiefs became kings (Rajas or Maharajas), the third class were the Vaishyas, or dealers, landlords, usurers. The fourth were the defeated Dravidians, the Shudras, i.e., slaves whose only right was to serve faithfully the three upper classes. This division into classes is rigid and strictly racial. No one can enter a class except by being born into it. The unsubmitted tribes, living in the jungles, forests, and other out of the way places were outlawed by the Aryan society, and became the Untouchables, who did not even have the status of true human beings.

The invaders destroyed the Indus Valley civilization and after many dark centuries, a new brahmanical civilization arose, and the Vedic religion, with its innumerable sacrifices to the gods, became the religion of the conquerors. The Shudras, or slaves, were strictly forbidden to listen even to Rig Vedic hymns. In fact, the Rig Veda is the mythologized narrative of the cruel war of attrition fought by the invading Aryans against the Dravidians. In the Rig Veda, the Aryan warriors were the gods, their Dravidian opponents, the demons. The slaves were allowed to have their own old religion and modern Hinduism originates from the blending of the two cults.

Many centuries later, the Aryans succeeded in totally wiping out the Indus civilization; not only eradicating the cities, but making them literally disappear under the surface of the earth, and any recollection of this civilization sank into oblivion in the memory of their descendants, the slaves. The Aryans, for centuries, made the entire world believe that when their ancestors, the "good" Aryans, invaded India, around 1500 B.C., they found the country only populated with savage aboriginals, whom they civilized. In 1925 however, this legend came to an end, when the British wanted to build a railroad to Lahore. The two English civil engineers in charge of this task were in trouble because in the plains they could not find stones to ballast the railroad. An Indian foreman told them, "You want ballast? No problem: under the mound you see up there are bricks by the millions." It was true! Amidst the bricks they found small carved objects with an unknown script, the famous Indus seals. The engineers had the intuition that they had, by pure chance, discovered the very old artifacts from an unknown and forgotten civilization. Archeologists came and dug out the cities of Mohenjo-Daro and Harappa, and still later, many more forgotten cities.

Knowing this, one understands that modern India is not a true monolithic society, but a conflictual one, tense with the relentless opposition between the matrifocal tantrics together with the descendants of the previous civilization, against the foreign, Vedic, brahmanical, patriarchal society, imposed on the Indian people by the power of war. Tantra originates from the pre-Aryan era, and is set against this patriarchal Aryan, oppressive system. The invasion of India by the barbaric Aryan tribes was a blast, but the counter-blast is to come when the shudras, becoming aware of their power, will no longer tolerate this. And this counter-blast could change the face of the world. Bearing the above mentioned facts in mind will make some statements included in this book readily intelligible, and explain why the brahmanical society is male-oriented and tantra the exact opposite!

With this brief history in mind, modern readers will have a new understanding of the concepts of tantra. This book takes the old theories and brings them into the modern world.

Part 1

The Tantric Outlook

Defining Tantra

Indian thinkers have the excellent habit of first defining the terms they intend to use. Defining *Tantra* is both indispensable and arduous given its myriad possible meanings, each with its own particular nuance. Depending on the context, *Tantra* means a shuttle (in weaving), the warp (of a fabric), continuity, succession, descendence, a continuous process, the carrying out of a ceremony, a system, a theory, doctrine, a scientific opus, or a section in a book. *Tantra* is also a mystical and magical doctrine or any piece of work based on such a doctrine.

According to S. N. Dasgupta, since *tan* comes from *tantri*, to explain, to expound, to expose, *Tantra* also refers to a treatise on a given subject. Consequently, the word *Tantra* is often found in the titles of books the contents of which have nothing to do with Tantrism, the reverse being just as true.

Today, for the Indian population at large, Tantra refers to any non-Vedic doctrine or cult. This highlights the antinomy, the fundamental antagonism, even, between the Aryan-Vedic-Brahminical system and Tantra.

In this book, I shall use the word *Tantra* to refer to a body of millenia-old doctrines and above all, practices. Some question this on the basis of the fact that the word was coined toward the sixth century A.D., which is not untrue. Nevertheless, equating the origin of Tantrism with its name's is rather specious: the word "sex" (from the Latin *sexus*, and the root *sectus* = separation, distinction) came into use as late as the 12th century A.D. But evidence points to an earlier origin of the act.

Tantra also means a "loom" or "weaving" which would seem to bear no relation with any form of doctrine. But Tantra perceives the universe as a fabric where everything is interrelated, interconnected, where everything impacts on everything else. If you add the instrumentality suffix *tra* to the radical *tan* (to stretch, to spread, to expand), you get *tan-tra*, literally, the *instrument to expand* the field of ordinary consciousness in order to reach supraconsciousness, the root of one's being and the wellspring of unknown powers that Tantra seeks to awaken and harness.

What is Here, is Elsewhere.
What is not Here, is Nowhere

These few deceptively simple words—an excerpt from the *Vishvasâra Tantra*—contain the very essence of Tantra. Their apparent simplicity belies breathtaking implications which dissolve the borders of our reassuring world of the senses and lead us to the very heart of the most Real of Realities.

But first, back to basics, that is, matter—understood in the contemporary sense: condensed energy—the homogeneity of which is expressed in the words of the title. For Tantra, all of the myriad energy forms in the universe—gravity, nuclear cohesion, electromagnetism, etc.—exist throughout the cosmos including right here where I am now sitting. Although post-Einsteinian generations generally accept the idea, we do tend to dismiss the "matter-energy" proposition to the realm of nuclear physics.

In so doing we fail to recognize that something gets lost in the translation: compact matter is thus reduced to single pure cosmic energy in spite of the multitudinous objects we perceive around us. Scientifically speaking, the universe is a gigantic continuum ranging from sub-atomic to astronomical dimensions. Tantrists have perceived this unity for over thirty-five centuries: no small achievement for people armed only with their senses, their intelligence and above all their intuition. Yet in our daily lives, this knowledge leaves our relationship with objects unchanged: for our senses, a grain of sand remains a grain of sand, a galaxy, a cluster of stars.

In dealing with life, the words of the title—*What is here, is elsewhere*—totally disrupt our habitual concepts in stating that life is present *throughout* the universe or even better (or worse?) that the universe itself is alive! The mind boggles: one can no longer live as if the earth alone supported life! Of course, many astronomers believe that in the billions of galaxies each containing billions of stars—there are more suns in the *known* universe than there are grains of sand on all of the beaches of our planet—there must be other planetary systems, other inhabited worlds. Organic matter has been found in meteorites. An interesting prospect, but the probability of life elsewhere fails to move us since we have no hope of ever contacting those undoubtedly very strange beings who live on planets uncounted light-years away from Earth.

Astronomers at the Kitt Peak National Observatory have stated that our galaxy might contain far more inhabitable planets than previously thought. A study of 123 stars belonging to the same thermal class as our sun shows orbital variations implying the presence of planets. Since our galaxy alone contains a hundred billion suns, even if one star out of ten had planets that would mean we are far from being alone in the universe, not to mention the millions of observable galaxies! Such remote possibilities notwithstanding, we in the West conceive of the universe as an enormous, frozen, and dead machine.

For Tantra, on the contrary, the universe is alive, each star is alive in the total sense of the word, and so it has a form of consciousness, just like each infinitesimal subnuclear particle. Conscious stars and atoms—mind-boggling, indeed! And this universal life which is One, is subdivided into innumerable planes of existence and consciousness! It is even present in the interstellar vacuum, according to Tantra. Unthinkable? Perhaps, but the vastness of the universe *is* unthinkable! Even for astronomers whose daily fare it is to think in terms of hundreds of thousands of light-years, these enormous distances are unimaginable and yet they are *real*! In Sanskrit, this gigantic cosmic being is called *Mahat*, the Great One. (*Mahat* is a Tantric concept first adapted then adopted by the classical non-Tantric Indian philosophy called *Samkhya*.)

Tantra views life as an ongoing process in space and in time, with no gap, hiatus or separation between any of the life forms, from viruses to Mahat.

I am part of the Whole and as such I am involved in the Whole and in the entire process. The cosmic energy continuum goes hand in hand with the continuum of life, the two being indissociable.

Tantra holds that the universe is both Consciousness and Energy, which in practical terms entails total respect for all life forms, be they animal, plant, or bacterial. It follows that harming any life form means harming one's own: ecology thus acquires a cosmic dimension.

But this also leads to contradictions, at least on the surface of it. On the one hand each blade of grass is just as important as a human being, but if a nuclear holocaust were to eradicate all life on our planet or blow it to smithereens, the explosion would barely be a scratch on the universe. However, the reverse is just as true and a statement by the British astronomer and physicist Eddington comes to mind: "a vibrating electron shakes the universe."

Let's go a step further: "Life" implies consciousness. Among our very few certainties, one is extremely dear to our individual consciousness: *cogito ergo sum*. In the famous phrase, "I think, therefore I am," the word "think" poses a problem. Germs may be denied the faculty to think, that is, possessing structured thought patterns, and humans seen as the only beings endowed with such a faculty, and yet one cannot deny that the former do perceive their own existence and environment and are therefore conscious entities. Evidence of this is found in the fact that unicellular beings can be conditioned, like amoebae, for example. So let us begin with the only truly undeniable fact: consciousness—although its source and nature may be a mystery to us, let's follow its path.

Let's assume for a moment that no one anywhere in the universe on any level or any plane is conscious: the universe would cease to exist!

But I, as an individual, have the feeling that first of all, my own personal consciousness is isolated from other minds, human or animal, and that secondly, it is located in my brain and thirdly, it is isolated from the rest of my body deemed to be unconscious. Tantra holds that each cell is a living being, that it is totally conscious, endowed with a mind, with emotions, and memory. Not some kind of vague or remote perception, but a form of awareness that is just as clear as cortical consciousness. Without a nervous system or a brain, a cell (or a microbe) develops its own world view that is a far cry from the one produced by the cortex, but in its own way and with its own capacities the cell is one hundred percent aware of its environment as well as of itself and its emotions. And so a cell can be happy, sad, or anxious, etc.

My Whole Body is Conscious

Consciousness no longer belongs to the brain alone, it becomes a property of the entire body. If consciousness and/or spirit exist in my brain—*what is here, is elsewhere*—they also permeate my entire body. The body is no longer a carcass, a burden, an obstacle to spiritual life, or—at best—a "faithful companion": spirituality exists at each and every level of my body.

The idea is breathtaking: *knowing* that one is made up of cellular individuals that are all alive and conscious, communicating with one another. There is no clearcut delineation between my cerebral consciousness and the consciousness of my cells, but a hierarchy of planes of consciousness reacting to one another. If in my mind I am optimistic, relaxed, happy, this feeling will permeate my entire body, right down to the very last cell in my toe, for example! And vice versa, affording my cells proper living conditions will make them happy, optimistic, and serene: and in my mind, in my brain, I will feel a kind of well being and energy the origin of which I fail to grasp. If, on the contrary, due to improper habits, I have fallen ill, each cell will have to become healthy before I am really cured. However, in order to be well once again, I can rely on the Higher Wisdom of the body, inherent in each and every cell, and on the "blind" devotion of each individual member of the cellular republic, on the condition that I afford it the material conditions to express and manifest itself. In case of illness, "talking" to one's cells—and conjuring up the adequate mental imagery—mobilizes our cellular task force, the white corpuscles, and boosts our immune system!

Tantra sees the body as a living temple. For centuries, the West has been caught up in the drama of opposing the flesh and the spirit, whereas for Tantra there is no border between the two, nor are they intrinsically different. Good health, far from being a luxury or a lucky draw, becomes a prime duty. A head-of-state unconcerned about his/her citizens' well-being would be remiss in fulfilling his/her most important task. And as far as "little ole me" is concerned, I who over-see billions of cellular individuals, my task is first and foremost to ensure the integrity, the good health, and the happiness of my cellular republic in general, and of each cell in particular. A way of achieving this is through Hatha Yoga, which logically and naturally stemmed from Tantra.

Let's go a step further! *What is here, is elsewhere. What is not here, is nowhere*: an unknown and unknowable force of which my ego is unaware generates the universe on a constant basis. According to Tantra, creation is not a single act that took place all of a sudden at the beginning of time. It is a permanent process (for the Kabbala as well). *Creation is happening here and now*. The creative energy that generates the universe is *actually present throughout the cosmos*, conse-quently in my own body, in my brain, in my cells. The cosmic forces which fashion life according to changing local circumstances are pre-sent here and now and I am an integral part of it all. At any given moment of my life a mysterious force is at work creating my body. It is the same mysterious force as the one creating the universe: aka kundalini.

Allow me a small digression: fortunately, Tantra is not a religion and so its world view does not conflict with the various religions of the world: one can be monotheistic and Tantric at the same time! Yet, if I belong to a given religion, it will take on a new dimension, enriched by the Tantric outlook. If God exists, then He is present here and now. *What is not here, is nowhere*, and if He is not here, then He exists nowhere else. Could a devout person conceive of a "hole" somewhere in the universe where there would be no God? A Tantric religious person does not think of his or her God as living somewhere up in Heaven, he or she feels His presence here and now, he or she lives "in" God. On the other hand, a Tantric non-believer acquires an extraordinarily enriched vision of the world.

Pascal, the French philosopher, felt that human beings are minuscule specks of dust hanging between two fearful abysses: the infinitely great and the infinitely small. A Tantrist feels the same thing, except that he/she feels linked to the two infinites, and that makes a world of difference!

The Tantric view shatters borders, or rather dissolves them, for they exist only in the mind. Strictly materially speaking, and except for my senses, there is no clearcut border between the various objects around me. For the physicist, matter is mainly a void where here and there clouds of electrons spin around the nucleus of an atom. This void is so considerable that if our planet were compressed so that all its atoms touched one another, it would fill a thimble! Inconceivable, but real: each and every second I am being bombarded by high energy particles from the outer reaches of the cosmos going through my entire body without touching a single atomic nucleus. It's worse than being a sieve! A hypothetical astronaut riding such a particle would distinguish no border at all between me and my chair; it would be like going through two energy clouds, two energy fields in contact with each other.

Does contending that consciousness is an ever-present dimension of the universe mean that a radiator, for example, is self- aware, as a radiator? Does a radiator feel bored, all alone in a room, is it happy or unhappy? The idea does seem far-fetched! What does Tantra make of it? Well, when the science of physics asserts that the universe *is* energy, that is already half of the Tantric concept whereby the cosmos = consciousness + energy. This means that any organized unit has a level of consciousness, including an atom or an electron. A few scientists, such as Jean Charron have flirted with this idea without going "all the way." Tantra holds that each atom of the radiator is coupled with a field of consciousness but the radiator as an *object*—a mere molecular aggregate without any kind of organic unity—has no single consciousness integrating the whole.

Modern physics has come close to this consciousness-energy unity, though its laws, such as the Boyle-Mariotte law predicting with great accuracy the behavior of a gas, give the impression that matter is blindly mechanical. Actually these laws are only *statistically* accurate and are valid only when applied to a large number of atoms (a mere centimeter of air contains billions of atoms, for example). However, the behavior of an isolated subatomic particle is indeterminate, "as if" it were guided by some form of intelligence. Delete "as if" and you have the cosmos-consciousness-energy concept symbolized by the Shiva-Shakti couple.

What is meant by the assertion that consciousness is a *dimension* of the universe? In this context, a dimension is understood as a component of the universe whose disappearance would automatically entail the disappearance of the cosmos itself. Let's be more specific: in measuring a beam, I may "forget" its height and say that it is a two-dimensional surface of, say, 6 feet by 2 inches. But this abstraction is only possible in my own mind. In actual fact, it would be impossible: eliminating one dimension automatically eliminates the other two. If in wanting to do away with its height, I wanted to plane it down until its thickness equaled zero, my last stroke would do away with its height, width and length all at once! The beam would have disappeared! And Tantra adds yet another dimension to the four of space-time: consciousness, the total suppression of which would make the universe disappear. In this particular context, I could have used the word "component" instead of "dimension" without changing basic Tantric thought. But the word "component" refers to a part sometimes isolated from the whole, whereas "dimension" is both abstract and concrete.

It must be pointed out that this is neither a dogma nor a precondition to Tantric *practice*. On the contrary, this view comes as a by-product as I discover that "I" am structured, organized consciousness-energy.

Tantra is not Dogma

Fortunately, Tantra espouses no dogma. However, this does not mean that a follower of Tantra must perforce reject his/her beliefs. If his/her chosen religion expounds dogmas, that's fine and well but Tantra expounds none! Tantra involves *inter alia* a search for reality and contradicts neither science nor religion. Nobody is forced to swallow the idea of consciousness permeating the entire material universe. It must be noted, however, that for Tantra, consciousness is not a supernatural metaphysical principle but a *fundamental property* of the material universe, in the wider sense of the term.

A Tantrist does not perceive himself/herself as cut-off from other beings, lost on a tiny planet, a mere speck of cosmic dust hurled into the frozen interstellar infinite. He/she knows himself/herself to be part and parcel of life from its very origins, in all its myriad forms and that life is an ongoing and conscious process embracing the entire universe. This is not, however, the equivalent of the much wider concept of "God"!

The idea that life and a certain form of consciousness exist at the sub-atomic level emerges now and again in the West, even in unimpeachable scientific circles. In an article published in April 1964 in the well-known British scientific magazine *Nature*, Professor D. F. Lawden suggests that for an outside observer, the electrical and gravitational characteristics of a particle reflect their mental qualities. Lawden provides evidence of the relativity of life and death: how can one know if a virus or a corpse is dead or alive? Without going so far as to accept the idea of a transcending life force, he does consider that a "materialist" scientist has to accept the continuity of life and consciousness in one form or another, down to the level of elementary particles. At the time, the idea created an uproar in the scientific community; however, it has not been disproven!

A Nobel prize winner for chemistry, Ilya Prigogine (quoted by Larry Dossey in *Space, Time & Medicine*, Boston, 1982, p. 83), once stated: "Here is the very essence of my message.... Matter is not inert. It is alive and active. Life is constantly changing in order to adapt to conditions of non-equilibrium. As the idea of a deterministic universe is swept aside, we can now gain control of our own fate, for better or for worse."

According to Prigogine, this means that first, matter is not restricted to our tiny planet, that the entire universe is "alive and active"; and second, that life, undergoing constant change, is inconceivable without consciousness, which is in keeping with Tantra.

Another scientist must be mentioned in this regard: the Swiss physicist Wolfgang Pauli who discovered that the electrons orbiting an atomic nucleus each settle at a given level of energy thereby excluding other electrons. This is known as Pauli's "exclusion principle" for which he was awarded the Nobel prize. When applied to crystals, his principle explains the way transistors work. All of this is fine and well but how does it tie in with Tantra? For Pauli, the mystery lies in the following question: *how* does the electron know that a given energy level is already occupied? Obviously, electrons are not like balls on a pool table, bumping into one another or falling into a pocket! There is no latch on a particular energy level that locks the door or says "occupied," like in the powder room! No mechanical model, no mechanistic system has heretofore explained this phenomenon and it would appear that electrons are informed of the fact—believe it or not—without having to go through time or space! For Pauli, who also worked with another Swiss, C. G. Jung, the phenomena of magic, alchemy and parapsychology are no more bizarre than the behavior of the elementary particles of "matter," and therefore, of energy.

It must be reaffirmed that the Tantric outlook does not rest upon or require the intervention of a transcending principle. According to Tantra, life, consciousness, the mind are all various aspects of cosmic

Abel Glance
Translator of the Invisible

C'est à l'instant précis où les
hommes prirent les empreintes différentes
de l'atome que les étoiles fondirent
en larmes.

L'Homme venait de découvrir
leurs secrets. Il n'y a pas d'en
haut. il n'y a pas d'en-bas. Il n'y a
rien de grand. Il n'y a rien de petit.
Les yeux se sont trompés depuis qu'ils
se sont entichés en remontant des
profondeurs marines. Les oreilles se
sont trompées. Il faut tout recommencer,
autrement. Ce sont les larmes, d'étoiles
qui me l'apprennent. Comment le saisir?
C'est une histoire bien incolorée que
j'essaierai de raconter quelque jour.
Si les mots clés des traductions de
l'invisible veulent bien m'obéir.

Abel Glance
1955.

A ma chère Nelly que seule, je
comprends

energy. They may be more or less subtle, but they are just as concrete, just as material as gravitation or electromagnetism.

Towards the end of the 19th century, the Viennese author Ludwig Anzengruber, mentioned earlier, wrote in colloquial German in *Die Kreuzelschreiber*: "*Es kann dir nichts geschehen. Du gehörst zu dem allem und dös alles gehört zu dir! Es kann dir nichts geschehen!*" which could be rendered in English as: Nothing can ever happen to you. You belong to all of this and all of this belongs to you. Nothing can happen to you.

Such certainty brings total serenity and can be achieved through meditation. Meditation also enables one to perceive the infinite potentialities within oneself, that is, the potentialities of the creative cosmic forces that are at work throughout the universe.

Actually, Tantric thought is quite natural and straightforward. But our prejudices, our preconceived ideas, our own senses (the veil of Maya, Illusion!) conceal it all from us. Both a visionary and a poet— surprisingly—Abel Gance, usually known solely as a film director, was a Tantrist without realizing it. In a letter he wrote to his sister in 1955, he said:

At the very moment man fingerprinted the atom, the stars began to weep.

Man had just discovered their secrets. There is no more up, there is no more down. Nothing is great, nothing is small. Our eyes have misled us ever since they cast their first glance while emerging from the depths of the sea. Our ears are mistaken. We have to start everything anew, do things *differently*. The tears of the stars have told me so. How do I know? It's a strange story that I may try to tell one day if I can ever grasp the keywords needed to translate this from the invisible.

To my dear Nelly who is the *only one* who can understand."

This letter is both cosmic and Tantric. Stars shedding tears? A ridiculous notion for our horse sense which would just shrug this off as yet another literary flight of fancy. But if the universe is endowed with consciousness, right to the very heart of stars, then this takes on a real dimension. Abel Gance was probably right when he said that *only* his sister Nelly could understand him, that is, as compared to the average Westerner. But Tantra provides us with the secret key to decipher his text which is more profound and condensed than many philosophical essays. I have often read and reread this text and pondered over the meaning of each word, with emotion. Especially when Abel Gance writes that we have to start anew, do things *differently*.

While such ideas might be tolerated if expressed by an artist or a poet, they appear to be the antithesis of the realistic and objective views held by science, at least for the time being. For there seems to be emerging here and there from within the scientific community itself, new ideas and trends indicative of change.

Evidence of this can be found in a book full of solid scientific arguments, *The Intelligent Universe*, written by the British astrophysicist, mathematician and biologist Fred Hoyle, whose views clash with the common Western idea according to which the universe being mere matter is *perforce* neither intelligent nor conscious. Asserting that consciousness exists at the interstellar level is at loggerheads with a certain form of obtuse, rationalist thinking.

The West maintains that consciousness prerequires a nervous system and a brain, i.e., a closed system. All right, but what is a brain? The obvious answer is: something made up of billions of nerve cells, each made up of material molecules, comprising billions of atoms. Let us consider the materiality of the brain at the atomic level and see what happens. Incidentally, we have opted for the outdated view espoused by Niels Bohr, in which the infinitely small reproduces the infinitely large, in other words where each atom is a mini solar system, as satellite-electrons gravitate round a nucleus, like planets. Of course, modern physics rejected this model of the atom some time ago, but since what it has to offer today can no longer be visualized, I shall retain Niels Bohr's solar system-atom for the sake of argument.

If I were to imagine that my brain was as large as a galaxy, there would be as great a distance, and therefore void, between its various atoms as between the hundred billion stars of our Milky Way. And if there were a hypothetical lilliputian cosmic traveler passing through this heavenly brain, riding a neutrino, it would not dawn upon him/her that the galaxy was actually thinking with all of its star-atoms. Yet that is what is actually occurring here and now in my own skull: thinking takes place thanks to my innumerable billion atomic constellations. This atomic galaxy is not static for there are constant sub-atomic constellation changes and exchanges happening all the time. So if I can think with my own atomic galaxies, why cannot Mahat, the Great One, think with stars? The former proposition is no more absurd than the latter.

Is a Tree Conscious?

Tantra believes that a tree is much more than just a source of timber or boards, it is a living being. A Tantrist does not feel separated or removed from a tree or a forest. "Normal" man or woman may admit that a tree is alive—the contrary would be difficult to prove—, but he or she does not see a living being in the tree, unlike some African tribes where men talk to the "spirit of the tree" before felling it. They dance around the tree telling it that they absolutely need it to make a dug-out and they promise that they will put it to good use! Of course, some people might condescendingly dismiss this as an animistic practice good for "primitive" peoples. Naturally, nobody claims or assumes that a tree is capable of rational thinking. Nevertheless, it does have a kind of consciousness, according to Tantra, even if our intellect deems this inconceivable. Plants are said to possess emotions and members of the Findhorn community talk directly to their plants, they send them love and the plants grow much better! And we're not talking about India or even something that belongs to the remote past, but taking place today, in Scotland.

Of course you don't have to believe in this to practice Tantra. Tantra holds no dogmas, and there is no prerequisite or act of faith required to practice it. Nevertheless, *"what is here, is elsewhere. What is not here, is nowhere,"* has straightforward and direct implications. For all of the secrets of life and death, of creation and of the dissolution of universes are all present right here, in my own body. (Notice that I did not say: "restricted to my body."). So what's the point of traveling all over the world, of going to the Himalayas or elsewhere to discover what is true and real, since I can find it right here. You don't need a microscope or telescope to discover the hidden essence of the world. Somewhere deep down in my cells "I" handle energies and subatomic particles like our ancestors did millions of years before modern human beings fingerprinted the stars, to use the words of Abel Gance.

Giordano Bruno

The place is Rome, the date, February the 17th, 1600, in the Campo dei Fiori, the square of Flowers. As gray as winter's last dying days, a lazy plume of smoke rises from the embers which have just consumed Giordano Bruno, a defrocked Dominican monk, and a remarkable visionary. He was a true Tantrist although he did not realize it. He could have escaped the stake by merely confessing his "errors," but he chose to be burned alive rather than renounce his beliefs. He spent seven years in a Roman prison after being arrested and put in irons at the behest of Pope Clement VIII. In spite of this, his head was full of stars and spinning atoms, and although he discovered or invented nothing, he was five centuries ahead of his time: intuitive genius but also the gravest of errors. The following excerpts reflect his vision and they are pure Tantra:

All of the body of the world is alive.... This table is not endowed with life per se, nor is this dress. However, being natural and composite objects, they possess shape and matter. All things, be they small, be they minute, contain spiritual substance [...] for the spirit is in all things and all corpuscles, however minuscule they may be, contain their share of, and are gifted with, spirit.

It is obvious that each spirit shares a certain continuity with the spirit of the universe...

Birth is the expansion of the center, life is plenitude, and death the contraction at the center.

Everything that exists is One. Knowing this unity is the be-all and the end-all of all philosophies and of natural contemplation. Whosoever has found the One, that is, the reason for this unity, has found the key without which one cannot enter into the true contemplation of nature." (*Planète*, Paris, p. 327)

Giordano Bruno proclaimed the permanent value of natural laws, thereby opening up the universe to the inquisitive eye of science thus freed from the fetters of dogma, but he also put forward the idea that our senses alone cannot grasp reality.

For him, the stars were so many suns that just might be the heart of inhabited planetary systems, like ours. He did not believe the Earth to lie at the center of the universe nor did he believe that it was without movement, thus contradicting Aristotle's cosmogony, still the law of the land.

For him the atom was a replica of the solar system, just like Niels Bohr was to conceive of it 350 years later.

He believed in the existence of many worlds.

But, above all, he proclaimed the existence of a diffuse psyche or mind, present even in the most humble elements: a meeting of the minds with another visionary, Teilhard de Chardin, who wrote: "From the biosphere to the species, all is but an immense ramification of psyches searching for one another through forms."

A Tantric Meditation:
Contemplating Our Mother, the Sea

A *meditation*, fine, but why *Tantric*? The answer is simple: although the approach may seem similar, the aims and themes of meditation in general and of Tantra sometimes express conflicting world views!

But let's first see what the two have in common. First, the choice of a comfortable, stable and motionless position in order to disconnect "the outside world" and to look inward. Secondly, contemplation—unlike the rational and discursive approach—is a process aimed at transcending the intellect and waking state consciousness in order to reach the secret inner workings of one's being and perhaps of the universe. That is why *contemplation* is preferable to meditation, the connotation of which is clearly reflective.

But the goals, and therefore the themes, are at variance. And in India they vary according to the movement one may belong to: Vedanta, Buddhism, or Tantra, the three major trends.

Vedanta holds that the manifest, concrete universe is unreal, an illusion (Maya). The only reality is Brahman, the absolute, uncaused Cause. Vedantic meditation calls upon followers to disconnect consciousness from the body and from the manifest world in order to realize that they are illusions and once one has become indifferent to names (*nama*) and to forms (*rupa*), one becomes lost in the Absolute, like surf on the sea. The body is an obstacle. It is to be forgotten, almost denied. For it belongs to the world of phenomena and is therefore unreal. Naturally, the themes of meditation correspond to this vision of the world. This explains Vedantists' ostentatious disregard for their own body and their often poor state of health. And many of them die at a very young age such as Ramana Maharshi (cancer), Ramakrishna (cancer), and Vivekananda (diabetes). However, they are not to be confused with yogis, especially Tantrist yogis for whom the body is sacred, holy.

In Buddhism—which has practically disappeared from Indian soil, its birthplace, for having dared to reject the Hindu pantheon and oppose the Brahmanical caste—contemplation makes up the greater part of worship. By meditating, one aims at attaining a state of emptiness (*nirvâna*) which, paradoxically, is a fullness freeing one from karma and the cycle of endless reincarnations.

Unlike Vedanta, Tantra holds that the universe, with its billions of galaxies, is real. It is constantly emerging from the union of the two ultimate and polar cosmic principles, symbolized by Shiva and Shakti. *"What is here, is elsewhere. What is not here, is nowhere."*

Far from denying or retreating from the concrete universe, a Tantrist becomes part and parcel of it in order to perceive its profound reality, either by spiritualizing sexuality, perceived as the ultimate creative impulse, or by other means such as contemplating our cosmic Mother or the sea of our origins as described below. A Tantrist may unite *concretely* with these cosmic principles with and inside his/her body-universe in order to experience the divinity of intelligent and conscious flesh and bones.

Neutral Contemplation

The following contemplation is neutral for it is universal: it can be
practiced regardless of one's religion or lack thereof. Traditionally, the
sitting position is the *âsana* for meditation, but this time, let us adopt
the fetal position: although the figure on page 19 is straightforward, it
must be pointed out that the crescent shape of the spine is the same as
in our mother's womb. This is an essential point because locked away
somewhere in its memory, our body associates the spinal position
with the fetal state and its richness, which is precisely what one is
seeking to experience anew.

The theme: a landscape at night. In our mind's eye let us imagine a
deserted seashore, several thousand years ago. In front of me stretches
out the immensity of the primeval sea. I may add to the dim twinkling
of the distant stars, a fine crescent moon. All of this is reflected in the
water. I contemplate this eternal view as the crescent slowly becomes
a full moon, thus extracting myself from linear time and entering into
cyclical time.

There is no wind, the night is warm, so is the sea. The ocean is
breathing: a soft wave lingers on the beach, covering it, creating some
foam before retiring back to the ocean. Another wave breaks on the
sand, foaming, then flows back, and so on and so forth. You may have
guessed: breathing will follow the ebb and flow of each wave. As it
rises, I breathe in, as it covers the sand and foams, I hold my breath,
and as it flows back into the sea, I breathe out, waiting a couple of seconds before breathing in again with the following wave. An imaginary OM accompanies the breathing in and breathing out. And so,
lulled by the waves, I become part of *marine life* to the point of perceiving the ocean as a gigantic living body, the cradle of all life and a symbol of the Undifferentiated.

How long should this contemplation last? As long as it feels comfortable.

Then, gradually, the horizon grows lighter and the sky reddens.
Slowly but surely, in all its real splendor, the sun emerges and rises in
the serene, cloudless sky.

I contemplate its orange disk above the horizon as it slowly becomes
spherical. Its soft warmth permeates the air, the water, the sand, and
envelops my body. The morning sun is sheer bliss! And yet, I have not
forgotten the waves in tune with my own breathing in and out, and the
OM. I feel both energized and soothed and when my mind decides to
turn away from the sun and the sea, I shall stop this inner contemplation, open my eyes and sit up—without haste, of course!

If this contemplation takes place at night, the sequence of events
has to be reversed: the sun sets as it drops into the ocean, dusk grows
darker, the quiet and serene night soothes my mind. The full moon

wanes, becomes a crescent and then disappears. And above, the stars and the planets sparkle away and seem to dance on the water. In the secure maternal ocean, life falls into a deep slumber. There is no better way to sleep tight—sweet dreams guaranteed!

But the scene does not have to be set in backward motion. If this "descent into darkness" is not suitable even at night, then the former sequence can be used. And lastly, this contemplation can take place in bed before falling asleep. In this case, it is to be done turned to one side (preferably lying on one's left side) and under the covers: this is even closer to the fetal position than the âsana in the drawing above. This reclining position, on the left side, would theoretically be better than the fetal position if it were not uncomfortable when not in bed.

As a matter of fact, it is likely that I will have fallen asleep before finishing the contemplation, which naturally poses no problem.

The above contemplation is totally divorced from speculative thinking; however, it may be interesting to review its symbolic richness.

A Spate of Evocations

The focal point of this contemplation is the immensity of the ocean and something in me—not my intellect!—*knows* that life began in the ocean, that the sea is my mother, the Mother of us all! If I were to go back in time through the genealogy of mothers, I would be going back through all of human and pre-human evolution and would reach the first unicellular beings in the primeval sea. Among our rare and unquestionable certainties, there is the following undeniable fact: The life beat throbbing here and now in my cells has been passed on without any gap, without a hitch in transmission since its first manifestation on Earth. I am the carrier, the bearer of this eternal life and am carried and borne by it. Could I go so far as to say that I am this universal and eternal life?

Moreover, as a terrestrial mammal, I am under the illusion that the air around me is my natural, vital, environment because if I were submerged under water for any length of time, deprived of air, I would drown. When Jacques Cousteau says that "we are organized seawater," that is literally true. My own lifegiving milieu, the habitat of my hundreds of billions of cells—each one made up of 95 percent water—is actually seawater at the same saline concentration as that of the tropical seas where life began. I am a walking aquarium *and my cells know it*! (A Tantrist meditates and contemplates just as much with and within his/her body as with his/her brain.)

Moreover, I spent the first nine months of my life in amniotic fluid, in the warmth of the womb. While I was in her uterus, my mother breathed for me and the rhythm of her breathing was like the rise and fall of the waves of the sea I now contemplate. In this suggested contemplation, harmony with the Mother is created by grouping three essential elements in the same image: the warm water of the ocean, breathing to the rhythm of the rise and fall of the waves, and the fetal position. Even if my conscious self does not realize it, my unconscious mind gets the message and very slowly the atmosphere of this crucial period of my life is re-created, a time when in my mother's womb I was without ego, without a name or nationality, without possessions and yet endowed with all my potentialities and fully aware. As a citizen of the world not yet belonging to the 20th century, I was without age and my mother was still the Mother.

By the Light of the Silvery Moon

To my knowledge, few people and notably few scientists have raised the following question: "What would our planet and life on earth be without the moon"? They probably had better fish to fry than seeking to answer such a futile and pointless question. We take the moon for granted. Yet it is the sheer luck of the astronomical draw that has endowed our earth with such a satellite. After all, we could have had several or none at all.

But let us raise this "silly" question anyway and not forget that for Tantra, the "water" element, which includes all fluids, picks up all cosmic rhythms. For billions of years now the moon has been controlling and timing the ebb and flow of our vast oceans, massive expanses of water that slowly chisel away at our seashores, but more importantly, became the cradle of life, thus influencing all of our own vital rhythms. Naturally, the sun has an influence, too, but it is eight light-minutes away, whereas the moon is only one light-second away, that is, 480 times closer. So, in spite of the sun's enormous mass, its gravitational pull is only one third of the moon's.

Living matter is actually waterlogged and as such, is extremely sensitive to cosmic rhythms: there are many tides in my own blood and even in my cells! For example, oysters open their valves at specific moments which correspond to the activity of the moon, and therefore, of the tides. In the USA, the "opening" time of oysters on the Atlantic coast differs from that of their sisters in the Pacific. As an experiment, a biologist, Professor Frank Brown, Jr. (Northwestern University, Evanston, Illinois), put East-coast oysters in a tank filled with seawater and placed it halfway between the two oceans. To eliminate the influence of daylight, the tank was placed in a basement and *in total darkness*. Progressively, all of the mollusks adapted to the time the tide would have been if the coast had been at that particular place: this is evidence that living matter perceives the action of the moon which influences our own vital rhythms. Somewhere in the inner recesses of living tissue "something" perceives this action and over the millennia, these lunar rhythms no doubt fashioned all of our biological rhythms.

For example, the influence of the phases of the moon on pinworms and on sleep has been well documented. The moon also regulates plant life through its influence on the rising of sap and also by its light which is polarized, therefore, organized. Farmers of yore knew this very well and their decision to sow or harvest crops depended on the lunar phases. Even in today's nurseries oldtimers know that tree grafts must be done when the moon is waxing, for at that time, its light has a healing effect and promotes growth.

Sea, Moon, and Sun

Nevertheless, Life gets its energy from the sun. Life on our planet became manifest through the union of the ocean and the sun without, however, being generated by this concerted action. For Tantra holds that Life and Consciousness—both indissociable entities—are universal properties, are dimensions of the cosmos and are therefore preexisting. A parallel can be drawn in this respect between Life end electricity: the latter was not *created* when Count Volta developed the first battery, it was merely rendered *manifest*! Life was made manifest thanks to the sun and it draws its vital force from the sun's light and the sun's energy. In order to live, we must "degrade" solar energy and "something" within me knows that too.

Bringing together the sea, moon and sun into a single image produces a very powerful symbolism which, when the fetal position is added, stirs "something" within me. Beyond our intellect and within the abyssal recesses of our unconscious mind, this contemplation can truly unite us with our Cosmic Mother.

The various ingredients of this contemplation can be extremely appealing and even fascinating, as witnessed by the sight of millions of sunbathers jam-packed on the seaside, stoically roasting themselves on our beaches' burning sand. This runs counter to all logic and yet, it seems so natural that we forget how absurd it really is. If we think about it, what could be less interesting than sand, water or sun? Logically, the diversity of the countryside or a mountain scenery is much more interesting or attractive. Could the fascination of this sea-sand-sun triptych be due to something else, could it not be a kind of pilgrimage back to the very origins of life? We never tire of seeing time and again, at sunset, the sun drop into the ocean; nor sitting on a dune at nightfall, do we tire of silently watching the moon rise and its reflection shimmer on the crests of waves.

There is so much more to say about this contemplation, but I shall stop here. When you actually do it—and I hope you will—forget my "spiel," the sole justification of which was to "soft sell" it.

Meditation on Life

Here is a second, shorter meditation which contains elements of the previous one but which nevertheless constitutes a whole.

Life and consciousness—which are inseparable—are fully present even in the most primitive of beings on our planet. And so the theme of one of the simplest and richest Tantric meditations is Life itself, and it goes as follows:

Sitting in my usual meditation posture—a yoga âsana or on a chair, the condition being a straight and well-balanced spine (not rectilinear!)—I first relax as many muscles as possible, without forgetting to relax my face. My eyelids are shut or just slightly open, and I try to focus on the tip of my nose without squinting too much—that might create tension. Then, I observe my breathing for a few moments and perceive the cooler air entering my nostrils and the warmer air coming out. I turn my gaze "inward" and become attentive to my body, I listen to it. Focusing my mind on my body, I try to sense and seize as many physical sensations and feelings as I can. Starting at the soles of my feet, I mentally feel my way up my legs, the torso, the nape of my neck, my head, and then, in my mind's eye, I begin again at the palms of my hands, up my arms, my shoulders, sweeping across the nape of the neck again and finally inside my head. The aim of this preamble is to calm the mind, and already my thoughts are less scattered. While remaining aware of my breathing in and out, I realize how marvelous it is to be alive, here and now, in a human body. How wonderful it is just to be alive. Then I become aware of the fact that this life was transmitted to me *through* my mother, and that she received it from *her* mother who in turn got it from *her* grandmother and so on and so forth. I try to conjure up the oldest happy memory of my mother and if there is a conflict—which is more frequent than generally thought—then, without lingering on this thought, I skip it and go on to the previous generation. And I also try to visualize my grandmother, if I ever knew her, so that the image is concrete. Then I become aware of the uninterrupted and anonymous lineage of mothers and lovingly I thank them for having passed on the flame of life down to me. Not just a kind of lip-service, but I try to feel a real swell of love: for meditation does not exclude feelings, on the contrary, they are its driving force.

Where will this trip back in time up the lineage of mothers lead me? Back to the very first woman? Far beyond that, for she is just a link in the entire evolution of life on earth.

If I could really delve into my unknown and unknowable but true genealogy, it would lead me to the very origin of life on our planet. This primeval life was passed on right down to me, through the myriad forms of evolution, from the primitive unicellular beings of the original seas, without a thousandth of a second's interruption. In other words, the life pulsating in me today is just as old and just as new as on the first day of creation. I and this life, existing for billions of years, *are one and the same*. With the full realization of this *undeniable fact*, my ego dissolves and I become Life. As an integral part of this extraordinary and mysterious process, I feel linked and related to this past life and also to the current life forms on the planet. Mentally reversing the evolutionary process, I shall at one point go through the fish stage, the larval stage, until I become anew the primitive soup which contained the dynamic essence that was to engender all subsequent life forms.

And did I not undergo the same evolution in my mother's womb as an embryo and a fetus? All of life's power and intelligence are present within me here and now. All of life's experience is present in my genes, my life. My own individual life becomes extraordinary and at the same time, negligible. Just imagine the incalculable amount of coincidences and twists of fate leading to my existence, my own being. If, per chance, my mother had met another man instead of my father, or if among the 500 million spermatozoa in my father's semen another one had been absorbed by my mother's ovum, another child might have been born, of the same sex, on the same day and maybe having the same first name as myself, but the child would not have been "me." And he might even have been a totally different person: dizygotic twins may be extremely dissimilar although from the same ejaculate. Personally, I owe my life to the First World War, and therefore to Kaiser William II. If he had not started the war, my mother would not have left her native Ardenne in Belgium to go to Brussels, and she would not have met my father who had been demobilized after the armistice. So "I" would not have existed! This is just to show the long string of events and chance that precede our coming into this world, both you and me! And this "chance," this good fortune, also occurred with my grandmother and my grandfather who might well not have met either, etc, etc.

Of course, the point is not to indulge in grand philosophical considerations but to realize how wonderful Life is, to become fully aware of the fact, and to feel borne by it, to feel that one is an indissociable part of all lifeforms on this planet. The tree is my brother, but so is a mosquito. Considering things in this light makes our concerns, our worries, great or small, seem relative and pale in comparison. If I tune in to this invincible force, nothing can happen to me and the vitality and incredible intelligence of life are here, present within me.

How long should one remain immersed in this meditation on Life? There is no upper or lower limit: one minute, five minutes, thirty, as long as it is comfortable.

With this meditation we can truly tune in to extraordinary forces without going against any religion and even an atheist cannot object to it. This meditation can also be done at night, in bed, and one may thus fall asleep in the bosom of the cosmic Mother of our origins: there is no better sleeping pill! Deep and peaceful sleep guaranteed!

Profane Time, Sacred Time

A Bavarian doctor is reported to have posted a sign in his waiting room, saying: *"It is later than you think."* Was it sadism or cynicism? In any case, it expressed in a nutshell the drama of "ordinary," linear time.

Stating, in the West, that one must free oneself from the fetters of linear time, the time of watches and calendars, gives rise to objections such as: "Time is something objective, it is self-evident. My watch measures it, therefore it exists! And why do away with it? What's wrong with it? Can one go against the grain?"

Linear Time

Without wanting to face these questions head-on from the very outset, let us first try to dissect our habitual concept of time deemed as self-evident and sufficing unto itself. This concept of time is *linear* because it is perceived as a straight, almost infinite line, upon which we stand or rather along which everything moves: "The date is May the 15th, 19.., the time is 11:33 A.M., G. M. T." *We* can live with this but scientists would like to be more specific: May the 15th, 15.223.967.492 A.B.B.—*anno Big Bang*—and entropy will bring the universe to a grinding halt in the year 48.793.538.193"!

Along this infinite straight line, the present, a mere infinitesimal point, steers a one-way course, always headed in the same direction—there is no turning back!—at a constant speed, oblivious to the events around it. Our common sense takes this so much for granted that it does not even dawn upon us that archaic mankind may have had another perception of time.

The dictate of our stopwatches makes us forget that this linear time is:

a) an abstraction,

b) a recent one,

c) and insidiously pernicious.

Newton who, like Adam, had a thing about apples, still had a cyclical view of time, like natural man and woman, but for us time elapses in a uniform way, like the sand in an hourglass: the upper part contains the future, whereas the past is building up in the lower one, and the sand slipping through the neck between the two vessels represents our evanescent present. The hourglass represents life: at birth, the upper vessel is full and then it empties inexorably until the bitter end. How much sand is left in my hourglass?

Time became linear in the 17th century, on the night of November 10th, 1619, when young René Descartes conceived of the universe as an immense machine where everything could be explained and fitted in perfectly. In other words, cosmic clockwork! He even went so far as to apply this mechanistic idea to humans as he wrote in his *Treatise of Man*: "All of these functions unfold naturally in this machine (the body) by virtue of the arrangement of its organs, just like clockwork." And in the 17th century as well, the Dutch astronomer Christiaan Huyghens invented the pendulum clock, an accurate and unending mechanism, relying upon gears, and this device materialized the Cartesian concept of a machine-universe and provided an "objective measurement" of the elapsing time. Clocks and watches, so inexpensive today that everybody can afford one (whereas a century ago they were still rare objects worn only by wealthy city dwellers) created the illusion of linear time.

Another familiar object was involved in "linearizing" time: the calendar. On the one hand it serializes and materializes the past—"that event happened on March 15th last…"—on the other it is an anticipation of the future which thus acquires a sort of preemptive existence. Cast in the concrete of our datebooks, Christmas seems so "real" that the spirit is with us already!

But the snag is that these time-measuring devices, be they an hourglass or a watch, eat away at our lives: what do we die of, what kills us if not time! "We count the remaining minutes of our lives and shake our hourglass to speed things up" wrote de Vigny, echoing the Bavarian Doctor and his cynical sign *"It is later than you think."* The implacable stopwatch materializes time which, like a rat, gnaws away, unrelenting, at my life.

The "logical" reaction is to go the whole hog. If time is limited, then let's fill it to the brim. And so one must produce more, enjoy things more, possess everything, right away, go faster and faster. Watches and calendars become considerable stress factors—this job *must* be finished before—in order to live more fully, we live faster, we run faster, drive faster, fly faster and faster. We suffer from an acute record-breaking compulsion. The result being that we also die faster: this rushing around puts our biological rhythms under tremendous pressure, thereby disrupting and disconnecting them from those of the universe.

In giving us the impression that life is slipping through our fingers, linear time makes us "time-sick" according to Doctors Friedman and Roseman. People constantly rushing about suffer from this time-sickness syndrome: they produce too much adrenaline, insulin, and hydrocortisone, their stomach secretes too much acid, they breathe too fast, have muscular spasms and their cholesterol increases. People always in a mad rush, under constant time constraints, die at an earlier age, from coronary disease, for example.

The corollary of linear time can be found in the myth of irresistible, continuous, linear progress. Of course, a computer can be seen as "progress" when compared to a mechanical calculator. And all right, new products are "better," than older ones: today's wash is whiter than yesterday's, but just wait until you see tomorrow's. This year's cars are a "step forward" vis-à-vis last year's models, etc. Science is constantly making great strides forward. The newer, the better, is the general feeling. Everything is changing, everything is developing, *consequently* things are getting better and better, progress is underway. This idea of progress as an absolute value is just as pernicious and abstract as linear time. And it constitutes yet another stress factor.

We consider unchanging life-styles—like in an Indian village, for example—as backward. And yet, this resistance to change—a fate worse than death for most of us!—erases linear time and almost erases time altogether. An old man strolling through his village is in touch with his own childhood. The well has not changed since he was a boy and it's the same well where his father or his grandfather drew water. Women wear the same saris, they carry the same copper jugs on their heads, children still play the same games. The huts have not changed nor have the fields.

Today resembles yesterday and so will tomorrow. (However India has already been contaminated by our time-keeping watches and clocks and our illusion of linear progress.) But when we Westerners return to our hometown, the church is probably still standing but everything else has changed, things have been disrupted, developed, "modernized." Only nostalgia remains. The only telltale signs of our youth are to be found in some familiar object forgotten in a drawer, in a dusty old photo album. (I'd like to point out in passing that I am not an anti-progress diehard, I just strive to realize the relativity of such a concept.)

Does "progress" exist in nature and in life? Is it because each year new, purportedly unbreakable sports records are shattered that humanity is physically improving?

Life is changing, life is evolving, but is that tantamount to constant progress? Is evolution a linear phenomenon? Has an oak today made any progress compared to an oak a million years ago? Have today's species "come a long way" compared to those in geological ages? All they have done is adapt to a changing environment. Does a rabbit represent progress vis-à-vis a dinosaur, or an ant vis-à-vis an elephant?

Modern humans are not necessarily, nor in all respects, superior to archaic peoples. Compared to pygmies, doomed to disappear along with the overexploited rain forest, contemporary urban man and woman are no positive case for progress, either in terms of strength or health, or from the point of view of their joie de vivre, in spite of the former's so-called primitive life-style. In any case, the idea of the "20th century" does not exist for a pygmy, nor does it exist for the rest of nature—but it's catching up fast—and with a vengeance!

Cyclical Time

You might object: why bother to see time in a different light, what would that change? Anyhow, we are all going to die, our days are numbered and each passing moment lops off a unit in our time credit-line.

Prior to considering "what" would change in so doing, we must first realize that the linear time of humans is just a convenient abstraction. Does a dog know that it's living in the 20th century and this is May 15th? A date is a totally meaningless concept for a dog, something incomprehensible, something it cannot grasp. And what about cats or birds or even trees? Some might say: well, for animals perhaps, but things are different for human beings. Well, no, archaic man's (and woman's, of course!) sense of time was not linear. He/she did not try to know if they were living in the year 12.322, for example, because their concept of time was *cyclical*, therefore, without a beginning, but also, without an end.

In a cycle things are continuously revolving, the loop is looped, the wheel turns! Even today, throughout the world, so many humans still live in cyclical time. They see the sun rise, cross the sky, set, and return the following morning. The moon waxes, becomes a full moon, wanes, disappears, but always returns. Winter is followed by spring, then summer, then fall and after another winter, the cycle begins anew. And animals are aware of this, too.

For archaic man and woman, nature is a process of constant renewal and its cycles regulate life. In the Hopi language there is no word to express linear time, nor is there any verb conjugation. Hopis refer neither to the past nor to the future. They live in an eternal present which includes everything that we called the "past." Even if they are given a watch, they continue to live in cyclical time. Notwithstanding such a lack of explicit reference to the past, present or future, the life of the Hopi Indians is very well organized, to our great surprise.

Of course, the sundial has been with us for a long time (by the way they did not call it a sun*watch*). The solar cycle can thus be monitored and dissected by following the shadow as it moves on the dial! Our modern watches are also endowed with rhythm, that of a vibrating quartz crystal, but we cannot see it: only the hands move or the displayed numbers change.

It should also be pointed out in passing that linear time as an absolute entity is currently out of favor with physicists. Better—or worse—no one is capable of defining precisely such "obvious" notions as time, the present, the past, or the future. Here is some food for thought: if tomorrow morning all of a sudden everything in our universe went twice as fast—or twice as slowly—who would notice? Would we live longer or shorter lives? Actually, nothing would have changed. The same holds true for space: if tomorrow morning everything in the universe had shrunk and was half its former size, nobody would realize it. Therefore, in a closed system (our universe), one can compare the evolution of a given phenomenon with another one (evaluate its time), or the size of an object with that of another one (the Earth can be compared with the sun, the sun with a galaxy, etc.). However, we cannot determine if our universe is fundamentally large or small. In order to do that we would have to compare it with another universe, thereby turning it into a new system and we would still not know whether or not it was large or small, etc. *That* is relativity, too!

Sacred Time

Rest assured, we need not delve into such subtleties and may now broach the topic of sacred time. Let us qualify the term first: *Sacred* is not synonymous with *religious* in spite of a certain overlapping between the two. Moreover, in India, these notions of sacred, cyclical, or linear time are neither explained nor even mentioned by Tantra, simply because linear time is a modern Western abstraction and unknown in that context! Furthermore, the Tantric ritual in India affords its followers a first class ticket to the very heart of sacred time: such is one of the goals of Tantra. But since I belong to the Western world and must perforce deal with linear time—from which I have had to free myself—I thought it useful to address the subject.

But back to sacred time and to what Mircea Eliade had to say about it in *The Myth of the Eternal Return* (Princeton, 1954, p. 34): "A sacrifice, for example, not only exactly reproduces the initial sacrifice revealed by a god *ab origine*, at the beginning of time, it also takes place at the same primordial mythical moment; in other words, every sacrifice repeats the original sacrifice and coincides with it. All sacrifices are performed at the same mythical instant of the beginning of time; through the paradox of the rite, profane time and duration are suspended. ....Insofar as an act (or an object) acquires a certain reality through the repetition of certain paradigmatic gestures, and acquires it through that alone, there is an implicit abolition of profane time, of duration, of 'history.'"

Let us highlight the keywords in the excerpt above: *repetition, gestures* and *by them alone.*

Tantra holds that sacred time alone is "real" and that—paradoxical though this may seem—it abolishes all other forms of time! The past, precisely because it has passed, no longer exists. The future, because it is still to *come*, does not exist yet! And is the present a year, a day, a second, a billionth of a second? Impossible to define in terms of linear time or even cyclical time. (The mind boggles!)

Let us go a step further. For Tantra, creation is not a single event that took place x billion years ago, it's a continuous process. Creation is *here and now!* The manifest universe is constantly emerging from the non-manifest, outside of time which is a mere mental category! What remains is an eternal *now*. (I deliberately chose the word *now* instead of the term *present* for people unconsciously situate the latter somewhere between the past and the future.)

The phrase, "at the end of time," is to be taken literally. When the universe is reabsorbed into the bosom of the Primary Cause during what we call the end of the world, even time-space will disappear and it will be the "night of Brahman." This will be followed by a new day, that is, a new universe, and so on and so forth in an infinite succession of universes.

This leads us to the essential concept of "process." Our reason and senses tell us that an oak is an independent, autonomous unit, distinct from other units and belonging to space-time. We know when it was planted, we could uproot it from the forest and replant it in the middle of the lawn. But that oak, as it stands here and now, contains all of its own "past." It bears the marks of every spring it has experienced, each and every rainfall. Its present is actually condensed past and it conditions the future, yet only its present exists. A Tantrist perceives the oak as a whole, as a process, from the acorn all the way to the storm that will eventually fell it and even beyond. For the oak did not begin with the acorn, a mere link in the overall "oak" process which in the meantime produces other acorns, etc. The real oak is the integral "oak" process, from the very first to the very last of the species and it is inseparable—except artificially or intellectually—from the forest which is in itself a continuous, complex process included in the total life process on our planet. Even felled, the oak still belongs to the "oak-forest-life" process which recovers it immediately.

Going from oaks to humans, let us consider a beautiful young woman. A male Tantrist feels the impact of her beauty, for him she embodies Cosmic Femininity, but at the same time he sees her as a process. As if superimposed upon her, he visualizes the baby she once was and the wizened old woman she will become. He also envisions her coupled with a man, taking his semen and perpetuating the process. Infertility would not matter because, come what may, she is part and parcel of the process called "humanity" which is itself included in the eternal process of cosmic and planetary life. Moreover, a Tantric man's attitude would be the same in front of a crippled old woman: he would visualize her as young and beautiful but also as an embryo or even a fertilized ovum in her mother's womb. Considered as a process, her life did not begin at the moment of conception and it will go on, after her.

Each human being having been posited as a process contained in another, wider, process, and so on and so forth up to the cosmos, have we not returned to Descartes' clockwork universe? Not quite; as a matter of fact, not at all. Each individual-process is endowed with its own ever-changing dynamism, it is not a mere cog in some mechanical construction and that makes a world of difference! The universe is alive and conscious!

This vision of time-beyond-time also applies to Tantric *maïthuna*, the ritual sexual union, which ceases to be profane with the awareness that creation is taking place here and now. Maïthuna reproduces in real time the initial human sexual intercourse, which itself duplicates the ultimate act of creation, where the cosmic feminine principle (Shakti) coupled with its male counterpart (Shiva) creates the universe and engenders it continuously. Maïthuna reproduces concretely, in sacred, therefore real, time, the original creative act belonging not to some non-existent, distant past but to the present moment which, alone, exists.

Once I *realize* this, once I become truly *aware* of the fact that I am encompassed in and borne by the process called "humankind," first I am instantly freed from the time of watches and clocks, then from time altogether. This liberating experience dispels all inner tension and brings a feeling of security and serenity. I also perceive that sweeping aside my ego does not change the process of which I am a part and which will go on indefinitely: the subsiding of a wave does not change the ocean, for the wave is the ocean.

This Tantric ritual *transposes the follower's consciousness onto another plane of existence* where he/she grasps and concretely experiences this ultimate truth, gaining access to the divine, to sacred time which abolishes both cyclical and linear time.

Although words cannot express it, attaining sacred time, thus eradicating profane time that gnaws away at our life, is a truly liberating experience. Thereafter, nothing is really urgent and even if we sometimes have to hurry, it need not be in a mad rush or stress-producing. Does it really matter if such and such a thing is done today or in ten years or not at all? I am part of the process and, well, no, nothing can happen to me!

Gaining access to the process, to sacred time beyond even cyclical time, does not mean that one must throw away one's watch—I still wear mine! The hands on it tell me that it's getting late and it's time to go to bed. Tomorrow the sun will rise again even if it's hidden by clouds. Nor have I thrown away my datebook: I have appointments tomorrow. But things have become relative, I don't get—or I no longer get—caught up in the game.

Linear time, cyclical time, sacred time? Allow me to reiterate: realizing that I am a continuous process which did not begin at conception and will not end when "I," a structure of convenience, dies, allows me to go beyond my ego. If, in a sudden flash of insight, I perceive the universe itself as a continuous process—to which I belong—in a state of perpetual emergence, then time is dissolved, be it cyclical or linear. I have reached timelessness. This elating experience makes everything simple, full of light, and I feel I have been freed. Clocks and watches no longer tick away my life with each passing second.

The Overmind

In Tantra, the concept of the *overmind* is an essential one and although I'm not crazy about superlatives, I *would* like to find one to describe the overmind: even "breathtaking" or "fantastic" do not measure up. For the overmind *refers to an autonomous mental level that includes and is greater than several individual sub-minds*. More than breathtaking, such a prospect is literally *mind-blowing*! But a more specific definition of the overmind follows:

The word "mind" stems from the Latin *mens, mentis*, the meaning of which goes beyond the mere intellect, such as in the expression "mental arithmetic." In this respect, the famous *cogito ergo sum* dear to René Descartes actually raises more questions than it answers! "I think, therefore I am" is just as obvious as it is insufficient. "I think," fine, but who is this "I"? And what is *thinking*? Such questions raise another thorny and basic problem, as yet unsolved in the West: the psyche. Invoking its Greek origin, *psukhê* (= "soul"), irks our rationalist friends and serves only to fuel their quarrel with our other friends, the spiritualists, the two schools of thought only agreeing to disagree and to oppose implacably, mind and matter.

To "I think, therefore I am" Tantra adds the corollary, "I am, therefore I think," it being understood that "to think" means first and foremost to be aware, to be conscious, and not to reflect. The *psyche* and *consciousness* are indissociable as the empirical basis of existence. Let's keep this idea on hold for the time being and forge ahead.

Tantra reconciles spiritualists and rationalists by stating that the psyche, therefore consciousness, is a dimension, a fundamental property of the cosmos: this Tantric axiom is of far-reaching import. (On this subject see the chapter "What is Here....")

In order to try to fathom the depth of this axiom, let us begin with our habitual concepts of thought and thinking. In this context, the idea of an immaterial or supernatural psychic entity, in a word, a soul, is repulsive to the rationalist for whom thought, like automatic data processing, stems from the activity of the brain and does not exist outside the brain. Moreover, even for staunch spiritualists, to think, to be conscious, implies a closed space—the cranium—and a unified material structure, in this case our brain, which an American humorist described as being the most sophisticated, miniaturized, and high-performing computer ever, 1° mass-produced, 2° at low cost, 3° manufactured by people without any special qualification, 4° in the greatest enthusiasm! Indeed, comparing the brain to a computer is pretty plausible. For its billions of neurons can be likened to so many chips, so many living microprocessors linked to one another by wires, i.e., their dendrites, the power supply being nervous energy.

The originality of the Tantric view is that each psyche (including the cell's, considered as possessing full-fledged autonomous consciousness) is a *force field*, a subtle energy system, therefore material in the wider sense, without being limited by specific molecules or atomic particles. My psychic force field oversees and encompasses all of my neurons, uses them, reacts with each one of them and vice versa. I think *with* my brain, *thanks* to my brain, although my psyche is neither limited nor totally identical to it. What's more: my brain is "in" my psyche rather than my psyche being in my brain! My individual psyche is the overmind of all my neurons, in fact, of all the cells in my body.

The following comparison may help to clarify this idea: my psyche is to my brain what a magnetic field is to a magnet. Iron atoms are "material," I can weigh them and even observe their structure under the electron microscope. Each iron atom is itself a miniature magnet encompassed in the total magnetic field of the magnet. And yet, this invisible, subtle, imponderable magnetic field is just as "material" as the iron in the magnet from which it is indissociable. Moreover, the magnetic field extends far beyond the limits of the magnet itself.

Now as regards our brain, physicists assert that neurons are made up of nice little material molecules which are themselves made up of atoms which are in turn made of subatomic particles. No cause for metaphysical angst yet! That's well and good, but my brain, like all matter, is mostly made up of void! This echoes an idea expressed elsewhere in this book: modern physics has asserted that, if matter could be compacted so as to eliminate all intra-atomic void, i.e., if all nuclei and electrons were in actual contact, then the entire planet could fit into a thimble. And what about our brain: thus condensed, it would not even be the size of a speck of dust. In other words, my brain is first and foremost a dynamic void, a force field sprinkled with infinitesimal energy specks, atomic particles. Scientifically speaking my "force field brain," contrary to the closed and compact structure perceived by my senses, is a cloud of energy in a relation of constant exchange with its environment, but above all it is a thinking void!

Now for an embarrassing question: suppose I were an ultra-Lilliputian sitting in the middle of such a "force field brain" to look inside this thinking energy cloud. Nowhere would I see the images which pop up in the "mind's eye" of the proud owner of the brain. These images make up the single content of our waking or dreaming consciousness, yet no one can say where or how they arise. For Tantra it's straightforward: it all happens in the mind, i.e., in the subtle force field that encompasses the entire brain and extends beyond its limits, like a magnetic field beyond the magnet's!

Tantra transposes this idea from the individual to the universe as a whole. The latter, with its billions of galaxies, is also a force field mainly full of void (the unimaginable vastness of interstellar space). Tantra holds that "something" thinks with the stars, just like I think with my atoms. And here once again we run into the concept of the universe as alive and conscious.

For Pascal, mankind is a "thinking reed," the weakest creature in all of nature. Tantra holds on the contrary that the universe itself is conscious just like any individual and each one of his/her cells. From the cosmic to the infra-atomic level, the universal psyche is stratified into an infinity of sub-levels of awareness or planes of consciousness that are both autonomous and distinct from one another, and interdependent.

The structure of the psyche corresponds to the structure of energy-matter, the two being inseparable. Einstein's energy-matter is One, from a grain of sand (or the minutest of particles) to a galaxy, to clusters of galaxies, to the universe as a whole. Each individual is made up of an infinity of planes of consciousness, from the cellular to the whole and beyond!

Witnessing the activity of a thinking brain is just as extraordinary as watching a starry sky at night and realizing that "something"—or someone?—is thinking with these myriad stars: from the individual to the universal, it's just a question of scale.

This stems from the fundamental concept of Tantric esotericism: the universe is alive and conscious at all levels; the psyche is one of its dimensions the deletion of which would annihilate the whole, as eliminating the height of an object would perforce destroy it. This idea of an intelligent and conscious universe is making headway in the West: I refer you to a book by the British astronomer-physicist-geneticist Fred Hoyle: *The Intelligent Universe.*

In his book, Fred Hoyle dissociates himself from the classical Western concept according to which consciousness and thought can only occur in a structure (the brain, of course) having reached a certain stage of complexity. This means that in the West, people have a hard time swallowing the idea—although it is a fundamental one—that each cell is alive, *therefore* conscious. Traditional thinking would have it that a cell has no brain, no nervous system, *therefore* it has no organized consciousness. The latter *therefore* is *de trop*!

From the One to the Many

Let us cast our mind back to the extraordinary marathon of the five hundred million spermatozoa—a single ejaculate!—all of which are doomed except for one, swimming with all their might toward the goal, the ovum, and survival. "My" die was cast when in the dark warmth of my mother's womb the ovum took in the winner: from then on "I" existed, although still ego-less. And I was ONE, for the first but also last time of my life, in the form of that tiny gelatinous droplet, barely a tenth of a millimeter in diameter, the fertilized ovum. For Tantra—*what is here, is elsewhere, what is not here is nowhere*—everything was already there, everything I have become or could have become, including the entire past of the human species as well as that of life ever since it began on Earth.

And in addition to the above—consciousness. For the very first cell is already endowed with consciousness, along with the formidable organizing dynamism that is set in motion as of the very first second. For Tantra, this evolving dynamism is not blind, robot-like, but a conscious organizing power, though strictly planned according to a time-tried process, repeated millions of times over millions of years. If I had been a testtube baby under the eyepiece of a microscope, an observer would only have seen a tiny gelatinous sphere with a few small filaments floating about, the gene-bearing chromosomes. Biology postulates that this single cell, devoid of a nervous system or a brain, ipso facto lacks consciousness. Tantra is convinced of the opposite and the science of biology, precisely, provides evidence in support of this point. Indeed, as a unicellular being I was like an amoeba, also a single-cell being. Now, an amoeba can express desires, preferences, a will of its own, memory: it can even be conditioned in the Pavlovian sense. Though lacking a nervous system and a brain, the amoeba *knows* that other unicellular beings, the acinetae, have poisonous tentacles when they reach the adult stage, but not at birth. So the amoeba slyly and patiently stakes out the young acinetae as they are released from the maternal ovary and gobbles them up! So, is the amoeba conscious or unconscious? Which actually begs another embarrassing question: *who* or *what taught it that*? Of course, the problem can be dismissed by stating that it is instinct, which explains nothing.

Now back to "me": I will not bask in my splendid unicellular unity for long! Soon I will divide into two, then into four identical cells and so on and so forth. And here, a truly crucial question must be raised: in so dividing, have I become successively, double, quadruple, eight-fold or have I remained *one*? The answer is that I was both *one* and *multiple* and so shall remain until the very end. From these four, eight, sixteen cells—all of which are conscious, each endowed with its own individual psyche—immediately emerges a unifying collective psyche, an autonomous overmind that is distinct from their individual psyche and which is superimposed upon the latter.

And then, as I grow and develop, as my cells specialize, become tissue, organs, autonomous and conscious sub-overminds are constituted at each level, in addition to the overall psyche or mind, thus forming a double *pyramidal and hierarchical* structure that is both organic and psychic. This Tantric concept involving organic overminds is less alien to Western thought than might be surmised. The famous physician and chemist, Jan-Baptist Van Helmont, born in Brussels in 1577, called them *archei*, in Latin, from the Greek *arkhê*, "principle." He identified the *archeus faber*, i.e., the main archeus which determines, makes, and preserves the overall shape of the body, ensures its harmony, organizes and controls the activities of the various organs, somewhat like a conductor. Then each organ had its own secondary archeus, responsible for its proper functioning. All of this ties in quite well with the Tantric view which adds to the *archeus faber* and the archei of the organs, greater archei (or overminds): one for the digestive system, one for the nervous system, one for the muscular system, etc.

For Tantric esotericism, each archeus or collective psyche is a distinct level of consciousness with its own memory and its own set of emotions upon which the central overmind may have an impact via the appropriate mental imagery. The central overmind can thus give it orders, encourage it, etc., and it works! It is also via these archei that negative emotions (anxiety, anger, envy, etc.) can disrupt organic functions and give rise to so-called psychosomatic illnesses. If "I" am depressed, I will end up demoralizing my cells. The reverse is also true: poorly oxygenated and poorly nourished cells can make "me" depressed as well. As regards Van Helmont, he was not yet another absent-minded dreamer: before his own *archeus faber* collapsed in 1644, he had notably discovered carbon dioxide, gastric juices, invented the thermometer and coined the word "gas"!

The Spirit of the Beehive

Something akin to the aforementioned archei or organic psyches can be found in the Esquimau culture. When an organ is ill, they say that "its spirit has left it"! They call on the shaman to travel into the beyond to bring back the organ's "spirit" and restore it to its normal state. This may seem to us naïve or even absurd, but there may be more wisdom in it than first meets the eye.

But back to the Tantric overmind. One thing is to accept the idea that my cells are so many conscious entities, each endowed with an individual psyche, a memory, emotions, and that my individual psyche is the overmind, the collective supra-conscious mind of my cellular republic. But that's a far cry from trying to swallow the idea of an overmind encompassing several distinct individuals—and yet, that is precisely one of the cornerstones of Tantric esotericism. But prior to applying this principle to humans, let us consider insect communities, honeybees, for example.

Accepting the fact that a beehive is a separate entity poses no problem. But endowing it with a psyche, an independent overmind which goes beyond and includes all the individuals, all the honeybees, is not as easy. And yet, I am all the more willing to cross this bridge as no other hypothesis explains the well-established facts mentioned below. Maurice Maeterlinck, in his book *La vie des abeilles* [The Life of Honeybees], Brussels, 1943, calls this overmind the "spirit of the beehive," and quotes from his book follow (the italics are mine):

> The bee is above all, and even more so than the ant, a being that belongs to a community. In the beehive, the individual is nothing, it only has a conditional existence, it is a mere indifferent moment, a winged organ of the species. Its entire life is a total sacrifice to the innumerable and perpetual *being* of which it is a part (p. 27).

The same holds true for each of our cells. In the following paragraphs which I would like to have written, Maeterlinck, referring to the aged queen bee in the springtime, adds:

> She is not a queen in the sense she would be amongst humans. She gives no orders and she comes under, like the very last of her subjects, this *masked and supremely wise power* that we shall call, until we try to discover where it resides, *the spirit of the beehive* (p. 32).
>
> And so, where is *the spirit of the beehive,* in *whom* is it embodied? It is unlike the special instinct of the bird which can build a nest skillfully and seek other climes when the day of migration returns. Nor is it a kind of mechanical habit of the species, a blind will to live that collides with the myriad facets of chance as soon as an unforeseen event disrupts the series of familiar phenomena.... It controls mercilessly, but with discretion and as if carrying out some great design, the wealth, the happiness, the freedom, the life of an entire winged people. It regulates day by day the number of births, which is directly related to the number of flowers adorning the countryside. It announces to the queen

when her reign has come to an end or when she must leave, makes her give birth to her rivals, rears the latter regally, protects them against the political hatred of their mother, authorizes or prohibits, depending on the generosity of the multicolored calices, on the advancement of spring and on the likely hazards of the nuptial flight, the first-born virgin princess to kill in the cradle her young sisters singing the song of spring... (p. 33).

This spirit is cautious and sparing, but not avaricious. And it apparently knows the sumptuousness and the madness of Mother Nature's laws in matters of love. And so, during the long summer days, the spirit tolerates—for the unborn queen will choose her lover amongst them—the cumbersome presence of three or four hundred heedless, clumsy, busybody males that are totally and shockingly idle, noisy, voracious, crude, dirty, insatiable, enormous. But when the queen is fertilized and flowers tend to open later and close earlier, it decrees their general and simultaneous massacre (p. 34).

Finally, it is *the spirit of the beehive* which sets the time of the great annual sacrifice to the *genius of the species*—the swarm—when an entire people at the height of its prosperity and power, suddenly relinquishes to the next generation its entire wealth, its palaces, its dwellings, and the fruit of its labor, to seek afar the uncertainty and the deprivation of a new homeland (p. 35).

On the day stipulated by the *spirit of the beehive*, one part of the people, and this has been strictly determined according to surefire and unchanging laws, leaves the place to its future hopefuls who are as yet without form. What is left in the city of slumber are the males amongst whom the royal lover will be chosen, very young honeybees who take care of the brood and a few thousand workers who will continue to gather nectar high and low, be the keepers of the amassed wealth, and ensure that the moral traditions of the beehive are upheld. For *each beehive has its own set of moral standards.* Some beehives are full of virtue whereas others are perverted, and the unwary beekeeper may corrupt a given people, may make it lose all respect for the property of others, may induce it to pilfer, or may give it habits of conquest and idleness that will make it feared by all the small republics in the vicinity (p. 39).

Forgive me for having quoted Maurice Maeterlinck at such length, but the text is beautiful and the subject of utmost importance. Still on the subject of the overmind of the beehive, a friend of mine, a beekeeper, told me regarding this puzzling phenomenon and the "spirit of the beehive," that when a beekeeper dies, his or her successor must go to each beehive and say aloud—really meaning what he or she is say-ing—: "I am the new master of the beehive," otherwise, the new bee-keeper will not be accepted. Is it "the spirit of the beehive" which hears and perceives what the beekeeper is thinking? Although the question is unanswered, the facts remain! My beekeeper friend also told me that when another beekeeper he knew, who loved his bees a great deal and took especially good care of them, died and was buried, a swarm of honeybees flew over his grave in the cemetery. Unsurprised, the villagers commented: "Look, old Thomas' bees have come to say good-bye." Unless this friend was lying (but why would he?) the story makes one wonder.

Before leaving the honeybees, a final word about the sexuality of the queen bee, for she is the true genital organ of the beehive. Should we feel sorry for this prisoner serving a life sentence in her royal apartment and who may never again see the light of the day, with her oversized and fertile belly which forces her to remain practically still, and who is compelled to lay some three thousand eggs a day, mean-ing as many fertilizations? She has sexual intercourse only once, dur-ing the nuptial flight, a woeful wedding during which she tears off some twenty-five million spermatozoa from her unfortunate lover of a single moment who dies immediately, his belly ripped. These sperma-tozoa will swim around until the end of her life in the seminal fluid located in a gland—a real sperm bank—just under her ovaries. She thus has within herself an inexhaustible male and thanks to the numerous, powerful and complicated muscles controlling the entry of her vagina, she "injaculates herself" with the gametes she requires. Another quotation from Maeterlinck:

> It is likely that this slave-mother whom we tend to feel sorry for, but who may actually be of a very voluptuous and amorous nature, derives a certain amount of pleasure from the *union of the male and female principles* taking place within her, like an after-taste of the rapture of the one nuptial flight of her life (p. 141).

Such a union of the male and female principles (Shiva-Shakti) is music to the ears of a Tantrist. And who knows, maybe the queen bee also has three thousand orgasms a day? Why not!

This "spirit of the beehive" emanates from individual honeybees without whom it is nothing, yet it outlives them, for the workers live for less than two months. It is entirely devoted to them and at the same time demands and obtains from each one of them total devotion to the community. When the bees depart in a swarm, it splits into two, accompanying the emigrating queen as well as constituting a new "spirit of the beehive" among the honeybees that have stayed on in the abandoned hive. Finally, since each apiary has its own overmind, the "genius of the species," to use Maeterlinck's words, that has guided and monitored their evolution for millions of years is the repository, the "keeper" of their past and the guarantor of their future. Could the same not hold true for humankind as well?

Before leaving the insect world I would like to quote an observation made by Prof. James S. Coleman from Johns Hopkins University: "Once, while I was sitting on the edge of a cliff, a bundle of gnats hovered in front of me, and offered a strange sight. Each gnat was flying at high speed yet the bundle was motionless. Each gnat sped in an ellipse, spanning the diameter of the bundle, and by its frenetic flight maintaining the bundle motionless. Suddenly, the bundle itself darted—and then hovered again. It expanded and its boundaries became diffuse; then it contracted into a hard tight knot and darted again—all the while composed of nothing other than gnats flying their endless ellipses. It finally moved off and disappeared....

"Such a phenomenon poses enormous intellectual problems: how is each gnat's flight guided as its direction bears almost no relation to the direction of the bundle? How does it maintain the path of its endless ellipse? And how does the insect come to change it when the bundle moves? What is the structure and what are the signals by which control is transmitted?"

The above is an excerpt from *The Great Evolution Mystery*, London, 1983 (p. 228) and the author, Gordon Rattray Taylor, makes the following comment about it: "I have often observed almost identical behavior in flocks of birds and I incline to believe that there are still processes of communication underlying behavior of which we have at present no more than an inkling. But birds, despite the opprobrious term "bird-brain," have quite efficient brains, weighing several grams. Gnats, on the other hand, have microscopic brains comprising only a few hundred neurones. Professor Coleman offers no answers to the question he poses; neither do I."

Tantra's answer would be that it is the overmind of the swarm of gnats, of the flight of birds, of the reindeer herd, of the shoal of fish, for such behavior has indeed been observed in all of these cases. A mere hypothesis? Perhaps, but scientifically, one is entitled to formulate assumptions until better ones are put forward!

Let's leave the insects behind and consider the realm of other animals. The collective psyche manifests itself notably in large reindeer herds when all the animals change direction at the very same instant. A school of fish behaves like a single individual, whereas the hens in a henhouse make up a hierarchical society, a "pecking order," endowed with a solid group psyche with the following result.

Let us consider the case of two sister-hens who do not belong to a given henhouse. If we introduce the first hen today, the alien is immediately attacked and pecked at by the other hens. However, she will gradually become a member of the group and of its collective psyche. When, later, the other hen is introduced, she will undergo the same fate and will be attacked by her own twin sister: the rejection phenomenon. After some time, she will eventually also become integrated into the henhouse. Come to think of it, this might shed new light on the rejection problem of transplanted organs. For each organ has its own group psyche—its *archeus* to use Van Helmont's expression—which is itself integrated into the overmind of the whole body. All of these overminds make up a kind of clan and transplanting an organ is tantamount to introducing an alien psyche which gets attacked just like the new hen or a foreign honeybee in the beehive. Rejection is all the more drastic as the donor and the recipient are less close. In the case of twins there will be few problems because their psyches are very close and in harmony with each other. On the contrary, the risk of rejection will be all the greater as it involves an organ that is highly responsive to feelings and emotions. Our heart reacts to all of our feelings and communicates them to our entire body. If our heart pounds away madly, this panic will be communicated to the entire cellular republic. That is probably why a skin graft is usually successful whereas a heart transplant entails so many problems. Applying this idea to organ transplants reflects a personal hypothesis and I am not expounding a Tantric view here. But since this might explain a good many things, why not mention it?

In the case of humans, there are fewer differences than one might think between an isolated, "self-contained" individual—me, for example—and a beehive, an anthill, a reindeer herd, a school of fish, etc. A beehive cannot move about per se, it lies in a single place, whereas its various parts (the honeybees) can. As far as "I" am concerned, my entire cellular republic moves about: I am a walking beehive!

The above introduces a disconcerting Tantric concept: I, as an individual, am a cell encompassed in various overminds that extend beyond me! Which brings us to the question of crowd psychology.

Crowd Psychology

When in 1895, Gustave Le Bon published *La Psychologie des foules* [Crowd Psychology], Paris, 1895 & 1947, his ideas were ignored. Since then, his book has become a classic and has been translated into at least fifteen languages. From the outset, in his preface, he goes straight to the heart of the matter:

> Observation has demonstrated that when a certain number of people are gathered, they constitute a powerful but momentary collective soul.
> Crowds have always played an important role throughout history, but never as considerable as today. The unconscious actions of crowds taking the stead of the conscious activity of individuals are one of the characteristics of the day.

In the Indian tradition, the age of Kali, the Iron Age in which we now live, is notably characterized by a surge of human masses, hence the increased importance of crowd psychology. But what exactly is a "crowd"? A great mass of people gathered together? Not necessarily. For Le Bon, a few gathered individuals may just as much constitute a crowd as may hundreds or thousands of people. A quote from his book follows: "The masters of the world, the founders of religions and empires, apostles of all creeds, outstanding statesmen and, at a more modest level, leaders of small human communities, have always all been natural psychologists, with an instinctive and unfailing knowledge of the soul of a crowd. And gifted with this knowledge, they easily became its master."

Then, Le Bon goes on to mention—surprise, surprise?—Napoleon: "Never, perhaps, since Alexander and Caesar, has any great man better understood how to impress the soul of a crowd. His constant concern was to be striking, to leave his mark on it. He thought about this in times of victory, in his harangues, in his speeches, in all of his acts. He was thinking of it still on his deathbed" (p. 47).

If Le Bon were alive today, he would have mentioned at least one other tragically famous or infamous name; need we spell it out?

But actually, what produces a crowd? How is one created? "Under certain given circumstances and only in such circumstances, a cluster of people possesses new features that are quite different from those of each individual making up the group. The conscious personality fades away, the feelings and the ideas of all of the units are oriented in the same direction. A collective, albeit transitional, soul is thus formed, displaying very clearcut features."

The collective soul, the overmind: "… makes up a single being and is subjected to the *law of the mental unity of crowds*" (p. 19). And yet: "A thousand individuals gathered by chance on a public square, with no specific goal or purpose, do not make up a psychological crowd" (p. 20).

The characteristics of a psychological crowd are as follows: "Regardless of the individuals making it up, whether their lifestyles, their occupations, their personality or their intelligence are similar or not, just the mere fact that they have become a crowd endows them with a kind of collective soul. This soul makes them feel, think and act totally differently from the way in which each person, individually, would feel, think, and act. This aggregate that is a crowd, is neither the sum nor the mean of its constituent parts, but rather a combination of these, as well as the creation of new ones" (p. 21).

In a certain way, the individual loses his/her personality and amid the acting crowd, seems to be in an unusual state, very close to the hypnotic state. Here is a first-hand account: in 1937, a young Alsatian girl was visiting distant cousins across the Rhine, whom she had not seen for years. She was surprised and shocked to see how involved they were in the Hitler Youth Movement and what gung-ho national socialists they had become. She told them what people in France thought of Hitler and the Nazis. They answered: "You don't know what you are talking about, come with us to Nuremberg to the party meeting and you'll understand." She was an inquisitive person and so she accepted, she was lent a uniform and she went with them full of negative preconceived ideas. Picture her in Nuremberg: everybody now has seen the newsreels of the time showing the enormous stadium with hundreds of thousands of men and women in uniform, so disciplined and well-organized. A profusion of swastika-bearing banners are flapping in the wind, there is military music and troops are parading. Heavy boots are rhythmically pounding the ground, people's arms are raised as hundreds of thousands of voices shout "*Sieg Heil!*" Then, at last, on the podium appears a figure dressed in a khaki uniform with a barely visible swastika armband, a figure rendered so small by the distance: the Führer! There is silence. Then, the hoarse voice, over-amplified by the speakers, drowns out the ardent crowd in its harangue. As the young Alsatian girl said, in her own words: "After a few minutes, I was convinced that I was in the presence of the savior of the world."

"Like everybody else around me, she said, I applauded, I raised my arm, I shouted *Sieg Heil*. When we got back home, my cousins who were so pleased to have converted me, told me: 'Now you see!' And indeed, I had seen! Once back to my normal life in Alsacia and no longer under the spell, I could not understand what had come over me and how I, a French girl, had become for just a few moments, a staunch Nazi supporter...."

The above sheds light on Le Bon's text: "As an isolated individual, a person might be educated, but in the crowd, he is pure instinct, in other words a barbarian. He has the spontaneity, the violence, the fierceness, as well as the enthusiasm and the heroism of primitive beings. The ease with which he may be impressed by words, images, and led to actions undermining his most obvious interests, brings him closer to such beings" (p. 24).

In the light of the above, where lies the difference between the haranguing of the savvy demagogue and a speech made by a member of the Academy? The latter makes intelligent, well-structured statements: he calls upon and speaks to the intellect, the reason of his listeners, not their passions. The audience applauds nicely but remains cold. An eloquent demagogue, through his passionate and charismatic discourse, fashions and addresses the overmind which is neither logical nor intellectual, even if the audience is made up of well-educated and sensible people. Crowds only react to primitive, archaic, tribal sentiments. That is why the nationalist theme, among others, is always so successful and popular! Just read, in a quiet environment, the actual written speech of such harangues: one is astonished that intelligent people could listen to such language and be taken in by it. Yet such things do happen (and do they ever!). For if the demagogue had said logical and intelligent things, he would not have moved the soul of the crowd, he would not have crystallized the overmind.

This overmind can also be reached at the national level and Le Bon has termed this, abusively, as a matter of fact, "the spirit of the race." "Spirit of the nation" would have been a better phrase, for a nation, in the true sense of the word, is formed even with very diverse ethnic groups, on condition, however, that they live together for a sufficiently long time and share a common geography and history. European nations, for example, are each an aggregate of various ethnic groups.

This "spirit of the nation" sheds light on the phenomenon of racism which is mainly xenophobia exacerbated by ethnic, religious, and other differences. This goes to explain how an intelligent, sensitive, and non-racist person can turn into a bigot.

In the overmind lies the real problem of ethnic minorities. The process repeats itself ceaselessly with its fearsome, inevitable consequences. It's perfectly normal for so-called aliens arriving in the U. S. to form communities—as in New York City, for example—where their compatriots already live. It's also natural for them to perpetrate their own lifestyle. In forming such clusters, they soon create an overmind distinct from the rest of the autochthonous people and as in the case of a transplanted organ, this gives rise to a reaction of rejection. Such a reaction will be all the more virulent as the ethnic differences and disparities in lifestyle are greater. However, if these immigrants had scattered throughout the country with, let's say, one or two families per town or neighborhood, no overmind would have been created and therefore no possible cause of rejection. After some time, these isolated immigrants would have learned the language, adopted the local lifestyle and been accepted and eventually integrated into the over-mind around them; in other words, they would have become assimilat-ed by the surrounding culture. But, in the case of heavily populated and closed communities, the rejection reaction is and will always be at the heart of the problem of all the ghettoes in the world. Sooner or later a demagogue, a leader, will rise and his or her passionate addresses will crystallize latent antagonism: it never fails. If one day, the afore-mentioned "I'm not a racist!" person goes to a meeting where this demagogue is to speak—such a speaker being a mere instrument—then, caught up in the overmind of the crowd, he/she will follow the pack. The rational arguments invoked, such as crime or unemploy-ment, that immigrants are proported to be the cause of, or any other ills, justified or not, are mere pretexts, rationalization in psychology parlance. The problem lies elsewhere in the realm of the irrational.

Unfortunately, there is no surefire medicine for this. In order to pre-vent the shaping of powerful overminds, it would be necessary—from the very outset—to prevent newcomers from creating such clusters. That would mean—which is not the case—that local authorities would have to be aware of the phenomenon and that they take due note of the seeds of conflict contained therein. The same holds true for the white minority in South Africa, who will also eventually and inevitably be ejected: the force of weapons can only delay the moment. Apartheid, even in the absence of economic discrimination, has given rise to extremely structured overminds, therefore creating conflict. Unless? Unless the Afrikaner, by skillfully opposing the overminds of the vari-ous black ethnic groups, lead them to kill one another.

A collective psyche can even be made up of just two individuals such as a couple or twins. In the case of identical twins, a collective psyche is created that is so strong that one can really talk about a sin-gle mind encompassing two bodies. An extreme case in point, instruc-tive without being enviable, is that of two sisters, Greta and Frieda Chaplin, from York (United Kingdom).

Up to age 37 they had never been separated, they dressed in the same identical way and walked at the same pace. They ate the same food at the same speed, raising their fork or spoon simultaneously and would finish eating at the same time.

Such total synchronism, which is extremely rare even in twins, took on a peculiar twist in the case of these two sisters: they could not stand to be separated even for just a few moments and when they were, they would moan and cry together, being extremely emotional and impressionable. The village children—kids are merciless!—were keenly aware of this and had great fun trying to scare them: the sisters would then wet their (identical!) pants at the same time!

But the most perplexing aspect of these twins is when they speak (and sometimes curse!) at the same time, for their sentences are identical, word for word, and synchronized as if they were speaking stereophonically! Such perfect synchronism is inimitable, even if two people decided to recite together a text they had learned by heart. This possibility was totally ruled out in the case of the Chaplin sisters, for the phenomenon would occur especially when they were angry or overexcited. They sometimes fought: they would then hit each other lightly with their handbags (strictly identical, of course!). Then they would sit down and sob in harmony as they embraced. Only the hypothesis of a single psyche encompassing two brains and using two bodies can explain this.

While we are on the subject of twins, systematic studies have been carried out, notably by David Lykken, at the University of Minnesota, who studied three hundred cases of identical twins, making encephalographic recordings which show that the brain waves of identical twins respond identically to similar types of stimuli. This corroborates the often-stated hypothesis that twins are in telepathic relation, unconscious perhaps, but constant.

You may object: "Crowd psychology, granted; OK for a kind of collective hypnosis which brings all of the people present under the control of a magnetic person. But accepting the idea of a supra-personal, *autonomous, conscious entity* having all of the features of a psyche (consciousness, memory, feelings), as asserted by Tantra, is another matter altogether."

A Strange Family

All right. So, instead of listening to a Tantrist, let us listen to a Westerner, one of the great figures of psychoanalysis, the Swiss C. G. Jung (1875-1961). The excerpts stem from Jung, *L'inconscient collectif,* published by the "Cahiers Jungiens," Paris, 1978 (translation).

The Jungs were a strange bunch indeed. Young Carl Gustav spent his childhood and adolescence in a presbytery in the country, for his father, Paul Achille, was a preacher. His mother was homely, obese, authoritarian and condescending, unlike Freud's mother who was young and very beautiful. That's probably why Jung thought Freud's assertion that each little boy is in love with his mother was absurd! This did not prevent Jung from writing: "Everything that is original in the child is, so to speak, indissolubly blended with the image of the mother.... It is the absolute event of the series of ancestors, an organic truth such as the interrelationship of the sexes to each other" (Jung, p. 37).

Jung's maternal grandfather, Samuel Preiswerk, was a Hebrew scholar and a theologian, and his second wife was Augusta Faber who bore him thirteen (!) children. This grandfather was, or thought he was, in contact with the spirits of the dead: in his den, there was always an empty seat exclusively reserved for the spirit of his first wife, who, he said, visited him every week. This caused no little distress to his second wife, the one who gave him thirteen children, his first wife having borne him only one! As regards his paternal grandfather, who was also called Carl Gustav, he was a legendary figure in Basel, where he was a very highly regarded physician, the rector of the University and a Grand Master of the Swiss Free Masonry. Although he never knew his father's father, young Carl Gustav identified with him to the point of becoming a medical doctor and not a preacher like his own father. In this strange family, his cousin Helen Preiswerk was a spiritualistic medium. Jung carried out experiments with her to the point of writing his medical thesis on her.

This biographic digression was useful and instructive prior to approaching one of the most well-known Jungian concepts although it might be the least understood of all: that of the collective unconscious. Between you and me it would have been a better idea if he had chosen instead to call it the "collective *supra*-conscious mind," as we shall see as we reflect upon the following excerpts from his works. Might I stress—and this is an important point—that Jung was a rationalist and a pragmatist, a very precious quality, especially in this field! He would say: "I cannot believe in what I do not know and I do not need to believe in what I know." Furthermore: "You know that I am not a philosopher but an empiricist. Thus, my idea of a collective unconscious is not a philosophical concept but an empirical one" (Jung, p. 32).

Jung's collective unconscious mind and the overmind of Tantra are as alike as two peas in a pod as we shall see!

...The collective unconscious appears to me as a continuum, omnipresent, a universal presence without length or breadth [...] It holds, side by side, in a paradoxical way, the most heterogeneous elements, including not only an unattributable mass of subliminal perceptions but stratifications deposited during the lives of forebears who by their very existence, contributed to the differentiation of the species" (Jung, p. 6). If the unconscious mind could be personified, it would take on the appearance of a collective human being existing above and beyond the specifications of the sexes, of youth, of old age, birth or death, and suffused with a couple of million years of practically immortal human experience. Such a being would, unquestionably, hover

over the vicissitudes of time. The present would bear no more significance for him than a given year in the hundredth millennium B.C.; he would be a dreamer of secular dreams and thanks to his inordinate experience, an oracle of uncomparable prognostications. For he would have lived the life of the individual, the life of the family, of tribes, of peoples, a great many times over and would know—like a living feeling—the rhythm of becoming, of blooming and fruition, of decadence.

[…]This collective being appears not to be a person but rather a sort of infinite stream, an ocean of images and shapes which emerge into the conscious mind in dreams or abnormal mental states.

It would be unfortunate to treat this vast system of experiences of the unconscious psyche as an illusion; our visible and tangible body is also a comparable system of experiences which still harbours marks of development dating back to the earliest age" (Jung, p. 6).

In Tantra, this being is personified as Shiva-Shakti and it corresponds approximately to Jung's Animus-Anima! And the following admirable text:

I am filled with the deepest sense of wonder and utmost reverence when I silently behold the abysses and the heights of psychic nature, a world without space which holds an incommensurable abundance of images, organically piled up and condensed over the millions of years of life's evolution. […] These images are not fleeting shadows, they are psychical conditions whose actions are powerful. We misappreciate them, but we cannot, just because we ignore them, rob them of their power" (Jung, p. 10).

The supranatural unconscious which exists throughout the encephalic structure is like an omniscient and omnipresent spirit which extends everywhere. It knows man as he has always been and not as he is today. It knows him as a myth. That is why the linkage to the suprapersonal or collective unconscious means an extension of man beyond himself; it means the death of his personal being and a rebirth into a new dimension, as precisely enacted in certain ancient mysteries (Jung, p. 59).

In Tantra, the important thing is not merely knowing that the collective supra-conscious exists, but going straight to the source of creativity, of real knowledge, of power. As a matter of fact, Jung was familiar with Tantra and thus came to understand the initiatory richness of

Tantric symbols and to discover the mandala and the archetypes, another central Jungian concept.

The Impact of the East

Jung also sensed the impact that the East would have on today's world: "The intrusion of the East is much more a psychological fact historically prepared for a long time but it is not the real, actual East, it is due to the collective unconscious which is omnipresent.

[...]"The truths of the unconscious mind are never to be invented but on the contrary, to be reached by following a course which all previous cultures, from the most primitive onwards, have described as the path of initiation" (Jung, p. 7).

Thus the overmind does not belong exclusively to Tantra although it is one of its cornerstones. The overmind makes it possible for us to grasp certain notions not readily understood otherwise. The Catholic church is fully aware of this. During catechism, when the parish curate whose cassock reeked of tobacco, used to briefly talk to us about the "mystical body of Christ," he would say that each Catholic, each member of the Church is a living cell in this Mystical Body. Then, he mentioned it no more. Maybe he believed, perhaps rightly so, that we, being children, were not able to understand what it all meant?

But did he, himself, understand this essential idea? For each and every Catholic, from the very beginning up to today and for as long as there are believers, is included in this extraordinary collective supraconscious mind, in which he/she immerses himself/herself and which is strengthened each time he or she attends a religious service, highlighting the importance attached to—and rightly so—the *physical* presence of the congregation at church for Sunday mass. This mystical body would have been constituted *even* if Jesus had not existed, *even* if he had been totally "made up"! Actually, do we know *who* he *really* was? But does it really matter?

Another quote from Jung: "Very early on, the true man-Jesus disappeared behind the emotions and projections which swirled around him, coming from all parts; immediately and practically without leaving a trace he was absorbed by surrounding religious systems and fashioned into their archetypal interpreter. He became the collective figure that the unconscious mind of his contemporaries had been expecting and that is why there is no point in knowing who he really was" (Jung, p. 57).

Over the centuries, this mystical body, this overmind, became imbued with the ritual of church services, for its memory spans the centuries. So, was the Church right in suddenly dropping the

Gregorian chant which for so many centuries filled cathedrals and the souls of believers and still haunts the memory of this gigantic overmind? This also goes to explain the Church's inertia, due to the passing centuries, in the face of some of today's current issues. You just don't push around or disrupt so easily such a formidable overmind with impunity.

What is the link between all of the above and Tantra, other than in theory? I'd like the Tantric couple, Arvind and Shanta Kale, to answer this question:

> It is from these dark wellsprings that the poet draws his inspiration, the gambler his instinct, and the telepathist his strange contact with other minds. It would almost appear as if all human minds were linked by telepathic bonds, at this level, as close as the cells forming a single human body.
>
> Esoteric Tantric doctrine contends that this single Overmind is the repository of all mankind's memories and if anyone can make contact with it he will know the totality of mankind's experience and knowledge; the senses, thoughts and abilities of every man and woman who lives today, or has ever lived, will become his.
>
> But because this Overmind is a racial-mind, individuality cannot exist within it. It is only a single racial "We" distinguished into the primal Male and Female. Tantrists believe that at the ego-dissolving moment before orgasm the minds of the partners make a fleeting contact with this Overmind. At that instant all Men are eternal uninhibited Male and all women at that moment are eternal Female. And both are merged in self-perpetuating ecstasy where, in common with the goal of most great religions, the selfish "I" is lost in the all-embracing "We."
>
> Tantra, therefore, seeks to use the rapture of sex to blast through the ego-protective barriers of our inhibitions and tap the incredible powers of this dark and omnipotent Overmind (Kale, Arvind & Shanta, *Tantra, the Secret Power of Sex*, Bombay 1976, p. 27).

Beyond a couple's experience, the chakra pûjâ—worship in a circle— creates a powerful overmind with sixteen participants, and this dissolves even more surely the impervious shield of the ego while at the same time arousing the extraordinary powers of kundalini.

An Unknown Universe: My Body

The body is the keystone of the Tantric cathedral. For Tantra, it is neither a humble servant nor the "trembling carcass," as Turenne referred to it on the battlefield, nor spiritualism's antithesis, the locus of crude appetites, a tattered envelope to be subjugated and mortified to save one's soul. For Tantra, the body is much more than a wonderful instrument of manifestation or an admirable biological mechanism, it is divine. A divine body? Well, one might possibly go so far as to "deify" the brain, the seat of consciousness, but our innards!

In order to fully comprehend this key thought of Tantra, one must realize that:

—my real body is actually an incredibly complex universe with its own secret life of which I am unaware;

—the body I experience as my own is actually an image, a representation, a mental construction and that is the only aspect I know;

—my body is produced and impelled by a Creative Intelligence, the very same one which created and keeps the universe going, from the most minute sub-atomic particle to the most gigantic of the myriad galaxies;

—in its inmost depth, my body holds untold potentialities, extraordinary energies, most of which remain untapped in ordinary men/women, but which can be aroused and developed by Tantric practice.

Objection, your honor! How can you say that my body is unbeknownst to me for I feel it, I feel it move, I know when it is hungry or thirsty, I know if my body is suffering or not! How can Tantra contend that I don't know my body? Here is the answer. The body we experience, we perceive, is a mere mental representation, something in our mind's eye, so to speak, which does not have all that much to do with the actual grandiose reality of our real body.

Let's reason it out: If I remove my watch and place it on a table in front of me, without realizing it, I am actually in the presence of two watches. The watch-object (outside) and the watch-image (inside) which I am observing in my own mind. The watch-object, that of physicists, the true one, is made up of atoms which resolve into minute specks of energy. Since Einstein's discoveries, we know that matter which appears so tangible and concrete to us, is actually energy. However, it is mainly void since, as stated earlier, by deleting the space between atomic particles, our planet, so they say, would hold in a thimble while retaining the same mass. And so my *real* watch-object is actually mere void, a field of swirling forces that my intellect cannot represent in my mind's eye. Although he/she may know that experimentally, the nuclear physicist is in no privileged position: for he/she can only "see" what I see, that is, the compact, reassuring, inside watch-image which only exists in his/her brain—or rather in the mind, according to Indian thought. The watch-image conceals the watch-object and it is this concealing veil that the Vedanta calls *maya*.

And now to the crux of the matter as regards my body, for I also have two bodies! A *body-object* (unknown) plus a *body-image* (perceived) and I confuse the two. Or rather, I am totally unaware of the former! It is less difficult to grasp this subtlety—pardon me, this fundamental truth—if you observe somebody else. So, look at me looking at my watch on the table. How does perception work? It's quite simple or at least it appears so: light bounces off the object, hits my retina which sends this message in the form of electric impulses, via the optic nerve, toward the cerebral cortex. That is how the watch-object I am looking at somewhere in my head, in my mind, pops up. And now comes the bewildering realization: all my life, I've been looking at *images* of the outside world in my mind, believing that I was actually seeing the outside world. Astounding and true. One might object that it makes no difference because we believe that one is the exact reflection of the other, just like the image of the landscape seen in a mirror is identical to the landscape itself. And we presume that the same holds true for images of the outside world which pop up in our mind. This is a grave mistake. For those images correspond as little—or as much—to outside reality as a city map corresponds to the city itself and to its inhabitants: it is just a useful diagram.

And now pay close attention! Let's go a step further and I shall put my watch back on my wrist. What's happened? Nothing has changed: my watch remains an image in my own mind. But what about my wrist? Here again, a distinction must be made between my real wrist, my material wrist, made up of energy and void, and the wrist-image in my mind. At this point in our thinking, many people get confused and I understand this because it took me months to truly distinguish outside *objects* from their inside *image*, i.e., to understand that these are two totally distinct, yet interwoven, phenomena.

Ay, there's the rub! (For most people, at any rate.) Granted, the real, outside, watch-object is one thing, and the inside watch-image is another and is actually the only one I "know." For all practical purposes and for my daily life, that suffices: no need for subtle distinctions between a watch-object and a watch-image since I can tell what time it is, regardless. Now my body is an altogether different matter: I feel it, so it is "*me*," isn't it? Well, that's what people usually think because it is normal and natural to extract, so to speak, one's body from the outside world: on the one hand, there is my mind and my ego associated with the body, and on the other hand, "outside," there is everything else, a multitude of beings and things. So, in thought, artificially, I isolate my body from the rest of the world, whereas it is an aggregate of atoms that are just as material and banal as all the objects belonging to the outside world with which I am in a relation of constant exchange: night and day, I absorb air and food molecules and discard as many. My body is an edifice that keeps its shape as bricks are constantly being replaced. Usually, this is an unrecognized fact: my body belongs to the material world from which it is indissociable: it is a cogwheel in the cosmic immensity. Naturally, my relation with my bodymatter is a special one. Actually my body, though material, is that special place in space where "*I*" structure matter, where "*I*" build this human body. "*I*" is placed in quotation marks because, needless to say, it is not my little ego, but the body's Higher Intelligence which creates and maintains it. Nevertheless, "*I*" am doing this and not some kind of external or metaphysical agent. Irrespective of any religion or philosophy, it is undeniable that all my planes of existence, whatever they may be, meet in my body, even if by virtue of my faith, I've always considered my body as more than a "mortal coil." The *real* body, I repeat, is an unknown universe and a gigantic one on the cellular scale, and not to be confused with the body-image in the mind. Naturally, at the beginning, this is a bit hard to swallow, for it seems to contradict what we experience each and every instant of our lives. A city map, a mere diagram, does have a connection with the city itself—the map of Paris is not the same as the map of New York—but nobody would confuse a city and the map of the city! And yet, that's what we do with the image of our body in our mind. The body we experience is a map, a representation, a "body image," distinct from the real body-object.

Let's go further. Butterfingers! Instead of hitting the nail on the head, the hammer lands on my thumb. Ouch! Don't tell me this pain is just an image in my mind and that a hammer full of vacuum hit my finger that is just as void as the aforementioned tool. And yet, that's the truth! Actually what hurts is the image of my finger in the image of my body, somewhere in my mind! Because physiologically my "real" finger feels no pain. The nerves thus hit send a message to the brain which translates it into pain. And so, somewhere in my mind—and there alone—is born the image of the pain in the image of the finger, in the image of my body! Another objection, your honor: it hurts! And so it does. And yet, certain sects—I know some of their followers—teach techniques whereby the message of "pain" can be turned into one of pleasure! They stick hooks into their bodies and grin and bear it. (Rest assured, that has nothing at all to do with Tantra.) Under hypnosis it is very common to change a subject's perception, for example, to make one of his or her arms totally insensitive and to stick needles into it without the person under hypnosis feeling any pain. The fact that pain seems to be such an inescapable part of our experience does not prevent it from being a *pure mental fact*, which is not synonymous with unreal in the absolute sense.

In the Bible (Genesis, III:16) God cursed woman: "I will greatly multiply thy sorrow and thy conception; in sorrow thou shalt bring forth children." Does not the pain of childbirth have the reputation of being almost unbearable? And yet, an English obstetrician, Dr. Carol Reed, has succeeded in reducing this pain and even eliminating it altogether by paradoxically asking the parturient to concentrate on her uterine contractions. As long as she disregards socially bred ideas of suffering linked to childbirth, she does not feel any real pain. If, on the contrary, she thought "pain," she would tense up to resist pain and would suffer. With the appropriate prenatal exercises, she becomes capable of feeling her uterine contractions as normal muscular tension and she accepts this, lets go and does not really suffer. The Tantric Shakti goes even further. She experiences her entire pregnancy intensively, she participates consciously in the development of this new life within her, knowing that at the time of delivery, by trusting the Higher Intelligence of the body and letting it act, she will escape the biblical curse.

Which brings us back to the Supreme Wisdom of the body. Whether I am a man or a woman, I must become fully aware of the fact that my body is *an aggregate of billions of cells*, that are all alive, all conscious, all intelligent, and that I shall forever be unaware of their secret, inner life.

A question that crops up time and again: Why worry about it since it works? (Does it always work so well?) Why worry about this *real body* that is different from the *perceived body*? And what if we just left it to the philosophers to argue out? That would be a great loss, for my unknown, real body is an extraordinary mosaic of untapped powers and this leads us straight to Tantric practice!

The Wisdom of the Body

What is this Higher Intelligence, this Supreme Wisdom which inhabits my real body, which IS my real body? It is not an intellectual abstraction, it is not some cold philosophical speculation but a living fact. In order to approach it concretely, I suggest the two following, moving, experiments.

The first one is to look through a telescope, even an amateur telescope on a warm summer night, at the star-spangled firmament, and to become conscious of the fact that each dot of light is a sun, a sun whose light traveled thousands or even millions of light years before reaching us.

This image of the sky is older than the human race on our planet which is a tiny speck of cosmic dust orbiting the sun, a rather modest star. Perhaps hundreds or thousands of unknown planets are orbiting other suns? They may be the homes of living species that shall remain forever unknown to us and vice versa. If our sun were to explode now—a cataclysm on the cosmic scale—millenia would elapse before the information reached other unknown planets orbiting faraway stars! As a matter of fact, some of the stars we see today no longer exist; they disappeared eons ago and we don't even know it. Our "present" is made up of innumerable "pasts."

The second experiment which may be a bit more familiar to us is still just as extraordinary: observing a droplet of sperm—one's own, preferably, if one is a man, of course!—under the microscope. Borrow your child's junior scientist microscope, the one he/she got for his/her birthday, and deposit the droplet on the glass slide, focus, look through the eyepiece and be amazed. Amazed at the sight of these thousands of genetic tadpoles wiggling around frantically in search of the elusive ovum. Although seemingly banal, sperm is actually a magic fluid: just imagine that *each tadpole contains your entire heredity*, your entire history as well as *all* your ancestors,' and probably that of life itself since the very beginning. Just think that each spermatozoon could fertilize an ovum and beget a different baby. And lastly, just realize that in addition to this immemorial past, each tiny tadpole contains the future of humankind, cradles the fate of future generations. Now, can you really find words to express this grandiose reality? If one day a superhuman emerges from today's man or woman, as different from us as we are compared to our Cro-Magnon ancestor, this being will perforce have evolved from the genetic potential of today, included in each spermatozoon.

I insist: the adjective "each" is essential. Let us now remove one of these gametes and call upon all the Nobel prize laureates on the planet, grant them an unlimited line of credit, build them an ultra-sophisticated laboratory and challenge them to manufacture a single spermatozoon identical to the one we have just extracted. Would they be able to do it? With our state-of-the-art science and technology, the answer would be no and I doubt whether they could in the future. And yet, for dozens of years in a male's life, two modest, unimpressive organs, the testicles, produce spermatozoa to the tune of thirty thousand or more per second, night and day: a single ejaculation projects up to five hundred million spermatozoa! Yes, that's five hundred times one million! That's enough to artificially inseminate millions of women! It's a fantastic race for life, an incredible marathon whose single winner— that is, the one absorbed by the ovum—immortalizes at the same time all the others, plus the cellular republic it came from...

But there they are, right under your very eyes! Just imagine that your, sorry, our own personal history began when one of these microscopic tadpoles met an ovum one tenth of a millimeter in diameter, in the maternal uterus. Testicles are not robots, they are living organs whose intelligent work exceeds both our comprehension and our imagination. It is the Supreme Intelligence of the body, the unknown body, which is thus at work silently, without "letting on," with no laboratory, at body temperature and normal atmospheric pressure. It is so discreet that until recently, man, the male of the species, did not even know what his specific role in procreation was, whereas the body has always known it otherwise we would not be here! And the phenomenon occurs just as well in the testicles of the village idiot as in those of Einstein, of the criminal or the saint!

I'd now like to broach the topic of the ultra-sophisticated work of each organ. I shall restrict myself to the incredible biochemical performance of each liver cell which simultaneously accomplishes hundreds of ultra-complex organic chemistry operations without our being consciously aware of it. I mentioned spermatogenesis because in such a case Cosmic Intelligence is at its most creative since it is—precisely— procreative. Such colossal energy located at the pole of the species, is sexual, it is Kundalini, or at least a part of this central concept common both to Tantra and to Yoga.

One can thus measure the abyss between empirical, discursive, cerebral consciousness, that which produces eloquent reasoning, and the ultimate, infallible Wisdom of the body whose innate knowledge knows no chemical formulae!

Take the case of this biologist, a pancreas specialist. In spite of long and patient research, in spite of in-depth studies, there are still many unanswered questions. And yet, all this time, the Intelligence of the biologist's own pancreas has been carrying out all its functions, without fail, in a breeze!

One of Tantra's goals involves establishing a conscious and trusting relation between the empirical ego and the body's Higher Intelligence. This is one of the secret keys of Hatha Yoga.

The Body-Universe is Sacred

Here is a new paradox: in order to become better attuned to the ultimate Wisdom of my real body, I must develop my perceived, experiential body, enrich my body image. In comparing the latter to a city map I should have specified that whereas a city map is static, there is a *reciprocal dynamic relationship* between one's body image and the real body. I handle my real body from my body image and vice versa. How can this relationship be developed? It's quite easy: during asanas for example, one must look inward, listen to what the body has to say, become more receptive to it and thus glean as many feelings and sensations as possible in order to become more and more aware of them. In this way, I can harmonize my conscious self, my conscious ego, with the work of genius carried out by the body's Higher Intelligence which is both cosmic and divine. For a Tantrist, Shakti—energy personified, the supreme cosmic intelligence—permeates, animates the body. A Tantrist perceives her work even in his/her most humble physiological functions; pleasure and enjoyment are not self-serving, just for the ego. A Tantrist feels and knows that Shakti experiences pleasure through him or her, is embodied in him, the man, or her, the woman. In suggesting that you observe sperm, I may appear to favor male gametes, but the actual reason is practical: first of all, sperm is much easier to sample than an ovum, and secondly, seeing a bunch of wiggling tadpoles is more spectacular than observing a single ovum.

In Tantric ritual, the first step involves meditating on the corporeal "divinity" of one's partner and oneself. In maïthuna, when there is a union of the sexes, this relationship is experienced as a tremendous, sacred event involving totally the two cellular republics which are made up of countless billions of subjects. The longer and the more intense the union, the deeper the participation of each cell in the event. Tantric maïthuna integrates the two cellular entities into a single one, thereby re-creating the primeval androgyne, the biblical Adam, both male and female.

Improving the relationship between the body's Higher Intelligence and the conscious ego develops my trust and confidence in it, and I slowly come to acquire a faultless intuition which guides me throughout life. This can be accepted without any major reluctance. However, what's the point of realizing that the real body is part of the outside world, that it is a vast energy conglomérate, an unknown universe that is distinct from the body image? But let's go back a little: I may go so far as to accept that all I "know" about my body is the image of it in my own mind, but is there no ultimate correspondence between my body image and the real body? When I raise my "mental" arm, doesn't my "real" arm do the same thing? What's the point of distinguishing the two?

The point is that it makes all the difference in the world. Indeed, the imagined, experienced movement and real movement of the body do match. I also know that such a commonplace movement as picking up an object involves extremely complex neuromuscular coordination, but since "it works," why cudgel my brains over it?

In order to better grasp the point of it all, let me revert to my earlier line of reasoning and return to the question of the outside world by having a look at things all around me. In the room where I am now sitting and writing this text, the various objects around me—my desk, my chair, the phone, books, files, etc.—represent for me so many distinct, static entities. But more than that, I see them as being "outside" myself. In reality, "I" see somewhere in my brain or rather in my mind, the image of this room and its contents and in addition to that I have projected the image of my own body.

But what about outside, really "out there," what is there? First of all let's see what is not there. Outside, there is neither light, nor colors, nor sounds, nor smells, nor heat, nor cold. Granted, it's not easy to accept this, and at this point in the argument, it is often objected that "since everybody sees the same thing, then that's what the outside, concrete world is like." Are we so sure? All right, it's quite likely that all humans create pretty similar images in their minds from the same exterior objects. But what happens to the same outside universe seen through an organism having different sense organs—for example, a dog, a cat, or a honeybee? What does this cup become in the mind of a honeybee whose eyes, bearing hundreds of facets, perceive ultra-violet light? Nobody will ever know unless they become a bee. Naturally, outside there are photons, wave-guided particles of light, but light and dark, brightness, colors, are *internal, mental phenomena.* Outside, the air vibrates, but sounds arise and exist only in the mind. Outside, there are odoriferous substances, but fragrance is mental. One might retort: "Well, everybody smells the same aroma when something good is cooking and everybody's mouth waters. So how can one believe it's all in our head?"

Well, I came to understand this notably in India, while watching scrawny-necked vultures meticulously tearing to shreds a dead cow carcass. For us, it stinks to high heaven! But is it the same in a vulture's mind? No, it's not. For a vulture, carrion gives off a delicious aroma and it must wonder at these strange bipedals who avoid it like the plague instead of enjoying it. And so the very same, real, outside molecules become a stench in the human mind and a delicious aroma in the mind of the vulture. The same holds true for taste! In gobbling up its pound of flesh, the vulture is probably thinking the same thing as humans nibbling on some nicely aged cheddar cheese: it's just right!

The same rationale applies to all of our other senses.

A Strange, Living Universe

The idea that the outside world, although real, is colorless, noiseless, odorless, is a disconcerting one at the beginning, granted. It is indeed strange to think that outside there is not even darkness but the absence of light, that's all. Moreover, once you *really* realize that the slightest outside and real object is incredibly complex, that it is a powerful force field (if released, the atomic energy contained in a grain of sand would correspond to the explosion of a single charge of plastic explosive) then the way in which one sees the world and one's relation to it are turned inside out, *the borders between beings and objects dissolve*, beings and objects become clouds of energy, force fields. And so I perceive that this book, far from being an inert object, is actually a dynamic process in constant relation with the environment, with the entire cosmos. This view is crucial. Every material object is dynamic, everything evolves and changes, everything is linked to everything and everything has an influence on everything else.

You can imagine what this means when applied to human beings! My body, behind an apparent, relative immutability, also contains a process, a tremendous event. As a fragment of the moving cosmos, it is ever-changing as well. Its essence is an intelligent dynamism linked to the whole. The world of objects and beings is not made up of isolated units, but of dynamic processes in a state of constant mobility as units. The tree is a force field which immediately enters into a relation of exchanges with me, another force field. A stroll in the forest becomes a new experience because I feel that my body is a part of it.

Seen in this light, Tantric sexual intercourse is experienced in a totally different way compared to ordinary, profane sex. In Tantra, you don't have a situation where Mr. and Mrs. Doe are "making" love—more or less successfully—but rather a meeting of two cellular republics, two universes. Both partners are attuned to one another and exchanges are taking place at all levels. Climaxing thus becomes a non-essential by-product. Instead of being totally focused on one's own egotistic enjoyment, each partner opens up to the corporeal universe of the other and to one's own. There is no refusal of orgasm per se, but it is not really important, neither for the Shakti nor for the Shiva. The ritualized, Tantric maïthuna, thus made sacred, creates a relationship that is a far cry from profane intercourse, by virtue of this attitude of contemplation vis-à-vis the other person and the event of their union.

In our Western world, one of the people to have grasped this alternative attitude is Alan W. Watts. Excerpts from his book *Nature, Man and Woman* (p. 165), follow:

> Given the open attitude of minds and senses, sexual love in this spirit is a revelation. Long before the male orgasm begins, the sexual impulse manifests itself as what can only be described, psychologically, as a melting warmth between the partners so that they seem veritably to flow into each other.... [T]here is nothing particular that has to be made to happen. It is simply that a man and a woman are together exploring their spontaneous feelings—without any preconceived idea of what it ought to be, since the sphere of contemplation is not what *should* be but what *is*. In a world of clocks and schedules the one really important technical item is the provision of adequate time. Yet this is not so much clock time as psychological time, the attitude of letting things happen in their own time, and of an ungrasping and unhurrying interchange of the senses with their objects. In default of this attitude the greater part of sexual experience in our culture falls far short of its possibilities. The encounter is brief, the female orgasm relatively rare, and the male orgasm precipitate or "forced" by premature motion.... The contemplative and inactive mode of intercourse makes it possible to prolong the interchange almost indefinitely, and to delay the male orgasm without discomfort or the necessity of diverting full attention from the situation. Furthermore, when the man has become accustomed to this approach, it is possible also for him to engage in active intercourse for a very much longer period, so affording the greatest possible stimulation for the woman (pp. 195-197).

Although the above is not, strictly speaking, Tantra, in which such a contemplative exchange is just a prelude, its main merit is to allow the experience to last: a must if each cell is to participate totally in the experience. Getting each iota of each partner's body involved takes more than five or ten minutes! According to the Kinsey report, the average coitus of an American couple lasts under 10 minutes in 75 percent of the cases surveyed, and under 20 minutes in 91 percent of the cases. A bit short for cosmic fusion, isn't it?!

During this extended contact, sexual intercourse takes place on the three following levels:

—the empirical mind which participates in the game and experiences joy;

—the usually unconscious level of the inner-depths of the body upon which every successful experience leaves an indelible mark;

—the psychic level where contemplation creates an intimate fusion down to the core of the unconscious mind (*manomaya kosha*).

So where does the difference lie? Well, to assess it, a comparison must be made between the above and profane intercourse, this forging ahead toward compulsory orgasm, toward ejaculation, a reflex spasm of no Tantric interest. How uninteresting this brief, final pelvic thrust, compared to the ecstatic contemplation made sacred, and I use these words somewhat reluctantly because nowadays they reek of mysticism. And yet, mystical ecstasy is sexual, even a saint's, such as Saint Teresa of Avila. It is significant that a mystic usually describes his or her ecstasy in erotic terms which is incongruous in our own cultural environment, obsessed as it is by the (artificial) antinomy between sex and spirit. We are given embarrassed explanations that such words are symbolic. But Tantrists know better.

Nevertheless, some mystical visions are truly symbolic. When Saint Teresa said: "An angel of great beauty pierced me right to the heart with his flame-tipped spear" (Bondet, p. 149), there is no point in calling on Sigmund Freud to decipher that!

Come to think of it, it is unfair vis-à-vis Alan Watts to imply that he was not really Tantric. It's relatively true inasmuch as he excluded the Tantric ritual per se, but actually his approach, as such, is cosmic. Let me quote other excerpts from *Nature, Man, and Woman*: "Without wanting to make rules for this freest of all human associations, it is certainly best to approach it inactively. For when the couple are so close to each other that the sexual parts are touching, it is only necessary to remain quietly and unhurriedly still so that in time the woman can absorb the man's member into herself without being actively penetrated" (p. 201).

He also says that "waiting with open attention is rewarding. When no attempt is made to induce orgasm by physical motion, the interpenetration of sexual centers becomes a channel of a vivid psychic interchange. While neither partner works to make anything happen, both are surrendering completely to whatever the process feels like doing.

The sense of identity with the other becomes extremely intense, as if a new identity were formed between them and this identity has a life of its own. This life—we could call it Tao—lifts them out of themselves and they are carried together upon a cosmic stream of vitality. This vitality is no longer what "you" and "I" are doing. The man does nothing to excite or hold back the orgasm, and it becomes possible to have an interchange for an hour or more, and the female may have several orgasms with a very slight amount of active stimulation, depending on how receptive she is to the experience as a process that takes charge of her. "When this experience bursts in upon fully opened feelings it is no mere 'sneeze in the loins' relieving physical tension: it is an explosion whose outermost sparks are the stars" (p. 204).

In the above lines, Alan Watts (*Nature, Man, and Woman*, pp. 201-204) becomes truly cosmic and the final sentence of the quote is not a mere lyrical flight of fancy or a stylistic device. Tantra takes this literally for it *perceives no border* between the human psyche and the cosmic psyche which includes all of the stars. Alan Watts also mentions the fact that the couple becomes a new entity that is distinct from each partner and may I refer you to my chapter on the Overmind.

Perceiving others as so many prodigious force fields is not restricted to sexual intercourse, mentioned here as a special relationship. It extends to any kind of contact, commonplace though it may seem. Other living beings, be they human or animals, are not mere specters, robots endowed with some vague form of consciousness, but processes rooted in the infinite and whose dimensions exceed their individuality.

Beings are not limited to the present: they are part and parcel of an eternal process. Tantrists are keenly aware of the notion of processes. In front of another human being, a Tantrist will perceive all of that person's dimensions, notably his or her astounding past. As each and every spring is imprinted and present in a tree, "I" am my entire past, since my birth, since conception and even before that. The spermatozoon—back to cell one!—that begat me, is the outcome of an incommensurable process as we have seen (now would be a good time to read or re-read the chapter on Sacred Time).

I am borne by life and this life is fragile, everchanging, and yet permanent and indestructible. I never tire of repeating that Life, of which "I" am a limited but integral expression, the Life which carries me and permeates me was transmitted to me by my mother who—obviously—received it from her mother and so on and so forth. In thus climbing the tree of those uninterrupted generations, one eventually reaches the original Eve and even beyond her; with no hiatus be it ever so short, one thus traverses all of evolution up to the first living cells in the warm ocean which gave birth to life. My life is as old and as new as at the instant if its creation. Life is a continuous, gigantic process that has been evolving for billions of years and that will go on for billions of years. This holds true for any being one might consider: a virus, a plant, an insect, an animal. Names and shapes (*nama* and *rupa*) differ and change but the single essence is timeless. Terrestrial Life is a unitary process that is constantly devouring itself and feeding on itself, where everything impacts everything else. Tantra perceives the earth with its biosphere as a single living organism, endowed with an independent and collective psyche that is inseparable from the cosmos as a whole. This also corresponds to the Greek myth of Gaia that certain scientists are re-discovering today! The sun's moodiness not only disrupts radio communications, it also influences all life on earth !

When applied to one's environment, the idea of a process, of processes becomes very enriching indeed: each object-event immediately takes on a cosmic dimension. I would like to mention here the example of the Ganges in Benares with its enormous flight of stairs, the ghats, that reach right down into the river. There are throngs of Hindus gathered on the ghats, performing their ritual ablutions in the sacred waters of Mother Ganga, for the river Ganges belongs to the feminine gender.

The Sacred River

Standing in the river, among a variegated and contemplative crowd, gathering water in my two cupped palms, I offer it the rising sun and let it slip through my fingers. And so the water returns to Ganga which I perceive in her totality, as a process. Ganga, beyond the here and now, beyond the ghats and the crowd, melts into the immensity of time and space. Ganga is a moving, changing unit: upstream, at its source, way up in the icy Himalayas from which it springs, thousands of miles away, and downstream at its mouth, in Calcutta, where Ganga and the ocean unite. The ocean of its origins where water evaporates, becomes a cloud, snow or a monsoon downpour, to feed some other river before coming back to her, ceaselessly, in an eternal cycle. Ganga is both here and now, yesterday and tomorrow: her banks have witnessed the birth and death of countless generations. And on her banks, Ganga saw the very first villages, the first settlers; Ganga provided water indiscriminately to the horses of all of the invaders: the Aryan barbarians, the cruel Moghuls, the British and others. Conquerors may come and go but Mother Ganga remains and she shall always be there, eternal, always the same and never identical: you never swim twice in the same river, as the ancient Greeks used to say. Majestic and serene, nobody, nothing can stop her languid flow.

Well, so much for Ganga, but the same applies to any object, to any being. Each person is a river, from conception to death and yet, we are just a mere drop, a fleeting instant in the immense human river of today, yesterday and tomorrow. But we carry within ourselves the entire cosmos, for "there is nothing in the universe which is not in the human body... what is here, is there and what is not here is nowhere" states the *Visvasāra Tantra*. Moreover "In the body there are the Supreme Śiva-Śakti who pervade all things. In the body is Prakrti-Śakti and all Her products. In fact, the body is a vast magazine of Power (Śakti). The object of the Tantrik rituals is to raise these various forms of power to their full expression." (Woodroffe, *The Serpent Power*, Madras, 1965, p. 50).

Death is Life!

Everything is alive;
what we call "death"
is an abstraction.
—David Böhm

As early as the tender age of 10, I already had an inkling of what death was because of a friend of the family, a science teacher. For the kid I was, he had all the allure and prestige of a scientist. He was an enthusiastic entomologist, doubled as a geologist and his hobbies were paleontology and prehistory, and in those capacities he would tirelessly comb the entire region. He had discovered, among other things, in a wooded dale near a rivulet, a so-called "neolithic work-shop" where he had dug up dozens of carved stone tools.

Since he was our neighbor, I used to visit him quite often and I believe my inquisitiveness amused him. He had gradually built up his own little private museum which fascinated me, especially his butter-fly collection of all shapes, colors and sizes, pinned in well-ordered frames. The greatest thrill for me was when he obligingly opened his special showcase, the one I called his treasure chest which contained all the stone tools as well as three human skulls. One day, he removed one of those anonymous skulls from the showcase and knocking on his or her forehead, told me: "You know, *somebody* used to live and think in there…" All of a sudden those old bones took on a strange human dimension and I mused that some day, some stranger might hold my own skull and say: "Somebody used to live and think inside that skull…" Without really frightening me it did make me think and that is probably why I later bought a skull-shaped paperweight that used to adorn my desk as a student. It's one of the few objects of that period that I still have today; it has now acquired a certain sheen and generations of uninhibited flies have studded it with little black dots.

Ever since—naturally this has nothing to do with Tantra of which I was obviously totally unaware at the time—the mystery of death has been a subject of thought for me, reinforced by the war which, like millions of other men, put me face to face with death many a time and in very concrete terms indeed.

On a lighter note and in order to introduce and support the title of this chapter, here is the story of two friends who have just met. One of them says: "Do you know that so-and-so died?" And the other one, shrugging his shoulders, answered: "Well, ole buddy, what do you expect, that's life..." Right! For Tantra, death is a vital topic which underlies our entire world view. A follower of Tantra lives not with the obsession of, but in constant intimacy with, death. In the West death means the end or *absence* of life, whereas for Tantra it is the *opposite* of birth.

These few words express the huge gap between Eastern and Western thinking about death and until quite recently the subject was almost as taboo as sex. Moreover in India, death is linked to reincarnation, a complex subject that I will not evoke here. I shall restrict myself to shedding light on the mystery of death from the point of view of Tantra, in order to grasp its deeper meaning.

Paradoxically, Tantra is first and foremost the cult of life in its myriad forms; it embraces all the implications of the above, joy and pain, life's constraints. Life must be experienced in its myriad forms, from its humblest aspects to its most sublime. Tantra realizes that life can neither be truly understood nor enjoyed if death has not first been conquered. Conquering death is not tantamount to denying its existence or not wanting to come face to face with it or wishing not to be subjected to it—that's obviously impossible. The point is to take the sting out of death.

At the root of all suffering, of all fear, lies death, either one's own or that of one's loved ones. I remember being greatly troubled as a child when I realized for the first time that my mother was a mere mortal and I could not bear the idea that some day she would no longer be here. Her first gray hair caused me great sadness because it meant that she was also subjected to the process of aging and I could accept neither her aging nor her dying. In order to make me feel better she yanked that first gray hair out.

Do we not sometimes think that if it were not for disease and death life would be wonderful? But how true is this, really?

First of all, dying is something that happens to other people: when my time comes, I will no longer be there to talk about it! And secondly, only the individual fears death, for it means his or her disappearing, whereas for the species as a whole, it is an indispensable blessing.

Religions may console us, reassure us, as they tell us of eternal life after death or perhaps reincarnation. Right or wrong? Who knows? To each his/her own opinion and that is why this chapter will be restricted to the biological field alone.

Death as the Driving Force of Life

Very briefly: in Tantra, death is the driving force of life for without death, life would lose all appeal, all significance. Now for a closer look: if I ("I" represents each one of us) am alive, it is because "others" have died, otherwise dinosaurs would still roam the planet. Pardon me ! There would be no dinosaurs for all the seas and oceans of the planet would be overpopulated by the practically immortal single cell organisms of primeval times. These multiplied by dividing, producing two strictly identical cells, mother and daughter being indistinguishable: they are both twin sisters and orphans by birth! "Real" death came about with the complex, multicellular organisms which paved the way for the birth and evolution of an infinite number of species. Life gives top priority to the species which is relatively immortal compared to its individual members. Each species reacts rather paradoxically vis-à-vis its members: on the one hand it has endowed individuals with a tremendous survival instinct and on the other it has programmed their disappearance. It's all quite rational: if the species were made up of immortal individuals, it would not be able to evolve. Thanks to death, each species, with each passing generation, safeguards its opportunity to evolve. *If death were eradicated, all extant species would become cast in concrete so to speak, stopped in their tracks.*

What applies to automobiles also applies to species: if the first Ford automobiles had been immortal, impeccably crafted, they would still be running today and would only add to the traffic congestion. Automakers also program the "death" of their cars: they deliberately limit their life expectancy and maximum mileage, thus new, more high-tech ones can be made! And so it is with life. Replacing its individuals provides each species with the indispensable plasticity required for its survival faced with the competition of other life forms and the challenge of a constantly changing environment. And so for the species, replacing its individuals is an inescapable necessity.

If we were to reason *ad absurdum* that life had declared compulsory immortality for all and sundry, what would happen? Quite simply, life would be totally and incurably blocked. Without death there would be no babies, no elderly people, only adults, immutably identical to one another. Death is a permanent process. Each and every day billions of cells die, those of our skin for example, and these cells are constantly renewed throughout our lifetime except, they say, for our nerve cells. My immortality as an individual would imply that of my cells as well, and I would be forever identical to myself!

There is another corollary to immortality: no more babies, therefore no more sexes! If nobody died anymore, imagine a world made up of permanent fixtures, unchangeable, irremovable and asexual adults.

Not even unisexual, for there would be neither female nor male genitalia! Flowers are the sex organs of plants and in a universe where everything is immortal, plants would be seedless, therefore devoid of corollas and pistils!

How Immortality Begat Boredom

As mere immortals and after spending a few billion years in an unchanging and unchangeable world, we would definitely begin to mope around and fret. Here is an idea! In order to pass the time of day, let us make love. But lo and behold, we have no sex! Never mind: let's cook a gourmet meal. Woe is me! Immortals have no need to eat, moreover salad would be just as immortal as the rest. No cheese: making cheese requires milk and immortal cows have no calves to feed and since there would be no eating, we would not even need a digestive tract! No sex, no stomach, no intestines.

We would all be together, all irremovable and immutable, for countless billions of years: unbearable! And that would only be the beginning! Such an absurd hypothesis, a world of immortal beings, requires as a corollary the invulnerability of those immortals. For if we were both immortal and vulnerable then as centuries elapsed we would invariably be full of wounds and scars or even have been amputated of a limb here and there! In what state would we be after "only" a few thousand years?

If we were invulnerable, however, we would be footloose and fancy-free and could indulge in all of our whims: just to pass the time of the day we could for example, jump off a cliff and land on the boulders below without ever hurting ourselves. Pursuing this line of reasoning would naturally lead to ever-greater absurdities.

Accepting the fact that death is the driving force of life, that without death Life would be unthinkable, absurd, that it would lose the greater part of its charm, that physical immortality would be unbearable, is all good and well, but as regards our own death, why should we have to worry about it before our time comes? Would it not be better just to forget about it, to be concerned only with living one's life? Why let the gloomy cloud of death darken the sky of our life?

Outside any religious considerations, why should the worship of life be incompatible with the thought of our own death? Let's try to understand why Tantrists combine the cult of life and a constant closeness, even intimacy, with death. The following story will help shed some light on the matter.

One day we got a phone call saying that some friends had just been in a car accident: the woman had a broken pelvis and her husband had a concussion. The next day when we went to visit them at the hospital, expecting to find them in a state of shock, devastated—surprise, surprise?—we found them in great spirits. As she sat up in bed, munching on an apple, her husband told us about the accident and how just before the impact he had realized what was going to happen. Then he blacked out and woke up at the hospital. The wife said: "Life is fantastic! I'd never realized it before: how great to eat an apple!." And the husband replied: "Actually, dying is easy. What's more, yesterday I had all these worries and concerns and the accident has swept the slate clean! Today, everything is new and I know what *really* counts."

This is not an isolated case and you have probably encountered similar ones. The lesson is clear: coming face to face with death dramatically heightens one's sense of being alive. Here is another example: the countless tragic events that took place during the Second World War included arrests, arbitrary rulings and death sentences. Thousands of people lived with the idea of their imminent death. Almost without exception, these people on death row, locked up in their cells, had a lucid and courageous vision of death and displayed tremendous fortitude. Their perspective on life was different. And many of those who survived to tell the story—after the event, naturally—stated that it had been an enriching experience.

Tantrists do not wait until they come face to face, by chance, accidentally, with death to perceive the true meaning of life: we shall see how below.

Since death does exist, one must come to terms with it and take it into account. We don't really fear *being dead*; what we really cannot stand is that we have to die first! Not having lived in Lincoln's days does not affect me either way—and pardon my "off-color" humor—but being dead in a hundred years from now leaves me cold!

Let us look death straight in the eye. The species has sown in each individual a survival instinct whereby he/she tries by every possible means to escape death's clutches and live as long as possible. As regards suicide, it could be pointed out that what really prevents many people from terminating their own life is the "transition." We hang on to life like an apple clings to the apple tree, come hell or high water. And yet when the October winds blow and the leaves turn brown, the apple is ripe and it falls naturally from the branch, without any regrets, without any resistance: such a simple and easy "death" just might be what life originally programmed in our genes. The body's Higher Intelligence fights for its survival until the bitter end, but if the incurable failure of an essential organ makes this end inescapable, then the very same Intelligence of the body triggers the "death process," pre-planned and programmed. For it is a complex and rather slow process. *People don't just up and die*, even if they have been guillotined; that is just the beginning of the dying process. Upon severing the convict's head, the blade of the guillotine merely sets off the death process. First the brain is going to die. It is stunned by the shock and soon it will suffer irreparable damage: when deprived of oxygen, brain cells die after just a few minutes. Conversely a man's beard—which should be awarded first prize for obstinacy for failing to be discouraged by countless close shaves—tastes sweet revenge at last: it will "survive" and grow for several days, as will hair and nails. Consequently the exact time of death is impossible to ascertain. In the plant kingdom things are even slower and less precise. A gardener once planted all around our house trees supported by stakes. Two of those trees failed to grow, however their stakes did! Buds formed, branches grew, roots developed and these stakes are now strong trees. Planting them in the soil reversed the process, otherwise they would have become firewood. Exactly when would they really have been "dead"? The question remains unanswered.

At the same time as the physical body dies, the subtle, psychic body—which is also material, according to Tantra—disintegrates slowly, probably over a period of several weeks. That is why Indian Tantrists are buried so that the disengagement can take place normally, and not cremated, as is the usual Aryan custom. Another question: is death the end? Whatever the case may be, human beings survive in their own children, their grandchildren and beyond them, in their eternal genes. And if one has no children, one survives in the process of humankind.

The Gentle Transition of Natural Death

My second encounter with death also occurred when I was about 10 years old and it revealed to me that real death, natural death which should be the norm, is neither frightening nor painful. When I was a child, the house next door (we lived right outside the city, almost in the country) belonged to a retired mason whose garden was his pride and joy. His flowerbeds were unimpeachable, perfectly aligned, and nowhere was there a weed to be seen. After toiling in his garden and when everything seemed just right, he would sit down on a wooden bench he himself had built to oversee his modest estate, and admire his radishes and lettuces. One day as he was sitting on his bench, warming himself in the May sun, his calloused hands resting on his thighs, I jumped at the opportunity and bombarded him with questions from my side of the fence, about the "good old days" when he was a young man: we used to have such grand conversations from time to time. That day I was all ears as he told me about his father's life and times, relating stories that were over fifty years old, i.e., for the kid I was, about as old as Methuselah! This habitually tight-lipped old-timer would narrate for me in lavish detail his father's life, how up at dawn he used to walk in his wooden clogs to the quarry six miles away, carrying his jug of coffee and lunch in a knapsack. This stonecutter would work for up to ten or twelve hours a day depending on the season, wielding a twenty-five pound hammer, under a flimsy, makeshift shed, come rain or come shine. In the evenings, at home, he would work in his garden or tend his animals. Never a day off, not even Saturday afternoon, except for Sundays and religious holidays and he'd never even heard of the word vacation! One night, when he was over 90 years old, he said: "I'm tired!" Then he went up to bed and on the following morning they found him dead. Had he perceived the "transition"? That's the only time my neighbor ever heard his father—who had never had a sick day in his life—use the word "tired."

Is that it, the natural death, the one that comes in its own time when the body has lived out its life, with no suffering, like sleep, death's brother, descends upon us? Actually it seldom happens in this way, even in nature where violent death is more often than not the rule. Yet even in the case of violent death it would appear that far from being a terrifying experience, dying is on the contrary almost exhilarating, interesting, luminous. How can we know since nobody has ever come back to tell us? However, with modern resuscitation techniques, clinically dead people are resurrected and there are thousands of accounts of dying people forcibly brought back to life who describe these near-death experiences or pre-death as something ecstatic. Very often these survivors are furious at having been revived and are extremely disappointed to wake up in a hospital bed with tubes running in and out of them! Therefore we have good reason to believe that the much feared moment of death is actually the final peak experience of life.

My third encounter with death was accidental and took place at about the same time, when I was about 10 or 12. My father was a First World War veteran and would never tell me about what he had experienced in the trenches, in spite of my inquisitiveness. One of his friends, however, was more talkative.

Accidental Death

My father's friend told me about the time when during an artillery fire he had taken refuge in a trench and a shell exploded nearby, burying him. He described how each time he exhaled, the loose earth would collapse further upon him, compressing his chest, and making it impossible for him to breathe in. He could no longer breathe or even move any part of his body and he thought he was going to smother to death, thus becoming a "beautifully" intact corpse, for he had not actually been wounded. His initial, frantic anxiety was followed by a strange feeling of calmness and—a classical occurrence which I was unaware of at the time—he relived entire chapters of his life and saw, inter alia, his long-dead mother walking back from the village fountain carrying two pails of water.

Meanwhile his buddies were hard at it, trying to dig him out as fast as they could. They got to him in the nick of time, saving him from an apparently awful death. This experience had left a tremendous impression on him and so struck was I by his story that to this day I remember its every detail. I am convinced that life is kind toward the dying.

This reminds me of another story which took place during the Second World War in which a soldier who had been "shot dead" by a death squad, told me the true story of his execution, but so that nobody gets touchy about it, since similar events took place in most of the warring nations, the circumstances and the place shall remain nameless. This soldier was taken as a hostage and locked up in a barn along with other unfortunate souls. All night long the soldiers guarding them kept on repeating to the beat of their fingers drumming the butt of their rifles: "Tomorrow morning, bang... bang...." At dawn they were led to a field and forced to dig a trench. Then they were lined up behind their future common grave as the soldiers aimed: "Ready, aim, fire!" ordered the commander as the machineguns fired away and our hostage "blacked out," those were his very words. He passed out and collapsed and when he later regained consciousness he was lying on the ground under the other dead men who were also gradually coming to: the soldiers had fired just above their heads and were laughing about this great practical joke! Then they released their hostages, considering no doubt that the lesson had been enough. Conclusion: if those men had really been shot dead, life would have been kind enough to spare them the throes of an apparently absurd death.

But back to Tantrists for whom death is the ultimate guru. Their regular flirting with the fact of death and its meaning aims at the following objectives:

—to reveal the true meaning of life which then conditions the right attitude toward oneself, others, and human values in general;

—to discover the innermost secret of being;

—to make it possible to prepare oneself to consciously experience one's own death;

—to go beyond all fears, in other words to overcome the fear of death which is the substratum of all other fears.

This is neither a morbid nor an obsessive attitude but rather a permanent awareness of the impermanent, precarious nature of life. Acceptance of the above dispels all anguish, but what counts is deriving practical lessons from this in order to live one's life, of course, but also to prepare one's death.

The best way to prepare to die—seriously—is to do one's utmost to live as long as possible. Is this not the only way to reach natural death?

Shava Sadhana

I have no intention of suggesting that anybody carry out the fearsome experiment described below, I only mention it to show that Tantra knows no bounds and goes "all the way."

When tradition stipulates that the follower of Tantra must live close to places of cremation, this is sometimes symbolic but oftentimes literal: let us be neither disturbed nor shocked by it but rather let us try to discover the meaning behind it. Remember, when India was conquered, the losers who accepted defeat became serfs (sudras), whereas the rebels, rejected by the system, became "untouchables." Tantrists, being opposed to Brahmanical racism and its ultrapatriarcal system, and given to the female cult, belong to the resistance to the invader which has been going on for over a thousand years and still exists today. Some of today's Tantrists belong to the *Chandala* tribes about whom Manu's laws state:

"Near well-known trees and burial-grounds, on mountains and in groves, let these (tribes) dwell, known (by certain marks), and subsisting by their peculiar occupations" (X.50).

Given the Brahmins' strong distaste for work—deemed shameful—and corpses, one measures the degree of abjection that these men come under, deliberately. Thus many Tantrists have lived close to places of cremation. Faced for thousands of years with death and corpses, they turned it into a spiritual experience, the *shava sadhana* described in *Tantra, its Mystic and Scientific Basis* (Lalan Prasad Singh, Delhi, 1976, p. 148):

This *Sadhana* is done for the unification of the *Kundalini* with *Param Shiva*. Performed with a dead human body at the dread of night on the New Moon day, it is the most difficult form of spiritual practice. Detailed rituals have been laid down for this *Sadhana*. The *Sadhaka* has to observe the esoteric principles very strictly. Violation of any rule or ritual results in disastrous consequences.

This is the most secret part of Tantric mysticism, but has been greatly misunderstood due to its non-Aryan character. The dead body should be fresh, complete and uninjured. It should not be mutilated or deformed. No part of the body should be distorted. Even if a finger is missing, or the dead is one-eyed, it is unfit for Tantra Sadhana. It is against the principle of Tantra Shastra.

Then the follower is left all alone in the dark night with the corpse and maybe even sitting on it. Then he or she meditates on what makes him or her different from this other human being who was still alive yesterday. The Tantric follower, in his/her mind's eye identifies with the corpse, experiences the disintegration of the body to discover within himself/herself the "living principle." This is a fearsome trial that one should never undertake without being guided, even in imagination only.

In another ritual, called *Kâpâlika Sadhana*, a human skull is used instead of a corpse. In the "5 M" ritual, the wine is drunk either out of a real skull (preferably a Brahmin's!) or from a cup which symbolizes a skull. Some Tantrists live and meditate in huts whose walls are literally lined from top to bottom with human skulls. Sometimes sexual

rites take place in cemeteries, among corpses, in order to perceive the complementarity of death and its antidote, sex.

Without actually practicing these rites and meditations, we should nevertheless be aware of the fact that Tantra does not have only pleasant sides and it is good that we grasp the origin of this intimacy with death.

What parts of this can be put into practice in the West? Very little indeed, except that we can often reflect on the meaning of life from the perspective of death, to discern its presence all around us and to realize that for Life, death is no tragedy. When we watch swallows fly, do we think that each dive means the death of an insect? Does this bother us or make us sad? And yet, from the mosquito's point of view, things are quite different... For the insect-individual it's the end of the world, but for the "mosquito" species it's of no importance. It's all part of the plan and its response to death is a tremendous reproductive potential. Kitty gets yelled at for pouncing on a robin, but who worries about the torment of a worm being swallowed up like spaghetti by a blackbird?

Death is an Abstraction

Soon emerges the Tantric perception that *death is an abstraction* and that *only life exists*. Of course there are corpses which are immediately recovered by life but, I repeat, only life has any real existence and letting go is easy when one is "ripe" for the great departure: remember the ripe apple falling from the tree. But in the meantime why not measure, size up our values by comparing them to the death standard rather than the gold standard? If our typical Westerner, over-ambitious, hyperactive, aggressive, asked himself/herself each morning whether he/she *really* wanted to become the richest skeleton in the cemetery, that might change his/her outlook. I knew a businessman some time ago—and this is not an isolated case, far from it—who was a real workaholic, setting up one business after the other, and was very successful. He was very rich and owned a beautiful chateau which he seldom visited and when he did he spent most of his time working. The only person to really enjoy his park was the gardener! He died (the businessman, not the gardener!) two years ago and he is no doubt the richest corpse in the cemetery. But does he really get anything out of it now, in the beyond?

However, the true response to the enigma of death is to be found in its Tantric definition: *death is life and dying is the opposite of being born*. Furthermore, I must realize that my life did not begin the day I was born nor even when my father's spermatozoon penetrated my mother's ovum; I must realize that *life is a continuous process* and that *I am* this process.

The chapter titled "Profane Time, Sacred Time" sheds light on the notion of process which frees me, releases me, from death.

Imminent death may sometimes lead to a very powerful, high-level spiritual experience. I remember getting a phone call from a friend one morning: he was very upset for he had just learned that he had leukemia and had only six months to live at the very most. What did he expect from me? Advice? Sympathy? I don't really know. And I confess being embarrassed: what can one say in such a case? Several months elapsed and I had no news. He called me back a year later and of course I did not say, "Well, looks like you're still around!" So I waited for him to explain. He said, in a nutshell: "At the beginning I was extremely upset. Then after some time I began to live fully each and every minute, to enjoy each ray of sunshine. Everything took on a fantastic relief. A mere flower that I never would have noticed before became something wonderful. Playing with my grandson was extraordinary. I felt myself alive through him as I did through my own children. I also meditated a lot and one bright morning I accepted without reservation the fatal outcome that had been announced to me. From then on I realized, I perceived, that I was part and parcel of the universe around me and that this would always be the case. My life has changed, I am happy. Now I know what's important and what is not. My leukemia? Oh, the doctor made a wrong diagnosis and I should actually be grateful to him! No kidding!"

Voilà! As a matter of fact, are we not all suffering from a 100 percent fatal disease—life? Should we have to wait for such a direct threat and a medical diagnosis to live fully, in spite of, or thanks to, the shadow of death?

There is a facet of the death question which I may seem to be skirting: the suffering that often precedes death, i.e., senility, disease and the pain they cause. Unfortunately these ordeals are all too real and nobody is denying them, but are they really inevitable, part of nature's plan? Naturally, the only way to live long is to grow old, but senility is neither unavoidable nor an inescapable outcome premeditated by Mother Nature. No illness, no disease, not even cancer is inescapable. At first sight, life is like a feast which begins with dessert, a happy childhood, and finishes by punishment, illness, suffering, senile decrepitude. Actually this is not at all part of nature's plan. Life provided for natural death as illustrated by the case of the man who slipped into the beyond while asleep, unknowingly, without ever having been ill.

Yogis contend that senility and illness are escapable outcomes: throughout their lives "civilized" people write "bad" checks that will bounce later on. They do not lead healthy lifestyles, eat or breathe properly, are too sedentary, letting their bodies get all "clogged up," becoming ill and senile. I've often mentioned the incredible youthfulness of Tantra masters and followers. It is very real but one has to lead the appropriate lifestyle, in other words practice yoga and I refer you to my books, which should come as no surprise!

And so that is how, for Tantra, death is the supreme guru.

Our "Dying Behavior"

Obviously the subject of death and demise would require an entire book. However for the practical purpose of living one's life, we can retain the following elements which stem from the above: "I" am an emanation of the "Life-process" and my life began neither at birth nor even at the moment of conception. Regardless of my religious faith or lack thereof, Tantra teaches that death is not the end, for the life process extends beyond the dissolution of my ego.

As a continuous process, I evolve within other processes that are infinitely greater, those of life, those of the cosmos! As a minute, yet gigantic atom, I embody the organizing dynamic force of the species as well as the conscious and creative power of universal Life.

In short, terrestrial Life as a whole is a tremendous single organism constantly devouring itself thanks to which it has proliferated ever increasingly, while diversifying to the extreme.

Powerful words? Perhaps… But beyond mere words, a powerful reality.

You might reply, and rightly so, that all of the above boils down to mere philosophical considerations, theory, and fails to solve the problem of *my own* death whose time will inevitably come: what does Tantra have in store for *me* and how can I prepare myself concretely?

Tantra's response to death is imbued with total serenity. Earlier I touched on the throes of senile decrepitude and its ills which we think necessarily accompany the dusk of our life. These days people feel that dying from a disease is the "normal" end of human life. And yet we know that for Tantra such suffering was not planned by Mother Nature and is escapable. Consequently, a Tantrist who is aware of his/her duties vis-à-vis the cellular republic, notably the duty to ensure its integrity, to lead a healthy yogic lifestyle, i.e., a long and happy one, thus prepares a natural and gentle death.

As regards dying proper, a Tantrist cultivates the awareness of his/her own mortality while at the same time, paradoxically, not worrying about it. Why? Because the dying behavior which has been programmed in my genes, will begin when the time comes without my having to worry about it. My body *has always known how to die*, even if "I" am unaware of it.

And that is actually what we did in our mother's womb, unknowingly, of course. Just think of the trials and tribulations of an infant worrying about its own birth, wondering how it is going to get out of its cozy uterine "prison": what a time he/she might have squeezing through the vaginal gate! Fortunately he/she doesn't worry his/her pretty little head about that! And unknowingly still, the baby trusts the body's Intelligence which, of course, *already knows what to do*. At the right time, the "program" will start and the child is informed of what it must do. It takes two to be born: the mother's body's Higher Intelligence dictates to her her "delivery behavior" to which responds the baby's "birth behavior," programmed and "run in" over the passing millions of years.

In the same way, our "dying behavior" pre-exists within us, in each one of us, and our intellect should not be concerned about it nor try to anticipate it: it will take place naturally, without our having to think about it. All I need to "do" is let go and give in to the instinctive behavior that will be revealed to me as the dying process takes place. I don't have to think about it beforehand. Most people already have such an attitude, you might say: they know they are going to die but they try to forget about it and when faced with the idea, they repress it. Tantrists do not try to obliterate the fact of death and they prepare for it by abiding by, as closely as possible, the natural and foreseen end of their lives. In the meantime, they let death lighten up their existence, not darken it, without pre-empting the dying process that they entrust to the body's Higher Wisdom which is that of Life.

No Dying

The following sign should be posted in hospital lobbies: "No dying." For medical science, "losing" a patient is experienced as a failure, almost an affront to the Medical Establishment. Doctors try to keep patients alive as long as possible, at whatever cost: they don't let people die any more. It is true to say that gentle, natural death has become an incongruous anomaly in a society where it is felt that you have to die of something, in other words, where it is inconceivable that one may die in good health, simply because the time has come.

Moreover, physicians try to eliminate or at least alleviate as much as possible their patients' suffering and no one blames them. But the peculiar corollary is that when the battle is eventually lost, the M. D.

will administer strong medication to the patient so that he/she slips into death unawares. This ultimate mercy, as it is perceived to be, actually deprives the patient of his/her right to "enter into death with your eyes wide open," to quote Marguerite Yourcenar.

Nowadays, the normal, almost decent thing to do is to die in an anonymous, almost clandestine way at the hospital. Yet, current evidence on near-death experiences confirms the fact that the transition, i.e., death, is an elating experience filled with light, thus confirming what people in the East have always asserted, notably the Yogis.

All of this is gaining wider acceptance in medical circles, I'm not denying it. A physician friend of mine confided in me that at the time of the great departure he would ask to be taken home to die among his nearest and dearest, like it used to be. That's what all Tantrists wish for as well, while at the same time knowing that the best way to prepare for one's own death is to live as long as possible and in good health!

I would like to close this chapter in repeating that as stated at the outset, only the "biological" side of death has been dealt with. The question of what happens after death was not raised in this chapter for it is the purview of religion. It is up to each and every one of us to decide where we stand on this matter, on the basis of our own beliefs. Moreover, an in-depth review of such a subject would require at least an entire book.

Woman:
Her Worship, Her Mystery

Woman is the Creator of the universe.
She is the very body of the universe;
woman is the support of the three worlds,
she is the very essence of our body.
There is no other happiness as that which woman can procure.
There is no other way than that which woman can open to us.
Never there has been, there is, there will be
a fortune the like of woman, no kingdom,
no place of pilgrimage, yoga, prayer,
mystic formula, asceticism, wealth.

Shaktisangama-Tantra II.52

The Mother-Goddess, the initiator, the origin of all life, the source of enjoyment, the path toward transcendence: woman and her mystery are at the heart of Tantra, are the very essence of its age-old message.

It might seem that the above emphatic enumeration has nothing to do with our daily lives, with the flesh-and-blood women we live with, meet every day: our mothers, sisters, wives, lovers. Is the mystery of Woman concealed in *them*? Where?

Fathoming the abyssal depth of the Woman hidden in actual women and gaining access to this, is precisely the stuff that Tantra is made of. The *Kaulâvalî Tantra* says: "One should bow to any female, be she a young girl, flushed with youth, or be she old, be she beautiful or ugly, good or wicked. One should never deceive, speak ill of, or do ill to, a woman and one should never strike her. All such acts prevent the attainment of *siddhi* (i.e., success in religious exercise)."

The way the woman is worshipped in Tantra far exceeds the claims of any women's liberation movement. I am not being critical of this movement which has become a necessity in our patriarchal society and which has at least placed women on an equal footing with men. "Equal" not being the same as "identical." Tantra believes that first and foremost Woman must emerge from the woman. She must become aware of what she *really* is, and she must integrate that awareness into the way she views herself and the world, as it becomes part and parcel of her life.

A male Tantrist's attitude toward women is very different from the ordinary male's. Indeed for the former, all women embody Shakti and they are not a sex object to be courted for their favors or game to be hunted. Tantric men are neither Casanovas nor Don Juans. Even if she is alone with a male Tantrist, she has nothing to fear; she is totally safe and free to act in any way she pleases. She is respected and will never be bothered or harassed.

Actually Tantra's message concerns both men and women. Every Tantric shakti is, or seeks to become, a *true* woman, one who dares to delve into her own being to discover her inner and ultimate well-springs.

She is the goddess, that is, the incarnation of the living and the present, the ultimate cosmic energy, although she may be unaware of it. So not only must men's attitude change, but women's as well, vis-à-vis her own mystery which she generally fails to perceive: "I am neither mysterious nor holy, nor divine," she may think. And for men, the mystery of women lies in their whimsical, capricious, unpredictable and irrational nature which makes them elusive and unattainable. Whereas *her true mystery is the mystery of Life*; for be we a man or a woman, our own personal life began in our mother's womb. But with the spectacular achievements of genetics and biology what actually remains of the so-called mystery of life? For primitive peoples, conception and birth were shrouded in mystery, but this is no longer the case even for our children: storks and cabbage patches belong to a bygone era! At school they are taught how the sperm fertilizes the ovum and how the embryo develops in the uterus. Genetics has therefore demystified—or desacralized?—the secrets or our heredity, especially in our age of gung-ho genetic engineering. We can film a fetus' development in utero and with a simple injection plan the baby's time of birth, give or take 15 minutes: fewer and fewer deliveries take place at night, a modern labor-saving device much welcomed by gynecologists!

In spite of all that, the mystery of life, embodied by and in women, remains abyssal. A mother represents infinitely more than a walking incubator even if her little conscious ego is unaware of it. Her mystery lies in the *creative powers* within her. A Tantrist (both male and female, of course) realizes that in a woman's womb, "that" which produces the ovum is the ultimate creative power. There, in the dark warmth of her belly, the primordial cosmic forces emerge, whether the ovum is fertilized or not. Understanding what is *really* at work and acting in her uterus, is grasping the mystery of the universe. That fantastic creative dynamism which gives rise to atoms and galaxies, makes wheat sprout, makes bacteria proliferate, is present and active at all times, not only during pregnancy, in all women, in all females. Am I being over-lyrical in evoking this grandiose reality? Is it too much to want to worship it? Women actually do *make* a baby: they don't just sit back and watch it grow inside of them.

Naturally the fertilized ovum's inherent dynamism, its genetic code, regulates the fetus' development which of course continues after birth. But the ovum is produced by the woman and not by some sort of mechanics. Lying dormant within her, involute, is the entire experience of all past generations through the entire evolution of humankind, even pre-human life. It is via her generative powers that the woman carries forth the species, via the creative powers of nature locked away within her. But does not the male of the species also contribute half the genetic capital, are the same forces not also at work inside of him? Does he not produce each and every day millions of spermatozoa, those torpedoes of heredity? Indeed. However, biologically speaking, the basic blueprint of any species, including human, is female. Therefore, a man is basically female, and the male was only "invented" in order to disseminate genes.

Woman was humankind's initial religion and the mother-goddess the very first divinity. Was, or is? It is an open-ended question. Suffice it to point out that she is found throughout the prehistoric world. She is represented by the first clumsy attempts at sculpting a human figure. She is the mother-goddess and also embodies the eros principle. She is the Shakti, the primordial energy whence the manifest universe emerges.

A religion of Woman also comprises its priestesses and magicians, i.e., cosmic go-betweens. Woman's mystery is not restricted to her sex: it pervades her entire being, including (and perhaps most of all) her psyche, her mind. Women are intuitive because they are in tune with their senses and attuned to cosmic rhythms. They know the secrets of life and health, of plants, of flowers. In archaic cultures, women were/are generally in charge of agriculture, notably because it was/is believed that their life-giving power could/can influence the fertility of the soil. A woman understands the human soul's wellspring, for in her unconscious mind and through it, she is directly linked to the major currents of the mind which bear us and carry us forward. She both attracts and terrorizes. Each man holds within him the image of the ultimate, absolute Woman but if he were actually to meet her, it would be tantamount to being struck by lightning: more powerful than love at first sight, he would remain forever attached to her. Actually, all his life, every man searches for her. Those who have met her are extremely few and far between and one might almost say: it's just as well! This is the dream, the unattainable ideal that men project in movie stars, for example: Greta Garbo was "divine" because she represented the ideal woman for millions of men, for whom all men feel a nostalgic longing. Such an "underground" worship of woman is actually thriving: its icons are, for example, pin-up girl posters, our contemporary caricatures of the real woman, created by men for men.

Feminists are critical of women being used as sex objects in advertising, and yet it is a tribute paid to women, albeit a clumsy one. One day I had to mail a package and went to the local post office in a small rural train station. The man behind the window was far from good-looking and piles of papers littered his counter. A single, naked bulb cast its dim light on the contents of flimsy shelves. Fixed onto the no-longer-white wall with rusty tacks was the torn, fading poster of a shapely and scantily clad pin-up girl: there was the Shakti in living color, right there in the train station, although the image of the pin-up girl did certainly not represent the paragon of the *true* woman!

What, and who, is the true woman? That is the question! Although each and every woman embodies the ultimate female principle and eros, the true Shakti is becoming ever scarcer. Who is to blame? Women, or the patriarchy which stifles them? Today, our women are like zombies, like attractive caricatures of true women. In matriarchal cultures, women can reach true fulfillment, and so can men, for the latter can evolve and grow only if they are in living contact with true women: by stifling women, men have stifled themselves. Throughout pre-historic times, matriarchal civilizations spread from the Mediterranean all the way to Dravidian India where they still exist today, in some regions, such as Kerala.

Outside India, the Trobriand Islanders, whose culture has been well documented, are one of the happiest peoples in the world: in spite of—or because of?—their matriarchal structure, men are neither repressed nor exploited and the women are free, open, radiant.

Mother Nature is matrifocal, that is, revolving around the mother: kittens suckling their mother's milk, purring away, could not care less about the old tomcat that sired them! And everybody's seen an old pussycat buried in a blanket or a piece of fur, kneading away, "making biscuits" with gusto: what is it doing if not repeating its behavior as a small kitten nestled against its mother's warm belly, an image still alive and present in its cat-mind. As for its genitor, well...

Knowing who the mother is, is easy and beyond the shadow of a doubt; as for the father, well, that's another kettle of fish! In the patriarchal system, the lineage goes from father to son: the estate used to go to the eldest son, or at least such was the case in most of our countries until the law was changed. The situation is different in matriarchal cultures and I would like to quote Alain Daniélou, *Les quatre sens de la vie*, Paris, 1976, p. 227: "The matriarchal system where the entire family estate belongs to the woman and the daughter inherits from her mother, is the system still in place today in Kerala, in South India. Even in royal families, the throne is passed on from mother to daughter and the king is a mere consort. This practice is deemed to be the only effective means of ensuring that royal blood is passed on. According to the ancient Indian saying: 'When a father says this is my son, that is faith: when a mother says it, that's knowledge.' Social institutions must rest upon certainties and not beliefs."

In the patriarchal system involving a father-to-son lineage and where the estate is inherited by the eldest son, in order to ensure that the kids are really chips off the old block and that "like father, like son" is a reality and not a taken-for-granted assumption, what must men do? Obviously they *must* gain control and take possession of women and their sex; they must be locked up physically, in a harem for example, and socially, in a network of rules and constraints which includes all manner of punishment to deter them from adultery, and they must remain virgins until they are married. When pushed to the extreme, this male argument leads to the "sewn-up women" (there are millions of such women in Muslim Africa): the clitoris and labia minora are excised—without anaesthesia or antisepsis—and the vaginal opening is sewn up leaving only a tiny orifice for the menstrual flow. This guarantees their virginity better than any chastity belt! On the wedding night, the husband opens up his glorious way to paternity with his dagger. And the next day he proudly shows the blood-stained weapon and linen for all to see. The ultimate male refinement: young women are sewn up by older ones, so except for deflowering them with their dagger, men don't have to dirty their hands!

The same patriarchal logic leads to abasing women, consigning them to their kitchens, and giving them as their sole purpose in life to serve their husbands and perpetuate the human race. In Brahmanical India, the laws of Manu and *Sati* thus describe the duty of the wife: her husband is her Lord, a living God whom she must serve and worship, even if he is as ugly as sin, even he is cross-eyed and mistreats her! Still in Brahmanical India, unfortunate is the widow, for she brings bad luck and her husband's death goes to prove it. Only yesterday, widows used to throw themselves onto the funeral pyre of their deceased husbands, maybe because this was expected of them but also because they knew what fate awaited them otherwise. In Aryan society, the widow is deprived of all comforts, she must live as a recluse and only wear tattered clothes and eat leftover food. She is a living ghost and any grooming or coquettishness is prohibited. She is a bird of ill omen and may attend no celebrations, no social gatherings. She may not look at men, not even male animals! And remarrying is out of the question, even if her husband died young and in combat, for example. Since her life ends in any case when her husband dies, her auto-da-fé spares her a life of harassment and suffering.

You might object that all of this belongs to the past and in any case pertains only to India. It is true, the practice of sati has been banned by law and widows no longer immolate themselves on their husband's funeral pyre. However each and every year in India, thousands of women burn to death in their own kitchens because their parents cannot afford the extra dowry demanded by the in-laws: with those kerosene burners, "accidents" happen.

In our Western nations, there has been, on the contrary, a reversal of the trend: women are becoming more and more aware of their own worth. That is a fact. But not only must men and women be equal, but women must become real women. Yet, real women have disappeared. How and why? Louis Pauwels—whether you like him or not—has addressed this question in his "Imaginary Lecture" called *La Femme est rare* (literally, Woman is Rare, i.e., Real women are few and far between).

La Femme est Rare*

"The problem is that there are hardly any women left. I contend that women have disappeared, that there has been a catastrophe, that the race of women has become scattered, annihilated under our very eyes, unbeknownst to us. Gentlemen, Woman, the descendent of paleolithic and neolithic times, our mother, our female, our goddess, the being whom I shall call *the woman of man*, and whom we cannot even conceive of today, was hunted down, touched in her physical and mental body and hurled back into the void.

"The earth's entrails are replete with buried forests, with the remnants of extinct animal species, the ashes of human and superhuman races whose history, if ever revealed to us, would defy our wildest imagination. Our true female is also mixed in with the humus of these subterranean abysses. Why? Just think, Gentlemen! She has borne the brunt of the formidable, merciless war waged against the West's primitive religions. That war: here you have the entire history of the so-called civilized world. Do you think that in those territories where the religion of the Roman legions never took root, in Gaul for example, or in Great Britain, the soldiers of Christ found a land devoid of all thought or God? In a thousand and one places of our old Europe, in our moors, in our menhir-strewn plains, out in the bush or on the banks where Pan used to sing, the indigenous religion from the dawn

---

* From a lecture given by Pauwels and published in Planète (Paris, 1964).

of time still existed, the true religion of Western man. Gentlemen, I hold to be self-evident the fact that for millenia Europe thrived on high mystical thought, itself inherited from other times, devoted to the Horned God and the exaltation of the feminine principle. I hold as true that this original spirituality was swept away violently, in flames and in blood, by an alien religion from the East: Christianity. The Horned God, the protector of ancient humankind in the West, was labeled the Devil and damned.

"Immemorial idols were cast down, and along with them their foundation had to be destroyed: woman as mother, woman as goddess, woman as female, the real woman.

"Today's lofty minds denounce the evils of recent colonialism: quashed Indians, the stifled magi of Africa, martyrized black civilizations. But why do they not mention our own toppled totems of yore! Why do they not mention our own God who was demeaned, accursed and hunted down! Why do they not talk about our own priestesses who were exterminated! And our women taken away from us! Old Europe was also colonized and marred. Yes, Gentlemen, I dare to assert all of this. From the strictly anthropological viewpoint which is mine, the history of the Christian Church is the history of a war waged by aliens against a very old, very powerful, and deeply-rooted indigenous cult, and of a successful crime committed against the entire female human race. We have lost half of ourselves, Gentlemen. Killed. And I shall prove it.

"My purpose is not to accuse. This fantastic crime was perhaps necessary. And it was perhaps fatal. Civilization would not exist as we know it today if the true woman still existed. We would still believe in heaven on earth. The human spirit would not have embarked upon new paths. We would not be today on the verge of reaching distant galaxies, we would not have opened up wide doors in the universe through which one may already hear the call of the ultimate God in whom all our gods will merge, in whom the spirit of the planet will be reabsorbed one day, having fulfilled its mission. But let us review the crime. I shall mention hundreds of thousands of real women called witches and burnt as such, as well as millions of other women vanquished and changed by fear. I refer you to *La Sorcière* (The Witch) by the visionary Michelet, an admirable and misunderstood piece of work. Extermination by propaganda, the most effective of all weapons as we now know, and more effective at the time than the strappado, the boot, or the sulfured shirt. A revolutionary war waged by knights against the real woman and in favor of a new idol. Lastly, on a wider, more mysterious and yet concomitant level, a downward mutation of the species. So that gradually the authentic female was replaced by a different kind of being.

"Gentlemen, the being whom we call woman is not *the* woman. She is a degeneration, a copy. The essence has gone, the principle is absent, our joy and our salvation are no longer there.

"[...] What we call women are beings who only look like women, we embrace imitations belonging to a species which has been entirely or almost entirely destroyed.

"*La femme est rare* (woman is rare) said Giraudoux. Most men, when they marry a mediocre imitation of a man, a slightly slyer one, a slightly suppler one, are actually marrying themselves. It is themselves that they see walking in the street, with fuller breasts, wider hips, clad in silk, so they run after themselves, embrace themselves, marry themselves. After all, it is less cold than marrying a mirror. Rare is Woman, she wades through floods, she topples thrones, she stops the passing years. Her skin is like marble. When she does exist, she is the impasse of the world.... Whither go rivers, clouds, lost birds? They all flow into Woman.... But she is rare.... If one encounters her one must run away, for when she loves, when she hates, she is implacable. Her compassion is implacable.... But she is rare.

"The real woman, from the beginning of time, the woman that was given us, belongs body and soul to a universe alien to man's. She radiates at the other end of Creation. She knows the secrets of water, stones, plants, and animals. She can stare at the sun and see in the dark. She possesses the keys to health, rest, and the harmonies of matter. She is the white witch perceived by Michelet, the fairy with wide, moist flanks, with transparent eyes, who awaits man to begin a new heaven on earth. If she gives herself to him, it is in a movement of sacred panic, opening up to him in the warm darkness of her belly, the door to another world. She is the fountain of virtue: the desire which she inspires consumes excitement. Immersing oneself in her returns one to chastity. She is sterile for she has stopped the wheel of time. Or rather, she is the one who plants her seed in man: she delivers him anew, she reintroduces into him the childhood of the world. She returns him to his manly work which is to elevate himself as high as he can. We talk about superman, but never about superwoman; for woman, the true woman, is the one who makes man into more than he is. And for her, just existing is enough in order to fully be. Through her, man gains access to his being, unless he chooses other forms of asceticism, where he will meet her yet again, in a symbolic form...

"Gentlemen, discovering the true woman is a grace, a blessing, a gift. Being unafraid of her, is yet another. Uniting with her requires God's benevolence.... What a strange encounter! She appears suddenly amongst the herd of false females and the fortunate man who spots her begins to tremble with desire and fear.

Change is happening; how much longer can we go on fooling ourselves?

Je vois tes seins s'épanouir
Et parfois ton ventre frémir
Comme un sol chaud qui se soulève
Tu m'appaises et je m'étonne
De ces pouvoirs que tu détiens...

[Freely translated as]:

I see your breasts blossom
And sometimes your belly quiver
Like the warm earth rising,
You appease me and I marvel
At your powers...

I confess that I hesitated to include such a lengthy excerpt but I did want to share with you this admirable text, one of the best I have come across. In the above paragraphs which are deeply Tantric, some parts may prove shocking to Christians for whom I have the utmost respect, but was I to censor Louis Pauwels?

Actually two conclusions can be drawn from the above. First: man must go through her in order to be. Woman—all women—is the true initiator of man, his way toward Being. Secondly: the patriarchal system has deprived man of real women who are a threat to his supremacy. In response to that, each woman must become aware of the Woman lying dormant within her: it is high time She left her cocoon!

This vital task can be accomplished and our modern world, gone astray, can be saved, thanks to Tantra. The fact that most Tantra followers in the West are women goes to prove their intuition. They *know* that this path of evolution is fruitful indeed and that it will lead them towards the Real Woman buried in them, in order to become once again the Ancient One, the Eternal Shakti that they should never have ceased being.

As for man, if he is to be worthy of the real Woman, he must first accept the idea, then restructure his life around feminine values. Our patriarchal system has created a technocratic civilization devoid of any soul, ideal, or true love. It is based on false values and leads to cataclysms, to wars. Actually, it is in a state of bankruptcy on all levels, including the social and economic ones. To emerge from this, man must be willing to rediscover his own hidden, repressed, femininity. Sheer utopia? No, because the cult of yore is making a tremendous comeback and the chapter titled "The Witches Are Coming, The Witches Are Coming... Back!" demonstrates the extent of the phenomenon.

The Mother-Goddess

The Mother-Goddess, the Great Ancestor, was humankind's first religion and the focus of an extensive cult as testified by the countless female figurines belonging to paleolithic and neolithic times, discovered throughout the Indus Empire, France, Spain, the entire Mediterranean region, Yugoslavia and as far north as Siberia.

Actually, this is quite logical. When man wonders whence he came, the obvious answer is "from my mother's womb"; and she herself came from her own mother's womb and so on and so forth. By thus going back up the uninterrupted chain of mothers, we reach the very first one, the common ancestor, the mother of all humans. And so it is quite understandable that we should make a goddess out of her, *the* Goddess!

But why did prehistoric sculptors depict her in such a caricatural way, with an almost grotesque figure? Far from awakening our esthetic sense, those shapeless, distorted, outsized Venuses should on the contrary stifle it. And yet there is a strange fascination generated by these matrons whose obesity is almost preposterous. Obviously, symbolism, more than esthetics or realism, guided the rough hands of these anonymous artists. Even if you accept that the technique of those Magdalenian sculptors was primitive, the deformity of the Venus of Lespugne, for example, is obviously intentional. How better to symbolize the inexhaustible fertility of the Mother-Goddess, the mother of men, beasts and plants, than by an enormous belly, the only one capable of bearing all her children. Indeed, how better to express the fact that she forever nurtures and feeds her countless offspring, than by breasts just as disproportionate as her belly? The very feminine slenderness of the rest of the body (the head, the bust, arms, the legs under the knees and the feet), in striking contrast with the almost monstrous belly and breasts, is just as deliberate: sculpting an obese woman would not have symbolized the Cosmic Mother, the Great Ancestor. Conversely,

Brassempuy, the "Hooded Head" as youthful as ever 20,000 years later.

when prehistoric artists wanted to represent actual women they did so incredibly skillfully.

Let us note in passing that in both Tantra and Hinduism, the strictly maternal dimension of women is remarkably absent: no pregnant goddesses to be found and representations of the mother-child couple are few and far between.

Female Values

The gods whom I worshipped demanded the Dance of Death...
Perhaps women should be entrusted with
the responsibility for the world
for they are guided by emotions
and not by intellect.

Who wrote these words? Some Tantrist, with a nostalgic longing for the matrifocal culture of the Indus civilization before barbarian and primitive Aryans invaded their territory, wreaking havoc high and low and enslaving survivors? Guess again! They were written by an Aryan, the representative of a patriarchal and totalitarian regime given to the worship of these war-gods who demanded the Dance of Death. And they are alive and well and living in rocket silos, standing by to home-deliver their missiles anywhere in the world, along with hordes of armored vehicles poised for a new Dance of Death. How can we avoid the total collapse and self-destruction of civilization and humankind? According to the author mentioned above, we should entrust the responsibility for the world to women! A utopian idea? Perhaps.

But back to our little quiz: have you discovered the name of the author of the quote? No? The answer: Adolf Eichmann, in his confession written in prison, in Israel, while awaiting hanging after being sentenced to death. Indeed! Coming face to face with death makes you think, especially your own death, even if your name is Adolf Eichmann. The prosecutor, Gideon Hausner, banned its publication and David Ben-Gurion, who was Prime Minister at the time, ordered the document to be kept for fifteen years in the secret archives of the State of Israel. Naturally one may have doubts as to the sincerity of such a confession in which Eichmann states he was never anti-semitic, displaying a macabre sense of humor. Nor did he ever show any remorse, either during, or after his trial.

And yet, written by such a person, in such circumstances, these words take on a new dimension through both an acknowledgment of failure and an apparently unique solution: entrusting women with the responsibility for the world.

Actually such a shift would be unattainable. Although the female cult or rather the worship of femininity is one of Tantra's cornerstones, toppling the world's leaders just to put women in their place would be preposterous. And nobody would even seriously advocate such a move. The fact that successful professional women hold top jobs does not mean a new matriarchal age is dawning. These women are part of the system, the establishment.

It is more a question of *values* than people and our civilization will thrive only if female values are allowed to play a central role. Nevertheless it is naturally desirable for women to be more directly involved in the concrete management of society.

In order to restructure our lives and society around female values, man, the male of the species, must discover—or rediscover—the hidden, feminine dimensions of *his own* being. A difficult task in a society that systematically stresses male values, not only in men but in women. Becoming aware of these feminine values, accepting them, developing them, and centering one's life around them, *that* is the cult of femininity!

Whence the following question: biologically speaking, which one is the dominant sex, it being understood that "dominant" is not synonymous with "superior"? Another (outrageous?) question: what exactly is sex?

The usual answer is a naïvely simple definition, restricting everything to the genitals, "G-string stuff." Far from being limited to the contents of one's underwear, sex marks each cell and organ of our body, even our blood: in the Olympics, a blood test proves without a doubt if an athlete is male or female. Well before birth, our brain is programmed for a type of behavior corresponding to our sex. If all goes well, we end up with either a male or a female brain and the corresponding mind. Consequently "my" sex includes all typically distinctive male or female traits, both physical and mental.

The English language commonly refers to the *fair* sex and the *stronger* sex, "therefore" the dominant one. In the patriarchal system, wielding his mighty biceps, the male of the species imposes himself and his gender: our species is called "Man," "Mankind," "Homo Sapiens," etc. Yet biologically and scientifically, the dominant sex is *not* male but female!

According to the latest findings of research work that began in the USA in 1950, notably at Kansas University and carried out by Charles Phoenix, Robert Goy and William Young, the basic organic and cerebral structure of mammals was first female, then male! Tom Alexander concludes that the myth of Adam should actually be reversed: scientifically speaking, Adam is a modified Eve! During its early developmental stages the fetal brain has a "blueprint," as well as latent neurological circuits, that will determine its future behavior as either female or male. But if left to develop on its own, that is, in the absence of any specific hormonal input, the fetus *always* develops into the female form! At the very beginning of the embryo's development, male and female gonads are homologous and very similar. A minute quantity of androgen hormone—we still don't know what triggers it—sets off a chain reaction leading to the formation of a male. This includes the activation in the embryo's brain, of neurological circuits that will control male behavior. Only later will the gonads—well differentiated at this stage—produce specifically male hormones.

Nevertheless—a capital point for Tantra—the female circuits have not been totally disconnected. Throughout the normal male's lifetime, they continue to influence his behavior, which fits in pretty well with Tantra's thesis that woman is the primordial human being and man must become aware of his own feminine aspects!

Greater height and physical strength are not tantamount to, or proof of, superiority, but in patriarchal cultures, they more often than not allow the male to lay down the law, his law. In nature, women are mostly mothers and men must defend and protect them physically, as well as their offspring, against wild animals and possibly human enemies. If women were the stronger, from the muscular point of view, in addition to caring for their children, they would also have to protect the men!

Even the generative powers of the male show that he is expendable. Theoretically, unless she repeatedly has multiple births, a woman can bear about twenty children, which isn't bad, whereas a man can theoretically fertilize two or three hundred women per year! If all but a few males came to be exterminated, the tribe could be reconstituted within a period of just a few years.

Developing man's feminine aspects does not imply a loss of virility, on the contrary! It leads to a new outlook—or perhaps a return to a fundamental, ancient, conception—for both men *and* women!

In our patriarchal societies, the woman must be subservient to the man. Her sexuality is repressed, for if allowed to assert herself, she would challenge the male order. In giving priority to the feminine side of humans, Left-Hand Path Tantra opposed the Aryan patriarchal order in India and has had to suffer unrelenting harassment and persecution for it.

We inherited the patriarchal system from traveling nomads who became the invaders and enemies of the settlers whose territories they crossed. The warrior and the male values he stood for became vital for the tribe's survival. Moreover these same male values are also those usually associated with the intellect. They find a contemporary means of expression in the exploring and conquering of our material world, in science, technology, organizational skills, industry, etc., in short, activities of the diurnal, solar type. Eichmann contrasted feminine and masculine values in his statement, "women are guided by emotions and not by the intellect," but since he was not a philosopher, one must try to interpret what his idea of emotions and intellect was.

The intellect is understanding, discursive reasoning, cold logic. It should not be confused with intelligence, which is more intuitive than discursive, and includes irrational, emotional elements of the feminine type. An intellectual is not *ipso facto* intelligent and vice versa. "Emotions" must therefore be understood in the wider sense of affectivity rather than unreasoned, uncontrolled emotionalism.

Changing Our Values

Female values are: love, affection, genuine relationships, being in touch with nature and life. Naturally this includes motherhood and children. I confess I did not mention the latter fundamental aspect first lest some women readers suspect me of trying to lock them up in the all-too-well-known three "K's" of the Nazis, that is, *Kinder, Küche, Kirche*, (children, the kitchen, the church).

Music, dance, poetry, and literature are also feminine. And feminine is the warmth of the home, enhanced by art, flowers, animals and also children, why not! Nevertheless, *the truest, deepest feminine values are those which transcend the rational mind, which delve into the irrational*, a world that intellectuals, scientists and the patriarchal system in general are extremely wary of.

The unrational lies in the deeper layers of our psyche, the ones habitually called the unconscious mind, the world of instincts and drives. Women are intuitive and I would like to endorse what J. Guenther, in *Yuganaddha, The Tantric View of Life*, Varanasi, 1979, p. 172 said: "A woman's consciousness is different. By a woman many things are already seen, while the man still pokes about in the dark. A woman is aware of the attendant circumstances and of the possibilities connected with them which, as a rule, a man is unable to see. For this reason the world of the woman appears to the male as getting lost in ages and cosmic infinitude. But, as a matter of fact, it is this expansion into the infinite, ageless, and transcendental which can give most valuable hints and impulses. Because of this transcendental character, it is aptly called wisdom. And wisdom is more than intellectual knowledge. [...] The woman and all that is connected with her is to the male a strange and yet most intimate world, waiting to be realized."

Indeed, such values also exist within man, but patriarchal education and upbringing have repressed them and it is a far-from-easy task to discover them. Actually the first step is realizing that there is nothing to understand, and everything to perceive, to feel. That is why in the Left-Hand Path, which involves the concrete participation of a woman, *she* is the initiator. She opens up for the man the secret doors to the abysses of his own being, to the ultimate, the cosmic. If Tantra were a religion, women would be priestesses and the priests would be men having developed, thanks to women, their own feminine qualities, the qualities of intuition and transcendence.

A Tantric man may access this feminine universe by entering into the secret world of the actual, concrete woman, the one he shares his life with, but only on condition that he open himself to her. And for their part, women must try to perceive their own masculine aspects. Allow me to quote Guenther once more: "Whenever man comes into contact with his female counterpart, which is a certain aspect of life not lived by the individual and excluded from his conscious attitude, whenever a man comes into contact with his latent femaleness or a woman with her hidden maleness, thus giving up the one-sidedness of conscious life, their whole being will be enriched. This enrichment is of utmost importance for the whole future life (p. 47).

"Femininity which is experienced by the male through the objective woman and through the unconscious forces of his psyche, is more deeply rooted in the realm of possibilities than are the male forces which, though they operate conjointly with the female forces, more often combat them and are in danger to lose the contact with the deeper layers of life" (p. 171).

Tantra in Daily Life

In Tantra, the woman—and this includes my own wife, of course—is the initiator, which does not imply subordinating the man. So what happens in everyday life? We could describe such experiences as "cosmic," but they must be translated into concrete terms. Allow me to evoke an experience of my own: After having lived for too, too, long in the city, one of our dreams finally came true: to build our own house out in the country. What an undertaking! If you have ever had a house built you will understand! Especially during the design and construction phases, I came to realize how much my wife sees everything through her feminine, mental "glasses," and men through their male glasses. These are two very different ways of looking at the world! While discussing the blueprints and the design, the architect and I talked in terms of space, building materials, various heating systems,

In spite of appearances, the Venus of Lespugne is not steatopygic. The head, the bust, the arms and legs are normal. The head remains anonymous. The artist wanted to represent in this way the fertility of Woman.

etc. Whereas the shakti was mainly interested in living space and how things would look, the decorating and the garden!

After the bulldozer finished grading the land, the masons came in and erected scaffoldings and walls. The house gradually came into being, a simple house, well-integrated into its environment with lots of windows and open spaces to capture every precious ray of scarce Belgian sunshine!

We would often visit the site. On one particular day the architect and I stood there admiring a beautiful, typically Belgian brick wall about to be completed. The shakti said: "That wall is really ugly! All of these walls are awful." The architect and I looked at each other, not knowing what to think: through our own male mental glasses, we thought those walls were beautiful and they were! But my wife would not change her mind: "All of these naked walls are ugly! When we move in I'll hide them with plants and trees and bushes!" And so she did! She planted and planted and year in, year out, it all grew. And now she likes those walls because they have practically disappeared behind her vertical garden. In May, when the clematis is in bloom, my wife is radiant and I confess I don't mind! From my home office where I am now sitting as I write this text, I see a green cascade of flowers hanging onto the façade. Birds scared away by the construction work, have returned and made their nests in the clematis. The nestlings are chirping away and their parents are busily flying to and fro between the plum tree and the nest, trying to keep them fed. The wall is alive with honeybees, ladybugs and a host of other insects: a real micro-universe. At night in our bedroom, it's a good feeling to know that close to us, warm in their nests, the nestlings are cozily tucked under their mothers. Now I see those walls with my wife's eyes and I like them. She was right: those naked walls were dead, therefore ugly.

I have also discovered our garden through her eyes. The man sees the garden in a general, synthetic way. Whereas the woman sees it analytically, shrub by shrub, flower by flower, but above all, she *lives* according to the rhythm of the garden, she feels it.

For the woman, the real "scoop" at winter's end, is the first crocus, a promise of spring, even if the outside temperature still hovers around freezing point. Now as far as I am concerned, if I just listen to my male mind, the news is interesting, but that's about it. What really matters to me is my 10:30 appointment! Then my 11:15 appointment. But if I look at that crocus with the eyes of the shakti, it *becomes* the thing that matters.

Living along with the garden is sharing its life. Whether it be for the shy forget-me-nots or the powerful cedar tree, the shakti behaves like a mother toward all plants: she knows them personally! She knows, she feels whether this plant or that one likes a particular spot, otherwise she will plant it somewhere else until it finds the place it really likes, where it will be happy and will be able to grow. Then the shakti is pleased.

When spring comes, she finds all the nests and shows them to me. She watches the nestlings and conjectures as to when they will be able to fly. She understands the language of the birds as they place all the shrubs on red alert when a cat gets too close for comfort. Whereas I merely notice whether or not there is any wind, she knows if it's the east wind or the north wind, if its direction has changed, if the wind is humid or dry. And there is also the vegetable garden. She knows whether or not the radishes are thirsty and she waters them, not merely in a utilitarian way so that they will grow larger, but simply because they are thirsty, which does not prevent her from harvesting them! Plants are not objects, mere things to eat, but living beings with whom she is in constant rapport, in the strong sense of the word.

First thing every morning: opening the curtains just to see what the air is like, what the new day promises to bring forth. Check out the sky: is it cloudy, will there be rain again today, or will it be sunny? Her mood does not really depend upon all of this, but it does permeate her physical and mental environment, the general atmosphere of her life. I have gradually entered into this feminine universe and she has become the initiator.

Naturally this is not restricted to walls and gardens, and if I have chosen such down-to-earth examples it is in order to better express the idea that the Tantric worship of femininity is not restricted to the ultimate dimensions of life and that this outlook can and should permeate the myriad facets of daily life. Through the shakti I am able to discover my own secret feminine universe and gradually the repressed feminine values within myself emerge from my own inner self, in all fields, including the female sexual experience.

The Immaculate Conception

Bernard Icart (*Religious Ceremonies and Customs*, 1733, vol. IV, p. 472) wrote:

> In China, one of the most important of the nature goddesses was *Shing-moo*, the holy mother, or the "mother of perfect intelligence." She was a counterpart of the Egyptian Isis, the Hindu Ganga, and the Greek Demeter. When the first Christian missionaries arrived in China, they were shocked to find that the image of this goddess bore a striking resemblance to the Virgin Mary, and they were further startled and disconcerted to discover that

Shing-moo, too, had conceived and given birth to a savior son while yet a virgin.

As regards the well-known and insoluble "chicken and egg" dilemma, nobody has ever thought that the egg might have come first! The same logic prevents us from considering that the human species was born of an original male. At the beginning there is the Great Female Ancestor, the Mother-Goddess, but since there is no male to fertilize her, she, the mysteriously pregnant virgin, must perforce give birth to the first male child. Naturally, biology and mythology do not always live in harmony, but at least the myth of the immaculate conception is on the right side of logic. It is therefore not surprising to encounter it in more than one religion. By proclaiming the dogma of the immaculate conception, did not the Church co-opt and assimilate a fundamental myth of humankind?

The Witches Are Coming,
the Witches Are Coming—Back!

Sure, gone are the times when witches were burned alive and, gone, too, the image of the wicked witch as an ugly, old woman riding a broomstick and having intercourse with the devil. If a modern woman says she is a witch, either people would give her an ironical smile or she is alarming. To Starhawk, Witchcraft is the oldest religion in our Western culture. It existed long before Christianity, Judaism, Islam, Buddhism or Hinduism and is very unlike these. The Old Religion as Starhawk calls it, is very close to the American Indian's religion or to Shamanism. Like Tantra, Witchcraft prescribes no dogmas, no strictly codified beliefs and has no sacred books. The witch gets her instruction from nature: the moon, the sun, the stars, the flight of the birds, the cyclical return of the seasons and the slow growth of the trees.

According to our legends, says Starhawk in her remarkable book *The Spiral Dance* (New York: HarperCollins, 1979) on which this chapter is based, this cult existed for more than 35,000 years when Europe's climate was becoming very cold and ice was descending slowly southwards. At that period Shamanism and the archaic religion of the Mother-Goddess arose and expressed themselves through a set of images: the Great Mother who engendered everything, and the Horned God, the hunter and the hunted, who again and again had to pass through the door of death in order to make life continue.

The male shamans wore horns and were clothed in animal skins to identify themselves with the god of the herds, and naked priestesses embodied the goddess and directed fertility rites. Life and death were perceived as a continuous process. Like the skeletons discovered in the Empire of the Indus valley, they buried their dead in the fetal position together with their tools and ornaments, so they could be reincarnated.

In Siberia and in the Ukraine, the goddess was the Lady of the Mammoths, and her image, with its opulent charms, was carved in bone or in stone. In the huge temple-caves of Europe, in Southern France and in Spain, her rites were secretly being performed. On the walls, unknown stone-age artists painted great polar powers, like the bison and the horse, and when seen in the flickering light of the torches, they are like dreams.

When the ice receded, some tribes followed the bison and the reindeer to the far north, and others crossed the small strip of land to Alaska and to America. Those who stayed in Europe became hunters, fishermen and gathered plants and shells. Dogs watched over their campsites, and new tools were made. The camps became villages where shamans and priestesses shared their knowledge and put their forces together. The first convents arose at that period, says Starhawk. In harmony with nature, human beings domesticated what they had formerly hunted: wild sheep, goats, pigs and cows. Seeds no longer were gathered but sown. The hunter-god became the god of agriculture who was sacrificed in the autumn and buried at the time of harvest, buried in the goddess' uterus in order to be born again the following spring. The Lady of the Wild Things became the Mother of Harvests, the cycles of the sun and the moon marked the time to sow and to harvest.

In that part of the continent which had been ice-capped, a new power was being discovered. It was a force which, like a spring, flowed through the earth itself. Short, frail-looking men with tanned skin started erecting huge stone blocks in circles where the priestesses could unravel the mysteries of time and the hidden structure of the universe. Mathematics, astronomy, poetry, music, the knowledge of the powers of the human mind were discovered and unfolded, alongside the unfathomable mysteries of life. These were the people who erected Stonehenge and so many other megalithic temples not only in Europe but in India as well.

One might consider the megalithic period to be very remote in time and the stone-age people to be savages, but this is not quite true. The people who lived near the sites where their ancestors built the first megalithic temples became rich and powerful. All through the ages, the European country-folk remained ethnically very stable, numerous invasions nothwithstanding, and the neolithic blood still rushes, at least partially, in our blood. And these peasants went on worshipping old beliefs, some of which survive even in our modern age. This remarkable ethnic stability lasted until the second half of our century. Until just before the Second World War, one was born, lived, toiled and died on the farm of his ancestors. To marry a girl from another village was not forbidden, of course, but frowned upon. People mixed very little.

During the Bronze Age, on the northern steppes, the tall, sturdy, courageous nomads who followed the herds and had become hunters and warriors started to breed cattle. To conquer new grazing-grounds for their herds, in successive waves, they slowly migrated to Europe, the Middle-East and India taking the land, destroying the settled civilizations, enslaving their inhabitants, and enforcing their patriarchal values. This system still endures today!

Meanwhile, the "fairies," or descendants of the priestesses of old, who bred cattle on the stony hills and lived in round huts, perpetuated the Old Religion. People celebrated the great feasts with processions, chants, incantations and lit the ritual fires. In many places, some invaders joined in and mixed marriages followed.

In the beginning, the advent of the new Christian religion did not change things very much. With the birth of Christ, at first, the peasants saw only a variation of the legend of the Mother-Goddess and her child. At the festivals and in the villages, some Christian priests participated and sometimes even led the Sabbath dances! Still, according to Starhawk, the convents who kept the knowledge of the subtle forces alive, were called *wicca* or *wicce*, from the old Anglo-Saxon word meaning "to fold," "to mould," hence our word *witch*. These convents knew how to mould, to bend invisible forces at their will. Healers, teachers, poetesses, and midwives, these women were the central figures in each community.

Later on came the persecutions. The 12th and 13th centuries had witnessed a revival of the Old Religion. The poems of the troubadours which seemed to be addressed to the noblewomen were, in fact, love-poems to the Goddess. Cathedrals were erected to honor Mary, who had taken on many aspects of the old Goddess. "At all times, and in all countries, the deities of rival religions have been looked upon as devils. The Hebrews, and later the Christians, conceived every deity other than Yahweh to be a devil. [...]

"In the early days of Christianity, the Jews, who refused to admit the divine conception of Jesus, looked upon the risen Christ as a devil. Those who confessed to the possession of familiar spirits were accused of conferring with the Devil; thus Socrates.

"The witches of medievalism, like the idolaters of paganism, did not look upon their chief as an evil spirit, but as a god. [...] The solidified witchcraft of the Middle Ages merely took the place of the ancestor worship of paganism, as this had ousted the sun and serpent-worship of barbarism. [...]

"Witchcraft was just as much a religion as Christianity, or Mohammedism. It had its god, its spirits of the dead, its ritual, its sacrifices. Originally and fundamentally a phallic cult, its observances were mixed up with a good deal of promiscuous fornication, as is evident from the reports of the witch trials.

"Nothing in connexion with witchcraft achieved such notoriety as the Witches' Sabbath, mainly owing to the fact that it was at this festival that was celebrated the infamous Black Mass. The Sabbath was really a gathering of the witches and wizards of the whole district or community. It was equivalent to a gathering of the worshippers of God in the local church, except that these worshippers who gathered together at the Sabbath were making their obeisances to Satan and the meeting-place was some secluded spot under the stars of heaven. For the Sabbath was held in the dead of night. It commenced at the stroke of midnight, and usually the ceremonies continued until cock's crow" (pages 99-101). (Or. Qu.).

The Old Religion became a too formidable contender to the new one, Witchcraft was proclaimed to be heretical. In the following century, wars, crusades, epidemics and upheavals raged all over Europe. The Church's stability was shaken, the feudal system crumbling. The Church could not let things go on and tolerate competing cults without reacting. In 1484, the Pope Innocent VIII launched the Inquisition against the Old Religion. In 1486, the publication by the Dominicans Kramer and Sprenger of the *Maleus Malificarum*, literally the "Witches' Hammer," laid the basis for a terror directed primarily at women and this was to last until the middle of the 18th century! About nine million so-called heretics were executed, 80 percent of whom were women, young girls, even children who were believed to have inherited the "evil" from their mothers. The asceticism of early Christianity, tied to the flesh, had degenerated in the Church into a fierce hatred against woman. In the Middle Ages woman-hate became the central theme of Christianity. Woman and her sex drive became synonymous to Evil. According to the *Maleus Malificarum*, "All Witchcraft stems from carnal lust, which is in women insatiable." The resulting terror became indescribable: a woman, denounced, for instance, by some envious neighbor, was accused of sorcery, brutally arrested, and, if unable to "prove" she was not guilty, was condemned. The worst atrocities, tortures of all kinds: these were the horrors of the Inquisition.

The indicted woman was tortured until she signed a confession, duly prepared by the Inquisitor where she recognized she had had intercourse with Satan. If she agreed to sign, the "reward" was to die strangled. Those who went on protesting their innocence were burned alive. Witchcraft, like tantra in India, went underground and became the most secret of all religions. From then on, the Tradition was only conveyed to absolutely trustworthy women, those generally belonging to the same family. All links between the convents were severed. There were no more meetings like the Great Festival where the knowledge and the results of the rituals could be shared. Whole chunks of the Tradition were irreparably lost or forgotten. Nevertheless, quietly, secretly, behind closed doors, camouflaged in fairy tales and folk songs, and buried deeply within the collective unconscious mind, the seed survived.

During the 18th century, an era of disbelief replaced the persecutions. The memory of the old Witchcraft faded away, and the remaining ugly stereotypes seemed either tragic or ridiculous.

According to Starhawk, only in this century are the witches able to come out publicly. She says that because the word *witch* implies so many pejorative connotations, many ask why we still use it. She responds that, to proclaim oneself a *witch*, is to claim the right for the woman to be powerful, and for the man to see divinity in the woman. My question: is this not pure Tantra?

To be a Witch, Starhawk goes on to say:

Is to identify with nine million victims of bigotry and hatred and to take responsibility for shaping a world in which prejudice claims no more victims. A Witch is a shaper, a creator who bends the unseen into form, and so becomes one of the Wise, one whose life is infused with magic (page 22).

According to Starhawk, Witchcraft was known as a religion of poetry but not theology. The legends and teachings of Witchcraft are recognized as metaphors for "That-Which-Cannot-Be-Told," a reality that human minds cannot know, mysteries that cannot be explained in words, mysteries that are intuited. She says that ritual acts are used to trigger altered states of awareness, and it is theses altered states of awareness that reveal insights that go beyond words (page 22).

The primary symbol for "That-Which-Cannot-Be-Told" is the Goddess and She has infinite aspects and hundreds of names. She is the manifest deity in each of us. The Goddess is not separate from the world, but is the world and all things in it. Starhawk teaches that the flesh and spirit are one. The Goddess religion is both an old and contemporary religion. And the renewal is being spurred by women who are actively reawakening the Goddess.

When the Goddess religions declined, women lost religious models and spiritual systems that addressed female needs and experiences. Male images of divinity characterized both Eastern and Western religions, and the symbols, prophets, and gurus were usually male. Women were not encouraged to explore their own strengths. Today, in modern Witchcraft, women are seeking the old powers (page 23).

Although many Eastern traditions excluded feminine values, Starhawk's comments exclude Tantra, for what follows is genuine Tantra. She says:

The symbolism of the Goddess is not a parallel structure to the symbolism of God the Father. The Goddess does not rule the world; She is the world. Manifest in each of us, She can be

known internally by every individual, in all her magnificent
diversity. She does not legitimize the rule of one sex by the other
and lends no authority to rulers of temporal hierarchies. In
Witchcraft, each of us must reveal our own truth. Deity is seen in
our own forms, whether female or male, because the Goddess
has her male aspect. Sexuality is a sacrament. Religion is a matter
of relinking, with the divine within and with her outer manifestations in all of the human and natural world.... The image of the
Goddess inspires women to see ourselves as divine, our bodies
as sacred (pp. 23-24).

Starhawk goes on to say that the Goddess is very important for men,
for the Father-God-ruled patriarch is oppressive for them, too. Men
from the patriarchal religions are also split internally, for the "spiritual" self is supposed to conquer the "base" animal and emotional
natures, which indicates that an internal war with themselves must
eventually take place. They try to conquer "sin" in the body. In the
East, they are required to conquer desire or any form of ego (page 24).
The Goddess allows men to experience the feminine side of their
natures, which means that the Goddess doesn't exclude men but contains them, as pregnant women contain the "child."

No Tantrist would argue with Starhawk when she talks about the
fact that religious models have affected our relationship with Earth,
and that when God is thought to be outside of nature, people have
plundered Earth's resources and have lost respect for Earth. She says
that Witchcraft is an ecological religion, for its goal is harmony with
nature (page 25).

Except for the modern witches themselves, few people realize the
foremost importance of this misunderstood religion. Knowledge of
the Goddess helps us prepare for the future; it is a non-violent revolution, an evolution of all the values upon which our failing civilization
is built. Our salvation will come from feminine values, from this
movement which is spreading slowly throughout the USA and Great
Britain. The followers of the Old Religion are forming covens, small
groups of twenty to thirty people, most of them women, who have a
great cohesiveness. No single central power enforces the liturgy or the
rites that are practiced to celebrate the Earth. Contrary to the male
model, this celebration has no hierarchic pyramidal structure. This
could be seen as a "weakness," but, in fact, the lack of structure makes
it invincible because it can't be overthrown or dissolved. Some covens
state that they are continuing practices handed down to them without
interruption since the origin of the practice.

For Witchcraft, and for Tantra as well, each act of love and pleasure is a ritual. Sex, which is the direct expression of the life force, is

sacred and is free to express itself, provided that it is guided by love. Marriage is a serious commitment, a magical and spiritual and physical bond, but it is only one way among many others to express love and sex. Sex is also magic, a way to feel and mold the subtle forces of the world; it awakens the deeper levels of consciousness beyond rationality.

The rites of Witchcraft are a kind of magic, and similar to Tantric rites, everything begins by forming a sacred circle. Starhawk says that each ritual begins by forming a sacred space, and the "casting of a circle" establishes a temple, whether it be in the middle of a forest or in the middle of a room in our home. The Goddess and God are invoked (or awakened) in each person in the circle, and are considered present within the sacred circle as well as in the bodies of the worshipers. That subtle force that shapes reality is what we called power, and it is raised by chanting or dancing, or can be directed through the use of a symbol, or by visualization. Ecstasy comes with the raising of the cone of power that may lead to a trance state where visions can be seen and insights be gained. (This would also explain the cone of power in the hat that we associate with Witches.)

Tantric is the vision—one that even modern scientists would accept—that Starhawk gives us: "All things are swirls of energy, vortexes of moving forces, currents in an ever-changing sea. Underlying the appearance of separateness, of fixed objects within a linear stream of time, reality is a field of energies that congeal, temporarily, into forms. In time, all 'fixed' things dissolve, only to coalesce again into new forms, new vehicles" (page 32).

The Charge of the Goddess, which Starhawk and others use, resembles the description of a Tantric pûjâ: "Once in the month, and better it be when the Moon is full, you shall assemble in some secret place and adore the spirit of Me who is Queen of all the Wise. You shall be free from slavery, and as a sign that you be free you shall be naked in your rites. Sing, feast, dance, make music and love, all in My presence, for Mine is the ecstasy of the spirit and Mine also is joy on Earth. For My law is love unto all beings" (page 90).

Let's be very clear that I am not saying that Tantra is trying to take over Witchcraft. Tantra and Witchcraft are not competing in a race to see who wins. But by comparing Tantra and Witchcraft, we can see that there is harmony between the two visions, and that our mutual visions probably share the same origin.

Any Tantrist would readily agree with Starhawk that the symbolism of the Goddess is an electrifying power for modern women. For women to rediscover the "matrifocal" civilizations is bringing a deep sense of pride in women's ability to sustain culture, and of course we all knew that, as our culture has survived. The Goddess is ancient and primeval, the first of the deities, the patroness of the Stone Age hunt and of our mythology, for it was under her guidance that the herds were tamed, healing herbs were discovered, crops were harvested, works of art have been created; the Goddess was the inspiration for song and story.

There is a common boundary between Tantric Shakta and Witchcraft, for when Starhawk tells about the Craft, she says that women do not believe in the Goddess, they connect with her—through the moon, the stars, the earth, the trees, the animal world, and through other human beings. The Goddess is here, within us all; she is air, fire, water, earth, essence, the body, mind, spirit, emotions, the seasons. The elements of Witchcraft are the elements of Tantra. The Goddess is Earth, the dark nurturing mother who brings forth all life. And Tantrists call her Kali to experience the true Tantra! The Goddess is fertility and generation, the womb, the receptive tomb, the power of death. Everything proceeds from her, says Starhawk, everything returns to her. She is the body sacred. Womb, breast, belly, mouth, vagina, penis, bone, and blood. No part of the body is unclean, no aspect of life is stained by sin. This is exciting to hear, for Tantrists feel the same way! Birth, death, decay, sleeping, making love, eliminating body wastes—all are manifestations of the Goddess.

If we replace the word "Goddess" with "Shakti" then we have Tantra. For, as Starhawk says, worship can take any form and happen anywhere. Witchcraft does not need a liturgy or a cathedral. To follow desire to the end is to unite with the Goddess. For Starhawk, the Goddess is the symbol of the innermost self, the liberating power within woman, for the cosmos is modeled on a sacred female body. In Witchcraft, life is sacred. The Goddess awakens the mind, the spirit, and the emotions, in a way that we can know the power of anger and aggression, as well as the power of love, which means that sacred life allows for all forms of life, rather than espousing only "good" and hiding anything that is deemed "bad."

Men in Witchcraft are seen in a similar way to the Tantric viewpoint. The male image is a "Horned God," an image radically different from the masculine image in patriarchal cultures. The male image doesn't fit a "macho" male, but is rather gentle, tender, comforting, yet a hunter. The Dying God is always in the service of the life force. He is also untamed sexuality—his is a deep, connective, powerful, sexuality that embraces the power of feeling. This is an image of what men can be if they are liberated from the binding constraints of other religions.

Starhawk tells us that the image of the "Horned God" was perverted by the medieval Church, and became the image of the Devil of Christianity. Witches don't believe in the Devil, nor do they worship or fear the Devil; it is considered to be a concept peculiar to Christianity. The Witch's God is sexual—and sexuality is considered sacred. Sexuality is not considered to be obscene or blasphemous. The Horned God wears the horns of the waxing and waning Moon, the symbol of "animal" vitality. The image is sometimes seen as black, not because he is dark and fearful, but because his power comes from the night (page 94). For the Witch the Horned God represents non-violent positive male qualities that have nothing to do with the emotionally crippled men in present-day Western society. To be free to be "wild" without being cruel, to allow anger without violence, to be sexually free without being coercive, to have a spiritual life without giving up sexuality, and to be strong enough to truly be able to love—this is what the male image of Witchcraft is (page 109).

It is interesting to note that Starhawk feels the pain and barrenness in men who are not allowed to feel, who are conditioned to function only in a military mode, who must ignore the messages that come from their bodies (pain, discomfort, fear) so that they can appear aggressive at all times. Western men's need to dominate women rather than celebrating them means that we all lose, because we wind up with a "war of the sexes" rather than experiencing mutual understanding, appreciation, and the all-encompassing power of love.

My friend Jonn Mumford, from Melbourne, a modern Tantrist, has fully understood the importance of the Wicca. In his book *Sexual Occultism* (1975, p. 27) he writes: "The emergence of modern Witchcraft in England and America is an atavistic resurgence of staggering proportions. Any successful system presupposes a need, and I would suggest that modern Witchcraft is the Tantra of Western man emerging in the twentieth century to quench his thirst for the vigorous and vital in the inner life."

> Startling similarities between Tantra and modern Witchcraft indicate that the primal layers of the unconscious in East and West seek satisfaction in an earth cult which is matriarchal and feminist...
>
> Tantra centers around Shakti as the active feminine pole responsible for dynamic manifestation. This is the direct equivalent of the Great Mother Goddess which is the focal point for worship by members of Wicca.
>
> Chakra puja, or the circle of worshippers, alternating male and female, is the paradigm of the coven, with an emphasis upon ritual nudity prominent in both groups. The purpose of a circle (in itself a womb or feminine symbol) is to enclose and entrap the psychic (pranic) energies exuded by the naked, living flesh of the participants. As their sexual-emotional excitement

increases, more radiation or 'steam' is produced for occult use. This energy forms a 'cone of power' over the group and is similar to the whirling vortex of psychic force released during copulation.

At the risk of appearing trite or simplistic, the resemblance between the Shiva Lingam (the central phallic symbol of Tantra) and the witch's broomstick and cone hat must be pointed out" (page 69).

In the same book (pages 70 and 71), Jonn Mumford summarizes the essentials of modern Witchcraft, published in 1973 in *Gnostica*:

- Recognition of polarity in all manifestations, including the manifestation of Divinity as Male and Female Forces.
- Recognition of Divinity manifesting within all life—including the Divinity within Man and Woman.
- Recognition of the Feminine as the "flower" of the race—that woman incarnates beauty and fruitfulness and through her we reach fulfillment.

Gnostica adds to this the following points (summed up):
- The woman as a flower bears and transmits the fruits of love, magic, and human endeavor;
- The woman becomes the criterion of our work, the goal of which is seen as beauty, fruitfulness, fulfillment;
- Our attitude toward woman is our attitude toward the race and toward life itself;
- It is Divinity as feminine, our Goddess, who is our Queen. We set her above us, not as a ruler, but as one we adore;
- It is our rule that that woman who fills the role of High Priestess in our covens must express the feminine at its fullness;
- There is in that essence of femininity, woman's monthly cycle, the source of our symbolic understanding of the Feminine Force in nature. Thus her symbol is the Moon, and we say that our Goddess is the Earth Mother, and her daughter (who is also herself) is the Moon Goddess, and behind her is the Great Mother, like itself.

What else can we say, except to repeat that this vision of Witchcraft corresponds totally to the essence of Tantra? And to say yet again that it would be easy, but a pity, to underrate the importance of modern *Wicca* because it is an underground movement. It carries hope of saving our crumbling civilization by the revival of the values of

Womanhood. The label does not matter, be it Witchcraft, Tantra or any other, provided it happens.

Because this trend is universal and eternal, it cannot be reversed and is invincible. I am perhaps overdoing the quotations, but how could I resist the following, coming from an entirely distinct source:

"In the woman this nature is revealed as the Eternal Feminine, which infinitely transcends all its earthly incarnations—every woman and every individual symbol. But these manifestations of the Archetypal Feminine in all times and all cultures, that is, among all human beings of the prehistoric and historical worlds, appear also in the living reality of the modern woman, in her dreams and visions, compulsions and fantasies, projections and relationships, fixations and transformations.

"The Great Goddess—if under this name we sum up everything we have attempted to represent as the archetypal unity and multiplicity of the feminine nature—is the incarnation of the Feminine Self that unfolds in the history of mankind as in the history of every individual woman; its reality determines individual as well as collective life. This archetypal psychical world which is encompassed in the multiple forms of the Great Goddess is the underlying power that even today— partly with the same symbols and in the same order of unfolding, partly in dynamic modulations and variations—determines the psychic history of modern man and of modern woman."

These sentences are filled with hope and they deserve to be read again and again. Eric Neumann, the famous Jungian psychoanalyst wrote them in Tel Aviv (*The Great Mother*, 1965, page 336), a city which is regarded as being a stronghold for patriarchy. Stronghold? Today, yes, but tomorrow? Did not Jeremy, the Prophet report how, on his arrival in Egypt, angry Jews blamed him for his loyalty to Jehovah, which they considered to be a male God, an usurper and the cause for all their woes. Defying the holy man, they told him they would return to the ancient customs, burn incense to the Queen of Heaven, offer her all kinds of gifts and drinks "as we did before, we and our forefathers, our kings, princes in the towns of Juda and in Jerusalem. At that time, we had plenty of food and were happy." In this text I would like to stress:

a) "We and our forefathers" and "our ancient customs," which implies a continuity in time;

b) Not only our forefathers but "our kings and our princes" which indicates a diffusion through the entire population;

c) The "cities of Juda and Jerusalem," means the cult of the Queen of Heaven was not a local and temporary phenomenon but included Israël as a whole.

But then, one might say, "this is past and gone." What about the future? By writing this down I remember the wives of some Jewish friends from the Diaspora. Believe me, far from supporting patriarchy, they are rather feminist-minded.

Tantra, Zohar, and Kabbalah

Every day, every male Jew in his prayers has to thank God for not having made him female, which is quite opposed to what Tantra teaches. Are Tantra and Judaism therefore really incompatible? The answer to this question is not as obvious as it seems, even if we can be sure that tomorrow we won't see the orthodox Jews in Jerusalem practicing sexual rites!

Nevertheless, at the end of a lecture on Tantra, a friend of mine, himself an orthodox Jew and director of a Hebraic College, told me: "A Kabbalist would not speak otherwise." This was the beginning of exchanges with regard to the Kabbalah, first with him and later on with other Kabbalists. In fact, Kabbalah means "what is received" from the One and the Masters, similar to the Tantric tradition. In Israel, a Kabbalah is (also) the tip given to a taxi-driver!

Initially when one learns about this tradition, one discovers it has much in common with Tantra. What is more, in the Kabbalah, the essentials of Tantra are included, even its views on sex.

The first common point: like Tantricism, the Kabbalah has no single sacred book like the Holy Bible, the Gospel, the Koran or even the Vedas. Kabbalah is a treasure of secret teachings from ancient Israel, orally transmitted from mouth to ear, from initiate to disciple. Another similar characteristic: like Tantra, which remained hidden up to the sixth century, the Kabbalah and its concepts first became public about the 12th century, but its mysticism dates back to the most remote Jewish tradition.

The Kabbalah's basic principle is: "What's on earth is like what's in Heaven," and this is pretty close to the Tantric saying "What is here, is elsewhere; what is not here, is nowhere." But, to proceed further, we have to refer to an essential 13th-century work, *The Zohar: The Book of Splendor* (New York, 1949, Moshe de Leon). This work is based on the teachings of Simon-bar-Jochaï, the great teacher of the second century. Even if this is not entirely true, there is no doubt that Moshe de Leon's teachings rely on the most ancient Jewish oral transmissions. When the Zohar was first published, it was not appreciated to its true value but it made its marks in the next half-millennium. Kabbalism also has influence on the Hassidim (pious, in Hebrew). Among the great modern Hassidim are: Martin Buber, Marc Chagall, Elie Wiesel, the philosophers Heschel and Levinas, not to forget Gershwin.

For the Hassidim, and the Tantrists alike, "Every created object, even the humblest, like a pebble or even more trivial ones, bear witness to God and have a soul. This very idea that every object in our universe, atoms included, has a soul, and hence some form of consciousness, is really at the core of Tantra as well."

Even more surprising in this form of Jewish mysticism and included in a patriarchal system, is the importance given by the Zohar and the Kabbalah to the *Shekina*, the female aspect of God. According to the oral tradition of the Kabbalah, God is both male and female, indissolubly united. Shiva and Shakti? The *Shekina* is the Divine Presence, the Veil of the Unknown, the Mother of the Origins, the Motherly Space. For the Kabbalah, every woman stands for the Shekina and is under her direct protection. And when the Kabbalah says a man is only whole when united to his *Shekina*, this is no metaphor.

The Zohar says (III, 81a) "When does man become One? Only when male and female are sexually united (*siwurga*). Come and see...! As soon as the human being, male or female, is united, by keeping his thoughts holy, he is perfect, without any blemish and is said to be One. Man should behave in such a way as to have the woman experience orgasm when both form a single Will—and both should keep this union in mind." No doubt this is not symbolical but very realistic and expresses the essence of the Tantric maïthuna whose aim is to sanctify sex as a way to the ultimate realities of our universe.

Louis Rebcke writes (*Prâna*, Deventer, 1982, page 89): "As soon as the union of the believer and his beloved is completed, the unity of the soul of the two lost halves, namely man and woman, is restored." According to the Jewish tradition, this reunification must take place to restore the primitive divine order of the Creation. For the lover of the Shekina, and the Seeker in general, this fullness is the only true solace in this sad and violent world.... Thus, the Kabbalist finds the key to a new start, and he knows that the Seeker who faithfully follows God's path will find the house of his beloved.

For Louis Rebcke, the genuine Kabbalist is a lover who never leaves the *Shekina*, who represents *woman* in the Creation. "Without any hesitation, he comes close to her and listens to the words of wisdom and love she addresses to him from behind the Veil. These words give him the vision and the inner knowledge (*derasch* in the Kabbalah)." This Veil, does it not mean that the actual woman veils the cosmic Shakti within herself? Is it not she who is the initiator as in the Tantric rite? This means that the kabbalist, like the Tantrist, should always be in touch with the outer and the inner woman.

In Zohar, the Book of Splendor (New York 1949, Gershom G. Scholem, page 36) writes: "According to secret doctrine, the Cosmic Mother is together with the male only when the house is in readiness and at that time the male and the female are conjoined. At such times, blessings are showered forth by the Cosmic Mother upon them. Likewise, the lower Mother is found together with the male only when the house is in readiness, and the male goes in to the female and they conjoin together."

In a translation of the Zohar (page 55) by Jean de Pauly we read: "God blessed *them* and gave *them* Adam as their name." This clearly means that Adam is neither male nor female, but man and woman united.

Julius Evola, in his *Métaphysique du Sexe* (Paris 1959, page 227) evokes the existence of some form of sexual magic among the Kabbalist. Speaking of the Sabbatians and according to the teachings of Jacob Franck, who goes so far as to assess that the mystical power of the Messiah, whom he believes to be a symbol, has been hidden in the female, he (Franck) says: "I tell you, all the Hebrews are in a great misfortune because they expect a Savior to come and not the Woman." And we could say the same thing today in the 20th century.

To quote Mircea Eliade, in his *Histoire des Religions* (Paris, 1964, page 354): "Many rabbinic commentaries confirm that Adam sometimes has been regarded as being androgynous." The "Birth of Eve"would have been the parting of the primeval Androgen in two beings, the male and the female. In the beginning Adam and Eve were joined back to back and with his axe God separated them. Others think the primeval Man's right half was male, his left female, but God separated them in two (*Bereshit rabbâ* I,1, fol. 6, col. 2).

Of course this is all to be taken symbolically. Here we encounter the myth of the Androgen—the Tantric *Ardhanari*—and at the same time the Latin origin of the word sex, derived from *sectus*, to cut! Add to this the fact that the right side is male, the left, female, and therefore, the Path of the Left (side) is the feminine way.

On the other hand, we could also compare the Zohar's theory of the *Sephiroth* and the subtle energies of Tantra, as well as the chakras. But this would lead us too far away from the scope of this book.

Let's be very clear about it: this, of course, is not an attempt to pocket the Kabbalah or to transform it into some Tantric mysticism. I want to show only that Judaism is much less ultra-patriarchal than it looks, provided one takes the trouble to look at the orally transmitted esoteric Tradition.

Tantra and the Indian Samkhya philosophy have many common features with the Jewish esoteric, for instance, the structure of the human soul, made of several "layers"(which is the exact translation of the Sanskrit word *kosha*) and of four "winds" to shape it. Both in Tantra and in the Jewish esoteric, these "winds" are subtle forces (*vayu* in Sanskrit) which animate the human body, and we find also the same elements: earth, water, air and fire. The Samkhya adds a fifth element, namely the *akasha*, which is "dynamic space," but this is not unknown to the Jewish occult philosophy: "Thus, by the most secret mystery, with the sound of the Verb, struck the Infinite void (or space)."

Another non-Aryan concept in India which appears in the Jewish esotericism as well is reincarnation. Jean de Pauly writes: "Juda and other tribes have known this mystery; they knew that as long as a soul did not achieve her mission on earth, she is being again transplanted on earth, as it is written: 'And man comes back on earth' (Job XXXIX:15)."

But the souls who did fulfill their task whilst being on earth will have a better fate: they stay with the Holy, blessed be He. This is the meaning of the Scripture: "I prefer the fate of the dead to the fate of the people still alive" (Ecc.IV, 2). Blessed is the soul who does not need to come back in this world to make up for the sins committed by the human she previously made live! (I. 187b, 188a).

To the Western Tantrist, it is not essential to take a stand about reincarnation, to accept or to reject it. To the Tantrist, the main thing is the present, to know one to be part and parcel of the continuous process of the rising of the manifested world, oneself included. Reincarnation or not, what counts here and now, is to live as fully as possible my fate as a human being, and to fulfill my tack. To me, for the time being, it is to write this book!

A Cosmic Sunbath

It is true that a good many aspects of Indian Tantrism are not exportable. Yet each and every one of us can grasp its essence which, need I add, has nothing to do with bizarre or perverted sex rituals. Although Tantra deliberately includes and uses sexual energy, many of its practices are not eros-related at all. Actually Tantra is above all the expansion of one's awareness, becoming conscious of having a direct insight into the cosmic aspects of life. Any experience, however commonplace or trivial, can take on a Tantric dimension. Let us take a concrete example: the "Tantric sunbath."

It's a cinch! Consider my non-Tantric fellow sunbather and myself, both of us stretched out on the beach, taking in the golden rays. I try to become aware of as many sensorial inputs as possible: feel the heat, the texture of the beach towel on my skin, my toes as they dig into the warm sand, really feel the wind blowing through my hair, the smell and quality of the sea breeze, etc. This is the first step. Now I must "cosmicize" the experience by becoming deeply aware of the "Sun-as-an-Event."

In my ordinary perception, the sun represents the same thing it did in ancient times: a large fireball way up there in the sky. When a Greek thinker asserted that it might be as large as the Acropolis, he encountered nothing but incredulity and even hostility! Today any school kid knows that the sun is one million times larger than the Earth, but do we truly realize it? Probably not. Moreover, knowing that the solar energy we now perceive was still inside the sun only eight minutes ago doesn't really "hit home" even if I know that light travels over 186,281 miles-per-second, the equivalent of almost eight Earth circumferences. In order to translate this enormous distance into concrete terms, let us imagine a highway running from the earth to the sun. If I were to drive at a hundred miles an hour, twenty-four hours a day, without ever stopping, how long would it take me to cover that distance? So as I lie on the beach, I'm trying to transform these abstract figures into a concrete reality. Let us imagine the immensity of the frozen void (- 273° C!) between us and the sun, and experience its light as a shower of mini-missiles, the photons constant-ly hitting and penetrating us.

Better still: light is actually solar *matter* which, only eight minutes ago, was still a part of the sun. It is therefore a continuous flow of mat-ter linking the star to me. So I am literally bathing in sun-substance, I am absorbing sun-matter. And I can also try—in vain, really, given its enormous size—to visualize its erupting mass, spewing incandescent matter hundreds of thousands of miles up from its surface. Even if it were physically possible, a close-up would be terrifying. Just think of how awesome an erupting volcano can be. Now consider our entire planet transformed into a single, huge volcano multiplied by 33,000! No human mind could stand it. When astronauts return from the moon after a pitiful, one-light-second hop, coming face-to-face with the cosmos—even for so short a time—entails a total change in their world view. Every astronaut having walked on the moon's dusty sur-face knows this. Tantric or not, even the farthest stretches of human imagination pale in comparison with that kind of reality.

Still lying on the beach, in the warm sand, I try to soak in the sweeping reality of our "sun-event." To fully grasp and become aware of what these streams of energy (solar matter constantly showering the total surface of our Earth) really are, I can think of the entire sur-face of my own skin, which represents under six square feet and only half of which, of course, is now exposed to the sun. In the summer-time, at high noon, that square foot is getting so hot that I have to go and sit in the shade. On the level of the entire planet, millions of square miles are offered up to the sun! And yet our planet, that tiny speck of cosmic dust, only captures an infinitesimal part of the total energy spewed forth by the sun in the interstellar void. Our sun has been "slimming down" to the tune of hundreds of tons per second for billions of years and is none the worse off for it.

But it gets even better: I am literally cooled down sun! Each atom of my body, each grain of sand, each and every object around me, is actually solidified sun, for the Earth was once also incandescent side-real plasma: it is a shred of cooled star. Therefore, I AM, in my flesh and bones, condensed sun. Sun is life, it is my life. To wiggle my pinkie finger, to think or to sleep, I must degrade solar energy. In order to live and act, I must get my energy either from plants which are canned sun, or from meat, which is transformed grass, therefore sun turned into beef! The fuel in my car is fossil solar energy, as is coal: the list is practically endless! In short, I am writing this text and you are reading it thanks to solar energy.

Intellectually *knowing* that we are made of condensed sun is inter-esting, at best, however, *experiencing* it, even fleetingly, is fantastic, is

Tantric! My senses are naïve and conceal from me the true sun, which only my intuition can reveal to me. Still lying on the beach, feeling the immensity of solar energy and the distance it has traveled, in real-time and on-line with cosmic energy, the borders between the star and myself fade away, dissolve, and I am able to perceive and feel the Shakti of Tantra, the ultimate creative energy of which the universe is a manifestation. *That* is Tantra.

Meanwhile my fellow sunbather is probably thinking about his buddies (or girlfriends!) admiring his beautiful tan, or perhaps he has simply dozed off. As my profane sunbath becomes cosmic, the sun's ultraviolet rays continue to burn my skin just as much his, but at least (a consolation prize!) *my* sunburn will be Tantric! In the same way, my entire life can be transmuted, made cosmic, which does not exclude pleasure and enjoyment, on the contrary. Whence a formidable expansion of my view of the world and of myself, especially my body, a universe unto itself.

Here is another example of "cosmicization": a dip into the sea or a river may be solely health or fitness-oriented. Let us imagine that I am doing my ablutions in the Ganges, in Benares, along the famous ghats, amid throngs of devout Hindus, a scene often depicted in documentary films on India. This bath can be a simple "here and now" affair, an ordinary act of everyday life. But everything changes as I realize that the river is not limited to just "here" and if I perceive the Ganges as a whole, that two-thousand-mile link between the Himalayas and the ocean. That changes everything. And everything becomes different too when I perceive its relation with all the seas and oceans of the world, when I realize that the Ganges of today is the same as yesterday although it is never twice identical, for it's never the same water flowing between its banks. As witnessed by an outside observer, there appears to be no difference between my ablutions and those of my non-Tantric fellow bathers, but my inner experience expands and is enhanced.

Therefore Tantra is first and foremost another way of being and feeling. That is what Tantra really is about although it has evolved concrete forms of expression such as special techniques and rituals.

However we must not fall into an intellectual trap! Our intellect—a precious asset indeed—affords us the objective and scientific tool making such insight possible. But what counts is the overall intuitive perception of the event. It is arduous to shift from the sensorial perception of the event to the concept of it (of the sun, a river, or anything else), and further on to the direct experiencing of its ultimate aspects. Yet that is precisely how the commonplace becomes ego-transcending and how the dullest of lives is "de-trivialized."

Tantra is fully aware of the difficulties involved, and has responded with art, rites, and symbols. More than any other Indian philosophy Tantra intentionally uses art as means of accessing the cosmic dimension concealed in the commonplace.

Part 2

Human Sexuality:
The Other View

When Sex is a Problem

After a couple of millennia of repression—give or take a few "slack" periods—sex has become unbridled, obsessive, and by virtue of the law of the pendulum, a new Puritanism may emerge which is all the stricter as the debauchery has been great. But regardless of its future trends, the undeniable fact of the day is that our society is hypersexual. Just one telltale sign: how sex is used in advertising to sell coffee, soap, fruit juice, cars, etc.! There is nothing accidental about this evolution. On the contrary, it is an almost inevitable consequence of our industrialized civilization which has created overpopulated, tentacular metropolises.

Just a few generations ago, 80 percent of the population were farmers or villagers, whereas now the opposite is true: farmers, i.e., 6 - 7 percent of the population, feed the entire US and produce considerable surpluses that are exported. For the peasants of yore, sex existed, of course, but it was no big deal. Prior to mechanization, at harvest time, the reapers would rise at dawn and cut the mature wheat, mowing slowly and rhythmically. The women and children would then tie it into bundles which, all stacked up, were indeed a promise of abundance: Breughel depicted this simple life in a famous painting a copy of which adorns my home office. People would barely take time to eat a bite and would toil from sun-up to sundown and return to the homestead dead beat, ready to sleep. In my native Belgium, in 1940, after our capitulation to the Germans, I led this rough life myself. I escaped and hid away in a farm where I reaped, stored and threshed wheat with a flail! It was hard work, especially for a city boy, and I know that in the evening, after your soup and fried potatoes with bacon, all you are interested in is sleep! Sex? The thought does not even cross your mind! In these rural areas, the purpose of sex was basically procreation and not much else.

The value system was and still is different in rural areas: what counts is not so much a piece of the action but the weather, getting the harvest in on time, healthy and well-fed cattle. These varied and down-to-earth tasks keep sex off people's minds.

Now let's take a trip to the city, to one of those ant-hills, our modern highrise office buildings and see what sex is like there. Farmers live in a relatively natural environment, whereas city folk survive in an artificial one: the buildings, windowpanes, wall and floor coverings, furniture, machines, computers, paper, and even the light, are all man-made, artificial. The city dweller's office, perched up on the thirtieth floor, overlooks a sea of roofs and the streets are like narrow canyons where tiny mechanical insects, lines of cars, thread their way in and out of the traffic. Nature has all but disappeared, except for the token parks that speckle some of our cities.

Living on a farm means living in closer contact with animal life: one is awakened by the sound of the rooster's cock-a-doodle-doo, baby chicks squawk under mother hen, the cat stretches lazily. Pigs grunt, cows chew the cud as their calves frolic in the meadow. In their rural environment, people were surrounded by goats, sheep, sometimes draught horses and of course, birds, insects. Peasants were in closer contact with farm animals, their source of livelihood. But in our cities, except for pets, where is animal life to be found today?

In their air-conditioned offices, city dwellers have lost all contact with pure, fresh air, with the rain, the wind, trees, brooks, birds, forest animals and even domestic animals. People are sequestered in their prison-offices that they themselves have built and where rural values have no place. Their work is seldom a barrel of fun and is usually a bread-and-butter job. Industrialized society has intentionally organized things so that people are not distracted from their work, to maximize the output of these producer-consumers in an environment that would have been sheer science fiction just a century ago. Now for such penned up people what represents the greatest interest if not the opposite sex? At the end of their workday it's the usual mad rush in the subway or traffic jams, amid a sea of people with whom relations are aggressive or sexual, rarely friendly. And in our leisure time, in movies, on television, etc., sex is omnipresent. The entertainment industry proposes escape, en masse: sex is a get-away holiday from the boredom and problems of everyday life. Hypertrophied sex thus becomes a problem.

Such pressure indeed shatters the barriers of hypocritical puritanism, but it also leads to the extreme opposite excesses. One remarkable fact is seldom mentioned: puritanism always goes hand in hand with dictatorships, be they military, political or spiritual. Under Franco and Salazar, just to mention two dictators, puritanism reigned. On the beaches, bikinis were banned, even for tourists, and going topless, unthinkable! Religious dictatorships such as Iran, are no exception, on the contrary. It's quite logical, really: the sexual energy that is thus repressed and building up behind the barrage of puritanism, actually feeds and fuels a kind of fanaticism which the ruling ideology absolutely needs, both to stay in power and to further conquer.

Tantra of the Left-Hand Path rejects puritanism and considers that neither prudishness nor all-out promiscuity solves anything.

What are the alternatives? "Healthy sexuality," free from guilt, is an acceptable alternative and certainly preferable to puritanism or vulgar pornography. You know, visiting a sexshop—although hopelessly monotonous—can actually be instructive, for you there can see on display the entire gamut of human sexual misery. X-rated movies are incredibly boring and rather anti-erotic. "Healthy sexuality" should be the norm, but that is not the case because of our lack of real sex education. What we are taught in this field could be called at best "reproductive information."

The other alternative and true solution to the problem is the *spiritualization of sex* as proposed by the Left-Hand Path, and which is perfectly suited to our times. It is for people who refuse both prudishness and pornographic pseudo-eroticism, for those who would go beyond "healthy sexuality." The Left-Hand Path solves this sex problem via liberation in the highest sense of the word and an access to the sacred. Tantra asserts that in our decadent and destructive time (Kali Yuga) only the Left-Hand Path can lead to true spirituality.

Allow me to quote Julius Evola: "Sexual union understood in this way, suspends the law of duality, provokes an ecstatic opening. The law of duality being thus suspended in the simultaneity of the ecstasy, the orgasm and rapture uniting two beings, a state of identity can be triggered which prefigures absolute illumination, the unconditioned state. The *Kularnava Tantra* goes so far as to state that the supreme union can only be obtained via sexual union" (*Le Yoga Tantrique*, Paris, 1961, pp. 191-192).

If we do not go back to respecting Mother Nature and the practice of magic-erotic rites whereby human beings can enjoy greater fulfillment and harmony with other beings, the destruction of the entire race is sure to follow.

I would like to conclude in quoting René Guénon: "What would be involved would be a reconstitution of what existed before our modern deviation, with the necessary adaptations to the conditions of another epoch.... The East may assuredly come to rescue the West if the latter is willing, but not to impose upon it alien conceptions as some seem to fear, but to help it renew with its own lost tradition" (*La Crise du monde moderne*, Paris, 1954, pp. 46, 129). And I might add: especially as regards sexuality.

Sex Education Revisited

In patriarchy, the man plays the active role in sexual intercourse: the penis is the essential organ and the vagina merely a pleasant receptacle. The penis penetrates, moves in and out, imposes its own rhythm, climaxes, i.e., ejaculates, and the male is satisfied, or at least contents himself with this. Due to centuries of male domination, most women accept the passive role, take it for granted, and live with it. Even the etymology of the word is eloquent: *vagina* is the Latin word for "sheath." Compare the Dutch word *schede* or the German *Scheide* which indistinctly refer to the sheath of a sword or the vagina. Obviously, the sword is the important object the sheath only having a protective purpose.

Even the most habitual lovemaking position in the West, the so-called missionary position, expresses male domination and reduces the possibility of the woman actively participating. An awful German proverb states: "Nach dem Essen sollst du rauchen, oder eine Frau gebrauchen." Literally: "After dining, you should have a smoke or use a woman." Sic! The proverb even goes so far as to put *rauchen* (smoke) first!

Moreover, men are supposed to have innate knowledge of all things sexual and very often, women do not even dare point out to them their ignorance or their clumsiness, or both.

One of the saddest parts of the story is that they are not to blame, really: when I was growing up in Europe, teenagers of both sexes still lived in "splendid isolation," cut off, as they were, from this reality. Sex was a veritable taboo and teenagers—even adults—simply hadn't a clue.

Because of the systematic repression of all forms of sexuality, many young males, especially in denominational schools, had no idea, at age 18 or 20, or even until they were married, what female genitals looked like: the science curriculum had "neglected" to include those "details"! If materially possible, I think they would have concealed from us the very existence of our own genitals!

The naked body was such a taboo that many women, now grandmothers, remember the time when at nuns' schools prim and proper young girls would take their bath in their underwear! You might object that Indian women still bathe in the Ganges, fully clad in their saris. That is true but it stems from the same logic, Victorian puritanism having contaminated India.

You might point out, with a knowing look, that in the meantime these former schoolgirls have become mothers, and that apparently their upbringing did not prevent them from bearing children! Indeed, but in what conditions? Officially, sexual intercourse before marriage was out of the question and boys and girls were raised and educated separately. Naturally, circumventing adults' painstakingly developed plans to keep them apart, they nevertheless made their secret rendezvous and "did it" on the sly, in helter-skelter circumstances. With no sexual initiation to speak of, boys were per force awkward, therefore disappointing, therefore disappointed. And the girls were no more skilled or knowledgeable. The whole experience was often steeped in feelings of guilt and sin, plus the fear of an unwanted pregnancy. Under such conditions how could a married couple expect to have a happy and fulfilling sex-life and become a close, sexually-united couple?

Sex education is now on the school curriculum, but the term is a misnomer: it amounts to little more than reproductive *education* and is not actual sex education. Teaching anatomy, the physiology of the sex organs and providing information on genital processes is good and well but is a far cry from teaching sexual *behavior*. Admittedly, this would be inconceivable in our schools, unless classrooms were converted into dormitories, or rather "sleeping" quarters. In this respect we might learn a lesson or two from certain "wild" tribes in India, especially those who have organized sex education socially in the form of the *ghotul*, or youths' dorm. Although the *ghotul* is not exportable to our countries, it may nevertheless serve as an enlightening eye-opener for Westerners as we discover its inherent wisdom.

Elwin Verrier (*Une vie tribale*, Paris, 1973) who lived among several Indian tribes for extended periods of time and even married into one, wrote: "Sex is more natural for those sharing the tribal life. Young boys learn about sex before their puberty by observing adults and by word-of-mouth. As they grow older, they imitate sexual play and gradually go on to premarital relations. Male adolescents consider young girls in their entirety and thus form an opinion of them, as do the girls (p. 196).

"[...] Premarital sex is not objected to in the tribal framework on condition that the rules governing the choice of a partner are abided by (p. 198).

"[...] The *ghotul*, now on the decline, provides a socially safe and secure framework for premarital sexual relations. Partners still meet one another in this way. In these tribes, a simple, innocent and natural attitude prevails vis-à-vis sexuality. And in the *ghotul*, this attitude is further reinforced and supported by the total lack of guilt and by the freedom which stems from the absence of outside influence or interference. They are convinced that sex is a good thing, promotes health, well-being, and is beautiful when shared with the appropriate partner, at the right time and place. The youngest of the girls and boys initiate themselves by imitating love and sexual behavior. Making love begins by smiling, laughing, and dancing together in the dormitory, which does not exclude meeting in deep forests or remote places. And so at a tender age, boys and girls learn sexual techniques through both example and their own personal initiation. In other tribes, like the Santhals, who do not have such institutions, youths have many opportunities to meet one another, during festivals, at weddings, dances, while visiting other villages and even while working in the field. This gives them ample opportunity to get to know one another better and eventually for sexual intercourse. These premarital relations often lead to happy marriages (p. 199).

"[…] In terms of sexual intercourse *per se*, even after marriage, some enter into extramarital relations, relics of a free sex-life prior to marriage and a very free psychological attitude developed during adolescence (p. 201).

"[…] In the tribes, certain festivals were the usual opportunity for extramarital sexual relations. One could quote in this respect the festivals of the Santhals, the Hos, the Mundas, etc. when a person is free to choose a partner for sexual intercourse. The other facet of tribal sex-life is the multiplicity of marriages. When a man is not sexually satisfied with his wife and if his sexual appetite is not totally fulfilled, he may have affairs with other partners just to make love or just as an extramarital relation, or even in the usual ceremonial fashion" (p. 201).

Naturally, adopting the above tribal customs is out of the question. However, the knowledge of such customs and their advantages may prove useful to us, if only to better gauge our own social conditioning. In these tribes, possessiveness, jealousy, crimes of passion for "cheating," divorces painful for parents and children alike, are thus avoided, without mentioning the lack of sexual frustration, all of which creates a solid psychological balance. Granted, these mores cannot be transplanted outside their original communities. We should, however, be capable at the very least of judging them on their own merit, impartially.

It is true that times are changing: a growing need for more and better sex information is felt by men who would learn the techniques to bring a woman to orgasm, the "magnum opus" of the male. Countless books on the art of loving are bought by these men in the hope that after filling in their own "cultural" gaps they can fulfill their partners!

This modern male learns everything he ever wanted to know about foreplay, erogenous zones and kissing. He becomes a real name-dropper as he begins to pepper his speech with words like cunnilingus and fellatio. He knows the one-hundred-and-one love-making positions and their variants. In short, he has become the Perfect Lover. Or has he?

The snag is that these are books for men, by men written perforce from the male point of view! But I hear you object: *this* book was also written by a man: True! I do "confess" to belonging to the male gender. But come on, ladies, what have you been waiting for to write something for us? Even the Hite Report, which is none too flattering for us males—among other things—is not the long-awaited and hoped-for book, i.e., the one in which a woman tells us men, at long last: "Gentlemen, this is who we are, what we like and how we feel, and this is how we want to be loved!" Current publications may be missing the real point, *that* is, the need for a radical change in men's attitude toward women and sex, that is what Tantra can bring, inter alia!

In sexual play, they must also let the woman lead the game. And when he approaches her, it must be with total respect for her *femininity*, her *femaleness*; he must open up to her female sexuality. I do not mean "lip service," I mean the acute perception of the formidable female sexual potential. To attain this perception, a dialogue must be established between the man and the woman. Unfortunately, women are all too often reluctant to share their feelings about sex and themselves with men. Why not tell their partners in an open and straightforward way what they really expect and want from a man? Why not express to him her innermost needs and desires? Why can the woman not be the initiator? The gross ignorance of many a so-called lady's man can be quite amazing!

Agreed, Tantra is more, much more, than ordinary sex. Nevertheless a Tantrist, that is, both the Shiva and the Shakti, must be able to satisfy his/her partner, even in a so-called normal embrace. Moreover, a Tantric union is possible only when both partners are capable of run-of-the-mill, mutually fulfilling, sex.

Sex manuals high and low never fail to include a chapter on foreplay and the fancy technicalities thereof. In contrast, Tantric foreplay does not involve so much this or that caress, or kissing any specific part of the body. The *real* prelude to maïthuna (Tantric union) involves creating an atmosphere of intimacy, both physical and psychological, so that both partners may become deeply attuned to each other. To this end, each one immerses himself/herself in the other's presence, becomes filled with his/her being totally, is permeated by the partner's sex (not synonymous with the genitalia). Opening up to one another in this way—often without actually touching—allows a subtle contact, an energy flow to happen. As the woman's perception of the maleness of the man so deepens, her *rati* (passion) is activated, and vice versa, in the man, there is an awakening of his *virya* (virility). Stroking, caressing, the whole kit and caboodle of habitual foreplay need not be totally discarded, but takes on meaning only inasmuch as the kind of contact mentioned above has been established, in which case they become practically superfluous.

When *rati* and *virya* are thus awakened, the yoni opens up and its warm and humid corolla invites the man. The lingam must not actively *penetrate*, it must be taken in and slowly *absorbed* by the throbbing yoni. The lingam is not a hammer drill!

Alan Watts had a keen understanding of this. In *Nature, Man and Woman* (p. 201), he wrote: "For when the couple are so close to each other that the sexual parts are touching, it is only necessary to remain quietly and unhurriedly still, so that in time the woman can absorb the man's member into herself without being actively penetrated."

At this point, good vaginal muscle control is an undeniable asset. For the controlled contractions of the yoni absorb the lingam and the Shakti may then feel that her partner has become part of herself, that they have become a single flesh, a single being, they have re-created the original androgyne. How long does it take to achieve this? Well, there is nothing to achieve, really: just let it happen!

Our Bipolar Sexuality

Human sexuality is dual or bipolar: the "species" pole and the "individual" pole. The former is located in the lower part of our body, in the genitals (*muladhara* and *svadisthana* chakras), literally the immortal enclave of the species within us and whose single finality is procreation, the perpetuation of the human race. The individual pole is located at the other end of the spine, in the brain, the One-Thousand-Petaled Lotus, the *sahasrara chakra*, that is, the seat of individuality, of the "I," the ego.

The sexuality of the species, whose physical "seat" is the genitalia, is expressed in the irrepressible vital *élan* which makes all life proliferate, it is the *Kundalini* of Tantra. This basic, animal sexuality—not meant as derogatory—fills women with sexual desire during the fertile days of their menstrual cycle. It is innate, it has been programmed, and it guides the woman's instinctive sexual behavior, when she unites with a man, which triggers almost mechanically the rhythmic movements of her hips and her vagina's contractile waves to make the fertilizing sperm flow forth so the species' design may be accomplished.

This compulsive impulse is obvious and well-known. The other type of sexuality, the more specifically human one, that of the individual pole, often goes unnoticed or is confused with the former. However, it is very important to distinguish the two as regards Tantric maïthuna. Naturally, Tantra neither ignores nor underestimates the power or the vital force of the species pole, but the goal of ritual maïthuna is not procreation. Indeed, the continuity of the species could be safeguarded with very few *coiti* in the course of a lifetime. In theory, twenty ejaculations spread over a twenty-year period, at the right time, would suffice to beget a score of offspring, more in the case of twins. On the basis of such procreative logic, some ultra-prudish sects, such as Hare Krishna and others, have banned sex altogether, except for married couples who may have intercourse once a month. Even Gandhi shared such an anti-Tantric view.

Tantra calls upon both forms of sexuality, with a clear-cut preference for the one that is not purely animal or reproductive. The specific location and the reflex, almost mechanical, nature of the sexuality of the species can be evidenced in the praying mantis. It is said that while mating, the female praying mantis sometimes severs the male's head from its body when he is not active enough. She thus eliminates the individual pole as the species pole continues to mate more vigorously, eventually fertilizing the female who then devours him! True, some entomologists consider this is to be no more than a myth. Nevertheless, it has been proven experimentally in certain butterfly species that if the male's head is cut off, the rest of the body continues to mate actively, demonstrating the autonomy of the species pole vis-à-vis the cerebral pole. In humans, it is a known fact that male paraplegics can get erections and fertilize their female partner: the spinal cord has been cut off so the species pole alone is active, and no feeling reaches the brain.

Consequently, the individual pole has its own sexuality which is quite distinct from the animal impulse of the species pole. It is indirectly genital and it also rests upon the polarity of the sexes. Eroticism is to pure sex what gastronomy is to animal hunger and it is the expression of the individual pole's sexuality.

Heaven and Hell

What does the science of physiology have to say about this? Believe it or not, the evidence confirms Tantra's assertions: the center of cerebral sexuality, the individual sexual pole does exist, it can and has been located! It is also the locus of bliss, of ecstasy.

An American researcher, Olds, implanted an electrode into a rat's brain to study the impact on its behavior of electrically stimulating specific points. He already knew how to electrically provoke, in the rat, extreme anger, fear, apathy, etc. On that particular day, the rat's behavior was rather strange and atypical. Instead of running away from the scientist, it kept on obstinately returning to the place where Olds had triggered the stimulation: the animal was obviously experiencing considerable pleasure, it was "in heaven" to quote Dr. V. Levy of Leningrad (V. Lévy, Les mystères du cerveau). Olds located other heavenly points forming a cross-shape in the hypothalamus, near the base of the brain. Unfortunately, he also discovered a sort of cerebral "hell" where the electrical stimulation terrorized the animal whose expression seemed to be: "No, never again!"

Mother Nature has been merciful: in the rat's brain, heaven is seven times larger than hell. Cerebral heavens and hells have also been identified in fish, birds, cats, dogs, dolphins, rabbits, etc.

These are interesting findings for Tantra. Olds also discovered that when their "heaven" was stimulated, well-fed laboratory animals experienced bliss to a much smaller degree. Conversely, when hungry, they felt greater enjoyment, which corroborates the Tantric assertion that "stuffing oneself" blunts the more subtle forms of eros. This should not prevent anyone from enjoying healthy and even refined food, on condition that one be frugal. The caricature of the plump and rubicund monk confirms that over-indulging in food and filling one's belly compensate for sex and facilitate continence!

Following in Olds' footsteps, a host of scientists taught self-stimulation to laboratory animals that learned to press the lever which triggers the electrical stimulation of their brains. They were very quick to learn. Once they knew the trick, they could not get enough: they would stimulate themselves hundreds of times in a row, never letting up, giving themselves ripples of orgasms to the point of exhaustion! Another crucial finding: these electric orgasms are dependent on sex hormones: neutered animals ceased stimulating themselves but if given an injection of male hormones, they would resume the self-stimulation with renewed energy.

In Tantric maïthuna, the powerful and protracted excitement of the species pole stimulates the gonads and boosts the production of male hormones which are indispensable for a maximum activation of the "heaven" in the brain.

Dr. Lévy (1979), commenting on Olds' experiments, recognizes that: "In all fairness to the rats, as long as they could, they were pretty reasonable, seeking to eat as much as to enjoy the electrical self-stimulation, except when the electrode was placed in specific points of their brains and the excitement thereof made them forget all other forms of pleasure."

Moreover, Olds discovered that rats which ate little but stimulated themselves, were stronger and perkier: this electromania—I would say the stimulation of their individual pole—made them more alert, more energetic, as if this newfound pleasure filled them with renewed strength. Compare this to the fact that Tantrists both male and female, even well-on in years, remain strikingly youthful, alert, dynamic.

What extrapolations can be made from the above findings and how do they apply to humans? Our cousins may help us with the answer. Dr. Lévy, who has also studied primates, wrote: "This monkey sitting in his special armchair is not suffering in the least and seeks not to release himself. On the contrary, judging by his expression, he is having the time of his life. He is exulting. On his head is a helmet through which run electrodes planted in his brain. There is all the less cause for concern as the experimenter is John Lilly, who is well-known for his humaneness towards animals, and is a great expert on the language of dolphins. The animal is experiencing ultimate bliss because the current going through the electrode has been planted in its own heaven. For twenty straight hours, except for short breaks for a little snack or even while eating, he sends the electrical current to his brain and then, exhausted, falls asleep. When he wakes up, he presses the lever again, ceaselessly. He has become a totally different monkey! Whereas he used to be irascible and full of fear, he has now become docile, playful, stroking the experimenter's hand instead of scratching it.

"[...] Although an animal's cerebral self-stimulation may correspond to what we consider to be a sort of gross enjoyment, in other cases, its inner state may be comparable to the inexpressible feelings of bliss, enthusiasm or ecstasy that we may feel for various, more complex, reasons."

Further questions could be raised: does the above prove that such a heaven is a) erotic, b) our second sexual pole and c) that it is applicable to human beings? The answer is yes, and here is at least one piece of evidence, still according to Dr. Lévy: "The first case of human electromania was observed (by chance) by Natalie Bekhtereva, a neurosurgeon in Leningrad. A patient whose "heaven" points were repeatedly excited, began to go out of her way and do her utmost in order to be able to feel this again. She sought every possible occasion to go to the laboratory, to strike up a conversation with her doctors, literally staking them out. She used various maneuvers, and was irritable and impatient, behaving in a provocative way. Even more, this patient fell madly in love with the experimenter, pursuing him in a particularly annoying manner, expressing excessive gratefulness for his care. Let this be a warning! I believe that you will agree that although the person was a patient, the above does confirm the erotic and orgasmic nature of our cerebral heaven and therefore, of the individual pole.

Incidentally, I have quoted Dr. V. Lévy at length because the former Soviet scientific community was not overburdened with any spiritualistic bias, which adds even more weight to his comment: "We sometimes get the impression that in many cases, modern science which has chosen the brain and the mind as objects of study, only broaches from another side phenomena which we constantly deal with in daily life and that one could easily understand oneself through introspection and the most basic observation. It seems indeed that we could have realized long ago that cerebral systems existed, without having to stick electrodes into brains."

Naturally, Tantra shares this point of view: it has been exploring for millennia the strange and fascinating universe of the human being and his/her psyche, without planting electrodes into people's brains! But since experiments have been carried out, let us take them into account and take note of the fact that they confirm the Tantric thesis.

Before reviewing the Tantric implications of our dual sexuality let us keep in mind Dr. Lévy's caveat which also applies to Dr. Delgado from Yale University, a real sorcerer's apprentice: he pushed the experiment a (giant) step further by planting electrodes inside the brains of apes which he stimulated remotely via a radio signal. The animal became a kind of remotely-controlled zombie, blindly obeying the experimenter. Such a remote stimulator exists, it is the size of a pea and can be inserted under the scalp. To this day experiments have been carried out on primates only, but NASA considers that remote stimulation would be the ideal means of controlling the behavior of astronauts, directly from Earth. They could be put to sleep, made to eat, made indifferent to loneliness, their attention could be increased tenfold during emergency situations. Fortunately these devices are not available to the general population. Will it ever be possible to "mass produce" according to need, intrepid warriors, super-kamikazes or on the contrary ultra-docile citizens, and so on and so forth? Lastly, cerebral electro-stimulation could become the absolute drug of the future.

This aside was also necessary to specify that Tantra, on the contrary, seeks to *liberate human beings* by giving them direct and self-controlled access to the immense psychic and other energies within themselves: a Tantrist is the antithesis of a remotely controlled robot.

Total Ecstasy

Another phenomenon highlights the distinction between the two types of sexuality: erotic dreams. In our dreams, we sometimes experience sexual ecstasy, mental orgasms far more intense than actual intercourse with a real partner. Dream ecstasy is a typically individual-pole phenomenon involving only mental imagery, i.e., psychical in nature, although oneiric orgasms extend beyond the cerebral realm and impact the species pole, in the genitals: young men long-deprived of the company of women (soldiers, prisoners, sailors, etc.) often have so-called wet dreams.

The two types of sexuality are distinct but linked, each impacting the other in a mutual feedback relation: a full bladder can provoke an erection which in turn may trigger an erotic dream.

In a nutshell, *the aim of Tantra is total ecstasy*, to experience the merging of the acme of the species pole, that formidable powerplant of ours, with the cerebral ecstasy of the individual pole, involving feedback between both poles. That is why in Tantra, the genital area is deliberately stimulated, in a conscious and controlled way. Upon being awakened at the species pole, the kundalini is then mentally guided up by the thought process, through the rachis to the cerebral pole (*sahasrara chakra*), where it encounters the heavenly centers of the brain setting off ultimate ecstasy. In the oft flowery and metaphorical language of Tantra this is known as the secret marriage of Shakti (Energy) and Shiva (Awareness) in the One-Thousand-Petaled Lotus.

To stimulate the individual pole and through it, the species', no electrodes are required! A moviegoer about to enter an X-rated movie theater is not too excited—yet! But after a few moments the erotic pictures on the screen begin to stimulate his/her cerebral pole with the expected impact on the genital pole. A Tantric situation? No way! Tantrists are by no means prudes—heaven forbid!—but crude, vulgar pornography is not their "trip," either. The point is to show how easy it is to awaken the energy of the species pole with the appropriate mental imagery. Tantra often resorts to erotic imagination, first to stimulate the species pole and then to guide the sexual current thus engendered up the spine to the cerebral pole. This notably involves the kriyas which are mental processes aimed at channeling energies in the body, be they sexual or not. For what purpose? For pleasure? To climax? Actually, yes, in a way, because according to Tantra, the experience of bliss brings humans closer to the ultimate. Dr. Lévy has another key for us: "Prior to the onset of one of his epileptic fits, Dostoevski felt an ineffable ecstasy, a supreme felicity, divine sincerity, and for a brief moment, *he seemed to discover the meaning of all existing things*. In some people such a state is created by music, even and especially if it is highly rhythmical."

The above sentence is worthy of our reflection and alone justifies Tantric sexual rites as the most direct means of reaching the state of ecstasy which "enlightens" and unveils as in a flash of lightning, the very foundations of our being and the cosmos, without electrodes or epileptic fits! Let us note that music can also trigger this state, whence its role in the Tantric rite (and all the more so, given the very erotic nature of Indian music). Moreover, for Dostoevski, this ecstatic and lucid vision of ultimate reality took place immediately before an epileptic fit which is, literally, a "brainstorm," therefore a phenomenon pertaining to the individual pole.

As an epileptic fit conceals ordinary, empirical consciousness, so the emergence of the cosmic vision takes place on a level of consciousness other than the ordinary one. Bliss, plus the transition to another state of consciousness are two of the conditions providing access to ultimate realities.

"Another state of consciousness" may seem mysterious or even fill one with apprehension, as happens when dealing with the unknown, in the case of epilepsy, for example. But actually, going from one level of consciousness to another is a very ordinary, commonplace occurrence which takes place every day, as in falling asleep or dreaming. And yet who—pathological cases excepted—is afraid of the Sandman?

A Unifying Cosmic Experience

Tantra has always known that the acme of sexual experience brings about a state of bliss that is a far cry from simply climaxing and produces a split from ordinary, waking consciousness associated with the ego. *Changing planes of consciousness is therefore a well-tried means of transcending the ego and gaining access to a unitary cosmic experience.* Going beyond the ego thus involves no mortification, no tedious asceticism which often creates more problems than it solves.

You may have noticed that in referring to this peak experience I deliberately avoided the word *orgasm*, both too specific and too vague, and chose *acme*, instead. I also discarded *climax* and *paroxysm* which both imply extreme tension that is totally alien to the Tantric experience. Without rejecting ordinary orgasm, Tantra considers that it is too dependent on mechanical, genital reflexes and prevents any conscious control. The female orgasm is a sort of spasm that is almost as irrepressible as the male's ejaculation. In this mysterious Tantric alchemy, the Shakti need not forfeit her genital orgasm on condition that the Shiva not lose his sexual control because of it: she must gradually transcend ordinary orgasm so that the energy thus awakened may activate the "heavenly" part of her brain. In the same way, the Shiva must go beyond his ejaculation, which implies that he has already mastered it. In both cases, the psychic, mental, orgasm is the acme.

Both our sexualities, the genital one with its orgasm, and the cerebral one with its acme, unite in the Tantric experience, although the heavenly one is given top priority, it being the only one capable of opening the doors to the cosmic experience.

Even without any Tantric initiation, some women may experience something very close indeed to the "real thing." A woman describes her experience as follows: "First, my feelings are concentrated at the genital region, then they flow over by great waves in my whole body. I become my feelings. I am all sensitivity. At times, I feel like singing, as if the sensations were reaching my vocal chords and made them vibrate on a still to be discovered tone.

"I have wonderful feelings of wholeness. It is difficult to describe this. I feel electricity running through my whole body and live intensely the bodily and spiritual union with my partner. At times, I pray God to become united to him, and feel the bliss of ecstasy!

"This kind of orgasm is to me a dive into the metaphysical, in another world, a religious world. I have the feeling of climbing a mountain. This all happens within my head which flows over with emotion, and compels me to stay emotionally close to the man with whom I am.

"Orgasm is a compulsive sensation of light; this light comes from his head and flows into my own, and I too start emitting light. Within my body everything becomes light. I am blinded by a dazzling light, which shines from behind my eyes, I hear nothing more, I do not feel anything precise, but each part of my blood starts dancing, every pore irradiates, and the spiders in the closet, the ants on the floor should feel it and be joyous to receive such love" (translation from *Le rapport Hite*, Paris, 1977, p. 178).

This excerpt is easy to decipher once you've realized there are two types of sexuality and two types of experiences. Obviously (and unknowingly), this Shakti awakened her Kundalini; her genital orgasm was the first stage of the rocket that propelled her toward another state of being, toward the heavenly experience which she herself explicitly locates in her brain (in the above quote the italics are mine) rather than in her yoni. Moreover her experience is spiritual, cosmic, and maybe even mystical, but it is unlikely that she will be able to reach this state each and every time. The same is true in Tantra. The Shiva must realize that if and when his Shakti reaches such a state—and the ecstatic expression on her face will tell him—she has become "disconnected" from the species pole: the "best behavior" for the Shiva, in this case, is to stop moving, be still and psychically share the Shakti's experience.

In a way, Tantra has democratized the experience with its rituals and processes which set the appropriate mental and corporeal conditions. True, this type of experience is not within the immediate reach of each and every woman, be she a Tantrist or not. But it is also true that each and every woman is potentially capable of attaining it. Moreover, such an acme is not the only door to the state of cosmic fusion (cf. the chapter on the Path of the Valley). Furthermore, exercising her anti-frigidity muscles and sharing maïthuna with a Shiva capable of ejaculatory control will gradually release the Shakti's dual sexuality and she will eventually be able to have such an experience and share it with her Tantric or non-Tantric partner.

As a follow-up to the above, you may proceed directly to the section starting on page 316.

Woman as an Erotic Champion

How strange: why do Eve's daughters, our partners, assert themselves more as *women* than as *females* while men are so proud to be *males*! Probably because sexually, women are an exception and in this field differ from female animals; whereas men—give or take a few details—behave like any other male on the planet.

What is so unique about women? First, all female animals without exception have specifically-timed rut periods. When a bitch is in heat, everybody knows it! Even if you lock her up, all the male dogs in the neighborhood get the message and lay siege to your house. If she manages to escape, your front yard becomes the scene of a real orgy. Fortunately for our social life, women do not experience a heat period, otherwise just imagine the subway at rush hour! Calling a woman a "bitch" is a serious insult. And to call a man a "son of a bitch" is also to insult his mother, the sacred being *par excellence*. Actually, there are biological grounds for such a reaction: human females differ from *all other females*, including their distant monkey cousins. This deserves to be underscored: the fact that human females do not experience the frenzy of the heat period is absolutely unique in Nature. In humans, the estrus, which marks ovulation, has practically disappeared. The rare residual signs are so discrete that they usually go unnoticed: during the "baby making days" of the month, the vagina merely secretes a little more colorless lubricant, a woman's temperature rises by one degree Celsius, her breasts are more tender, but that's about it. A woman really has to check her body, keep a daily record of her temperature curve to know what point she has reached in her cycle. Whereas a female monkey in heat gives off a strong sexual odor which irresistibly attracts and excites male monkeys; her genitals are turgescent and she aggressively incites the male to mate: none of this occurs in humans.

In female monkeys, despite certain common elements shared with their human counterparts, such as the clitoris and a similar menstrual cycle, ovulation triggers a heat period that lasts for about ten days. During that time the female chimpanzee or baboon only wants one thing, sex, promiscuously mating with several males and displaying all the signs of intense pleasure. The inescapable consequence of her coital marathon, the sole aim of which is procreation, is pregnancy. Once she has become pregnant, sex is out of the question both during and after her pregnancy and even prior to the weaning of her offspring. So, no dates, no fiancés, no love before two or three years' time, which reduces her sexlife to a few week-long interludes throughout her entire simian lifetime!

Male apes and monkeys, "better off" than all other male mammals which only have a once-a-year copulatory period, mate approximately every month. Incidentally, compared to monkeys and apes, human males have by far the largest sex organ. The penis of a 250 kg gorilla is nothing compared to Tarzan's!

Can women thus be considered as all-out sex champions? Without a doubt! Forgotten are the days when, not so long ago, women were not supposed to have any sexual urges and "decent" women did not have orgasms, the prerogative of "loose" women only. Since then, we have almost gone to the other extreme, becoming hell-bent on having orgasms each time, every time, come rain or come shine! And yet even in our "liberated" societies, we continue to consider that frigidity is restricted to women and women alone: do we ever label an impotent man as frigid? Actually, hidden within every so-called "frigid" woman there is a sexual athlete unaware of her potential, more often than not stifled by patriarchal morality that is as repressive as it is hypocritical. Except for physiological accidents that are very few and far between, female frigidity is usually acquired.

Elsewhere in this book, I have stated that there is no such thing as a frigid woman, only "refrigerating" men, *inter alia* bumbling lumps and premature ejaculators. I say this somewhat in jest—fortunately—for theoretically, no woman is really frigid and each and every female could be sexually active and reach orgasm without a hitch. However, some women *are* inhibited and their partners are not necessarily personally responsible. The numerous causes range from a puritanical upbringing to a lack of sex education (see the chapter on this subject).

Did Nature create woman for love and eroticism? Helen E. Fisher in *The Sex Contract*, London, 1983, has the following answer: "We are a species devoted to sex. We talk about it, joke about it, read about it, dress for it, and perform it regularly.... Why? Because the human female is capable of constant sexual arousal. She is physically able to make love every day of her adult life. She can copulate during pregnancy, and she can resume sexual activity shortly after having a child. She can make love whenever she pleases. This is extraordinary. No females of any other sexually reproducing species copulate with such frequency (p. 3).

"What a remarkable evolutionary twist this is. Because a woman has no obvious period of heat, a couple who wish to have a child cannot tell when the woman is ready to conceive. So they must make love regularly. It is almost as if nature had wished human beings to make love daily, for the human female is particularly designed to do so.

"It was not until the 1950s that investigators documented a second extraordinary human female endowment. Not only can she make love with impressive regularity (and has to if she wants a child) but her sex organs generate intense sexual pleasure—even more pleasure than the human male derives from intercourse. For nature has provided the human female with a clitoris, a bundle of supersensitive nerves designed solely for sex. Furthermore, about four or five dense masses of veins and nerves congregate in the muscles of her genitals—and during intercourse these sensitive aggregates sharply distinguish her sexual performance from that of her mate.

"As a woman becomes sexually excited, blood pours into the vessels of the genitals and the general pelvic area. The nerve bundles begin to expand. The muscles around the clitoris, vaginal opening and the anus begin to swell with blood.

"Shortly, the spongy sacs that surround the vaginal opening expand to three times their normal size; the inner lips double their size, and the muscles of their entire genital area become engorged with blood" (p. 10).

(I wonder whether Helen E. Fisher's above description is the female equivalent of the male erection or whether, on the contrary, the male erection is a "copy" of the turgescence of the vagina?)

Then she goes on to compare female and male orgasms: "First the wall of the uterus pulsates, followed quickly by the muscle of the outer third of the vagina, the sphincter of the rectum, and the tissues around the vaginal opening and clitoris. About every four-fifths of a second a new contraction hurls blood from the pelvic area back into the general system."

She then describes the male orgasm as following the same principle. Physical arousal begins with a thought or touch and blood flows into the penis. The penis tissues fill with blood, the pressure becomes intense and the blood-laden muscles contract. Here men and women are different. A man normally feels three or four major contractions followed by a few minor ones, all localized in the genital area and sex is done. The penis goes limp, and the male must start from the beginning to achieve orgasm again.

"The female pattern is different, for women feel five to eight major contractions and then nine to fifteen minor ones. They diffuse throughout the pelvic area. For woman, sex may have just begun. Unlike her mate, her genitals have not expelled the blood, and if she knows how, she can climax again and again if she wants to. The more orgasms a woman has, the more she can have, and the stronger they become."

Helen E. Fisher contends that this is far from being the case for American women, most of whom are unaware of their own sexual potential. Nevertheless, each and every woman is physically capable of having multiple orgasms. It is just a matter of practice, she says. These orgasmic bursts may follow one another so closely that they merge into a single, continuous orgasm. She notes that from the point of view of procreation, the female orgasm is useless, even counterproductive, given that the orgasmic pulsations go downward.

On the basis of the aforementioned, the title of this chapter should have been: "woman as a genetically programmed, all-star erotic champion." More accurate, but too long.

Sex on our minds amounts to neither fornication, nor depravation, nor lust but is the hallmark of human destiny. Our species is destined for eroticism, a subtle game where sex, decoupled, freed from its procreative, animal drive, becomes a means whereby a human couple may accede to the spiritual dimension of being through the total union of two beings in amorous ecstasy. In the animal kingdom, the female of the species takes in the sperm to be fertilized, and that's that. Beyond her immediate enjoyment, she seeks no other form of merging on any other level, such as in meditation à deux, for example, which gives humans access to the cosmic dimension. In animals, once the male has ejaculated, the female rejects him like one spits the pit out of a piece of fruit.

Although Helen E. Fisher provides a good description of the difference between the male and female orgasms, she does skirt the issue of the first female orgasm being just a beginning, whereas ejaculation leaves the man drained and puts an end to the experience: with ejaculation control the balance can be restored, benefiting both partners.

But, you might object, if male sexual control has to be learned, is it not artificial, even unnatural? An affirmative answer would be tantamount to condemning everything that distinguishes humans from animals, right down to the ability to speak. We learn how to speak in early infancy. If we had to wait until adolescence, we would never truly be able to speak as evidenced by the case of children having survived alone out in the wild and discovered years later: they never catch up. A dog that falls into a river can swim, whereas a human who has not learned, will drown. But by learning to swim, a human may become an incomparably better swimmer than a dog.

A capital fact, seldom mentioned in this context: being bipeds compels us to learn just about everything, but also makes us *capable* of learning. Who knows why our distant forbears stood erect on their hind legs making us humans the only true bipeds. In any case, freed from locomotion, our front paws became hands.

This made us capable of producing tools, therefore work, therefore play! The brain and its extension, the hand, are constantly enhancing, perfecting each other. Moreover, the vertical position has entailed a larger skull, therefore a larger brain.

But the upright posture has even more crucial consequences. A vertical rachis requires a restructuring of the pelvis and there is a price to pay: a narrower passage and a larger fetal head means "in sorrow thou shalt bring forth children."

Animals are born "ripe"—a baby zebra, for example, can run on all fours shortly after birth—whereas *the narrower pelvic passage ushers us into this world as premature babies.* Is this a handicap? Well apparently and in the beginning, no doubt. During the first month of its life, a chimpanzee is more precocious, cleverer and quicker than a human baby still clumsy at age 1 or 2. A child must learn to walk and does so rather painstakingly. It takes it several years to be truly mobile. Whereas in animals, instinct provides them with almost everything at birth and the learning process, when there is one, plays only a limited role. But human babies, precisely because they are born premature, have an incredibly plastic body and brain which can be shaped and fashioned almost at will, and they must—and can!—learn everything, acquire everything. Humans are very quick to catch up with the clever monkey. An adult ape is identical to its ancestors that roamed the earth 20,000 years ago or more. But what a gulf separates modern man (and woman!) from Neanderthal man, at least as far as knowledge, skills, and capabilities are concerned. It is the very plasticity of the premature baby that makes education, culture, and all civilizations, past, present, and future, possible. Without it, humans would never have invented art, built the pyramids and cathedrals. Human beings must learn just about everything from scratch, except smiling, except laughing! A normal human baby loves to laugh: what about cats, calves, or even orangutangs?

So, just like everything else, *it is normal for us to learn, to become educated, acquire knowledge and know-how about our own specific sexuality* that is so different from sheer animal instinct and urges. Our physiology has provided us with the possibility of maximum sexual intensity: this has been *deliberately* planned and is inscribed in our genes. Moreover, it is both *legitimate* and *rightful* on condition that it be without drugs, medication, or anything artificial or unnatural. I would even add that not developing this potential of ours becomes a source of unconscious but real frustration, a sort of "self-*un*fulfillment" in a most vital field!

We are Made for Eros

Being bipeds influences our sexuality in yet other ways. In quadrupeds the sex organs are practically concealed: you must take a closer look to distinguish a female cat from a male one. On the contrary, a standing man in the buff exhibits his penis in an almost aggressive way. The Venus de Milo flaunts her sex organs despite the artful draping of the fabric that conceals her lower body. Female mammals have teats but women have breasts whose erotic vocation eclipses their "nourishment" function. Does a bull get excited at the sight of a cow's udder? Moreover, a female monkey's teats possess, proportionally speaking, neither the size nor the fullness of a human female's breasts.

Lastly, the tilt of the pelvis is appropriate for face-to-face love-making, a human—and reportedly occasional gorilla and orang-utan—prerogative. The face-to-face position allows for much more personal, intimate and intense exchanges than the rear coitus of quadrupeds. Moreover the human female body is "tailor-made" for it, so to speak: indeed the vagina has the exact appropriate angle. Tantra does avoid this oh-so-common position initially because the ejaculatory reflex is so closely associated with it. Deconditioning is made easier by adopting another position, without the "missionary" position being ruled out, per se. Moreover, all straddling positions, like the ones with the Shakti sitting astride the Shiva, are also face-to-face positions.

Since we are on the topic of rapport and exchanges, this is probably as good a time as any to wonder why we are indeed naked apes, as Desmond Morris has stated. Where, when, how, but above all *why* have we lost our fur? And what advantages lie therein from the survival viewpoint? Apparently, none. In any case it has not prevented us from "being fruitful, and multiplying and replenishing the earth." Did the tropical climate of the Africa of our origins incite our forbears to part with their hair? A plausible assumption if we had not been the only ones. For our simian cousins who still live in a tropical environment are certainly not "naked." If this really constituted an adaptation to the climate why are not Eskimos as furry as polar bears? And are they hairier than we? Not in the least. Lastly, why have certain specific hairy areas on our body been preserved by evolution: pubic hair, eyebrows, beards, the hair on our head? What about our armpits: what is the point for our survival and our evolution as a species? Let us note that our attachment to this residual hair is inversely proportional to its surface. Humans spend billions of dollars on shampoos, hair dyes and countless cosmetics to have a thick, lustrous mane (or to try to hold on to it)!

For want of a truly convincing explanation, here is a consequence, at least: in animals, sexual contact is restricted to the genitalia, their fur preventing any direct, skin-to-skin contact. In humans the entire surface of the skin, that cosmic antenna with billions of sensitive captors, is caressed, allowing extensive tactile exchanges. Imagine what human love-making would be if we were as hairy as gorillas.

All of these exclusive differences add up to the confirmation that our species, and above all women, are designed, are made, for sex and eroticism, more than any other on this planet. A human being is a basically sexual being and the only one capable of endowing intercourse with dimensions other than procreation. Consider the following figures. At the reasonable rate of two contacts per week, the average forty-year conjugal life would include about 4000 *coiti*. Therefore, a mother of four, a large brood in this day and time, would have had 999 "wasted" contacts, procreatively speaking, for every "useful" one, i.e., a fertilizing one! Which goes to prove to what extent human sexuality has become divorced from its procreative goal, the sole end of animal sexuality. And also that it has been genetically programmed in us.

Tantra cottoned on to this thousands of years ago.

The Unisex Hormone of Desire

In humans, the erotic hormone is unisex and male: testosterone! True, men *and* women produce both male and female hormones, but men secrete ten times more testosterone and ten times less estrogen than women. The reverse applies to women, naturally, but actually only the *male* hormone eroticizes the female of our species.

What is significant is that humankind is hormonally programmed for Eros. In female animals, the *female* hormone (and it alone) triggers the heat, or rut, and its irrepressible coital impulse. Here is proof: if a she-cat gets a female hormone injection, she will immediately go into heat. Such an injection would not, however, influence a woman's sex drive.

Throughout the natural world, the human female is the sole instance of an almost *total hormonal dissociation between eros and procreation*: reproduction depends on the ovaries which secrete female hormones, whereas the *adrenals* distill the small amount of male hormone required to excite a woman's desire center located in her brain.

In women, nature has genetically dissociated sexual desire and ovarian functions—therefore reproduction—and that is why, thanks to the male hormones produced by her adrenal glands, a woman's erotic potential remains intact long after the menopause, in fact, throughout her life.

If testosterone is the unisex hormone of desire, what makes a man different from a woman? Quantity, that's all. Ten times less male hormone is required to stimulate desire in a woman than in a man whose testicles produce most of it. That is why a cold water shower on the scrotum every morning, as recommended in my book *Je perfectionne mon yoga*, page 62 (not yet translated into English) keeps the male genitals youthful and has restored the dwindling sex life of many a man, to the delight of both partners!

The following case related by Dr. Sherman J. Silber, *Understanding Male Sexuality* (London, 1983) evidences the role of the male hormone in female sensuality and the hormonal split between eros and procreation. It is the story of a couple who more than anything wanted a second child, a perfectly legitimate wish. During a checkup, the woman told her doctor she had suffered from extreme fatigue and had been to see another doctor who, as a kind of "booster," prescribed megadoses of testosterone. This semi-frigid woman had become insatiable and her exhausted husband (for he had never heard of Tantra) could not keep up with her sexual appetite! Despite their repeated efforts, there was no baby in sight: the testosterone exacerbated the woman's sex drive but also inhibited her ovarian hormonal output. Still on this question of the unisex hormone of desire: an injection of male hormone does stimulate the female sex drive but the reverse is not true. In men, the female hormone produces the exact opposite effect. Injecting a sex fiend with female hormone inhibits his production of testosterone, entailing a loss of interest in sex, a lull in his urge and a total absence of sexual imagery!

In closing this chapter, I would like to mention a great (dashed) hope and also raise a question. Is it possible, as was long hoped, if not to cure, at least to help impotent men by giving them male hormone therapy to rekindle their dwindling fire? No, help must be sought elsewhere, for even impotent and very old men—give or take a few rare exceptions—have a normal testosterone level. The cause of their impotence lies elsewhere.

Despite this fact, swindlers eager to make a quick buck will send misleading "information" to doctors advertising testosterone-based preparations purportedly capable of curing precisely what ails these prospective male patients. They boast income-generating (for them) testosterone pills (instead of the much less lucrative testosterone injections) but taking the hormone orally is pointless for it is destroyed by gastric juices!

Moreover, testosterone is highly toxic for the liver. When the "medicine" does work, that is most probably due to the placebo effect and the power of mind over matter!

Homosexuals and Tantra

Over the thirty-odd years it has taken me to carry this book, my brain-child, to term, I have not remained silent and have had ample opportunity to speak on the subject of Tantra to very diverse audiences. And I always encounter reactions that surprise me.

At first, in denouncing the ills of our macho civilization and in advocating female values, I expected to be accused of high treason by men, or seen as some sort of defector from the male gender. But nothing of the kind occurred. When I did encounter resistance, it more often than not stemmed from women afraid of the new role they would have to play in another type of civilization. These women were often content to stay put in their comfortable, traditional roles: the sex object, the submissive wife.

Moreover I thought the Church would raise a lot of hue and cry, particularly with respect to Tantric sexual practices. Here again, I was wrong and many a priest after listening to my lecture on Tantra would come up to me to offer support and approval, although there *were* a few qualifications and reservations here and there.

My third surprise came from the questions put to me. Contrary to (my) expectation, one topic did seem to preoccupy a good many interlocutors: "What about Tantra and homosexuals?" Was this in reaction to the considerable gay phenomenon witnessed in our nations today? Whatever the reason(s), I thought the readers of this book might also wonder about this and I must say the answer is straightforward and applies to a host of other domains as well.

Actually let us reverse the terms of the question: instead of Tantra's position vis-à-vis homosexuality, can gays accept Tantra? *That* is the question! I remind you that Tantra is *a*moral, *a*religious, *a*theistic, *a*political, etc., i.e., Tantra espouses, imposes no moral code, no "-isms," it is neither a religion nor a theological doctrine. You don't become a Tantric "convert," you don't have to enroll, sign or pledge anything! Tantra judges no one, nothing.

It is therefore up to each individual to establish *his/her own* moral, on the basis of *his/her chosen* religious beliefs, freely, without preconceptions. Tantra has no organized structure, there is no dogmatic or centralized authority, therefore no one is empowered to speak on its behalf, not even a guru who at best represents one particular *current,* one particular Tantric *trend* and not *all* of Tantra.

Before answering the question, it is important to make sure that "straights" understand "gays." Let us consider the range of factors that determine homosexuality, with a distinction between female and male homosexuality, the former often appearing more socially acceptable (or perhaps less "objectionable") than the latter.

A female infant has a sensual, "homo-sensual" relationship with its mother, the male baby experiencing the opposite, naturally. This sensual bond (not "sexual" in the usual sense) is extremely important as so many things are determined during those crucial moments right after birth.

The newborn babe is like a small animal (no offense!) in a timeless world: it belongs neither to our culture nor to our century—not yet. Fresh-delivered from its mother's womb, it is still very much a part of her. Suddenly expelled into an unknown, potentially hostile world, it needs the warmth, touch and skin-to-skin contact of its mother's naked body: it expects and awaits this, as would any newborn, be it in prehistoric times or now.

By "need," I really mean need! That is, a necessity as vital as food. And beyond touching its mother's body, it must discover it. This is truly a sensorial and sensual relationship. Very often, if not always in our contemporary world, babies are swaddled in rags called clothes and it is an equally "wrapped-up" mother that baby touches: its first frustration.

Secondly, instead of enjoying endless moments in naked-body-to-naked-body contact with its mother, the infant spends many hours physically separated from her. This is a wrenching experience for the baby thus torn from its mother. From its cradle it can hear mother's voice which it recognizes, having heard it *in utero*, and although reassuring, it cannot replace skin-to-skin, flesh-to-flesh touching. Not so long ago in maternity wards, newborns were taken from their mothers and placed in a common room where they joined in the general bellowing. These babies must have felt practically abandoned by their mothers and such a situation which they had no means of understanding, must have been traumatic for them with—no doubt in my mind—untold, unforeseeable, and unsuspected consequences right into adulthood. In little boys, such a trauma may lead to poor relations with women, encouraging them to turn to their own sex.

In addition to the above, the segregation of the sexes is another cause of non-fundamental homosexuality. It is a well-known fact that in boarding schools, barracks, aboard ships, in prisons, the lack of heterosexual partners leads to "incidental" homosexuality which often disappears when heterosexual partners are available, but which may also remain a permanent sexual preference.

Another cause of non-fundamental homosexuality lies in the inadequacy of heterosexual partners. I once knew a young and attractive widow who had become lesbian. I asked her why, she, the mother of two, had decided to become a lesbian. Her answer was short and sweet: "I simply cannot stand the idea of having a man around the house, smoking, coughing and griping all the time, and who masturbates in my vagina at record-breaking speed, every Sunday morning at a quarter to eight." I pointed out that although most men do grumble from time to time, they don't all smoke or cough incessantly. Moreover, I added, a woman can just have a boyfriend instead of a husband. She answered: "Having a girlfriend is less conspicuous than a boyfriend. When she comes over, the neighbors don't gossip. And there's no chance of getting pregnant!"

In women's letters, the real clue is often found in the postscript. So the actual reason was probably conveyed in her final remarks: "You know, you men, you really don't know how to go about it! You've finished before you've begun and your sole concern is your own pleasure. You haven't a clue as to caressing, stroking a woman's body. A woman's beautiful body is considerably more appealing than the pudgy, hairy, unshaven and sometimes none-too-clean body of a man." What could I say ? I could have mentioned Tantra—if I had known at the time!

Feminine friendships under the sign of Lesbos are often characterized by a deep and lasting affection. I was once told of the case of two women who had been living together for over thirty years and who shared a degree of affection and happiness that many a heterosexual couple would have envied.

My point is not to draft a panegyric of male or female homosexuality but to highlight the fact that it often stems from the inadequacy of heterosexual partners. A woman may well find in a member of her own sex what she sought for, in vain, in the opposite sex. This inadequacy comes from ignorance which in turn stems from a lack of sex education which is characteristic of macho cultures in general, unlike matrifocal societies.

The situation is somewhat different for men, for homosexuality is often more "fundamental" in gay males than in gay females: I shall come back to this. In addition to purely incidental male homosexuality (prisoners, sailors, etc.) the problem of sexual inadequacy also exists but is of a different nature.

Lastly, there is the question of so-called fundamental homosexuality. We know that the basic sex is female and that the male is an adaptation required for the horizontal distribution of genes. But it does happen—much more frequently in men than in women—that a female "soul" chooses the "wrong" body. Although some men become transvestites—the resemblance can be striking—others go so far as to undergo protracted, painful and extremely expensive medical treatment and become transsexuals so their feminine soul may at long last inhabit a female body.

There are other cases that are also more specifically male. In all men lies a dormant, latent, and unavowed nostalgia for the female state. That is why some male heterosexuals occasionally accept, as a sort of experiment, being penetrated, which may lead to bisexuality.

And what about Tantra in all of this? A male homosexual couple is actually a heterosexual couple although they may not realize it. One penetrates as the other takes on the female part. You have Shiva and Shakti! If they perceive the sacred nature of the sexual drive and the divinity of their partner, their relationship can be Tantric. I'm not judging anything or anybody: as we have already seen, Tantra teaches no moral. For lesbian women, things are slightly different, although very often one of the two partners is more male in her behavior than the other. But naturally a woman can very well perceive the "goddess" in another woman, and notably her partner.

In Tantra, in its texts and in the pujas, only Shiva-Shakti relations, i.e., heterosexual relations, are mentioned; this does not imply that homosexuality does not exist in India, but to my knowledge, it belongs to the non-Tantric world.

Finally, Tantra is also a way of looking at life and the world, of having another outlook on it. It is therefore not restricted to sexual matters. It is not a religion and knows no "all or nothing" attitude. There is no converting to any religion or accepting dogmas and in Tantra each and every person defines himself/herself on the basis of what he/she is here and now, either homosexual or heterosexual!

Before closing this chapter I would like to mention the gay communities in Los Angeles and San Francisco who were the first victims of the AIDs epidemic, more often than not because of their unbridled sexual practices, some men having hundreds of different partners on an annual average, in "special" establishments. Even with loads of comprehension and sympathy, it is difficult to find anything sacred in these practices. Nevertheless, the human solidarity, the closeness, warmth and support shown throughout the gay community in the wake of this scourge are exemplary and rarely witnessed in non-gay circles. This must also be highlighted.

Yoni Soit Qui Mâle Y Pense

Caveat, Male Ego and take heed all ye gentlemen out there: the male is an accessory created for merely practical reasons by Mother Nature who often purely and simply dispenses with him! The female alone is truly indispensable for the survival of multicellular beings. *Voilà!*

Actually the reproduction problem was posed billions of years ago, when Life "invented" multicellular beings, spawning an infinite number of species. Parthenogenesis would have been the simplest, most logical and efficient solution. To implement the Biblical *be fruitful, and multiply, and replenish the Earth,* "parthenogenetic" species have a dual reproductive potential with a single female procreating as much as a couple. Life could easily have ensured reproduction without the male: consider the molly, a Central American fish no larger than a human finger. The species includes only females, each daughter being the spitting image of her mother.

In the words of V. Dröscher (*Ils se déchirent et ils s'aiment*, Paris, 1975, translation): "In the history of evolution, the male was invented at a relatively late stage. A being which gives birth is, and will always be, a female. No female, no descendants. The male could be dispensed with altogether.... However via the male, improvements were made to the reproduction process but at a cost of countless problems.... Adam did not precede Eve, nor was she created later with one of his ribs, referring to the Biblical allegorical representation. The reverse took place" (p. 28).

Biologically speaking, parthenogenesis is not totally inconceivable in humans, but the ovum would have to contain the entire human genetic capital instead of only half. However, barring parthenogenesis, the ovum must wait for the male gametes, which raises the problem of their transfer. Admittedly, Mother Nature has found a pretty charming solution.

At present, artificial parthenogenesis is a scientific possibility! If my memory serves me well, I believe the Frenchman Jean Rostand carried out an experiment in which he stimulated frog's eggs with a tiny drop of acid and obtained perfectly well-constituted female tadpoles without a daddy frog! It is technically feasible to extract a human ovum from a woman's womb, stimulate and fertilize it without spermatozoa, and reimplant it inside the uterus. The mother would then give birth to a fatherless test-tube baby. Nature, the ultimate Mother of Invention, could have saved herself the trouble of creating the male.

So, why the male? Well, consider the hypothesis of single sex parthenogenesis where each female would beget a vertical lineage of descendants strictly identical to their mother. These branches would evolve separately, each in their own way, in parallel, with no possibility of cross-genetic exchanges. If for example, at a given point, one lineage underwent a favorable mutation, the beneficial information could not be passed on to others.

But enter the male and nothing is the same! In polygamous apes, for example, when a male fertilizes several females, there is an intermixing and rapid horizontal dissemination of genes. Monogamy would slow down, but not alter, the process. If males only fertilized their own mothers and sisters, the lineage would close in on itself. That is why the rules of sexual play seek to avoid transfers that are too closely related: the incest taboo prevents the partitioning of the species into isolated, vertical lineages that would have the same drawbacks as parthenogenesis.

If a favorable mutation occurs in a male, he will inject it into several females with a positive outcome for the species as a whole. If the beneficial mutation takes place in a female, no problem: her male descendants will willingly take it upon themselves to disseminate it!

To guarantee a "horizontal" dissemination of genes, Mother Nature has endowed the male with a genetic potential thousands of times greater than the female's who at best (?) can bear one child per year, whereas a man *could* fertilize a hundred, two hundred, or even three hundred women per annum (and even more with artificial insemination!). Given the fact that one ejaculation includes as many as five hundred million spermatozoa, one male could theoretically inseminate, via a sperm bank, all the Indian women that could be fertilized in a single year, at least!

Moreover, nature has refined the process of passing on beneficial genes: in sea-elephants, for example, only the strongest male fertilizes his entire harem-herd. If challenged by a rival, they both fight for the right to the females and territory. Few males actually get to procreate under such circumstances. A fate worse than death? Yes, if you translate this into human terms: indeed, barring a man from fathering children on the basis of physical strength alone would be unthinkable. But for sea elephants as a species this is a positive phenomenon because at each generation, the entire female population is fertilized by the strongest males.

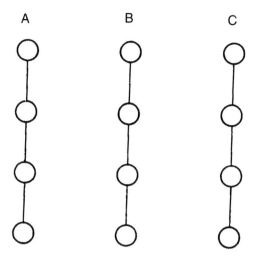

With parthenogenesisno genetic link is possible between lineages A, B, and C.

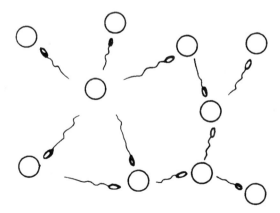

The spermatozoon is invented and there is an immediate circulation of genetic information.

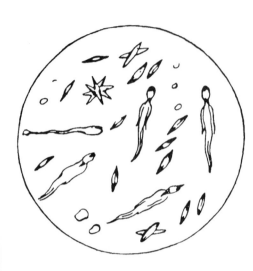

Van Leeuwenhoek was the first, in 1703, to observe spermatozoa under the microscope, an invention of his, by the way. He thought they were homunculi, each complete with a head, arms, and legs (his drawings, above). Here was "evidence" in support of the idea that "daddy plants his seed in mommy's flower pot," of the "supremacy" of the father and his sons and patriarchal domination in general, with its corollary: the subjugation of women.

Y spermatozoon.

X spermatozoon, larger and with an oval head.

"Is there any trace of the spermatozoon left in adult human males?" I wondered, as I watched on television the flow of thousands of wriggling runners competing in the Paris and New York marathons! Past the finish line the winning male gets to kiss the beautiful woman who has been waiting just for him: talk about symbols! And guess what it reminds me of when the winner celebrates his victory by shaking a bottle of champagne and generously spraying the cheering crowd with white foam!

Come to think of it, was not the medieval custom known in French as *droit de cuissage* or *jus primae noctis,* to use the Latin phrase (whereby the lord of the manor was entitled to deflower every young bride of his fiefdom on her wedding night), a limited application of the same principle? The supposedly biologically superior nobleman thus "enriched" the genetic capital of the future child by virtue of his noble sperm. This may explain the privileges of the eldest son who (alone) was entitled to be a bastard of the lord and whose "noble" genes would eventually trickle down to inferior serfs. On that assumption, the level of the people would indeed have "risen," gradually. Seen in this light, the *jus primae noctis* custom is almost tantamount to philanthropy! However, reciprocity was denied the lord's spouse to avoid inferior sperm, a commoner's, a villain's, polluting the feudal lord's lineage!

Thus the female is the original life form. In his cult of the Mother-Goddess, in worshipping Woman, his first religion, archaic man was actually in harmony with natural biological laws.

SeXYness *vs.* SeXX Appeal: Who's Got What?

Modern genetics has confirmed Tantra's intuition: the male is a modified female whose purpose is the dissemination of genes. That is why there is a latent feminine side deeply ingrained in men.

From the point of view of their respective chromosomes, it could be said that women have seXX appeal whereas men are just plain seXY! In addition to the 44 chromosomes that carry their entire genetic capital, the man has an X chromosome and a Y chromosome and the woman has two X chromosomes. We know that gender is determined by the X and Y chromosomes.

This would seem to confirm the Biblical version of creation according to which Eve was made from Adam, pointing to male pre-eminence: apparently the spermatozoa determine the embryo's sex. Indeed, the ovum is always X whereas the spermatozoon can be either X or Y. Daddy's X plus Mommy's X makes a baby girl. But if Daddy's Y is added to Mommy's X, you get XY = a baby boy. Hence the apparent domination of the spermatozoon: although latent during the first six weeks of its life, at the moment the ovum absorbs the spermatozoon, an embryo's sex is determined. After the sixth week, the embryo's undifferentiated gonad develops into testicles or ovaries (i.e., the entire female genital apparatus: uterus, vagina). So Dad is the boss, here: = Q. E. D.

But are we so sure? The above version conflicts with the findings of Professor Alfred Jost from the *Collège de France* (Paris, France) and Dr.

Stephen S. Wachtel, a New York biologist. These scientists have observed that if in a pregnant doe rabbit the embryos' gonads are excised before their gender potential has become manifest, *all* the embryos, be they XX or XY, will *always* be females. If, however, the testicles of a male embryo are excised, this *never* produces a male. Which goes to prove that the primordial sex, both in animals and humans, is female, and that the male is also built from the same "blueprint." These recent findings have been confirmed for other animal species, as well. Castrating an XX-embryo (female potential) before differentiation does not prevent it from developing into a female, whereas an XY embryo (male potential) castrated prior to differentiation *always* reverts to the female form. In short: when deprived of its embryonic gonad, a potentially female embryo will become a female and a potentially male embryo will become a female. Shorter still: a castrated embryo *always* becomes a female.

What if Males did not Exist?

The drawing (page 157) shows the status of a species prior to the "invention" of the male, with the following consequences:

1) It includes females only;

2) All daughters are strictly identical to their mother, whence stereotyped lineages;

3) The species is made up of isolated lineages, rendering genetic exchanges impossible;

4) Consequently, a favorable mutation in a female can only be transmitted to *her own* daughters, not to other lineages.

Let There Be Males!

Then Life invented the male! Instead of being contained in a single, complete egg (or ovum, if you prefer) the genetic capital is now split into two halves. To deliver the genes of the male half-egg, i.e., the spermatozoon, Life invented the penis. Let us consider this new situation:

1) The species instills in its male and female members the urge to unite, whence sexuality;

2) Genes are exchanged between lineages that are henceforth genetically linked;

3) Any mutation enhancing the species' survivability is rapidly disseminated throughout the entire species, each male being capable of fertilizing several females;

4) To avoid lineages closing in on themselves: the incest taboo. Males disseminate their genes far away or at least not too close to the original strain;

5) Genetic intermixing produces individuals that are highly differentiated and no longer stereotyped;

6) Natural selection will eventually eliminate the carriers of an unfavorable mutation, often before their sexual maturity.

In conclusion: the male is a very beneficial functional invention but the basic blueprint of a species is and remains female. The male is a modified female. Some men, such as transsexuals, experience a sort of nostalgia for the female state but the reverse is rarely true.

The Incantatory
Magic of Mantra

As you might not have guessed from his name, Elwin Verrier is one-hundred-percent British. This Anglican clergyman left his native soil to conquer India, mind you, but was conquered by her! Not by Brahmanical India but by the India of the aboriginal tribes, the Dravidians and others, long-forgotten in her jungles. He was conquered to the point of spending thirty years of his life among these "primitive aborigines," leaving the priesthood and marrying a beautiful Dravidian woman, Lila, "as soft as a moonbeam," who gave him happiness and two children! This man probably came to know more about these tribes than any Indian or Englishman, and he has related in his fascinating book titled *Une vie tribale*, Paris, 1973 (The Tribal World of Elwin Verrier, Oxford, 1964) that one day, while driving through the jungle in a convertible car with the top down, accompanied by his old friend Baiga, they came face to face with a colossal tiger. Elwin Verrier confessed he was terrified and understandably so! "However," he wrote, "old Baiga, sitting next to me, remained unruffled; he mumbled some magic formula, some incantation, and a couple of minutes later, the tiger quietly returned to the thick of the jungle."

This account from a reliable source reflects, at the very least, the total faith Indians have in the power of magic formulae, or *mantras* as they are called. Naturally one might object that the above outcome was not due to the mantras but to the absolute trust in their effectiveness and that is why old Baiga remained so cool, calm and collected and the tiger felt it: you can't fool babies or animals, especially wild animals. Their lack of fear and aggressiveness inhibited the tiger's attack reflex. This is a rational explanation that might well be partly true, at least, for animals do indeed smell fear (apparently fear has an odor and this influences their behavior).

However, it is also a fact that animals are very receptive to sound. I remember the case of a French woman whose name I have forgotten: when encountering her for the first time, the fiercest of dogs, the kind that will tear an intruder to shreds, became as mild as lambs, crouching at her feet and licking her hands. What was her secret? She knew how to "talk" to them. She knew which sounds made them aggressive and which ones soothed them. In other words, she *knew* canine mantras! Mantras are absolute sounds, that is, having no conventional meaning, and they work on the body and the mind by virtue of their vibrational quality. Tantrists have developed to a high degree this science of sound—for it is indeed one—to a level inconceivable for us Westerners.

Writing a book on Tantra without mentioning mantras would be like describing our civilization without talking about electricity! I do confess, however, to being slightly embarrassed. On the one hand I owe it to you, the reader, not only to evoke this topic but also to give you pointers on the practice of mantra, for speaking about the question in general terms would be pointless. On the other hand, there is unanimity across the board in Tantric tradition that mantra is a living thing and *must* be transmitted "person to person," orally, for its pronunciation has to be just right, otherwise it would have no effect or worse, would entail certain dangers. So impossible though it may be to convey to you this science in its entirety—a whole library would not suffice—I can provide you with some specific phonetic pointers that will enable you—after a little trial and error—to pronounce correctly a sufficient number of effective and beneficial mantras.

Before entering the magic world of mantra, allow me to quote Max Muller, the famous Indian scholar, who wrote in *Six Systems of Indian Philosophy* (London, 1928, p. 360): "We must guard against rejecting as absurd what we do not understand at once, or what seems to us fanciful or irrational. I know from my own experience how what seemed to me for a long time unmeaning, nay absurd, disclosed after time a far deeper meaning than I should ever have expected."

Moreover, Sir John Woodroffe, alias Arthur Avalon, wrote in *The Serpent Power* (Madras, 1969, p. 83): "There is perhaps no subject in the Indian Shâstra which is less understood than Mantra. Mantra science may be well founded or not, but even in the latter case it is not the absurdity which some suppose it to be. [...] The creative power of thought is now receiving increasing acceptance in the West. The doctrine is ancient in India, and underlies the practices to be found in the Tantras, some of which are kept in general concealed to prevent misuse. What, however, is not understood in the West is the particular form of Thought-science which is Mantravidyâ.... There is nothing necessarily holy or prayerful about a Mantra. Mantra is a power (*Mantrashakti*) which lends itself impartially to any use."

For millennia now, Tantra has known and used the healing and revitalizing powers for the body and mind of *prânavâ* (ôm) and of the six seed-syllables (bija mantras) *hram, hrim, hrum, hraim, hraum, hrah,* each of which impacts a specific organ or part of the body.

But since we Westerners always need to know the whys and wherefores, here is the story of Leser-Lesario, a man who for thirty years studied the action of sounds on the mind and body. He was born in Vienna and was a fragile child, with a delicate constitution. Studying became his consuming passion and his parents, overjoyed at the excessive "bookworming" behavior of their son, granted him unlimited access to books and more books, which eventually ruined his health.

When he was 18, his health hit rock bottom: among other illnesses, he suffered from acute rheumatoid arthritis. His physicians lost all hope. He felt abandoned, a total "goner," until the day he discovered the benefits of restorative sound and life-giving breathing.

He wrote: "One day a neighbor brought over to our house her baby for my parents to baby-sit. The presence of this healthy baby made me forget my own suffering for a while. It lay there on its back, gazing up at the ceiling and cooing away *lah... lah... lah...* I asked our house-keeper to undress the baby and place it next to me in my bed, which she did. Sitting up with great difficulty, my starved eyes eagerly took in the sight of that beautiful little body, a perfect, divine creature, especially when compared to my own, so puny and sickly, for which I felt such loathing.

"After looking at me, the baby soon returned to its most serious business of singing his *lah... lah... lah...*'s. It was a delightful sight indeed and I held my breath in order to catch every sound. I noticed that each *lah...* made his three upper ribs vibrate. I was intrigued by this and decided to try it on myself : I was astonished and excited as I obtained the same result. I further experimented with *poh... poh... poh...* and each time I felt the vibration lower and lower in my abdomen."

Leser-Lasario gradually came to several realizations: first, that each sound reflected a given mindset, revealed a certain mental attitude. In this case, the child was visibly happy. Second, the vibratory effect was very pronounced. Third, the baby repeatedly uttered its *lah... lah... lah...*, in a single out-breath, without taking in any air, breathing out until its lungs were totally empty. Fourth, he would breathe in deeply, hold his breath, with his lungs full, then contract his abdominal muscles, deeply and rhythmically, briefly drawing his diaphragm in and up, before resuming the *lah... lah...* cycle.

Leser-Lesario decided to imitate the child: lying on his back like the baby, and trusting the natural order of things, he began to vocalize monotonous sounds for hours on end. "At first I could not keep it up for very long, I would get dizzy, but I gradually got used to it. I always tried to equate a given sound with a mental attitude. The *eee*'s were bright and gay, the *oooh*'s were more serious and somber, without being sad." In a few weeks' time, his bodily functions became more efficient and his arthritis receded. Invariably, the sounds produced specific and focused effects. The *eee*'s would clear mucus in his throat and bronchial tubes, for example.

Leser-Lasario wondered whether it was the breathing combined with the vibration or the change in his emotional state that caused the improvement. The bottom line, thirty years later and after completely healing himself—as well as thousands of others—is that he realized that in combining breathing and sounds, one can, at will, direct the bloodflow—and, Tantrists would add, Prana (life-energy)—to any part of the body. He also discovered that sound vibrations act on the sympathetic system and endocrine glands. Unwittingly endorsing the Tantric thesis, Leser-Lasario stated: "He who would establish a limit to the power of sounds and their use, would be very foolhardy indeed!"

His way of vocalizing sounds is also akin to Tantra: first you must imagine the vowel, imagine it emotionally, then hum it. Each vowel has its own specific field of action:

"I (long E, as in "meet") vibrates upward, toward the larynx, the nose, the head and dispels migraine headaches;

"E (eh) has an impact on the throat, the vocal cords, the larynx, the thyroid; (Leser-Lasario claims to have thus cured many goiters);

"A (ah) on the oesophagus, the three upper ribs and upper pulmonary lobes (antituberculosis);

"O (oh) on the thorax and diaphragm center (tones, boosts blood supply to the heart);

"U (oo, as in "root") on all abdominal viscera, including the stomach, liver, intestines, and the gonads."

Leser-Lasario used thirty-two sounds and sound-combinations he would adapt to a person's individual needs. His method was simple and totally "in tune" with Tantra: "Your attitude must be one of devotion and reverence. Concentrate on the emotion awakened by the selected vowel. Remaining in the same frame of mind, breathe in through your nose, hold your breath effortlessly while concentrating on the vowel you are going to enunciate. How long you hold your breath matters little although the duration increases with practice."

Then hum the sound, concentrating on the place where you feel the vibration, exhaling as slowly and as completely as possible but without exerting yourself.

This vibratory massage releases into the bloodstream toxins that have been building up in tissues, thereby eliminating them. Moreover the influx of well-oxygenated blood feeds and vitalizes the cells.

Unfortunately Leser-Lasario's book is out of print and in spite of all my searching I have never been able to get hold of a copy. All I have is what is reproduced above. Apparently, his legal heirs have objected to his book being republished. I wonder why! Whatever the case may be, Leser-Lasario only discovered the outermost aspect of mantra, i.e., vocalizing the sounds aloud. Tantrists consider this important but only as a first step.

In the Beginning was the Primordial Sound

"Before," both *everything* and *nothing* coexisted, this *Everything,* this *All,* was cosmic energy in a state of equilibrium, of rest.

Nothing was not even the void, it was the unmanifested state, without space or time.

Without anyone, save the Eternal, knowing why, in the *akâsha,* the "dynamic ether," exploded the Original Vibration. "In the beginning was...": the Word for Saint John, the Big Bang for the physicist, or *damaru,* Shiva's drum, for the Tantrist. As it begat space-time dear to Einstein, the original sound—whose echo will vibrate throughout the universe until its final dissolution, *mahapralâya*—diversified into an infinite cascade of beings and forms.

Matter being energy and vice versa, all things—from a galaxy to a grain of sand—are force fields in a perpetual vibratory state.

For Tantra, "in the beginning" was Shakti, undifferentiated energy, the *OM,* representing cosmic energy in its pure state, the primordial sound which gives forth galaxies. *OM* is the mystical syllable through which humans may come into intuitive contact with ultimate reality, with the very root of the Universe. *OM* is the seed-syllable of the Universe, the *bîja,* whence all other sounds stem. In India, *OM* is unanimously accepted: for the Vaishnava, *OM* is Vishnu, for the Vedantist, it is the Atman, and the Brahmin never fails to include the *OM* in his Vedic sacrifice and rituals. For the Shakta Tantrist, it represents the Female principle, which in dynamic union with the Male principle, generates the universe. *OM* vibrates high and low throughout India, in her ashrams, her temples, and her homes rich and poor, regardless of caste.

However, this universality conceals major differences in the way the sound is actually vocalized. The *OM* of the Brahmanical system as taught by non-Tantric swamis and gurus, in India and in the West, is the "goldfish *OM*" as I call it. If I recite *OM-OM-OM-OM* in succession on a single exhalation, I open my mouth for every *O* and shut it for every *mmm,* like a goldfish in its bowl!

The occult Tantric *OM* is different: whether pronounced just once, for its own sake, sufficing unto itself, or to initiate another mantra such as *OM namah Shivaya,* or the well-known Buddhist *Om mani*

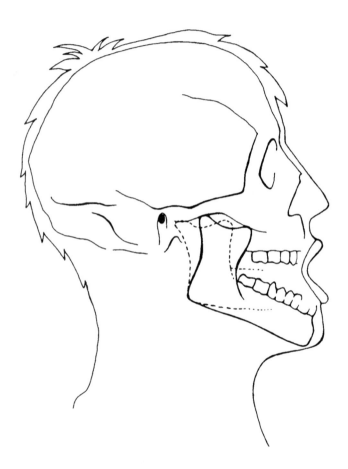

This drawing shows the wrong way of opening one's mouth, i.e., by jutting the chin forward and down.

The dotted line shows the initial position of the lower jawbone and the full line indicates its position when the sound is to be emitted: a forward movement.

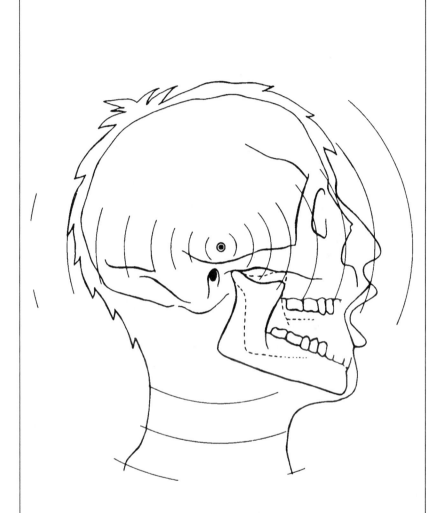

In this illustration, the dotted line shows that the far-end of the jaw-bone, both at the beginning and the end of the sound, remains in the same position.

The mouth thus opens as wide as possible whereby a rich and full sound can be emitted.

The sound can be modulated at will, by changing the position of the tongue, even with an immobile lower jawbone.

The habitual ॐ represented above is a stylization of the original and authentic drawing below as it was, and still is, drawn on palm leaves today (none have been retouched).

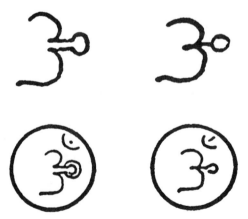

padme Hum, or repeated in a string of *Oms*, the mouth remains open during the entire emission of the syllable. In certain cases the mouth remains open even during inhalation.

How can a person working alone, unaided, find the right way of vocalizing the Tantric *OM*, without having been duly initiated? Here's how: open wide your mouth, yawn and begin exhaling *aaah* as if your doctor were examining your throat! It's like gargling! The tongue is flat at the very back of the mouth as the lips pucker slightly, forming an O. This produces a cross between a deep *aaah* and an *oh*, i.e., neither a true *ah*, nor a clear-cut *oh*. The sound originates somewhere between the two ears and makes the palate, the skull and the thorax vibrate: you can perceive this clearly if you place your hand flat on your sternum. The deeper the sound, the more the thorax vibrates. Now keeping my mouth open, I direct the tip of my tongue towards the lower back part of my mouth to block the glottis: the *oh* sound ceases and becomes a hummed *mmmm*. So in Tantra, the O is not a true O and the M is not a true M! It is written *M*, but should actually be pronounced *ng*, a nasal sound like in the word long. This *ng* sound generates vibrations in the nostrils, the palate, the cranium and the thorax! And one should try to feel the fullest vibrations possible.

I continue the exercise, still with my mouth open, and let the *ng* vibrate freely: the sound is purely nasal, in the skull. Then with a slight forward movement of the tongue, the *ah-oh* is vocalized again and fills the space around me. The difference? Listening carefully you can distinguish a permanent vibration, the *ng* sound which forms a constant sonorous background in which the *ah-oh* sound comes and goes. *Ng* is a continuous sound, whereas *ao* comes and goes. It is not *ah-oh* first, then *ng*, sequentially, but both at the same time, as superimposed on each other.

Seems complicated? On paper, it does... Let's just agree that for practical purposes, *OM* shall hereinafter be written *OM* but pronounced *ONG*!

Stay tuned, folks, there is more to come! A little trial and error will eventually lead me to the right *ngaong*, that is, the one that suits me, the one I like best: it fills me and extends beyond my body. It vibrates from my face and thorax, from the back of my skull, my back, my sides. It surrounds me and I feel it permeating the entire room, that everything around me is pulsating!

Granted, you have to work a little to find the true *OM*, but it is well worth the effort, for it is Tantra's basic mantra, the root of all sounds, the one which accompanies all other mantras. *OM* is so important that it is called *Prânavâ*, that which carries and modulates prâna, life-energy, or *ômkar*. For Tantra, every feeling, every being, every object has its own basic vibration: from the finest crystal wine glass to a plain flower-pot! *Vice versa*, every sound has its own visual representation: *OM* is *drawn* (not *written*).

As regards the (mesmerizing) representation of *OM*, most Westerners take it for granted—as I too did for a long time—that it is Sanskrit. For us, it's simple: you just draw 🕉 and pronounce it *OM*, *and voilà!* But we are left in the dark as to its actual significance.

In order to grasp the secret meaning of 🕉, let us remember that *OM* is the vibration which generates worlds and that the universe is begat by the cosmic maïthuna of Shakti-Shiva of which human maïthuna is the concrete expression on the terrestrial plane.

OM enables the Tantrist to better concentrate his/her power of mind on this Ultimate Reality and gain access to it: in our focused mind, the vibration of *OM* and its graphic representation 🕉 , the *visible form* of the vibration, becomes one. Whether this be achieved through contemplating an actual drawing or through visualization, matters little. The point is to seize its hidden meaning.

Not unlike hieroglyphics, 🕉 is a *yantra*, a mystical and magical diagram, as well as a *mandala*, a symbolic drawing within a circle showing the deployment of universal creative dynamism. 🕉 is no doubt the most compact, the most concentrated and powerful mandala of Tantra.

Prior to Sanskrit, and even *Devanâgari* writing, *ômkar* was drawn in soft clay and on palm leaves.

People still represent it graphically today, and not only in the context of Tantric esotericism, as related in, for example, *Tantra, the Erotic Cult*, by F. D. Colaabawala (Delhi, 1976), or *The Soul of Symbols* by Jaya Raja, quoted by Colaabawala.

This yantra includes a host of essential elements, a prime one being the circle (see *chakra pûjâ*) which protects everything it encloses. The circle symbolizes the manifestation, it creates a sacred space and develops around a focal point. The drawing represents the ritual and concrete maïthuna of Shiva and Shakti as well as the cosmic union of the Female and Male principles. ☾ undoubtedly represents the crescent of the moon, the female lunar principle, whereas the dot is both *bindu* (the seed, the sperm) and *anunâsika*, the sign of nasalization.

It is amusing to compare 🕉 and ♡ which lovers carve on tree trunks or those naïve scenes depicting a cherub (the future baby) shooting its fateful arrow! Honestly, try as we may, the real, organic heart is not easily recognizable in this symbolic heart of love, a hallmark of our culture and found everywhere, from playing cards to advertising. While my conscious ego may be "in the dark" about its hidden significance, my unconscious mind puts two and two together! Of course, I am not forcing this "shocking" (?) explanation down anybody's throat.

Some people vigorously reject the above; non-Tantrists, that is. Naturally, they are free to choose their own interpretation: if the more soothing and "neutered" *OM* suits them better, that is their perfect right. No harm is done, but they have missed the whole point, to my mind! However, the person who chooses to immerse himself/herself in the profound meaning of the esoteric *OM*, can gain access to the roots of his/her being and those of the cosmos: I am the fruit of ॐ, of the union of the spermatozoon and the ovum, in the same way the cosmos stems from the sacred maïthuna of Shakti and Shiva.

Brahmanical ostracism vis-à-vis *Om*'s sexual symbolism stems from outdated Puritanism or ignorance, or both.

A perfect example of the deliberate camouflaging of a mantra's real meaning is the well-known Buddhist mantra, *Om mani padme Hûm*, nicely translated as "jewel in the lotus," which doesn't mean a thing. Buddhistic prudishness (which is equal to, or even exceeds that of neo-Brahmanism) has bent over backwards trying to find a pretty convoluted explanation.

What *is* the true, hidden meaning of this mantra? To fully grasp it we must go back in time, not as far back as Methuselah, perhaps, but to the day and time of young Prince Siddharta, the future Buddha. In those days, the rajas and princes were locked in a power struggle with the Brahmins who vied with one another as to the greatest number of gods and propitiatory ceremonies they could create. All of these sacrifices, you see, required the duly remunerated intervention of the Brahmins whose numbers were also increasing and all of this soon became outrageously expensive, even for wealthy princes. If you add the arrogance of these very same Brahmins who as "exclusive divine delegates" took it upon themselves to regulate public and private life, you will readily understand the irritation of the rajas who became more and more reluctant to part with considerable fortunes they would much rather have spent on their luxurious courts, harems, and armies.

Prince Siddharta crystallized this antagonism. At first, he rejected the entire Hindu pantheon *en masse* rendering all sacrifices nugatory. He went so far as to say that Brahmins are made, not born, which enraged them. (Ironically, Siddharta, the future Buddha, rejected all gods, but was eventually deified by his own disciples!)

He distanced himself from the caste system, allowed widows to remarry, but above all he opposed the Brahmins. More than the founding father of a religion, Siddharta was a revolutionary, albeit a peaceful one. In his campaign to undermine the Brahmins' authority, he received support from his peers, the princes and the warriors. That is why the emperors erected the tens of thousands of Buddhistic stupas seen throughout India. The Brahmins, however, were quick to learn their lesson and keeping a low profile they gradually recovered their influence. They eventually "licked" Buddhism which was driven out of India, its country of origin, and went on to conquer a large part of Asia.

Here is the connection with Tantra: the Buddha preached in *Prâkrit*, the language of the people, not in Sanskrit which was the prerogative of Brahmins and learned pundits. This was much to the liking of Tantrists who also opposed the Brahmins and their system. These Tantrists found allies amongst certain Buddhists and initiated them to Tantra whence the Tantric branch of Buddhism, *Vajrâyana*, which includes sexual rites, including chakra pûjâ, worship in a circle.

In the light of the above, let us now decode *Om mani padme Hûm*. *Mani*, the jewel, is the Buddhistic equivalent of *vajra* (diamond), the male organ. *Padme* is the lotus flower which symbolizes the yoni, the female principle. The real translation is: *Om* = lingam in the yoni, *Hum*. Perfectly clear and pure Tantra. In his book *Sexual Life in Ancient China* (Leiden, 1961, p. 340), R. H. van Gulik, who lived for a long time in the East, notably in China, has confirmed this: "The vajra is also called *mani* "the (indestructible) jewel," that penetrates *padma*, the lotus flower, symbolizing the vulva. There can be little doubt, therefore, about the meaning of the much-discussed Lamaist prayer formula *om mani padme hûm*. Since sexual mysticism is the essence of the Vajrayâna, one need not wonder that the formula designating both mystical and carnal sexual congress in succinct form came to occupy such a predominant place in Tibetan religious practice."

As additional confirmation, let us note that in Tantric terminology, *Vajra* is the male organ and *Vajra-Nadi* is a subtle energy channel that ends in the penis. In Tibetan, it is *rdo-rje*, a sort of ritual scepter whose sexual symbolism is obvious. Likewise, another sexual symbol of Tibetan Tantrism: the bell (yoni) and its tongue (lingam).

One Buddhist text instructs the adept that he should "place the *vajra* in the *padma* but should retain the *bodhicitta*." This sentence is a good example of the code in which most sexo-yogic treatises are written; the literal meaning of *vajra* is thunderbolt, that of *padma* is lotus, and *bodhicitta* means mind of enlightenment, but here the words mean, respectively, penis, vagina and semen.

Impressive and erudite volumes have been written by non-Tantric Buddhists (including Anagarika Govinda), about *Om mani padme Hûm*, without ever revealing its true meaning. Why? To keep it secret so that only initiates can use it? Out of hypocrisy? Both, most likely.

The science of mantra includes a respiratory component, i.e., an obvious link to *Prânayama*, the title of my book on this subject in which I do not, however, broach the topic of mantra.

Mantra and Breathing

Pronouncing a mantra requires a deep and protracted exhalation, followed by a fuller inhalation. Repeating the mantra spontaneously establishes a regular *rhythm*, another essential element of the science of mantra and of pranayama.

Let us first consider the outbreath. It must be long and deep, and must "flow like oil," *dixit* Tantra. For as long as the vocalization lasts, the sound *OM* must be stable and uniform which requires finely controlled and relaxed expiratory muscles. No quavering! No "wasting your breath." Check with the palm of your hand: bringing it close to your mouth—a couple of inches away—your palm should not feel the warm, exhaled air, even during a strong and resounding *OM*. The outbreath *is* felt, though, as it rises above the upper lip toward the nose.

As this slow and long exhalation draws to a close, the abdomen contracts, may even vibrate, and a spontaneous *Mula Bandha* (contraction of the sphincters and the elevator muscle of the anus) sets in. This may be deliberately intensified.

After breathing out fully, you must breathe in again, naturally! After a full and resonant *OM*, I may close my mouth and breathe in again, silently, through my nose. When my lungs are full and I am on the verge of chanting the next *OM*, I may do so either by reciting a single *OM* per exhalation, or in a cascade of multiple *Ongongong*'s per outbreath, with the tongue modulating the *ng*'s. In the latter case, the heartbeat usually paces the string of *Ongongong*'s.

Several levels are involved in mantra vocalization, including *OM*, in its whispered form, notably. In the latter case, breathing in with one's mouth barely open and slightly closing the glottis, produces an almost inaudible *ah*. Exhaling (also with an open mouth) produces *ham* (actually, it should be written *hang*). If the above explanations seem somewhat unclear, just imagine, to find the right sound, that you are panting and trying to catch your breath by breathing through your wide-open mouth: the sound resembles *a-hang*.

A-hang is usually written *aham*, abusively translated as "I am That." Naturally each individual is free to give a meaning to the mantra, but that runs counter to its very principle: a magical, non-conventional, non-rational language having effects on the body via its vibratory frequency, and on the mind by the virtue of the *ambiance* it creates. A mantra is not a word or a sentence, although Vedic mantras, unlike Tantric ones, are often short phrases. By not giving any specific meaning to a mantra I may immerse myself in its pure sound. That is how it acts upon me. Whereas giving a particular meaning to a mantra deflects my attention from its actual sound and is not true

Mantrashastra. Beyond the question of right or wrong, it is more a matter of personal choice.

Last but not least, one may practice *japa* (the repetition of a mantra) without opening the mouth at all, by breathing in and out through the nose only. Sitting with my eyes closed, attentive to my breath, I listen to the flux of air as it passes through my nostrils and throat. If I close my glottis *slightly*, the airflow produces a *sotto voce a-ham* sound, with the expiratory *ham* lasting approximately twice as long as the inhaled *ah*. I can also imagine the sound *ssss* when I breathe in and the sound *ham* when I exhale. Combined, these sounds become a two-syllable "word" often written *Soham*, translated as "I am Him" subject to the same reservation as above.

Silently repeating *aham* is conducive to a deep state of inward focusing; it calms and stills the eddies of the mind and may constitute a complete meditation in its own right. Maharishi Mahesh used japa but called it *Transcendental Meditation*, a. k. a. T. M., a stroke of tautological genius: is there such a thing as *non*-transcendental meditation?

Renaming *japa* (the continuous repetition of a mantra) *Transcendental Meditation* is brilliant because if somebody suggests you practice *japa*, the idea may not seem too appealing. If, on top of it all, it is free, then it's *really* no big deal! People are like that. What's in a name? "Jogging" is bound to be better for you than just running, right? *Transcendental Meditation* sounds more "professional" than *japa*, especially if it costs money! Moreover, if you get your own personalized, customized, top-secret mantra in the bargain, it's like icing on the cake! (By the way, a "secret" mantra means you can give the same one to everybody.)

When T. M., supported by remarkable marketing techniques, flaunts encephalograms "proving" its effects on the brain, it is all true. But: first, it is a tried and true practice whose effects have been known for millennia; second, these are not T. M.'s exclusive prerogative; and third, the same results are obtained with any mantra repeated for a long time, in a state of relaxation. But for those who practice T. M., I say: keep up the good work!

It is true, of course, that in India, during initiation, the guru gives the disciple his/her personal and secret mantra. Even if there are no witnesses, the mantra is whispered to the disciple's ear and the new initiate repeats it *sotto voce* with the right intonation. This is a truly personal mantra. In this regard one must remember that even if a guru and his/her disciple do not see each other often, theirs is a very special and close relationship: they are much closer than friends or even brothers or sisters and this bond evolves and matures with the passing years. The guru knows his/her disciple extremely well and is able to assess the possibilities of his/her personal development. The guru will meditate for long periods of time until *the* personal mantra, the one that will trigger the desired echoes in the disciple's mind, finally emerges. Moreover, the disciple has already received initiation in other Tantric and/or Yogic techniques. Furthermore, the guru is by definition a master of mantra-vidya which he/she did not acquire overnight! Only in such cases can one really talk of a personal mantra that cannot be revealed to anyone else. But this is extremely rare, even in India.

According to the tradition, as mentioned above, mantra is a living thing, it must therefore be received directly, on line and in real time from an initiate. This would appear to contradict the approach suggested earlier in this book since I am obviously using the written word to pass it on. True, but mantras are like diplomas: the first sheepskin was awarded by someone who had never received one. In the same way, the original mantra was not received, but discovered! So rediscovering simple, key-mantras, is indeed possible with the indications provided in this book, even if at first you have to work at it a little. And all the more so since there are no risks involved even if the pronunciation is not quite right.

Having set this record straight, let us return to the question of mantra and breathing and focus on the end of the outbreath: after a full and resonant *OM*, the lungs are almost empty, the abdominal muscles begin to contract, throbbing slightly, and the anal sphincters also contract, in a spontaneous Mula Bandha. After this exhalation, when the lungs are empty, there are two alternatives: either repeating the cycle, i.e., closing the mouth and taking in air again through the nose, or pausing on empty lungs and not inhaling right away (*kumbhaka*).

Holding the Breath In and Out

In the latter case I do not breathe in immediately and stay on "empty" for a while. During this retention the (imagined) *ng* continues to resound in my mind: at this moment the power of mantra begins to fully unfold on all planes, the corporeal, the mental and the spiritual.

How long should I hold my breath out? No time limit can be set, really, for some people are comfortable holding their breath out for only 5 seconds, others for 20 seconds, etc., but in raw terms, the duration matters little.

Here is a fail-safe rule to check if I have exceeded *my own* capacity: as I hold my breath out, it is normal for my abdomen to contract spontaneously, rhythmically (see above), but when the retention becomes uncomfortable, it is time to breathe in again. Now everything is fine if I can *reinhale slowly*, without feeling short of breath or panting. Feeling you will "bust" if you do not reinhale at once indicates that you have held out your breath for too long. But our limits vary from day to day. That is why there is no point in timing oneself: the body and the body alone must be our guide. No stopwatches or other timers are required. Are any risks involved? No, if you abide by that rule.

When it feels like it is time to breathe in again, I let my lungs fill up at a comfortable, leisurely pace, then I hold my breath in, before releasing the next *OM*.

The sign of a properly executed retention (holding breath in) is seen in the effortless and prolonged *OM* which "flows like oil," without straining. I must regulate these successive exhale-pause-inhale-pause-exhale cycles so as to be able to continue indefinitely, without discomfort.

In conclusion, the *OM* is and remains the supreme mantra the repetition of which can literally cast a spell on, "enchant," the mind. We have borrowed from the Latin *incantare* (to pronounce magic formulae) to express the impact of such an action: to be enchanted, charmed. The incantatory magic of *OM* stems from the fact that it includes a maximum number of absolute vibrations, of non-conventional sounds. An absolute sound is understood by everybody. For example, if you announce to a classroom full of spirited young people that they are getting an extra day off, you will hear a joyful *aah*! After a long

*To prove that the habitual ॐ is **not** a "Sanskrit" design, let us write it in Devanagari characters as shown below.*

A + M

In Devanagari writing, the signs hang from a horizontal line.

Moreover, OM was not imported into India by the Aryans, for it does not belong to the Vedic cult. The reliable Monnier-Williams *Sanskrit-English dictionary confirms the fact that there is no trace of OM in Aryan texts written before the Upanishads, therefore several centuries after the Indian conquest.*

and cold winter, voluptuously stretching their bodies out in the new sun, people will frequently utter *aah* (that feels so good!). When people admire the crowning piece of a firework display against the dark sky they let out an *oh* full of wonder, not a strident *ee* or *oo*! Lastly, gourmets smacking their lips to better taste their favorite dish express their enjoyment and pleasure as *mmm* (delicious!). *Aaah... oh... mmmm...* awakens a range of feelings that can be modulated at will according to time and place. Still on absolute sounds, if I stub my toe and cry out "ow!" everybody understands, including animals!

With mantras, we can modulate and awaken *at will* a desired feeling and create an appropriate inner atmosphere for ourselves. It follows that we can dispel an undesirable, counter-productive emotion, as well. As the rising sun melts away the morning haze, so can *OM* chase away the blues if you allow yourself to become mentally, physically and emotionally filled with the radiance of the sun.

Yantra,
a Psychic Dynamo

Yantra is mantra's visual counterpart and the two are indissociable. The word *Yantra* stems from *yan* or *yam* (energy support, medium), plus *tra*, the suffix of instrumentality. In its habitual sense, *yantra* refers to any utilitarian gadget in the wide sense of the term: a robot, for example, as an elaborate gadget, is a *yantra*. In Tantra, *yantra* refers to a two- or three-dimensional magic-symbolic diagram which may range from a simple dot or triangle to a Hindu temple, in actuality a gigantic yantric complex endowed with occult properties.

Over the centuries Tantra has turned yantra into a veritable science and art. A science because in each yantra lies a dynamism, an energy, a Shakti and its construction must obey specific laws. An art form because its unique combination of symbolic lines and colors often produces genuine works of art and any Tantric art book worthy of the name includes yantras (although they more often than not fail to add the secret code to interpret properly and to use these yantras). Tantra is the only yogic-philosophical current to have given birth to works of art, but almost as a by-product, i.e., with no immediate artistic achievement in mind.

Beyond aesthetics, without yantra or mantra, no Tantric ritual, however simple or basic, is even thinkable. India in general and Tantra in particular attribute extraordinary, almost miraculous, powers to them, which may seem inconceivable or absurd to us. Indeed, how difficult it is for us to accept that inert, geometric drawings can generate dynamics of any kind!!

The Ultimate Abstraction

A photograph or portrait of a woman is restricted to the personal, individual, level: it is, let's say, a likeness of *my* mother, *my* wife, *my* sister. Whereas the anonymous, prehistoric statuettes of the female figure discovered (in the thousands) by archaeologists represent Woman in general. The unknown artists who sculpted these statues often accentuated, geometrized the female pubic triangle, the female genital pole.

If this triangle is considered separately, extracted, as it were, from the statue, it comes to symbolize the enclave of our species in the woman's body, and further, beyond her yoni, the genital pole of all females, both human and animal. Ultimately, this triangle represents Womanhood, Femininity, Femaleness, the Cosmic Mother: the abstraction of the symbol transcends the individual, representational level and reaches the Universal. In Tantra, a downward-pointing triangle symbolizes the Cosmic Mother, Femaleness, the Shakti.

Be it a line drawing or a *surface*, an area, the triangle delineates a *space*. One of yantra's functions of is to structure, to organize space and the triangle does so with a minimum number of lines. The downward-pointing triangle becomes the ultimate yantra of Femaleness when colored red (reminiscent of the menstrual flow). In India, family-planning billboards encouraging couples to have no more than two children, sport red, downward-pointing triangles: the meaning is obvious. In an Indian funeral procession, a red shroud indicates the deceased was a woman, a white shroud, a man.

Is this but a mere intellectual abstraction? A flight of fancy divorced from reality? Let me just point out that the voice of women who regularly receive megadoses of male hormone becomes deeper; further, specific hair growth is promoted, notably, an upward-pointing triangle of pubic hair like a man's! In Tantra, Shiva is represented by a white (color of sperm), upward-pointing triangle.

The impact of yantra's magic is considerable, including on the minds of people its symbolism escapes. For the *unconscious* mind *knows*, the *unconscious* mind *deciphers*. I once saw a Tantra-inspired play in Antwerp (Belgium), directed by Alain Louafi (who studied with French choreographer Maurice Béjart). At the end of the performance, a nine-foot-high, red, downward-pointing triangle, on a black background, came rolling down at the back of the stage: the audience just sat there, mesmerized. How could a "simple," banal, geometrical figure trigger such a reaction if not by its impact on the unconscious mind?

Symbolically speaking, a triangle obviously evokes triad. An isosceles triangle represents balance and harmony. Pointing downward, it also symbolizes water Pointing upward, fire. (Here we find two tattwas). The combinations of triangles are discussed on page 186.

To recap, the downward-pointing red triangle is a very powerful yantra which symbolizes, *materializes* the Shakti as the universal *creative power*, the *Cosmic Womb*. For a Tantrist, Shakti, the Great Goddess, is the eternal *dynamic principle* whence is continuously emerging, here, now, everywhere, all of creation. The upward-pointing white triangle (less frequently encountered) symbolizes the *static substratum* of the Universe, Shiva, the male principle, indissociable from Shakti. It is interesting to note that in the pyramid of Cheops, the entrance to the Queen's chamber is indicated by a triangle pointing downward.

The Point of it All

What could be more trivial, more insignificant, apparently, than a simple dot? Yet in Tantra, a dot is—literally—the point of It All! Every yantra is structured around a central core, a central dot, whether depicted or not. A yantra both unfolds from a focal point and returns to it. It can thus be "read" either way, outward from the center of gravity toward the periphery, or the opposite, inward from the periphery back to its center of gravity, the final point, the ultimate dot which absorbs it all, gaining in power.

The dot, the simplest conceivable yantra, is also—amazingly—the most concentrated, condensed of all. It is energy all the more powerful as the dot is small and compact. Consider the following comparison: we all remember playing, as kids, with a magnifying glass and trying to set a piece of paper or wood on fire, using the sun's rays. The closer the magnifying glass to the paper or wood, the larger the circle projected onto the object (although neither very hot nor bright). Conversely, the further away the magnifying glass from the paper or wood, the smaller, i.e., the hotter and brighter, the circle, until the paper or wood eventually begins to smoke and catch fire! Theoretically, an infinitesimal circle would be infinitely powerful. So Tantra considers the dot-symbol to be the most powerful of all yantras, above all the dot that is not actually shown but that one nevertheless perceives, lying there, invisible, at the center of gravity of the drawing, like the Kabbala's "hidden point."

Like all symbols, the dot is versatile. For a physicist, it might represent formidably condensed cosmic energy right before the Big Bang. In Tantra it is called bindu, literally, "sperm-seed" and the ovum united. The dot is therefore an object of profound reflection and meditation: each one of us began as a minuscule dot, so tiny it takes ten to make one millimeter, much smaller in fact than the period at the end of this sentence.

In bindu, in the dot, in the fertilized ovum "I" once was, are indissolubly united the (father's) male and the (mother's) female principles (Shiva/Shakti for Tantra). It contains "everything," as the fertilized ovum holds the complete heredity of my ancestors, of the human species as a whole and even Life since its origin on this planet (see "Meditation on Life"). From this ovum, my physical and mental self developed, according to the "blueprint" in bindu and the process will continue until the end of my individual life. Moreover everything is constantly returning to bindu, to the dot: in the untold secrecy of the species pole, in our gonads, in each spermatozoon and ovum, "I" am back to "square one," "I" am once again the initial "bindu." In the meantime, Life, the species, have become enriched with a new human experience, inexplicably, mysteriously.

Beyond the symbolism just described, yantras also serve to focus the gaze and the mind. Focusing attention multiplies the power of the mind, considered as a material force field. Yantra, notably its central dot, is to the energy of the mind what a magnifying glass is to the sun's rays. The magnifying glass—an inert, passive instrument—increases the power of the sun's rays without expending additional energy. Here lies one of yantra's secrets (and mantra's as well): this passive, geometrical drawing focuses, concentrates mental energy and reinforces the power of the mind. What are the limits of a human mind thus focused, thus concentrated? Who could say for sure?

Without the magnifying-glass-yantra, the sun's rays would not be powerful enough to set fire to the piece of paper. Conversely, the magnifying glass would be powerless without the sun's rays.

The Base Square

The square is *the* static base *par excellence*. It is both stable and firm and represents the substratum, the Earth element, the forces of densification, the plane of manifestation. It includes the four cardinal points and the four dimensions of time-space. Squaring this tetrad gives you sixteen, Tantra's sacred number. According to the science of yantra, the square is a sacred enclosure that opens onto the "outside" world through four T-shaped gates that are actually initiation thresholds. Most yantras are framed by such four-gate squares.

The Circle and the Lotus

The lotus is the Tantric flower *par excellence* and most yantras include lotus petals displayed around a circumference.

The seed (*bindu*) and the flower together reflect the never-ending cyclical process of seed to flower and flower to seed. The flower also represents the yoni seen as the incarnation of the organizing cosmic principle, Female Creativity, in short, the source of all form. The lotus, an aquatic flower, is a link to water, another female symbol.

Tantrists perceive swirls of subtle energy in all flowers. The actual atoms and molecules that constitute the plant are "immaterial," so to speak: a lotus flower growing elsewhere is made of different molecules but remains a lotus flower, generically.

The real "flower" lies in the mysterious and invisible organizing dynamism that has created the current rose, carnation or lotus I may be looking at, using the "material" particles of the universe outside.

Tantrists perceive this subtle dynamics and know it to be the same force at work in their own bodies, with each cell, each organ possessing its own organizing dynamism (cf. Van Helmont's *archeus*). Tantra represents these subtle energies that are particularly active in the *chakras*—those strategic loci in the body where such energies twirl and swirl—as yantras which always include a given number of petals and a "divinity," i.e., a specific anthropomorphized energy form. The latter is always female, evidencing the Tantric origin of the methods used in *Kundalini Yoga* to awaken these force centers. Moreover, there are sexual techniques (described in the section "How to Control Ejaculation," page 315) that activate them automatically.

An interesting aside: the importance of flowers in Tantric ritual is actually reflected in the word *pûjâ*, which comes from the Dravidian *pû*, "flower" and *gey*, "to do." In Sanskrit, the root *pûj* refers to a reverential attitude. By combining the two—*pûjâ*—you get "ritual worship with flowers," which is the usual standard meaning.

The circle—chakra pûjâ's focal symbol—expresses the manifestation's cyclical evolution, the cosmic force *par excellence*. For archaic men and women, the heavens were strewn with circles: the rising sun's disk, the earth's circular horizon—even the moon is round, for through its various phases, it unflaggingly returns to the full circle.

Native American culture is also suffused with symbols, the circle playing a prominent role. The following is a quote by a 48-year-old Native American woman, Catherine, who has kept her people's religious traditions alive and whose life is dedicated to passing them on. She knows the secrets of medicinal plants, she knows which incantations ward off evil spells. And Catherine talks to the Great Spirit: she is a medicine-woman, a shaman.

Her hair is tied back in a bun adorned with an eagle feather. She wears turquoise earrings and the jewels around her neck and on both hands bear the emblem of the sun. On her belt are silver moons and her dress is bright blue, like the azure of the sky through the vibrations of which she "tunes in" to the Great Spirit.

"Have a look on these drawings," she says, "for they tell my own and my people's history. This black line is the sacred mountain, Big Mountain, and here are we, the humans. In the beginning, we have been placed here on this mountain. The sun is our father, the earth our mother, and they begat twins: the Child-born-from-the-water, and the

Killer-monster. Thanks to the Child-born-from-the water, we survive. The Monster-killer brings tornadoes and storms. And here is a rainbow, and this dot is the earth. The whole nature is on this shoe. Inside, I have put the items for the ritual: the praying stick, the candles and the colored sand. Because the Powers of the Universe always act in a circle, heaven is round, Earth is round, the stars are round, the powerful wind blows in a whirlwind, birds nests are round, the heart of the tree is a circle, therefore our hoogans are round. Such is the sacred power of the circle and that's why we always dance in a circle. And we, the Navajos from Big Mountain are here at the center, the spot where man appeared. Here, thanks to the vibrations, we are able to talk to the Great Spirit, who gave us the magical herbs, solace, faith and courage. Why should we leave this and go? For money? Never."

Catherine closes her eyes. She is praying.

We 20th-century denizens know full well that celestial bodies are spheres, not circles. Likewise, yantras are also three-dimensional and meant to be visualized in relief. Even when a yantra is represented "flat" on a piece of paper, in two dimensions, it still possesses a three-dimensional dynamics which is very obvious in the lotus petals around a circumference. Bindu, the germ-seed, is three dimensional as well.

A circumference and its central point are a horizontal projection of a cone produced by a triangle pivoting on its own axis (reminiscent of the "cone of power" of the witches of yore?). Likewise, a square generates a cube.

A yantra placed inside a circle (instead of a square) is called a *mandala*. And a rotating circle forms a sphere.

Combinations *Ad Infinitum*

Each elementary figure—the dot, the triangle, the square, the circle, the flower—is a yantra in its own right, but in combining these "root yantras," Tantra creates often very complex ensembles in which each figure retains its own symbolism but whose power is multiplied, when thus assembled, the whole being more potent than the sum of its individual parts.

The following simple examples are easily grasped by the uninitiated Westerner: a red, downward-pointing triangle with the bindu as the center of gravity represents a pregnant uterus and/or the Cosmic Womb. The same red, downward-pointing triangle superimposed on a white, upward-pointing triangle represents the male-female union or the cosmic union of Shiva/Shakti (note that these *superimposed* triangles differ from the star of David, the latter being formed by two *intertwined* triangles).

Two triangles, apex to apex: two-dimensionally, they are the representation of the beginning or the end of Shiva/Shakti's union, the beginning or end of the manifested universe; three-dimensionally, they are the Dravidian drum that Shiva holds in one hand as he dances, they symbolize the original vibration which is constantly fueling the unbridled cosmic dance of particles inside matter.

In India, any complex Tantric mandala or yantra includes a complete cosmogony: at each crucial point, at each angle of the triangle or each triangle, in each petal, "resides" a "divinity," even if it is not explicitly portrayed. In meditation, the disciple starts at the focal bindu and mentally reconstructs, re-draws in his/her mind's eye, the entire yantra, in order to better penetrate it and be penetrated by it. Moreover, each crucial point corresponds to a basic vibration, a mantra embodied in a letter of the Sanskrit alphabet which the disciple vocalizes with his/her gaze focused. Tantrists use Sanskrit letters in this way for they cover the *entire* gamut of sounds the human voice is capable of producing. In this regard, the Sanskrit alphabet is indeed universal.

The reader will have surmised that for the more complex yantras, initiation— therefore a master—is required, perforce excluding Westerners. Let me point out, however, that Tantrists are not the only ones who practice the science of yantra, nor are they its sole inventor. They have, nevertheless, developed it into a sophisticated art, far beyond its original bounds. And let the Westerner be consoled: even simple yantras are powerful instruments with a strong mental impact.

Let us consider a Western yantra: the Latin cross. A Christian mystic gazing at the cross can become filled with its significance, the meaning of Christ's suffering, and may thus reach via the cross-yantra, a higher state of consciousness, in connection with his/her faith.

If you have any doubts as to the formidable power of yantras, just go to Beirut and scrawl the star of David on the walls of a shi'ite mosque, or a swastika on the wailing wall in Jerusalem, or better still (sorry, worse still!) add the mantra *Heil Hitler!* Any remaining doubts should be dispelled and the full power of the mantra-yantra duo should hit home P. D. Q.!

The Ultimate Yantra

In closing this chapter, I would like to quote an excerpt from Shashi Bushan Dasgupta in *An Introduction to Tantric Buddhism* (Calcutta, 1974, p. 146): "On the practical side, which obviously is the most important thing, is the stress laid on the body, as the medium in and

ETHER

AIR

FIRE

WATER

EARTH

Each basic geometric figure is highly symbolic in its own right. However, the dot, the circle, the upward-pointing triangle, the lunar crescent and the square also symbolize the five tattwas *or elements of Tantra.*

The two triangles with their apexes touching, opposite one another, represent the damaru, *Shiva's as well as Dravidians' drum, and symbolizes both the original vibration and the vibration which constantly ripples through matter, sustaining it, giving it being. They also refer to the beginning of the manifestation as the two triangles, Shiva and Shakti, meet.*

The lotus flower symbolizes the yoni as well as the ultimate manifestation principle. It also pertains to lunar symbolism, with its main circle and eight petals. If you count one couple per petal, that gives you sixteen, chakra pûjâ!

In combination, these drawings generate an infinite number of yantras and mandalas, each one endowed with its own mental, psychic energy. Life is no different: using only a few basic "bricks," Mother Nature has built (and continues to build) the planet's (the universe's) myriad life forms.

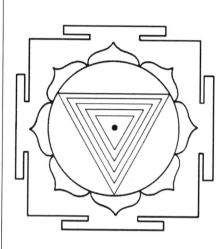

On the basis of these elements, this yantra can be easily decoded: you have the square with its four "gates", the circle, the lotus, the triangles, and the central bindu around which the whole structure develops.

There are two ways of looking at this yantra: two-dimensionally or three-dimensionally. The triangles make up a pyramid whose focal point is its gravity center, its apex and its point of origin, all at once.

The pyramid has been placed at the center of the lotus whose petals are pointing toward the sky. The square constitutes a base, a solid foundation, a sort of podium with its four gates opening onto the outside world.

For Tantrists, each angle of this square, each gate, each petal, each angle of the triangle, contains an energy of its own symbolized by a Shakti that the disciple visualizes at each of these points. This level of visualization is not habitually within the Westerner's grasp.

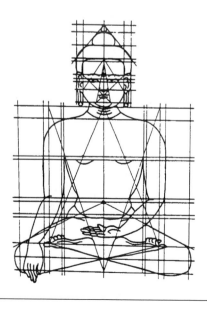

Even Buddhism is full of yantras concealed behind the canonical representations of the Buddha which all sculptors must abide by. Actually, the human body is itself considered by Tantrists to be the supreme yantra. Moreover each Indian temple is a giant, three-dimensional yantra, as seen inter alia in the famous Buddhistic Bârâbudur complex.

through which truth can be realized. All schools of Tantra hold that the body is the abode of all truth; it is the epitome of the universe or, in other words, it is the microcosm and as such embodies the truth of the whole universe. Many Tantras identify the universe completely with the body even by locating the seas, rivers, mountains, thus making the whole physiological and biological process a perfect *yantra* for realizing the ultimate truth."

Furthermore, *Ghandarva Tantra* adds: "Here (within this body) is the Ganges and the Jumna, here the *Ganga-sâgara* (the mouth of the Ganges), here are Prayâga and Banaras—here the sun and the moon (the masculine and the feminine). Here are the sacred places, here the *Pithas*—I have not seen a place of pilgrimage or an abode of bliss like my body. The *Tattwa* is within the house of our body: yet, curious indeed it is, that we generally roam about in the whole world in search of it" (Dasgupta, 1969, p. 89).

Getting back to the cross, practically all nations have adopted the Red Cross symbol except for Arab countries who, instead, use the Red Crescent: a Christian yantra would be unthinkable! And yet technically—and unemotionally!—speaking, a cross is merely two intersecting lines.

To recap, each and every one of us, be we Tantrists or not, should live with our chosen yantra(s): the cross for a Christian, for example. Tantric yantras are special inasmuch as they are universal and neutral, i.e., are not religious symbols, Tantra not being a religion as we understand the word. At the end of this book I suggest a Tantric ritual for Westerners: everybody, believers and non-believers alike, can practice it and add to it or delete from it, according to individual preferences.

Part 3

Myths and Symbols

To Believe or not
to Believe in Hindu Gods?

Ask me if I *really* believe in Hindu gods and my answer will be: "Like I believe in Santa Claus!" Straightforward? No, because I do "believe" in Santa Claus, well, in a way!

Was *is* a Hindu "god," actually? Let me first point out that unfortunately the English language—so rich and subtle—offers a surprisingly limited choice: god(s) or God. God (capital G) is the Supreme Being, the Creator, perforce the One and Only God, be we monotheistic or monoatheistic, ruling out the whole kit and caboodle of other gods, Hindu or otherwise.

If I am a Christian, a Jew or a Moslem, I have a single God, excluding *ipso facto* any other god(s) (little "g" and/or plural): "Thou shalt have no other gods before me." Naturally, the study of Hindu mythology is a perfectly honorable undertaking, academically, but believing in those gods or worse, becoming polytheistic, is a no-no. Worshipping those outlandish gods with countless arms would amount to nothing less than heresy and the price to pay would be excommunication! Rest assured, we are not in the business of advocating apostasy!

In the case of mono-atheism (with apologies to the Oxford English Dictionary) things are simpler still—thank heaven! Why worry about a slew of gods since, for some people, a single one is one too many!

For us Westerners, therefore, Hindu gods are (and will remain) as strange and remote as they are alien and sprung from a foreign land. So why bother? A legitimate question and I hasten to respond that Hindu "gods" and "goddesses" are a far cry indeed from our Western concepts of "God" and let us deplore once again the paucity of the English language unable to convey this subtle shade of meaning. The Sanskrit *deva* comes from *div*, to shine, to glow, and refers by extension, to a shining, celestial, divine, being. The least unacceptable compromise would be simply to use the word deva and forget about "god(s)"! (By the way, the operatic "diva" stems from the same Latin root as the French word *déesse* meaning a goddess.)

Upper class (or supposedly so) Aryans, the Brahmins and the Kshattriyas, are self-proclaimed "devas," sons of Light, as opposed to the demons, the forces of Darkness implicitly meaning the conquered indigenous peoples).

The Rigveda, the earliest Indo-Aryan work (remarkably preserved for thirty centuries) is the cornerstone of Brahmanic religion and it recounts and glorifies the epic struggle between Good, the devas, and Evil, the dâsas or demons. (By the way, take one "o" out of Good and you get God!)

But is this combat between Good and Evil purely mythical? Is it not, rather, the mythologized, deified, narration of the implacable war of conquest of India by the Aryans? An Indian professor at New Delhi's Nehru University, Malati J. Shendge, in her remarkable book, *The Civilized Demons: the Harappans in Rigveda* (Delhi, 1977), sets the record straight: "What do the constant references in the Rigveda to the wars between gods and demons mean? Are they really the wars between the forces of good and evil as it is generally assumed? Or, were they the wars fought by the Aryans with their predecessors in this land? [...] The events referred to in the exploits of Indra and Vishnu, the leaders of the Aryans in their conflict, probably took place historically. The opponents of the Aryans were primarily the Asuras, the Raksas, the Gandharvas, the Yaksas, and the Pisâcas. When the Aryans created a religion out of these events, they deified their leaders and arrogated to themselves the title of cosmic good. The opponents naturally became demons and represented the cosmic evil" (p. 2-4).

"In Hymn II.20.7 Indra is praised for having burst open the dasa fortresses which concealed the dark people (*krsna-yonih*) in their interior" (p. 35).

Since weapons alone could not quash the Harappans' resistance— they seem to have been tough cookies—the Aryans resorted to water and fire. The Mohenjo-Daro civilization was based on agriculture which depended on a remarkable irrigation system the water for which was supplied by the monsoon rain stored behind dams. Centuries before the World War II Allies blew up a dam in Germany to destroy enemy towns, Indra, the main Aryan god, killed Vritra, the Harappan war chief and guardian of the dam, and "released the waters," killing two birds with one stone, so to speak: on the one hand the flood wreaked havoc in its wake, people drowning in their inundated towns and villages, creating utter chaos and disaster. On the other hand, once the fields had been flooded and the harvests destroyed, the water shortage made farming impossible and the survivors starved to death.

Thus deified, transferred to heaven and glorified as the destroyer of fortresses, Indra, "He-Who-Releases-The-Waters" was promoted to the rank of a rain god, his weapon being a bolt of lightning.

Agni, the fire god, worshipped on an almost equal footing with Indra, is not the deification of a war hero but of a local element in the Rigveda sacrificial cult. The campfire played an essential part in the Aryans' nomadic lifestyle. Around such a fire would the clan gather during halts, to listen, notably, to bards who were later to become the Brahmins, the masters of the sacrificial fire. Thus promoted to the status of a weapon, an instrument of war, and deified as "Agni," fire became a pivotal element of the worship. Agnihotra, the fire sacrifice, is still practiced today as it was in Vedic times: I have personally witnessed more than one such ceremony. Nevertheless, people are careful and never say that it is in commemoration of fire's successfully annihilating enemies (the dâsas) that various ingredients are thrown into the flames, including seeds symbolizing, notably, the destruction of crops, towns and forts; nor are we told that the bits of meat thrown into the fire represent enemies to be burned.

Another mythical element of the Rigveda is soma. Indeed, even deified, Indra, the intrepid and turbulent warrior, remains very human. That fellow must have been fond of his liquor for the battles against "Darkness" were preceded by boisterous bouts of drinking. The Rigveda, in terms of boundless admiration, describes how Indra would swallow impressive amounts of soma, an intoxicating beverage which became "his" drink. Also included are spats with his wife who nags him as if he were a mere mortal, for having indulged in too much drink! Which does not prevent the other devas from guzzling soma, on the contrary!

In this paradise à la Breughel, there was never a dull moment: for their entertainment, these Vedic gods would call in nymphs and celestial dancers, the Apsaras, whose poetic name means "essence of water" symbolized as clouds in the sky. During land wars—like their Teutonic cousins, the Walkyries—they descended onto the battlefield to recover warriors (Aryans, naturally) slain in combat: they placed the duly adorned and flowered bodies of the fallen men on their chariots and took them straight to Indra's heaven. Even during the "off-season" the devas are depicted as fun-loving and frequently send the nymphs on a terrestrial mission to charm, entice, and even better, seduce, ascetics, rishis, and other forerunners of Saint Anthony: Aryan heaven is not a place of doom and gloom and the devas certainly enjoy painting it (bright) red!

Gradually, the already relatively sizable Aryan pantheon upon the invasion of India, came to include a host of new "gods" (annexes had to be added to the official celestial census!) The war of conquest produced countless Aryan heroes who were duly deified, like Vishnu, one of the members of the Hindu trinity. Varuna, a co-manager of

Aryan paradise along with Indra, and who, unlike his aforementioned partner, has no claim to sparring fame, "Knows-all-Sees-all," is Mr. FBI/CIA, all in one, the keeper of law and order. Here in the Rigveda, Rudra (a divinity also encountered in the myth of Shiva) is a mere backbencher: was he the defecting chief of a local tribe? In any case, he brought with him to heaven his sons and his supporters, the Maruts, a bunch of fearsome celestial firebrands.

Let's pause for a moment and recap this initial deification process. Superlative clan chiefs noticed on the battlefield for their uncommon fighting capacities are promoted to the status of heroes and are duly "emigrated" to Indo-Aryan Valhalla where they become devas. Apart from drinking and being entertained by the Apsaras and their dancing, their celestial R & R is spent managing (anthropomorphized) atmospheric phenomena, such as storms and the wind (Vayu and Vâta).

For the Aryans, the sun is not a unitary phenomenon. Savitur is the sun that can be "looked at," i.e., rising or setting. Surya is the name for the glaring or blinding sun. Conspicuous in this almost entirely male context is the charming Usha, the dawn that gives the sky its pink color. She is female because each and every morning, day in, day out, she gives birth to the sun: even in heaven, giving birth is a prerogative that men are happy to leave to women. The Rigveda has truly put Usha on a pedestal as a host of very poetic hymns are devoted to her. The other Aryan goddesses play but a subsidiary role as the wives of gods. In Tantra, on the contrary, goddesses are the focal point of worship.

The Ashvins, worshipped on an almost equal footing with Indra, control the pale light that looms just prior to dawn. And so the loop of the solar cycle is looped. They precede Usha who gives birth to Savitur which becomes Surya, then again Savitur at dusk. Complicated stuff!

Strangely enough, the Aryans did not take the stars into account at all.

Shall we call it a day or are you thirsting for more info on Indra, Varuna and other divinities? Actually, I have mentioned them mainly to differentiate them from Tantric divinities.

Far from being a proselytizing, spread-the-word missionary faith, the Brahminical religion has on the contrary adopted a racist and exclusive policy. As the strict prerogative of the "twice born," the Aryans, it bars all descendants of the conquered, the sudras, and *a fortiori* the untouchables. And what could be more logical? Why should they know anything about a religion which in actual fact glorifies their ancestors' defeat? All memory of their armed struggle had to be eradicated.

Over the centuries a curious osmosis has taken place. The Aryans of yore declared their Vedic religion "off-limits" to all conquered people, who could not own land, either. In fact, the "underlings" were given free rein to practice their own cults and worship their pre-Aryan gods. These indigenous gods gradually infiltrated the Brahmanical pantheon. After their Aryanization, some of them even came to supplant Vedic gods.

However, regardless of origin, Aryan or otherwise, no Indian god is ever equated with the Supreme Being, though each individual divinity personifies a limited aspect of It. As idealized men and women promoted to the rank of devas, they nevertheless remain very human indeed and are often jealous, vindictive, petty, resorting to prevarication and downright lying when they have managed to paint themselves into a mythological corner! Their allegorical myth serves to "prove" that humans can reach a state of perfection which Indian art has materialized in marvelous sculptures and bronze statues.

To symbolize their supernatural powers, they are graced with several arms, for example, as well as various accessories. Moreover, behind their sometimes dark, threatening or forbidding appearance, their true nature shines through. In Indian households they are almost a family member, and worthy of veneration. As heavenly beings they are endowed with supernatural powers and although they live on another plane, each idol can be reached through its own cult. In exchange for this worship they grant favors to their devotees or at any rate do them no harm. However, the bottom line is: these exotic gods, as such, will probably remain inescapably alien and remote for us.

Is there an equivalent in the West? Actually saints of the Catholic Church are very similar. Like the devas, our saints are idealized humans, they live in heaven and are supposed to be sensitive to the prayers and pilgrimages of earthbound devotees. The various cult forms involved (worshipping their statue, praying to them, offering flowers, burning candles...) are all quite similar both in the East and the West. The rural chapels found throughout Europe are not all that different, except architecturally, from the small temples in Indian villages. Our saints intercede on our behalf with the heavenly powers-that-be or use their own supernatural powers to heal people, for example. Devout Catholics are as close to their saints as Hindus are to their *ishta-devata*, their favorite divinity. Some control atmospheric phenomena, such as rain. Others, such as Saint Aloysius or Saint Barbara, for example, are the patron saints of guilds, sailors, and so on and so forth.

The Myth of Santa Claus is Alive and Well

Only those Indian gods incarnating universal archetypes or myths could ever be "transplanted" in the West without being rejected. An example of a successful transplant is found in Japan (after all, India is located halfway between the West and that Far-Eastern nation). The Japanese have imported and adopted Santa Claus and Christmas, which they call *Karusumasu*! Japanese kids' *Karusumasu* (= Christmas, onomatopoeically!) presents and toys are delivered by Saint Nick. Why not? After all, Santa Claus (or the British version: Father Christmas) is the universal archetype of the Father, the tribal Patriarch, engraved in the collective memory of all humankind. And dressed any other way (like a cowboy, for example) would he look as sweet? No way! His white beard, his red coat, his hood, all materialize his benevolence as does his sack full of toys (for good children!). His fur-lined coat means that he visits us in the frozen midst of the long winter night. The "bogeyman" represents the complementary, repressive aspect of the archaic Father "who art in heaven" (that is, on the subtle psychic plane). Later, when children "find out the truth," what do they gain by it? Nothing. Unless as adults and disguised as Santa, daddies partake anew in the myth of the Father!

By the way, I used to think that Santa Claus was as old as the hills. Not so. He was invented in 1850! But I was not entirely mistaken, for his lineage is reported to be as old as the ancient legends of the European peoples of yore: Gargan, the son of the Celtic god Bel, carried a knapsack on his back and distributed gifts, especially to children. Absurdly enough, in 1881, Cardinal Roques, the Archbishop of the city of Rennes, France, called this custom an "incredible stupidity involving an imaginary ragman called Santa Claus." In 1861 on the square in front of the Cathedral of Dijon, France—this is highly symbolical—250 "programmed" kids set fire to his effigy but the following day, he was reborn on the roof of City Hall! Archetypes die hard!

It is no coincidence that Christmas and New Year's Eve festivities occur at the same time of the year as pre-Christian celebrations of the winter solstice marking the rebirth of the sun and light! The Church, more realistic and clever than the Archbishop of Rennes, knew it could never hope to repress such a movement and so just converted the lot. Ever since the year of grace 354, officially, the Savior was born on December 25th (by decree of Pope Liberius), whereas His birth used to be celebrated either on January 6 (Eastern Church), April 10, or May 29. So the switch made everybody's day, so to speak!

But back to Santa. The more mythical, therefore unreal, a character, the more closely he/she is linked to his/her own stereotype. Everything in Santa Claus and his appearance is symbolical, therefore practically intangible. Any change in this symbolism would reduce his evocative impact. Santa wearing a green coat seems unthinkable. Red is a highly symbolical color and the child's unconscious mind registers everything, picks up on all these symbols. Shaving his beard, for example, would be preposterous for a smooth-cheeked Saint Nick would no longer incarnate the archaic Father. Even his height is important. If he were tall and towering, he would instill fear, whereas a short and stout Santa is a jolly and reassuring *bon vivant*.

Children could not care less about our grown-up hair-splitting analysis of Santa Claus. However, the unconscious mind of the child deciphers Santa Claus as the archaic Father. The child enters into the magical, enchanted world of parents' love for their little ones. Let us indeed feel somewhat sorry for kids who have been deprived of Santa Claus, who is neither American, nor British, nor Japanese, but universal.

Yes, Santa Claus is exportable and just as I "believe" in Santa Claus, I "believe" in Shiva, whose character, legend, and personality are all highly symbolical. A Westerner may wonder where and how he/she can be initiated to genuine Tantrism. Initiation depends, to a large extent, on coming into contact with and unconsciously deciphering the symbolic myths that Tantra proposes. Just as the pagan Santa Claus peacefully coexists with our Christian religions (and with Japanese cults), Tantric myths are compatible with any authentic religion for they reveal and even activate latent cosmic forces in our being and in the universe.

This lengthy preamble was necessary, to my mind, to better introduce you to Shiva and his symbolism, barring which one runs the risk of missing the point, the essence of Tantra.

Symbols to be Experienced

Symbols reveal by concealing
and conceal by revealing.

—G. Gurvitch

Words inform but symbols reveal. As a non-verbal means of approaching the ultimate realities of being and the cosmos, the symbol is one of the pillars of Tantra, indeed of any tradition. Naturally, the spoken word is a capital means of human communication and when it becomes The Word (a rare occurrence) it also has its rightful place in tradition. Indeed language is one of our most prized intellectual tools. Otherwise why bother writing or reading this text? Nevertheless it stays on the surface of things and beings.

Contemporary man and woman are drowning in a deluge of words. Unfortunately, we are now out of touch with symbolic language and it is significant that the following words (which best reflect Tantric thought on symbols) were spoken by a Sioux healer/clairvoyant called Tahca Ushte, talking to Richard Erdoes, a white friend of his: "What do you see here, my friend ? Nothing more than an old kettle, black with soot."

"This kettle has been put on the old stove which has been lit and the water in it boils. The steam of the boiling water goes up to the ceiling and lifts the lid. In the kettle, besides the water, are pieces of meat with bones and fat, and many potatoes.

"This old kettle does not seem to convey any message, and I suppose you don't even notice it, except for the good flavor of the soup, and this reminds you you are hungry. Maybe you are afraid to have found a stew made of dog's meat. But don't be afraid, this is only beef—not from a fat animal for festive days, for today is an ordinary day.

"But I am an Indian. I think of many ordinary things like this kettle. The water comes from the sky. The fire comes from the sun which blesses us all with his warmth—people, beasts, trees. The meat symbolizes all creatures walking on all four, our brothers the animals who sacrifice their life in order to make us live. The steam is the breath of life.

"The water goes up to the sky, becomes again a cloud. All of this is sacred. Looking at this kettle full of good soup, I think that in this simple way Wakan Tanka, the Great Spirit, takes care of us. Everyday, we Sioux, spend much time thinking of all these things, which in our mind are mixed with the spiritual. In the world around us, we see so many symbols which you, white men, don't even notice. You would notice them if you liked to, but you are always in such a hurry! We, Indians, live in a world full of symbols and images where things spiritual and everyday objects are united. To you, the symbols are only words you say or read in books. To us, they are part of nature, of ourselves—the earth, the sun, the wind and the rain, the stones, the trees, the animals, and even the insects or the locusts. We try to understand them, not with our head, but with our heart, and a simple hint is enough to reveal their meaning.

"What is ordinary to you, becomes marvelous to us, thanks to the symbolism. Funny: for "symbolism," we do not even have a word, and still symbolism permeates our entire being. You have the word, and that's all. Each and every day of my life, I see symbols in the form of some roots or some branches. I give them a special attention, because I am a seer, a yuwipi and the stones are my business. But I am not the only one, many Indians do the same. *Inyan*, the stones, that's what's sacred. Every human being needs a stone to help him in his life."

Yes, we all need a stone to help us "get by," to live better, and my wife and I "hang out with" a black, egg-shaped stone we brought back from India: a lingam.

The Lingam, an Absolute Symbol

The lingam is India's most common symbol. It is accepted by both Hindus and Tantrists of the left-hand and right-hand paths. In her book *Mother India*, Katherine Mayo wrote in 1927: "Siva, one of the greatest of the Hindu deities, is represented on highroad shrines, in the temples, on the little altar of the home, or in personal amulets, by the image of the generative organ, in which shape he receives the daily sacrifices of the devout."

Actually the lingam is the only common element encountered in practically all Hindu temples. It is also the only symbol that can be looked at and touched by all and sundry, regardless of religion, sect or caste. It plays a pivotal role in all Tantric rites, be they Shiva or Shakti followers.

By its very nature, the symbol reveals aspects that differ according to the eye of the beholder and for the same person, according to time and place, hence its richness; and the symbolic value of the lingam is extraordinary. It is universal, therefore believers and atheists alike can accept it!

Is it a phallic or priapic representation? That is what the first Westerners in India initially believed. In 1670 a man called Stravorinus, a captain in the Dutch East Indies Company was shocked by it: "Here and there are pictures of a god they worship under the name of lingam. This is the most scandalous cult of all the loathsome superstitions man has multiplied on earth."

No comment.

Tantra is the means of approaching ultimate realities that is the most readily accessible to humankind as a whole, regardless of racial or other differences.

At first sight, what could be stranger than Tantrist concepts, rites and techniques, notably lingam worship? And yet its impact on our unconscious mind is deep and far-reaching as we enter its mysterious universe.

In Tantra, the lingam is the male sex organ united with the female sex organ and not just the phallus, alone, although the latter is in itself a very powerful and universally encountered symbol, even in our Western nations.

George Ryley Scott, *Phallic Worship* (New Delhi, 1975) wrote: "It was natural that the ancient Britons should worship stones and pillars, as emblems of the male principle, just as did the ancient Hebrews, the Greeks, the Romans, the Egyptians, the Japanese, *et al.* Traces of such worship have been found in many parts of England, Scotland, and Wales, though it must be admitted that *realistic* phallic statues or priapi are remarkably rare. Such specimens as did exist have probably been demolished, and all records concerning them carefully eradicated by ecclesiastical and other authorities."

The same author quotes J. B. Hannay in *Christianity: The Sources of its Teaching and Symbolism* (p. 232): "It must not be thought that these phallic columns were uncommon in Britain. We have lengthy lists of such sacred columns in antiquarian writings. Many have been destroyed or thrown down, and some re-erected in a different form, others mutilated or weather-worn at the top; but where investigation has been made it has been found that they were phallic columns such as an Indian Sivaite would fall down and worship today, and others simply represent the glans like the forms the Assyrians worshipped."

On the prehistoric site of Filitosa, in Corsica, there are erect stones that are so explicitly sculpted that they are indubitably lingams, although archaeologists have modestly called them "warriors." Here again a parallel is drawn between a man's sexual virility and his sparring virility.

What would our friend Burgess have thought if he had witnessed the scene related by Captain Hamilton who saw a seven-foot tall and well-proportioned "sanctified rascal" who belonged to the Jougies' sect (sic:) "I have seen a sanctified rascal of seven foot high, and his limbs well proportioned, his body bedewed with ash and water, sitting quite naked under a tree, with a *pudenda* like an ass, and an hole bored through his prepuce, with a large gold ring fixed in the hole. The fellow was much revered by numbers of young married women, who, prostrating themselves before the living Priapus, and taking him devoutly in their hands, kissed him, whilst his bawdy owner stroked their silly heads, muttering some filthy prayers for their prolification (*A New Account of the East Indies*, Edinburgh, 1727, Vol. I, p.152, quoted by Ryley Scott in *Phallic Worship*, p.197). We can well imagine the shock that this subject of the British Crown must have felt upon witnessing such a sight! However, he failed to grasp that these women were not worshipping the man's penis but the lingam, the symbol of Shiva's creative power.

Oh, horror, oh, outrage! Another traveler saw a naked ascetic, sitting under a tree, hanging chains of flowers and other ritual offerings on his own erect penis! For the ascetic, the erection materialized the creative force that gives rise to new life and galaxies, out of the void, and it is the cosmic principle that he was worshipping. He was therefore able to dissociate his individual-pole (the conscious ego) and his species-pole. Of course this cannot be transposed to the West: think of what would have happened if the same scene had taken place in Times Square!

In India, the origin of lingam worship dates back to prehistoric times, to the ancient sexual fertility rites and worship of the Great Goddess. Men and women would gather near their fields and the purpose of their collective intercourse was to boost, by contagion as it were, the soil's fertility. This practice was certainly less toxic than modern pesticides. Then stones were erected to invoke pro-creative powers and there they still stand.

This cult is clearly older than the Aryan invasion of India: according to the Rigveda, the lingam was, if not the only, at least the main, pre-Aryan religious symbol. For not only was it unknown to the Aryans prior to their invasion of India, but they found it repulsive.

Terms of insult used to refer to Dravidians include: *akarman*, without rites, *ayajvan*, not making any sacrifices, *shishna-devâh*, literally "whose god is the penis" (VII.21.5, and X.99.3), which proves that the profound symbolism of the lingam totally escaped the Aryans. Lingam worship, thus condemned, was banned from Vedic rituals.

Nevertheless a turnaround was to take place: having taken deep root in their conquered land, with their self-proclaimed racial integrity protected by the strict apartheid of the caste system, the Aryans could well afford to be tolerant *vis-à-vis* other religions. So they let their serfs, the sudras, keep their own gods and old forms of worship.

Usually the conqueror imposes his religion on the vanquished. But in India not only did the Aryans not want to "Brahmanize" their serfs, they actually prohibited non-Aryans (and Aryan women!) from listening to the Vedas. And Manu's code provided for the swift punishment of offenders committing such a "sacrilege."

Nevertheless, the "lords" gradually annexed the gods, beliefs, and magical practices of the conquered, Aryanized and integrated them into their own cult and pantheon: the result of this osmosis is Hinduism. Initially abhorred, the lingam gradually became the most frequently encountered symbol in India. Aryan patriarchs were not too reluctant to accept it because for them, it represented above and beyond everything else, the male sex organ!

Lingam worship has lost none of its original fervor. The following is a quote from Mircea Eliade's *L'Epreuve du Labyrinthe*, Paris, 1978, p. 68 [The Test of the Labyrinth]: "The second lesson India has taught me is the meaning of the symbol. In Rumania, I was not drawn to religious life, churches seemed to me to be cluttered with icons. Naturally I did not consider these icons to be idols, but still... Well, in India, I once lived in a Bengali village and I saw women and young girls touching and decorating a lingam, a phallic symbol, to be precise an anatomically very correct stone phallus; and naturally married women, at least, could not have been unaware of its nature, its physiological function. I therefore understood the possibility of 'seeing' the symbol in the lingam. The lingam is the mystery of life, of creativity, of fertility, which manifests itself on all cosmic levels. This epiphany of life was Shiva, not the member we know. So this possibility of being religiously moved by an image and a symbol revealed unto me an entire world of spiritual values."

At first sight, it would appear that the lingam is indeed a purely macho he-man symbol, and yet when the penis becomes erect it is usually in response to the presence of a woman! A Tantric saying states that: "without Shakti, Shiva is but a mere *shava*, a corpse." An erection is proof of women's power! Forgive my mentioning a well-known example in the canine world. Usually things are pretty quiet in dog kingdom but when a bitch is in heat, all the male dogs go berserk! The female awakens the male and not the opposite!

So the lingam meets with everybody's approval (or so it would appear): the erect penis is paramount for the male chauvinist. The Tantrist is beyond the union of male and female sex organs, and perceives the cosmic principles thus symbolized. It is relatively easy to sculpt male genitalia, but it is technically impossible to sculpt a three-dimensional female sex organ. Because of such constraints, in Indian lingams, the female organ merely clasps the base of the male organ, the rest being left to the imagination of the beholder.

Why are lingams always carved out of stone, except for those in clay which are thrown into the Ganges? Why is the stone usually black? The answer is simple: because of the skin color of the Dravidians whose god was Shiva!

What is a linga-pûjâ (lingam worship) like in a puritanical environment such as the Rishikesh ashram, for example, in the foothills of the Himalayas? The officiant, sometimes Swami Chidananda himself, the ascetic, first strokes the smooth stone lingam for quite some time, almost lovingly, adorns it with garlands, then draws ritualistic and symbolic signs on it with yellow sandalwood paste. Throughout the celebration, the officiant and the participants chant together for hours on end: "Om Namah Shivayah" as they throw leaves and petals on the lingam which practically disappears under the offerings.

At the height of the ceremony, the officiating Swami pours onto the lingam a viscous white liquid made of milk and honey (whose symbolism is obvious) which slowly trickles down the stone and flows into the arghya and is then shared amongst the participants who drink it with manifest devotion. As in consecration, in a Catholic mass, for them, in that moment, Shiva is present in the lingam.

If anybody happens to mention the obviously sexual nature of this ritual, people are shocked and very sincerely protest that such is not at all the case. I once heard a Western woman, also in good faith, defending the same viewpoint. She even thought she had a subtle and watertight case in saying that if this really were the symbol of intercourse, the phallus would be horizontal, not vertical! In the most common Western lovemaking position, the so-called missionary position, that is indeed true, but not in Tantric maïthuna where the Shakti sits astride or atop the Shiva and the male organ is vertical. Indians—who know—never "let on"; they just flatly deny it.

Tantrists perceive that ejaculation is the procreative moment *par excellence*, i.e., when female energy seizes the sperm to create a new life. They believe that any act of creation is accompanied by intense enjoyment and creation itself stems from a permanent and orgasmic cosmic union that will continue until the end of time: each galaxy is the fruit of a cosmic orgasm. Any cosmic experience is perforce ecstatic, like the ecstasy of Western mystics, and that justifies the sexual rites of the left-hand path, the straightest path toward ecstasy. In Tantra, cosmic libido (may Dr. Freud rejoice in his grave) is the fundamental dynamism of creation: the universe is born of desire, like all living beings. Desire and enjoyment accompany any truly creative act.

In Tantra's sexual rites, all means available are used to awaken desire, to create intensely eroticizing situations in order to reach bliss and ecstasy through ritualized, sacralized, concrete union. This union becomes a spiritual one only if its holy, divine nature is perceived. Tantra holds that any form of pure enjoyment is of a spiritual nature. Sexual union is the most concrete, most symbolical "sign" there is and it goes hand in hand with the most ultimate bliss that can be experienced in a human body. All of this presupposes a different outlook from the quotidian one according to which sexual enjoyment and spiritual matters are incompatible. The following excerpts from holy texts confirm the lingam's symbolism: "The manifested nature, the universal cosmic energy is symbolized by the yoni, the female organ engulfing the lingam. The yoni represents that energy which gives birth to the world, the womb of everything manifested" (Karapâtri, *Lingopapâsana*, Siddhanta, Vol. 2, p. 154).

"This Universe stems from the union of an yoni with a lingam. Everything, therefore, bears the sign of lingam and yoni. It is the divine power, which, in the shape of individual phalluses, enters every womb thus creating all beings (p.163).

"It is by controlling sex, by making it a ritual and not by repressing it that one acquires physical and mental power. When the Hindus revere the lingam, they don't deify the physical organ, they pay homage to the eternal and divine form manifested in the microcosm. To ignore the sacredness of the phallus is dangerous, whilst by revering it one gets the enjoyment (*bhukti*) and liberation (*mukti*) as well" (p.165).

Or : "He who lives without revering the phallus is pitiable" (*Shiva Purana* I, 21).

"He who venerates the lingam, knowing it to be the primal cause, the source, the consciousness, the very essence of the universe, is closer to me than any other being" (I,27).

Two comments come to mind as regards these quotes from Aryan scriptures. First, they are a far cry from the Rigveda and its fulminations against "worshippers of the penis-god." Second, a little macho sleight of hand reduces the lingam to a mere phallus, whereas in Tantra, the lingam equals yoni PLUS the male organ, the two being indissociably linked. A world of difference.

I would like to conclude this chapter by quoting once again our Sioux friend Tahca Ushte (a genuine Tantrist unbeknownst to himself!): "To the white man, symbols are simply a pleasant thing that allows his mind to speculate about, a mind's game; to us, they are much more than that, so much more. We Indians have to make them live."

Therefore the purpose and relevance of speculation (including this text) should be to open the door to the rich world of symbols that speak directly to our minds. So that they may become "more than that," wordy dissertations must be left behind. Only then can symbols fully impact our unconscious mind: there lie our roots, then may we "touch base" with the living and dynamic forces of the universe. Here words like "giving birth" and "generating" take on their full meaning.

Let us return to the West: could the Christian cross actually be some sort of "closet" lingam? The question may shock (why should it?) Christians who see in the cross the supreme sacrifice of the son of God in order to save humankind. Does this perforce preclude seeing it *also* as the symbol of the union of the ultimate creative principles? Should not symbols be multifaceted? Is versatility not an asset, a richness, here? Is it a sacrilege to see it as a possible phallic symbol? I am, of course, neither a father of the Church nor a doctor in theology, but I do seem to recall that before the cross, the sign of Jesus Christ was the fish, an undoubtedly phallic symbol. Even today, in Southern Italy, the same word means both a fish and the male genitalia: if in doubt, go to the harbor in Naples and ask the fishwives.

Lingam—a Definition

The word *linga* means a "sign," "The sign through which we know the ultimate nature of everything is a linga" (*Shiva Purâna*, 1, 16, 106). *Linga* therefore refers to both the male *and* female sex organs, together, united, their union being the visible sign of universal creativity.

Regardless of a person's religious or philosophical background, the very existence of the universe implies that of a cosmic energy—the Shakti of Tantra—which generates forms, *ad infinitum*, from galaxies to atoms, from viruses to whales. The origin of all living beings lies in the union of the sexes, the union of the male and female principles. This cosmic dynamism is present and active in sexual intercourse. It symbolizes the transition from the non-manifested to the manifested world. For a new being, potentially present in his/her parents' genes, to be born in to the manifested world, sexual desire must be awakened. Maïthuna follows, and this is perceived, in Tantra, as the most "significant," most sacred of all acts. It has thus become Tantra's supreme symbol.

As regards the *lingam*, Guru Nishtûra Nanjanâcaryâ (who belongs to the Virashaiva branch) interprets it as Shiva, the Supreme, who can only be perceived through his manifestation, i.e., creation. He derives the word lingam from two roots *gam*, to go (out), to issue out, from which the idea of production is developed, or to go (deep), to penetrate in, to understand, and *lin*, to absorb, from which the idea of absorption is developed (*A Handbook of Vîrashaivism*, S. C. Nandimath, Delhi, 1979, p. 69). For Radhakrishnan, *lingam* also comes from the roots *lin* (to dissolve) and *ga* (to come out of, to produce) meaning "the ultimate reality where all creatures are dissolved and whence they emerge anew." Hence the two different spellings: linga and lingam.

Furthermore, and by virtue of the fact that an erect penis is the obvious "sign" that its procreative power has been awakened in a man, lingam also refers to the erect male organ.

Representations of the lingam range from simple steles with rounded tips to very elaborate symbols such as the one on the left. In the Shivaite temples in South India various allegorical-symbolical figures are carved on the lingam itself.

Shiva emerges from this stone lingam as the main figure. Above him is portrayed another member of the Hindu trilogy, Brahma (not to be confused with Brahman, with an "n," the Absolute) and below him, Vishnu, the third member.

A simple egg-shaped, erect stone is the most basic form of the lingam snugly inserted into the earth which is the feminine element.

An archaic form of the "sign," of the lingam, where the male stone is inserted into a rather realistic yoni.

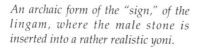

Here the egg-shaped stone rests upon an unusual base: it is bell-shaped, another symbol of the female sex organ.

One of the monoliths which stands erect on the prehistoric site of Filitosa, Corsica: an Indian Tantrist would immediately recognize a lingam. But is it not a purely male symbol? Where is the yoni, the female organ? Quite simply: the yoni is none other than the earth herself!

Denise Van Lysebeth examining one of the "lingams" of the prehistoric site in Filitosa, Corsica. This gives you an idea of their size!

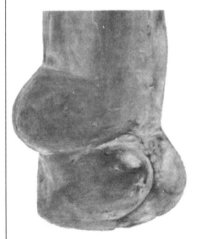

The lower half symbolizes female fertility: a woman's pregnant abdomen and well-shaped buttocks have been clearly represented!

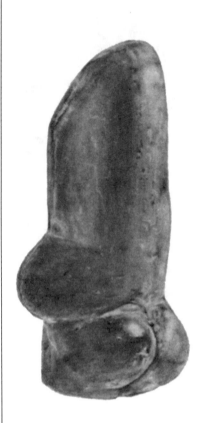 

This statue which belongs to the neolithic period and which was discovered in Italy, near Lake Trasimeno, is very original indeed: the artist managed in a very simple way to represent both the male and female principles. But only those who know can see them!

But if you consider the "back" side of the same statue, you will also notice a male organ, also well-delineated. The whole, which includes both Shiva and Shakti, deserves to be called a lingam, that is, a sign.

Shiva or the Career of a God

*Dance appears to have emerged
at the point of origin of all things, like Eros;
this primordial dance spawned
the choreography of the constellations, the stars
and the planets, in their harmonious relation
and interdependence...*

Aryans having heard of Shiva (most had not) despised him. Nevertheless, Shiva was to become, with the passing millennia, both a Hindu and a Tantric key-divinity. His upward mobility in the divine hierarchy to the point of becoming, along with Brahma and Vishnu, a member of the Hindu trinity, reveals his profoundly dynamic nature.

The well-known example of Santa Claus showed us how the subtle symbolism of a fictitious character makes it possible to gain intuitive access to deep mental strata that would be difficult to penetrate without him. Paradoxically, in awakening these archaic strata, he becomes more alive, more real than a real character.

Regarding Shiva, there is a wide consensus shared by Western and Indian scholars of Indian civilization according to which his worship dates back to the Dravidian civilization, rather than to the time of earlier, aboriginal peoples: "One may search from the foot of the Himalayas up to the Cape Comorin in vain to find even the slightest trace of any Tantric form of worship, of Siva or Kali, his wife, among these wild aboriginal people. Not even a phallic symbol of Siva has yet been found worshipped by these wild tribes" (N. Bose & Halder: *Tantras, their Philosophy and Occult Secrets*, Calcutta, 1956, p. 72).

Even his name is unknown, for it is so sacred and secret that people avoid pronouncing it. "Shiva" by which he is referred to throughout India, is a simple adjective meaning "the benevolent one," "the favorable one." "He is linked to the solar cult very common to primitive mankind; the name *shivan*, given to the sun, is similar to the tamil word *shivappu*, red, hence *shivan*, the Red one, meaning the rising sun. *Shivan* is also similar to the tamil words *schemmam* and *shemmai*, meaning prosperity, right-mindedness. Later on, the Red obe, *shivan*, became "of good omen," "prosperous," etc." (V. Parjoti, *Saiva Siddhanta*, p. 13). He is also called *Shambhu, Shamkara*, the kindly one, he-who-is-full-of-grace. Alain Daniélou believes that his true name is *An* or *Ann*, whereas others believe it to be *Hari*, that is, God, in the absolute sense.

Shiva, the enemy's god, was initially rejected by the Aryan invaders. But after conquering and subjecting the Dravidians, they became impressed by the worship universally afforded him by their serfs. They gradually got used to him and eventually took him on board. It is interesting, even amusing, to track Shiva's Aryanization process via his gradual rapprochement and assimilation with Rudra, a more than secondary Vedic god.

In all likelihood, the Rudras, like the Maruts, were defecting aborigines who joined ranks with the Aryans during the war of conquest, in exchange for which their chief Rudra was deified "very grudgingly, as a god of tears. He causes pain. The Vedic Rudra has not been given the same respect as the gods Indra, Varuna, Ashvini, Vâyu, etc. [...] Rudra has not been given any share of the offerings in the fire. His share, as a god of tears, is allocated outside the residential quarters in or near the cremation grounds" (Bhattacharya, *Saivism and the Phallic World*, New Delhi 1975, p. 216).

In the Shatarudrîya, Shiva-Rudra is sent out into the mountains and forests where he is likened to hunters, foresters, as well as robbers and thieves! What a reputation they carved out for him !

It is likely that the Brahmins, for whom this Aryan attraction to Shiva was growing tiresome, initially tried to make him as unsavory as possible: they went so far as to make him the god of diseases.

In creating Shiva, the incarnation of the male creative principle, the Dravidians acted in a way not unlike Voltaire's *mot*: "God created man in his own image, but man certainly returned the favor!" Shiva, i.e., the male creative principle, is one of the most powerful and ancient symbols of Tantra: he initially appears as *Pasupati* (the father and master of animals) on the Indus seal (p. 215), seated and surrounded by wild animals: the tiger, the buffalo, the elephant, the rhinoceros.

His horns symbolize lunar forces and/or the bull, his mount and the paragon of sexual vitality. Remember the bull's horns found in the sanctuaries of Tchatal-Hüyük and the horned god of the witches, who was turned into the devil in the Catholic Church's iconography. His three faces show that he gives rise to, maintains, and dissolves the universe. He is the god of yogis and his posture is such that his male attributes are well displayed.

After coming in through the back door of the Vedic pantheon, Shiva gradually climbed the rungs of its divine ladder and became

Vishnu's and Brahma's equal, thus constituting the dominant Hindu trilogy. However, this was done under the pressure of "popular demand," as we would say today.

Shiva was the Dravidians' favorite god. He embodied their resistance against Aryan occupying forces. There are countless legends about him and the following one expresses the enmity between the two Indias, that of the conquerors and that of the conquered. It starts with an idyll between Shiva and Sati, the daughter of the Aryan king Daksha. Sati is in love with Shiva. She marries him against her father's will and goes off to live with him on Mount Kailash, in the Himalayas. After many years spent far away from her family, Sati learns one day that her father is organizing a sumptuous reception. Although she is not invited, she wants to go for she yearns to see her family again.

Her holy husband advises against it but for the first time she takes no heed. When she arrives there, the entire Aryan *crème de la crème* is already in attendance: kings, princes, noblemen and their wives,

Steatite seal of a proto-Shiva, the Lord of Animals, sitting in a yogic position and with well-marked male attributes. The original seal is in the New Delhi National Museum and its size is approximately 3.5 x 3.5 cm.

everybody is dressed for the occasion. When her father sees this defector for love, clad in rags, he feels dishonored, and turning white with rage, he yells out abominable insults aimed at Shiva. This is too much for poor Sati. She faints, never to awaken.

The sad news spread like bushfire throughout the city. Upon hearing it Shiva was infuriated. All of his "supporters," the little people, rose and rebelled *en masse*. The rioting rocked the entire city. General resentment toward Brahmanical tyranny, pent up for so long, was let loose. The site of the ceremony was ransacked, desecrated and Sati's father, Daksha, was humiliated. The crowd demanded that Shiva be proclaimed the equal of the other Aryan gods. In order to placate the mob and defuse their rage, the Brahmins agreed to incorporate Shiva into the Hindu pantheon.

The legend describes the rebellion in such vivid terms and is still so popular today that it has been published as a comic book! The Indian subcontinent—remember one human being in five is an Indian—is a volcano, with pressure mounting underneath the crust of their millennia-old Aryan structure. When India explodes the world will indeed feel the tremors.

According to his iconography, Shiva's favorite weapons are first his trident, then his lasso. "Officially," the trident—not Neptune's or Club Med's!—symbolizes the three *gunas* of *Samkhya* (*sattwa, raja, tama guna*) or the three *nadis* (subtle energy channels) of yoga: *Ida, Pingala* and *Sushumna*.

But for those who know, its meaning stems from an altogether different source. The trident was the Dravidians' favorite weapon but its Aryan counterpart had four prongs. The Rigveda (152.7 and 8) states that: "Holding a four-pronged weapon (*Chaturashri*) they (Mitra and Varuna) kill the holders of tridents." The Indian Rajmohon Nath, in *Rigveda Summary* (Shilling, 1966, p. 83) includes the following comment on the above verse: "This gives a clue as to the ancient quarrel between the two sects, which still continues in India (to this day)." Most people keep this to themselves. Those who "spill the beans" are few and far between! Nevertheless symbols are open and everyone is free to see in them what they like. Therefore the official version is an option, too!

Shiva, the Divine Dancer

The above is interesting, no doubt, but honestly, we Westerners may not feel all that moved by Shiva's great adventures and misfortunes. However, the myth of Shiva, the divine dancer, may have meaning and relevance for us by virtue of its universal symbolism.

To better seize its significance, let us go back in time and review what dance has meant from time immemorial for humankind. Modern men and women only dance at parties or discos. Choreography has become an artform, a performance, the realm of professionals. For archaic people, on the contrary, and even today in "primitive" cultures, dancing was/is the most significant spontaneous tribal activity. Dancing punctuates every event of the tribe's life: marriage, birth, mourning. They have their rain dance, their hunting dance, their war dance, and can go on unflaggingly, throughout the night. Dancing is also a very special means of awakening the collective psyche, the overmind of the tribe. A state of ecstasy may thus be reached. The dancers can become attuned to the rhythms and mysterious powers of the cosmos.

The following text was written by the French dancer and choreographer Maurice Béjart who also expresses this very same Tantric vision of dancing: "To dance... is first and foremost to communicate, to unite, to join, to speak to the innermost depths of the other person's being. Dancing is uniting, the union of man with man, of man with the cosmos, of man with God.

"The spoken word belongs to the realm of illusion; even when we think we understand them, words conceal or unveil deceitful images, draw us into the never-ending labyrinth of the semantics of Babel. When men talk for a long time they seldom reach an agreement. To discuss is to argue. Language divides.

"To dance is also to speak the language of animals, to communicate with stones, to understand the song of the sea, the breath of the wind, to discourse with the stars, to approach the very throne of existence. It means totally transcending our poor human condition in order to fully participate in the profound life of the cosmos.

"When African dance was revealed to me, I experienced the purest, most complete, most human and most utterly real joy and certainty" (*L'homme et la Danse*, Paris, 1985, p. 75).

Former Senegalese President and poet Léopold Sédar Senghor adopted the same stance: "To express the highest spirituality, African dance uses the appearances of our visible world only to better penetrate them so as to grasp the archetypal images lying in the inner recesses of ancestral memory: the representational symbols that express spiritual surrealities. Its means are the same as Negro-African artists', for analogical images would be meaningless, they would not be symbols without a melody and rhythm, without singing and dancing."

In dancing, man and woman can also gain access to all things sacred. In powerful sanctuaries, such as the Lascaux caves, the ground still bears the traces of prehistoric dancers' footprints. Moreover, sexual rites probably took place there.

Dancing can be erotic. The Church knowingly prohibited the waltz and the tango deemed too sensuous (the sin of lust!). Dancing can be magic. Early neolithic farmers would dance near their fields at the time of sowing or the harvest to awaken human sexual potency in order to enhance, by contamination as it were, their soil's fertility. These rites also included collective intercourse.

In India, dancing has always played a special role for it originated in temples. At the beginning, these erotic dances were a prelude to ritual, therefore sacred, sexual intercourse, which took place in the temple itself. In those days dancers were genuine *dévadâsis*, servants of the god. Then the Brahmins came along. They were quick to spot the nice profit that could be made by exploiting the dancers. Consequently, the temples were eventually turned into brothels! See the chapter on this subject.

What is the connection between the above and Shiva, the divine dancer? Firstly, dancing means rhythm, and rhythm permeates the entire universe. In the final analysis, the essence of the cosmos is energy endowed with rhythm and consciousness: night and day, the movements of heavenly bodies testify to this. But rhythm also lies within the atom. The rhythm of the vibrations of the quartz in our watches measures the beats of the universe. Life is rhythm. Consider a simple hen's egg a few hours after being fertilized: a pulse begins where the future heart will beat. Rhythm precedes both the organ and the embryo.

Incidentally, dancing may provide us with an intuitive answer to a question which remains insoluble on a purely intellectual level: why did God go to such lengths to create a gigantic universe composed of billions of galaxies? Did not God suffice unto Himself? Why bother creating such an imperfect world? Tantra's answer is that the manifestation is Shiva-Lila, a game, a dance. For neither a game nor a dance requires any justification, they suffice unto themselves.

Shiva is surrounded by flames. In the Tantric perspective, he dances in the midst of the cosmic fire which sculptors have had to represent as a single ring of flames. Moreover, fire is one of humankind's essential symbols for not only is it our oldest companion but it exists throughout the universe, including in our bodies: life entails slow and controlled combustion. A corpse is cold. On the cosmic level, consider the countless galaxies, each one made up of billions of suns, with temperatures reaching billions of degrees: it is true to say that except for the planets, all celestial bodies are ablaze. Even on our own planet, cosmic fire lies beneath our feet, under the earth's thin crust, thinner than an egg shell, comparatively speaking!

Deciphering Shiva's Dance

In South India, the most famous variant of Shiva's dance is the *Nadanta*, represented on page 220. This is a sketch of a modern bronze statuette I found in Tamil Nadu a little while back. The worship of Shiva is alive and well in that "neck of the woods"! The keys to Shiva's dance are indicated on the sketch. These symbols may be self-evident for Indians, but we need a few additional clues to decipher them. The most striking feature of the sculpture: Shiva's four arms.

The *drum* he holds in his right hand confirms his pre-Aryan origin: Dravidians are formidable drummers. The drum, the *damaru*, represents the primordial sound, symbolically speaking. In the *Unmai Villakam*, verse 36, it is said that: "Creation comes from the drum..." Was this an early intuitive insight into 20th-century physics' big-bang theory? Both startling and uncanny, to say the least.

With his *right hand* raised in *abhaya mudra*, Shiva says: "I protect."

The *fire* which transforms and destroys, emanates from the hand touching the ring of flames. Shiva, all alone, holds the reins of the three cosmic functions: to create, to protect, to dissolve. For the Brahmins, on the other hand, Brahma is in charge of creation, Vishnu protects, and last *and* very much least, Shiva has the none-too-glorious power of destruction!

Finally, the *hand pointing* toward his raised right foot liberates anyone who has penetrated the myth by revealing to him/her the essence of the cosmos.

For Tantrists the *left foot* treading on an *evil dwarf* symbolizes Shiva's Aryan ex-father-in-law who was responsible for the death of his beloved Sati. "Officially," it represents the demon Muyalaka holding a cobra. The statue is mounted on a lotus-shaped pedestal.

His *hair* is peppered with symbols. Jewels adorn his braids and his curled, swirling locks show the impetuousness of his dance which maintains, upholds the universe. Another fantastic intuition: a grain of sand is insignificant and motionless to my eyes. Yet electrons spin around an atom's nucleus at a speed of thousands of miles per second. If all of a sudden all the electrons and all cosmic energy came to a grinding halt, the universe would collapse back into the "dynamic void" (*akasha*) whence it came!

There is a *cobra* in his hair but it does him no harm.

The *skull* is Brahma's! The *nymph* says that the Ganges springs from the top of his head. Add to this the *crescent of the moon*. He is crowned with a *garland* of *Cassia*, a sacred plant. On his right ear he wears a *man's earring*, on his left ear, a *woman's earring*, showing that both sexes are united within him. His *jewelry* highlights his divinity: he wears elaborate necklaces and his belt is studded with precious

Ganges

Hair

Drum

Destructive Fire

Cobra

"I protect."

"I liberate."

Flaming ring

Malevolent Dwarf

stones. He wears bracelets on his wrists, ankles and arms, and rings on his fingers and toes! He is *clad* in tight-fitting, tiger-skin breeches and has a scarf. And to flout the Brahmins, he also sports the sacred thread.

The overall impression is one of easy, light, graceful impetuousness: Shiva-Lila is a "game"! In spite of his frenzied dance, Shiva's face remains serene. In the middle of his forehead, his *third eye* is open, the eye of intuition which pierces appearances and transcends the sensorial world.

For those who can see and perceive it, Shiva's dance reveals, in a strikingly condensed form, the Ultimate. Shiva is thus *Nataraja*, the Lord of the Dance, the name of *Nataraja* Guru, precisely. What a symbol!

The *Tandava* is also one of Shiva's popular dances: Shiva-Bhairava dances wildly at night on cremation grounds, accompanied by frolicking imps. This is clearly a pre-Aryan dance and here Shiva is half-god, half-demon. This dance is performed in places as distant from one another as Elephanta, Ellora, and Bhubaneshwara.

The Myth of Shiva and Modern Science

Contrary to what too many people still believe, Tantra is more—much more!—than sexual worship. Tantra is first and foremost an initiatory tradition. Actually, this is almost tautological for a true tradition is perforce initiatory, that is, transmitted through symbolism and/or mythology. More specifically, "initiatory" means an intuitive, non-discursive, non-intellectual, non-rational approach to reality and its hidden wellsprings, to become better integrated into it. A tradition works in the opposite way of science. The latter is, by definition, an organized system of *information* on the facts and laws of the manifested universe. Science situates itself on the purely cerebral level . One of its self-proclaimed, key qualities is objectivity. But in spite of appearances, the Tantric and scientific approaches are far from being mutually exclusive. They are, on the contrary, complementary.

This does not apply to scientism and its adepts for whom symbols and myths are simplistic beliefs of the past. They might go so far as to consider them worthy of study out of pure historical interest, for example, but that's about it! Using them for their own personal development or to grasp the essence of the cosmos? No way! Strange? Not really. After all, our type of civilization owes the better part of its development and originality to science and its corollary, technology: never has humankind acquired so much knowledge in so short a time, never has it had so much material power at its fingertips. It was easy therefore to jump to the conclusion that this technical/scientific approach was the *only* valid one!

The price we have to pay for these undeniable accomplishments is a hypertrophied intellect, one that measures, weighs, computes, compares and contrasts, makes inferences and deductions. But for all its efficiency and effectiveness, this *démarche* barely scratches the surface of things and can never hope to reach the ultimate truths behind phenomena. Even when science splits the nucleus of an atom or discovers the cell's secrets, when astronomy explores the outer reaches of the inter-galactic void, it all remains superficial: the observer is supposed to remain neutral and not get involved.

Paradoxically, the more the intellect believes that it can, alone, approach ultimate realities, the more they slip through its fingers, so to speak. This endless chase reminds me of something that happened when I was 10 years old: there had just been a storm and I can still see in my mind's eye that beautiful rainbow, so bright and shiny against jet-black clouds. It was so clear and well-defined and seemed so real that it looked like it had been put there, on the waterlogged meadow in front of a row of willow trees. I jumped on my spanking new bike and rushed toward it for a close-up look. Boy was I disappointed! The closer I got, the further away the rainbow "moved" and when I reached the willows, it was way over there in front of the grove! Ultimate reality is like a rainbow that science is running after, in vain.

Such a quest *could* be exciting for science if it did not lead to an impasse. For science, the daughter of intellect and the mother of technology, raises and gives rise to more problems than it solves.

By definition, our intellect can only reason and compute "coolly." So when science claims to be "objective," that is literally true: it reduces the universe to a mere "object." The universe is thus made up of an infinite number of "objects." Everything becomes an "object," even living matter. Humans have created an abyss between their artificial, technological universe and nature; between intellectual abstraction and actual, living, experience. Instead of demystifying things as it purports to do, the intellect demythologizes, desacralizes.

When nothing is sacred anymore, not even life, what a free-for-all the planet becomes: natural resources are shamelessly and ruthlessly depleted, with barely any letting up even when human life is threatened! Animal-objects are subjected to man's "goodwill" as he unflaggingly mass-produces cows, pigs, hens, and what not, the name of the game being money and a blind eye to the animals' suffering. Who cares?

Is the root-cause of the current world crisis (that no one denies save those who would hear and see nothing) to be sought elsewhere? Humans have alienated themselves from nature and somewhere along the way from *their own* nature. We have uprooted ourselves and like an uprooted tree we shall disappear, unless we find our roots again. I raised the following question in my book *Yoga Self-taught*: "Should laboratories be shut down and scientists incarcerated?" I naturally answered "No," for I am convinced that science and Tantra (including Tantra's symbolism and mythology) are perfectly compatible. It would be unreasonable and unrealistic to want to do away with the intellect and its baby, science. But if we want to prevent this incomparable tool of ours from becoming barren and unproductive, we must urgently add to it a symbolic and even a mythological dimension. I believe modern physics, the spearhead of science, and Nataraja, *can* be reconciled.

Nataraja and the Physicist

Modern physics and oriental thought are compatible and complementary. As nuclear physics makes ever greater strides forward, our visible, familiar, reassuring world gives way to another strange and imperceptible universe which dissolves into the physicist's mathematical formulae. Objects which our senses present to us as impenetrable and solid become a void, whirling force fields of pure energy, the Shakti of Tantrism. Utterly confused, unable to keep up, our minds eventually give up trying to understand, and it is likely that over the years, the hiatus between our intellect and reality will increase, as will our feeling of helplessness. Through its myths and symbols which transcend the intellect, Tantra can quiet this mental vertigo.

Fritjof Capra described this in his book *The Tao of Physics* (Berkeley, 1975): "I was sitting by the ocean one late summer afternoon, watching the waves rolling in and feeling the rhythm of my breathing, when I suddenly became aware of my whole environment as being engaged in a gigantic cosmic dance. Being a physicist, I knew that the sand, rocks, water and air around me were made of vibrating molecules and atoms, and that these consisted of particles which interacted with one another by creating and destroying other particles. I knew also that the earth's atmosphere was continually bombarded by showers of 'cosmic rays,' particles of high energy undergoing multiple collisions as they penetrated the air. All this was familiar to me from my research in high-energy physics, but until that moment I had only experienced it through graphs, diagrams and mathematical theories....Later came the experience of the Dance of Shiva... which was followed by many similar experiences which helped me gradually to realize that a consistent view of the world is beginning to emerge from modern physics which is harmonious with ancient Eastern wisdom....

I also hope to find among my readers many physicists with an interest in the philosophical aspects of physics, who have as yet not come in contact with the religious philosophies of the East. They will find that Eastern mysticism provides a consistent and beautiful philosophical framework which can accommodate our most advanced theories of the physical world" (pages xv and xvi).

Sitting on that beach, Fritjof Capra had a spontaneous Tantric experience. His intellect had known for a long time that matter is condensed energy. But that had remained an abstract, "cold" concept, not something he had actually experienced. All of a sudden, his knowledge became a unitive perception and living reality revealed to him the hidden meaning of the myth of Shiva, the Cosmic Dancer. *That* is the essence of Tantra: through its symbols and myths, its rites and practices, to go beyond the intellect and grasp ultimate reality, without depending on a chance, spontaneous experience. When it does happen, all of a sudden the pseudo-borders between the illusory universe created by our senses and the underlying, invisible, but real universe, between the spiritual and the material worlds, are dissolved.

Fritjof Capra did indeed *perceive* the rhythmic vibration of the cosmos, *see* the energy-nature of the universe, *hear* its universal sound, not with his eyes and ears, but with his internal organ of perception, his intuition, his "third eye."

The time has therefore come to conciliate and reconcile science and Tantra. For the physicist, the direct perception of reality is a new and striking experience. And for Tantra, it is perfectly natural for modern science to confirm the Tantric view of the cosmos.

Shiva and Parvati (Bronze sculpture, Madras Museum).

Shakti:
Creative Nature

If such a thing as a Tantric coin existed, the obverse would be Shakti, female creative power, and the reverse would be Shiva, her male aspect, both inseparable. Like heads and tails, on either side of the same coin, they are united and indissociable. In Tantra, Shaivism favors Shiva, whereas the Shakta current, or Shaktism gives priority to Shakti on the basis of the Tantric saying: "Without Shakti, Shiva is a shava," that is, a corpse.

Translated into more habitual terms, Shakti is the creativity of Nature. But "Nature" is an abstract concept and the human mind abhors abstractions. When personified, Nature (Mother Nature as she is sometimes referred to in English), becomes a Tantric "goddess," the Shakti, the Universal Creative Energy that Tantrists perceive, beyond myths and symbols, as immanent in everything our senses perceive. A non-Tantrist taking a stroll in a forest may feel in harmony with nature. Great! But if I put on my Tantric "glasses" I see in this mighty beech tree the Shakti, universal creative and organizing dynamism: the forest suddenly becomes a gigantic swirl of vital energy.

A swirl in which each tree, each blade of grass, each living being is an extraordinary force field, a whirl of intelligent, pure energy in the infinite ocean of life, an ocean where all borders are dissolved. My own body is also this primordial energy. Energy and Wisdom! Energy and Intelligence. In the chapter "An Unknown Universe: My Body" (p. 53), I mentioned this Supreme Intelligence at work here and now, day and night, from conception (and even before) to the dissolution we call death (and probably beyond). Borne and guided by it, I feel safe and secure: it protects me at all times against the onslaughts of the outside world. It keeps me alive for it is Universal Life expressing itself through "me."

Through it, Tantra brings me back to the times of archaic man and woman who lived in a magical universe, whereas our contemporaries, obsessed with their desacralizing science, no longer perceive the magic of the universe or the magic in their own being, especially their own body. Our planet could have been a big arid stone, as dusty as the moon, lost in the frozen void. Instead, Life and its magic have given rise to the infinite variety of beings, a magic whose ultimate source science is not about to comprehend.

Archaic man and woman felt they were living in the midst of invisible benevolent or hostile forces. When they saw the myriad beings spawned by our fruitful and nurturing earth, they perceived its sacred character. As farmers (agriculture was invented by women) they named the Earth the Great Goddess, the Mother-of-All-Living-things. Then Women's and the Earth's fertility were combined, as expressed, for example, in an amazing seal found in Mohenjo-Daro (or was it Harappa?) showing a woman upside down, giving birth to an entire tree, with its trunk and branches!

Dravidian Goddesses *ad Infinitum*

While "giving birth" to this chapter, I was wondering whether or not I should try your patience by telling you about India's innumerable divinities, so alien and remote. I decided against it. Actually such an undertaking would be unthinkable: each and every Dravidian village has its own *amma* or *mata*, its own local "little mother," usually the deified spirit of a deceased woman. Imagine the task! Incidentally, they are always goddesses, not gods like in the Vedic pantheon.

They often possess a fearsome, terrifying side, for sometimes the goddess devours her own children. In the same way Mother Nature can be cataclysmic, wreaking havoc, especially in India where extreme environmental conditions are the rule: searing temperatures, devastating monsoon rains, lethal animals, deadly epidemics.

Among these fearsome divinities is Poleramma, the goddess of smallpox. When she is angry, she makes people sick, but when placated, she becomes the healer. Her temple stands outside the village and in order to be pacified, she demands blood. A goat, an ox, or a chicken are sacrificed to her. Villagers suffering major natural disasters used to believe that the ultimate sacrifice, a human sacrifice, was required to avert cataclysms. There were volunteers who received the highest honors, for, like kamikazes, they gave up their own lives for others. Superstition? Probably, and if I contracted smallpox, I would not resort to killing a hen just to placate Poleramma!

Indians are thus very superstitious people, especially in the South, and they live in a state of constant fear. Since they believe that misfortune mainly befalls happy people, they must avoid—at all costs—doing anything that might attract evil spirits. If you are invited to the home of an Indian friend, the worst thing you can do is compliment your host on his/her beautiful children or lovely house: that would only attract the evil eye. Politeness requires picking out flaws and being critical of everything. Uninformed Westerners are shocked upon hearing an Indian father call his son "idiot," "trash," "crooked"! But you *may* compliment the child on his necklace or clothes for that deflects the attention of evil spirits. Likewise, Westerners are disappointed when an Indian friend criticizes their designer house or snazzy new car.

Above and beyond these innumerable goddesses and for all their superstition, even the humblest of villagers knows very keenly that each local goddess is but one aspect, one facet of the Great Goddess. Nonetheless, over the centuries, a few goddesses have risen from the pack and their universal, archetypal essence appeals and speaks to our innermost being.

Tantric Goddesses

The above applies to Tantric goddesses, most of whom are married to Shiva who draws his energy from them. Unlike the dreary wives of gods in the Vedic pantheon, they are at least his equal, often his superior. Their legends have a significant symbolical and mythological content, like our fairy tales. In Himalayan heaven, Shiva and his wife Parvati spend their time making love or having philosophical discussions. When Shiva is the teacher, that is called *agâma*. Conversely, when his wife is the teacher, that is *nigâma*.

Another one of Shiva's favorite spouses is the faithful Sati, mentioned earlier.

But two goddesses are more specifically Tantric and symbolic: Kâli and Durga, who are actually a single goddess. We are more sensitive to their symbolism for they bring us back to the greater Alpino-Mediterranean area of our ancestors. In this respect, W. C. Beane (*Myth, Cult and Symbols in Shâkta Hinduism*, Leiden, 1977, p. 67) was struck by: "The fact of religio-symbolic resemblances between, apparently, the oldest Indian civilization and those of the Middle or Late Neolithic Mediterranean area or Central and Western Asia has led scholars, both Western and Hindu, to adopt conclusions ranging from theories of extra-Indian diffusion eastward to pan-indigenous religious development (but heading westward)," therefore toward India.

This made a very strong impression on—*inter alia*—Laksmanshastri Joshi, *Stone Age Cultures of Central India* (Poona, 1978, p. 25): "In the earlier civilizations of Egypt, Crete, and Mesopotamia are... found the Gods of Shiva, Vishnu, the Goddess Kali and the worship of the Naga (Cobra), Linga (genital organs), the moon, the Graha (the planets), and the ancestors.... Hinduism thus inherits a number of things peculiar to the civilization which arose along the banks of the Nile, the Tigris and the Euphrates and the Indus."

The above supports the thesis that the Dravidians, as Alpino-Mediterraneans, traveled toward India, along with their myths and symbols, the same ones as in Tantra, the ones which trigger echoes in our collective memory.

In any case, their direction—westward (my conviction) or east-ward—is immaterial, the main point being the constant ties between India and primitive Europe. One thing *is* sure, however: these Tantric goddess-symbols were *not* born of the barbarian and bearded Aryans. In their specifically Dravidian and Tantric form, I can nevertheless accept the hypothesis of a mixed origin, that is, a creation of the Dravidians and the pre-Dravidian, aboriginal peoples.

Kâlî, Kâla, Kalki

I have not hitherto indulged in etymological hairsplitting. But in the case of *Kâli*, the name's etymological ambiguity is highly symbolical. Starting with the Dravidian root *Kâl*, black, Kâlî becomes the black goddess, the horrible destroyer who wreaks terror, and Kâla, the black god, sometimes identified with Shiva. The Aryans borrowed the roots *kâl, kal, khal* from the Dravidian languages, then they equated *black* with *destruction*, turning the lot into Time, *Kâla*, the great Destroyer (male). However, neither he nor Kâlî-The-Black-One has a Vedic origin: the Rigveda mentions neither.

Kâlî, the black goddess, belongs to the realm of lunar symbolism. *Kâl* is the Dravidian word for "black moon," i.e., the last quarter, the non-manifestation phase. She is also the Goddess-in-the-Moon and in her iconography, where she symbolizes the entire cosmos, you find the number sixteen, the sacred number which represents the sixteen phases of the moon, as illustrated by her sixteen arms. Her forehead bears the crescent of the moon. She therefore belongs to cyclical time.

As Adyakâlî, she is without form, therefore inconceivable for the human mind. She is non-manifestation, non-time, without beginning or end, without attributes. When she becomes Kâlî, she generates manifested Time, the one in which we live, which produces the universe of which it is the fourth dimension. Like Chronos devouring his own children, she will, at the "end of all time," reabsorb everything she has generated.

Her symbolism is as ambiguous as the etymology of her name. Firstly, as the Great Destroyer, as the Terrible Mother, it is normal for her to wreak fear and horror. She is nonetheless portrayed over and over in a very rich iconography, and found throughout Tantric art: artists wanted to paint her as "black" (literally) and horrible as possible.

The ambiguity is twofold: first in her official symbolism, secondly in her more specifically Dravidian, "closet," significance. According to the official interpretation, she is portrayed as black, as dark as a moonless night, because black erases all differences, all distinctions. She is naked, clad in space, because she has discarded the veils of illusion. Her face is horrible: in order to better devour all her creatures, her fangs are as nasty as Dracula's. The blood she drinks is shown dripping from her mouth and she exhibits a tongue of fire.

When she is represented with only four arms, one left hand brandishes a two-edged sword (*khadga*), the other one holds by the hair the bloody head she has just cut off. One of her right hands holds a slipknot or a lasso (*pâsha*), the other one a lance (*khatvânga*) with a skull mounted on it. It is all very macabre, but that's not all: her necklace and her belt are made of rows of human heads; two dangling corpses hang from her ears and on her wrists are bracelets also made of severed heads or skulls. Lastly, she tramples on a corpse. Officially this means that nothing or no one can escape her grip, escape death or destruction. In the same vein, the scene often depicts corpses roasting or being torn to shreds by jackals.

Tantrists accepted the aforementioned official symbolism to which they added their own symbols. Sorry, reverse the sequence: in the beginning was the original Tantric-Dravidian Kâlî who was eventually superseded by the "official" one. If you want to fully grasp her secret, Dravidian significance, you must notice that all the heads, all the corpses are *male* and have either a *white* or a swarthy complexion: no women, no dark-skinned people.

Surprisingly, Aryan Brahmanism never noticed or took offense at the fact that there are only white corpses. But once you *realize* why, it all becomes clear! The Alpino-Mediterraneans were of mixed, indigenous origin, lived in the hot Indian tropical climate and had dark skin like Dravidians today. But their northern enemies were "pale faces."

This information provides the necessary clarification. In *Markandeya Purana*, we read that Ambîka, the protecting Good Mother, she-who-ensures-bumper-crops, "when expressing her wrath towards the enemies, her face becomes as black as ink.... Hence Kâli's terrifying aspect" (in Spain when somebody is furious, they also say that the person "becomes black"). Kâlî is therefore an emanation of the Good Mother, a manifestation of her ire toward her enemies. Now, who were the Dravidians' enemies if not the fearful Aryans? Kâlî thus incarnates hatred for the Aryans and in order to better fight and crush them she is heavily armed with the Dravidians' favorite weapons, except for the trident which is Shiva's prerogative.

The Indian war of conquest was a fierce one and the Dravidian warriors fought the Aryans every inch of the way. But the superior weaponry of the latter and above all, their chariots, were a decisive factor. The following excerpt from the *Puranâ-nûru*, Tamil poems translated by von Glasenapp, *Les littératures de l'Inde* (Paris, 1963) exude hatred and heroism:

> *Her veins became swollen and*
> *Her flesh fell loose on her body*
> *When the white-haired mother learnt*
> *Her son had turned and*
> *Run from the battlefield!*
> *Enraged, she swore if it were true*
> *She would cut off*
> *The very breasts that had fed him*
> *And she would cast them aside, herself.*
> *Carrying a sword,*
> *She rummages through the bloody battlefield*
> *And lo! underneath the slain bodies*
> *She finds her son, cut in two!*
> *Then truly her joy was greater than at*
> *The time she held him in her bosom.*

If possible, that mother would have turned into Kâlî herself, to avenge her son and all the other Dravidian heroes.... In this context, it is "normal" for all of the bodies slain by Kâlî to be both male and white since they are enemy warriors. This secret version, as logical as it is unofficial and which was passed on to me directly from the mouth of Nataraja Guru himself, casts a different light altogether on Kâlî and her image, her representation.

The Age of Kali, the Age of the Apocalypse

We are now living in the age of Kali, in *kali yuga*—do not confuse Kâlî with kali—that is, the Iron age, the twilight age before the end of time, as predicted by Indian scriptures. *Yuga* (not *yoga*!) means a quarter: the moon has four yugas. According to Mircea Eliade, *kali* means in this context "discord, conflicts, quarreling." It is an age in which human society reaches an all-time low of degeneracy, barbarism, disintegration. For Indians who are fond of playing dice, kali is the losing side of the dice, the one with a single dot.... The four yugas bear the names of the sides of playing dice:

Krita or Krita Yuga is the golden age of humankind, the side with four dots;
Treta or Treta Yuga is the silver age, the side with three dots;
Dvâpara or Dvâpara Yuga, the copper age, has two dots;
Kali or Kali Yuga is the one-dot, losing side.

As regards the aforementioned yugas, what do the ancient scriptures, the *Purânas*, say and predict? Nothing very exciting, I'm afraid: "In the Kali age, endowed with little sense, men, subject to all the infirmities of mind, speech and body, will daily commit sins; and every thing that is calculated to afflict beings, vicious, impure, and wretched, will be generated in the Kali age.

"In that end of the Kali Yuga, men will be united with heretical sects, they will strike friendship for the sake of women. This is without doubt.

"In the Iron age, there shall occur epidemics, famines, droughts, and revolutions. Men shall be devoid of virtue, possessed of slender powers, irascible, covetous, and untruthful.... There shall be a large number of beggars amongst the people; short life, lassitude, disease and misery shall prevail as consequences of sin and ignorance.

"...In the Iron age, even *Mahâdeva* the lord of all beings, the god of gods, shall have no divinity to man.

"The people shall steadily deteriorate by adopting a contrary course of life.... The people will be unholy, unrighteous and oppressed with disease and sorrow; and goaded by failure of rain they will be eager to destroy each other...

"Behold... the age of destruction is so horrible, that during it the clouds never fall on the surface of the earth as drops of rain for one hundred years. Being thus overpowered by what is wrought by time, the men gradually lead themselves to utter destruction" (Mukhopadyaya, *The Karma Purana*, pp. xxix, xxx).

"Hence, on the one hand the *Harivamsha* can tell us that in the last cycle will take place great wars, great tumult, great showers, and fears; know this to be the signs of sinfulness" (Harivamsha IV, *Barvishya Parva*, trans. Dutt, p. 827).

I have taken from Alain Daniélou's book *Shiva et Dionysos* (pp. 220-221), the *Linga Purâna's* most significant passages: "Men of the Kali Yuga are tormented with envy, irritable... indifferent to the consequences of their action.... Their desires are misdirected, their knowledge utilized for malignant ends.... Heads of State will be mostly of low origins and will be dictators and tyrants.... Thieves become kings and kings become thieves. Virtuous women are rare. Promiscuity is widespread.... The earth produces almost nothing in some places, and a great deal in others. The powerful appropriate the public weal and cease to protect the people.... Men without morals preach virtue to others.... Criminal associations are formed in towns and villages."

Other predictions in Indian scriptures are strongly reminiscent of the Apocalypse. But let us take heart: the age of Kali is supposed to last 432,000 years. In the *Mahânirvâna Tantra*, Shri Sadashiva has proclaimed that: "During the first three ages, this rite (of Tantra) was a great secret; men practiced all of that in secret and thus reached Liberation. When the age of Kali prevails, the followers of the Tantric rite Kula will have to declare themselves to be such and both at night and during the day, they will have to be initiated openly." W. C. Beane (p. 241) also mentions *Rudramayâla*: "I shall proclaim left-handed practice, the supreme *sâdhanâ* of Durgâ; following which the adept obtains *siddhi* speedily in this *Kali*-age."

The end of time, the end of the age of Kali, will be marked by the coming of Kalki, the last avatar of Vishnu. Both an avenger and a redeemer, he will come in the form of a warrior riding a winged white horse. In one hand he will brandish a sword, in the other a discus, for as the trident is Shiva's insignia, the discus is the insignia of Vishnu, the second member of the Hindu trilogy. Then he will destroy the world.

I would like to close this chapter with a question: should Kâlî become our favorite subject of meditation? Not necessarily, but it would have been unthinkable to publish this book without mentioning the fearsome Kâlî, since reality also includes terrifying aspects. Nevertheless, in the Tantric rite, the most accessible aspect of Shakti, of Primordial Cosmic Energy, is Woman, for every woman is a goddess.

Every Woman
is a Goddess

For Tantra, each and every woman incarnates the Goddess, *is* the Goddess, Absolute Woman, the Cosmic Mother. These words may make you laugh or shrug your shoulders; you may think they are but a stylistic device. Indeed, how is it possible to see in *every* woman you meet, a Goddess, in the total sense of the word? Consider a husband's reaction after a spat with his wife: "A Goddess? You've got to be kidding! More like a tigress!"

But for Tantra, the concrete perception of the divine aspect of each woman is a precondition to maïthuna and the Tantric ritual preceding this sacred sexual union aims at making one perceive this reality. How can we see the Goddess that is hidden in each and every woman?

There are several means. Firstly, save becoming an infant ourselves, we can at least consider the relationship between a newborn baby and its mother. The newborn is still a part of her flesh, and months, years will pass before it becomes, if not separate from her, at least autonomous. In the child's enchanted universe which revolves around mommy, she is the Ideal Woman. Let us be really nasty and portray her as an ugly, stupid and ill-tempered shrew. Does the infant see her like that? Of course not! As far as it is concerned, mommy is beauty, kindness and love incarnate, in a word, she is the Goddess. She is perfect, she knows everything, she cannot lie. Only later will the child discover the "real," commonplace, ordinary woman that his/her mother is, with all her faults, her hair curlers, her crankiness, her idiosyncrasies. For us adults who "know better," only the latter is the "real and true" woman, the rest is literature.

Is the baby's Divine Mother an illusion, a mere figment of its imagination? For Tantra, the child, not the adult, is right, because beyond appearances, a child perceives Ultimate Reality, the Divine Mother, Cosmic Life embodied in his/her "real," flesh-and-blood mother.

The other means of accessing the hidden Absolute in a woman (or in an ordinary man) is a very pleasant one indeed: all you need is love! We should feel sorry for any human who has never experienced

the wonderful state of being in love, the tremendous emotion trig-gered on meeting the (provisionally, at least) ideal being. Lovers embody for each other, beauty, perfection; they float around in a magic universe where everything is sheer rapture. A single word, the slightest touch, and they're on cloud nine! Then there is the first ren-dezvous, the first kiss, caresses, embracing: the great stuff that novels, plays and movies are made of!

But do lovers live in the real world, do they see reality as it is? We have all known a couple where a beautiful and intelligent young woman is hopelessly in love with a man who in our eyes, is neither handsome nor smart, nor young, nor even very rich! And we all think: "How on earth can she be attracted to that man? What does she see in him"? *We* know him, *we* know he is not very special, not very interest-ing, has no great personality or education. But *she* sees nothing of that! As far as she is concerned, he *is* the ideal man. A Tantrist would say: "He embodies Shiva." One day, when they are married, and perhaps when her bubble has burst, she will see him "really" and the couple will fall into the rut of daily routine, resigning themselves to their fate or eventually breaking up. The divine Shiva having vanished into thin air, people will say: "She has finally woken up, she now sees him as he is." Actually from the Tantric point of view, a woman in love per-ceives the ultimate reality that lies beyond the concrete, everyday character. And vice versa, for a man in love, his beloved is Shakti, the Goddess.

So we confuse what is superficial, commonplace, ordinary, with what is deep, real, concealed by appearances. Even physically, our actual body hides our true body: no one has fulfilled the potential of his/her true body, the one planned by nature, programmed in our genes. *That* is the real one, the one we pass on to future generations.

If, from conception to right now, I had had an ideal environment in all respects, corporeal, mental, spiritual, I would have manifested my genes to perfection and I would almost be a superhuman compared to what I am today.

The myth of the Goddess, of the Shakti, like the one of Shiva, includes all of that, plus all of the cosmic virtualities that are sealed in living matter. That is why a Tantrist worships the cosmic Shakti in all women. To *realize* this, to fulfill it, is one of Tantra's aims and is part of expanding one's consciousness, another aim of Tantra.

This involves Kundalini, that evolutionary dynamism which has compelled today's human to emerge from the prehominids of yore and which will perhaps, in the future, make him/her into a superhu-man, compared to us. Why not? But evolution is not linear: in fits and starts, it juggles with one or several species; in "lull" periods,

Kundalini is that mysterious dynamism which guides the evolution of a being from the fertilized ovum onwards. Tantra considers that Kundalini, located in the genitalia, the species pole, is linked to our life energy and sexuality. It is most often latent, "asleep," as symbolized by the sleeping serpent coiled around the lingam. Tantra seeks to "awaken" it, to materialize now some of the virtualities stored away for the future evolution of humankind.

Consider how far our short discussion on the Goddess embodied in each woman has led us.

The "Sinister" Path

A Western woman living in India where her husband had been post-ed, once wrote to me. She was surprised and troubled, she said in her letter, for a Catholic missionary had strongly advised her against Yoga which according to him "always leads to sexual practices." Actually, the comment made by this no doubt well-meaning priest reflected the Brahmins' loathing of Tantra and Yoga which they lump together, and rightly so, actually. Brahmanism contends that Tantra is a licentious, barbaric and odious cult leading to the most awful sexual perversions; there is no abjection, no crime that Tantrists have not been accused of and this is not a recent phenomenon, far from it! W. J. Wilkins, a good Anglican missionary, became so interested in Hindu mythology that he published in 1882, in Calcutta, a book so well written that an Indian publisher in Benares reprinted it in 1972 (*Hindu Mythology, Vedic and Puranic*, Varanasi, 1972) without changing a single word. In the chapter on Shakti worship, the author reveals the irreconcilable opposition between Hinduism and left-hand path Tantra:

"There is a cult of the Shakti, accepted and worthy of respect, named the Right Hand's Path, but there is another one, quite opposite to it, named the Path of the Left Hand. In the first, the ceremonies and rituals are performed openly and are not very distinct from those of other Hindu rites. The adepts of the Left Hand's Path take much care to keep secret to non-initiates the doctrine and practices which are their form of adoration. But what is known is enough to make one ashamed to have anything in common with this system. Eating meat, which is strictly forbidden to Hindus, drinking intoxicating drinks, as strictly forbidden, as well as gross obscene acts are part of this cult of the goddess."

Enough to ruin any Tantrist's reputation! The British, who on the faith of such assertions banned all public demonstrations of what they held to be unnameable excesses of lechery, merely managed to drive them "underground."

The Left-Hand Path which perpetuates the pre-Aryans' ancestral form of worship, involves sex because sex is indissociable from life: any view of the world denigrating such an essential aspect of being and of the cosmos is out-of-step with reality.

The Rigveda implicitly recognizes that the Left-Hand Path, Vama Marga, is Tantric, when it refers to the pre-Aryan god Shiva as "Vama" (Left).

As regards accusations and prejudices, D. N. Bose and Hiralal Haldar, in their book *Tantra, their Philosophy and Occult Secrets* (p. 9), have set the record straight: "It must, however, be admitted with reluctance that there are some prejudices even among the honest people against the Tantric creed on account of some of its rites and rituals, which would on superficial survey appear to be either highly licentious, or extremely cruel, or exceedingly loathsome. But if one only takes the trouble of going deeper into things he will find that they are neither licentious, nor cruel, nor loathsome, but they are some mystic rites and rituals (which have been degraded by the vicious people for their selfish ends and for the gratification of their animal appetites) calculated to help the devotee to advance along the path of moral perfection, which is absolutely essential for one's final emancipation."

The Left-Hand Path

In the minds of the (many) detractors of the so-called *Left-Hand* Path of Tantra, Tantrists are "sinister" characters, sexual perverts resorting to black magic, even human sacrifices. In this context, it is useful to remember the Latin word *sinister* = left. "Sinister" gradually came to mean "of ill omen" (by reason of being on the left), baleful, malign, nefarious, dismal, threatening, frightening. In India, a person's left *hand* is unclean for a very prosaic reason: having no toilet paper (practically impossible to find in India) a Hindu washes his/her anus with water and since this is done with the left hand, it must never touch food. One may well understand Indians' repulsion on seeing uninformed Westerners touching their food with their left hand: even if a Hindu were starving he/she would not accept food proffered by someone's left hand even if it had been thoroughly washed and sterilized! Speaking of hands, Hindus who abhor body-to-body contact, find the Western habit of the handshake repugnant. Only a tiny Westernized minority reluctantly deigns to shake our hand, even our right hand.

Brahmanism always makes a clear-cut distinction between disgusting, repulsive, *left-hand* Tantra, and *right-hand* Tantra, the only decent one as far as it is concerned. This reference to the left (hand) is purposely biased and tendentious for in Tantra, *Vama Marga* (*Vama* = left, *Marga* = Path) has nothing to do with the left *hand*!

I share the opinion of Francis King (*Sexuality, Magic and Perversion*, London, 1971): "A good deal of nonsense has been talked about these terms, 'left-hand' and 'right-hand,' by Western occultists who, following H. P. Blavatsky's erroneous interpretation of them, have endeavored to endow them with some moral significance—the transition from 'left' to sinister, and from thence to 'evil' is an easy, and misleading one for the European to make. In reality the terms have no moral significance whatsoever. They simply express the plain fact that in rites culminating in physical sexuality the woman practitioner sits on the left of the male, whilst in those in which the copulation is merely symbolic, she sits on his right" (p. 35). And I might add that in the symbolism of the androgyne, the female side is always on the left. Vama Marga is therefore the female path, no more, no less!

To follow the Left-Hand Path—and to assert it!—is to bring much neo-Brahmanical wrath upon oneself, including the swamis', most of whom belong to the "establishment." Aghehananda Bharati wrote: "Some subjects are tabu to the Brahmins and the Indian Pandits, and Tantra is the object of a very strict tabu" (*The Tantric Tradition*, London, 1965, p. 28). So when you hear Tantra spoken ill of and much maligned, which will no doubt happen, you will know where the attack comes from and why. I personally reconciled myself to the idea a long time ago. I just think of the Arab proverb: "The dogs bark, the caravan passes and it goes far."

The Myth of the Androgyne

The highly symbolical Tantric drawing on page 241 comes from Innmann's book, *Ancient Faiths*, published in India over a century ago, in 1868 to be precise. It portrays the *Ardhanari*, the Indian androgyne, half-Shiva, half-Shakti. Shiva is on the right, obviously, and we recognize his main attributes: his necklace is a cobra whose tail is curled around his neck and whose hood rises above the god's head. Shiva's hairstyle is typically male as is his earring; another snake—a sexual symbol in all traditions—obviously not a cobra, is coiled around Shiva's arm.

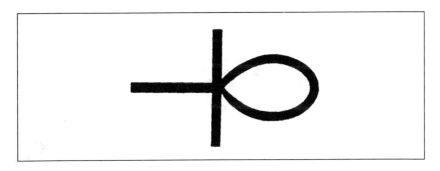

Ardhanari, the androgyne, symbolizes the unity of cosmic origins. The primordial Adam was also both male and female and each and every human being includes features of both sexes. Although he appears to be a male god, Shiva is actually androgynous. That is why he wears a woman's earring on his left ear and a man's earring on his right ear. Lastly, is it because our heart is on the left side of our body that the left is Shakti's side?

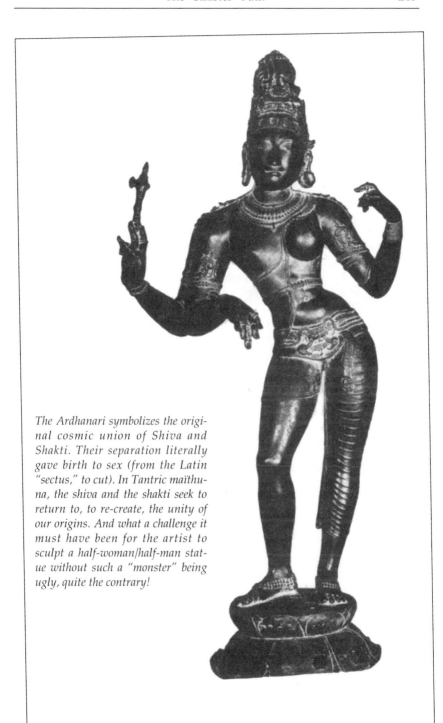

The Ardhanari symbolizes the original cosmic union of Shiva and Shakti. Their separation literally gave birth to sex (from the Latin "sectus," to cut). In Tantric maïthuna, the shiva and the shakti seek to return to, to re-create, the unity of our origins. And what a challenge it must have been for the artist to sculpt a half-woman/half-man statue without such a "monster" being ugly, quite the contrary!

The left half is Shakti, of course. One recognizes the curve of her hip and the fullness of her breast, as well as her earring in the same style as those worn by Indian women. Her half-necklace as well as her half-belt are also typical of those worn by women, as are her anklets. She is the goddess of fertility, therefore of plants and water, and she holds a lotus in her hand. The couple stands on an enormous lotus-flower floating on the primordial waters.

To portray their sexual union, the artist has very visibly placed, where the sex organs are, the Egyptian ankh, the loop of which obviously represents the yoni since it lies to the left, Shakti's side, whereas the cross symbolizes the male sex organ. The ankh, in this strategic and central position, captures the sexual union of Shiva and Shakti. If one refers to the etymology of the word "lingam," i.e., "sign" (of the union of the male and female principles), the ankh can indeed be considered to be a true lingam.

Given the trade relations (by sea and land) which have existed since earliest antiquity between India and Egypt, this correspondence should come as no surprise. Moreover, there is no point in trying to ascertain who borrowed the ankh from whom, the Indians or the Egyptians. The point is its symbolism and *that* is perfectly clear!

Purushâyayta: "Reversed act" missionary posture.

Upavishta: A seated posture.

Upavishta (or *Sukhasana*): The "Happy Posture" upon a seat.

Uttana Bandha: Variation of the missionary posture.

Tiryakâsana: The asymmetric or "sideways" posture.

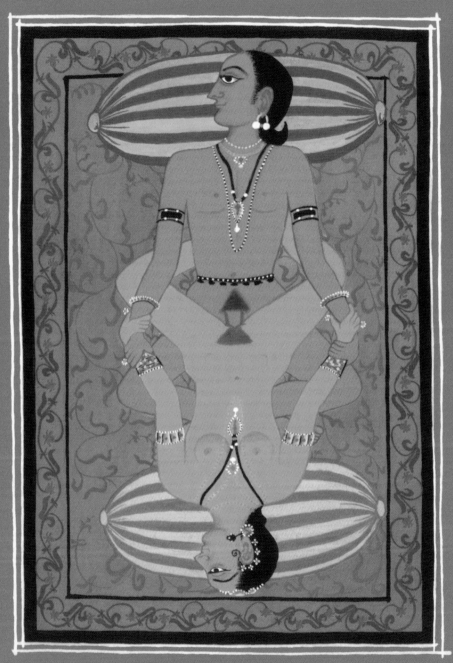

Janujugmâsana: The X posture.

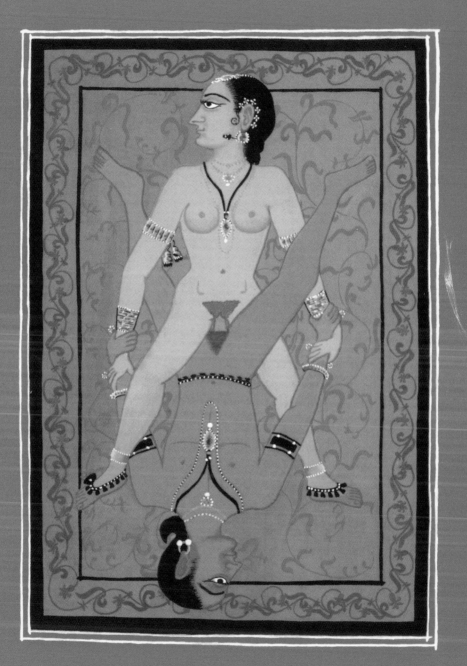

Janujugmâsana: Crossed variation of the X posture.

Janujugmâsana: Variation of the X posture.

Part 4

The Tantric Ritual

The Path of the Valley

The Tantric Path of the Valley is by far the easiest way to control the ejaculatory spasm, and is based on physical and mental relaxation. One might think that this method is not very exciting and this is relatively true. Nevertheless this practice opens the door to an entirely new world of feelings and experiences. It creates a sense of completeness and leads to the total integration of two beings, filling them with ecstasy—a state so unknown to today's "normal" couples who are always in a hurry.

A Divergent Experience

Thanks to the Path of the Valley, the Tantrist is able to "feminize" his sexual experience. To the ordinary male, sex is a convergent experience both in time and in space, convergent meaning that his erotic feelings revolve around the pole of the species, i.e., his sex organs. In other words, his experience becomes progressively narrower both in space and in time: the woman turns him on and as soon as he has an erection and his penis is inserted into her vagina, it becomes the focal point of his awareness, especially at its tip. At the same time, his experience becomes controlled by time: it concentrates on the short-lived moment of bliss caused by ejaculation. As soon as the spasm is over, his desire for sex vanishes, he withdraws his penis and turns away from the woman.

To the Tantrist, on the contrary, maïthuna is a divergent experience, much like the woman's. As far as she is concerned, far from being limited to the vagina and the penis it holds, her experience overflows and fills her entire body, and when the orgasm explodes, it is felt by every fiber, every cell. Her ecstasy tends to become more intense and prolonged as time elapses. Hours after the sex act, it still echoes throughout her whole being.

This is the kind of experience the Tantrist has: he does not make love to a vagina, but to a human being as a whole, i.e., the physical, psychic and cosmic woman, the incarnation of the cosmic Shakti. As soon as the lingam establishes an intimate connection, the Tantrist is of course aware of the yoni, but he shares the Shakti's desire and erotic emotion. The lingam becomes not an end in itself but the starting point of his erotic experience that, progressively, spreads to his abdomen and spine, causing each cell to vibrate. He intensely shares the Shakti's ultimate sexual emotion when she experiences a deep orgasm. This makes him aware of the sacred part of the woman, without trying to appropriate her body or her sex life. He does not think, nor say, "This is my wife, her vagina is my property, I own her sensuality." He perceives sex as the manifestation of cosmic creative power, which is suprapersonal. When united to the Shakti, his body as a whole becomes a sex organ and not only his lingam, which normally is the case in the sexual act.

Applying the Technique

First, which positions are best suited for the Path of the Valley? The most common in the West, the missionary, is not the best choice if the sex act is to last a long time because the shakti would soon become tired by the sheer weight of the man's body lying on top of her, especially if he relaxes, and this should be the case. This is particularly true if the encounter lasts for one or two hours or even more.... Sleepiness is a good thing, too, as when the man or both partners become sleepy, the best psychic and magnetic exchanges take place, and during sleep these exchanges occur on a higher, subtler level.

A Tantrist would rather prefer the "X" posture, either horizontal or reclined to the 45° angle position (see the next chapter about the maïthuna âsanas). This âsana is specifically designed for Tantra because it promotes the flow of subtle energies, allows for total bodily relaxation and good sexual contact, although motion is limited or nonexistent. What's more, this posture can easily be practiced while lying in bed. In our colder climate, it is often necessary to cover oneself because during relaxation the temperature of the body tends to lower quickly. Another big asset of this position: controlling ejaculation is not at all difficult.

Another suitable posture is the *Paryankasana*, in which the shiva lies on his side. It is the one von Urban spoke about. Though asymmetric, in the *Paryankasana* posture, both shiva and shakti can relax deeply, and it can also be practiced lying in bed, covered with blankets, like the first one.

In practice, the Path of the Valley implies that the partners remain almost motionless, and this applies to shakti and shiva as well.

Normally, only one partner is active, while the other remains totally passive and relaxed.

In Tantra, usually the active partner is the shakti, who maintains the erection that needs not to be very strong all the time. Even with a semi-stiff lingam the shakti can have a very deep sexual experience, and the shiva, too. If spontaneous, rhythmic and undulating motions start in the shakti's body, she should not try to repress them, unless these motions become too fast or too full. Too much movement could force the lingam out of the vagina if the penis is not fully erect, or cause an unwanted ejaculation. In the Path of the Valley, the shakti has the opportunity to achieve another kind of orgasm, which comes from within the brain's sex center rather than from the genitals, as in a normal sex act.

The reverse could happen as well, with the shakti remaining passive and the shiva being active with limited movements. In fact, one should let the body move by itself, while the mind watches what's happening, and lets it happen, unless movement becomes too great and causes ejaculation.

The roles can also be reversed: this means that first the shakti is the active partner then the shiva, or the contrary, both experience total immobility and enjoy the "secret language," where the vaginal and penile contractions answer one another. One should avoid willing or thinking about movement—avoid "intellectualizing" the act, but rather remain very conscious of what's going on. Both partners should be fully receptive to all the subtleties of the event, not only those happening in the sex organs but in the entire body. An inexplicable feeling of melting into one another is the normal outcome of the Path of the Valley technique—at least in principle— because at first it seems less enjoyable and satisfactory than the usual way of making love, but with a little patience the exploration of this new world of feelings becomes fascinating.

By the way, there is no need to "convert" oneself, once and for all, to one type of sexual encounter: one way never excludes others. The Path of the Valley makes it easy for the shiva to stay any length of time in physical contact with the shakti, and he will discover that inhibiting ejaculation is not a problem and does not reduce his sensual delight. Quite the contrary!

The Carezza Experience

Another sexual union similar to the Path of the Valley has also been discovered and practiced in the West: the Carezza method. Without being Tantra in disguise—it does lack Tantra's spiritual and cosmic content—this method shares many common points with the Path of the Valley and disproves one objection against Tantra which insinuates that it is not suitable for Westerners.

Carezza was "discovered" by an American citizen, John Humphrey Noyes, founder of the Oneida community, who called it Carezza, an Italian word needing no translation. Noyes also called it the "male retention." In the States, just before the First World War, this method was quite popular. At that time, Alice Stockham, a staunch supporter of the method, wrote: "Carezza is the highest and most perfect way of making love where neither the woman nor the man wants nor tries to have an orgasm." Another fervent supporter of the method in the U.S. was J. William Lloyd (*Karezza Praxis*, Zielbrücke-Thielle, 1966) and the following paragraphs are based on the writings of both authors.

For Carezza, the rule of the game is very simple indeed: everything is OK, except ejaculation, and if this happens, it should never occur in the vagina: the male must withdraw his lingam. The female orgasm is allowed provided it does not unleash the male ejaculation.

For Carezza, ejaculation and male orgasm are synonymous whereas for Tantra, ejaculation sabotages the male orgasm, and if it happens, it is in the vagina. Carezza comes close to realizing that male orgasm and ejaculation are two totally distinct things. Alice Stockham accepts the "possibility for the male to have an orgasm similar to the female's, who has no semen to eject." Now, let's see what Carezza, like Tantra, promises to its followers.

First, Carezza presupposes a deep love relationship between the partners and the desire to elevate sex to a plane other than the common one. J. William Lloyd wrote: "Man's first religion was based on sex and only through this medium can we rediscover our true origin," which is exactly what Tantra says. Carezza, like Tantra, considers the sex act to be a true feast of love, and ejaculation is seen as a clumsy, crude incident—something quite banal which kills sexual desire. The man who, a few minutes before, was seized by a frantic sexual desire, changes as soon as he has ejaculated and turns away from his wife, damaging her in her self-respect and her love as well.

To J. William Lloyd, a sexual union ending with an ejaculation is like a firework ending abruptly because the one in charge makes a mistake, and all the rockets explode prematurely. In his opinion, to ejaculate is often the surest way to kill true love and to make its sublimation impossible. To Carezza, the sex act is an exchange based on the most intimate of all human contacts which can be realized only if it is prolonged.

Carezza does not advocate any specific postures. It advises one to avoid long, rhythmic and accelerating motions, which would lead to an ejaculation; on the contrary, it recommends varying the motions until the danger of ejaculation is over.

Carezza rediscovered a major aspect of the Tantric maïthuna, i.e., the prânic, magnetic exchanges between both partners. Albert Chavannes, another Carezza enthusiast and undoubtedly a Frenchman, calls "magnetization" what Tantra calls "prânic exchanges," for to him the male and female sex organs are magnetically polarized.

According to J. William Lloyd, usually the male is the active sexual partner while the female is passive like a magnet attracting iron. This is why a man who wants to succeed in the Carezza technique should train himself in the art of caressing and of establishing magnetic contacts. He should view himself as if he is an electric battery, his right hand being the positive pole, his left the negative. When his hands happen to touch a receptive partner, an electric current is generated and spreads throughout her being. He should feel this magnetic current flowing from his left side to the woman's right and he should be able to achieve what he desires. If he touches the woman with one hand, only that part of her body should react to his magnetism.

For the expert in the art of love, this magnetism flows from his fingertips, his palms, reflects from his eyes, and is felt in the tone of his voice. He is able to transmit it to any part of the other partner's body even without any physical contact.

J. William Lloyd goes on to say that, when Carezza is practiced successfully, the sexual organs are as satisfied and demagnetized as after an ejaculation. The body of both lovers radiates with energy and joy and they rest together gently, feeling the kind of satisfaction one has after playing a happy game. On the contrary, if the male ejaculates, after a short relaxation, he feels weak and somehow disappointed: the wonderful world of love and desire has vanished, and his dream woman has disappeared.

Do these excerpts from Carezza literature seem too praiseworthy? I don't think so. My object in presenting them is to show how well the Carezza technique may suit couples in our Western culture.

Maïthuna, the Tantric Way of Love

During maïthuna, if the male remains quite still to avoid ejaculation, the shakti is active and controls the evolution of the ritual. It is irrelevant if the lingam stays all the time fully erect or not, provided the couple remains united, so as to attain greatest ecstasy. During intercourse, it is the shakti who gathers the cosmic rhythms while the shiva becomes immersed in her own magnetic energy until he feels the "divine vibration." To achieve this, all that's needed is to pay full attention to what is happening in each other's body, to the subtle exchanges taking place.

This union can—and should—last up to two hours or even more. Meanwhile, the shiva should remain totally aware of the woman, feeling her blood pulsating, vibrating to her rhythm and, most important, *breathing at her pace* until the ecstatic experience unfolds.

Nevertheless, neither Carezza nor the Path of the Valley insists that their followers stay always motionless. Over and above the "secret language" so favorable to subtle exchanges, all movement is accepted provided it doesn't cause an ejaculation. Most practicants are surprised to discover that what triggers ejaculation in an ordinary sex encounter becomes possible without the incessant concern as to how to control oneself.

Without much difficulty, Tantra frees the male from the ejaculatory reflex. Of course, a couple long used to "normal" love will not achieve this technique in the twinkling of an eye. At first, the male will most probably succeed only once out of two or three intercourses to avoid ejaculation, sometimes due to the lack of cooperation on the part of the shakti, who is also used to the "normal" outcome of the act. At first, both could find this kind of lovemaking less satisfactory, but if they persevere a little they will discover the thrill of the Path of the Valley, the easiest way to having meditation between two people.

The Rhythm of Maïthuna

Life is rhythm, rhythm is life! In ordinary intercourse, the male usually controls the event, notably the coital movements. Without noticing it, he will enforce *his own rhythm* on his partner and, more often than not, he will move against her rhythm. It is as if he would dance the tango whilst she would prefer to waltz! Agreed, at the ball, the male dancer guides the woman, but in this case this is not a bad thing since the couple follows the orchestra and therefore moves in harmony.

Maïthuna ought to be a dance where the shiva follows the shakti's rhythm, and this rhythm will not only vary from one woman to another, but from one day to the next—no, from one moment to the next! The male should know and accept the fact that nothing *has* to be done but that he simply should *let* it happen. With an experienced shakti, things are easy, and all one has to do is to wait until she starts the motions. Then he should follow her. If she has the habit of following the male passively, however, matters will be a little bit more difficult. He should remain fully aware of the woman's experience and watch the rhythm of her breathing, without moving. Usually, if nothing happens, one needs to wait only a little until, with the help of erotic tension, slight, spontaneous motions start, to which he should then respond. Yes, the shiva should respond to the shakti's motions and rhythm whether they be fast or slow, deep or shallow.

The shiva has nothing to lose by abandoning his dominant position, quite the contrary! Instead of having a woman who is as passive as a puppet, he will enjoy a true Tantric shakti.

This drawing from Rembrandt (ca. 1646) shows that the "missionary posture" was the usual one at that time. Although the couple is alone, they remain in their clothes. This kind of intercourse can pretty well satisfy the male's sexual urge and produce children, but is very distant from the Tantric experience.

The Maïthuna Âsanas

Any intercourse, be it human, animal or even vegetal, is sacred since it reproduces the ultimate creative act, the cosmic embrace of Shiva and Shakti, the reason for the existence of this universe. In ordinary sex, lovers do not know this, whereas Tantrists are very conscious of the true meaning of the sexual union, and this we should keep in mind while considering the maïthuna âsanas.

In Tantra both partners want to realize the "divine" aspects of their sex life, which is not only eroticism, otherwise the *Kama Sutra* and the *Koka Shastra* would be Tantric scriptures. The aim of these scriptures is only to heighten sensual delight—not bad in itself—and they offer plenty of sexual techniques, among them quite a number of coital positions. At first sight it would seem enough for Tantra to borrow from these postures.

In fact the traditional âsanas best suited for this "meditation to two," unique to Tantra, are few and the Tantric gurus selected them not only because they allow the partners to be relaxed together but above all because they allow a protracted union without needing to change position, and so disturb the partner's meditation. Some of these âsanas are so comfortable that they allow the partners to reach a very deep physical and mental relaxation, changing their level of consciousness, and, for example, falling asleep, which is not really a fault. For Tantric purposes, the maïthuna âsanas should promote magnetic and prânic exchanges as well as the control of the ejaculatory reflex, and that is why some are not very exciting!

This also explains why Tantra does not advocate, at least at the beginning, the most common sexual position in the West, the missionary (*Uttana Bandha* in Sanskrit), or the male being on top of the woman. This position got its name when Africans peeped through the cracks of the hut and saw the missionary and his wife making love! This position was unusual for them, they made fun of it, hence the name. By the way, in our modern culture today, some women stubbornly reject other sexual positions, which they consider to be obscene.

The only reason Tantra tries to dissuade people from this most common position is because it makes the control of ejaculation difficult. In fact, people who have been accustomed to a certain sexual position for many years have created a very powerful conditioned reflex (remember Pavlov!). It is easier—or at least less difficult—to control oneself by changing the rules of the game, and let's start with position.

According to Rajneesh, his neo-Tantra postures are irrelevant because we should not fix anything. Even to make love, he says, we now refer to books explaining how to act, and the whole process becomes intellectual. He is certainly right when he says sex should not become cerebral. But let's take an example. When I go for a swim in the sea, I do not plan anything. I let my body act, and, depending on my mood and the circumstances, I may use the breast-stroke and swim leisurely. The next day, if I have more energy, I may do a powerful crawl. In both cases, while swimming I do not have to "think" about the motions of my body. I simply enjoy the swim.

But how and why did I get this spontaneity if not from my lessons at the swimming pool? Of course, I did not invent the strokes! Now I can forget the swimming pool and the lessons. I swim and that's it! The same is true with the maïthuna âsanas and other Tantric techniques. Why should each couple re-invent the Tantric postures? Why should we deprive ourselves of this age-old knowledge? If a couple, for instance with the help of this book, discovers a suitable love-âsana, next time they make love they can forget the book. Of course, the Tantrist is not a typical performing-lover who has faithfully studied all the books about love-making and, in bed, starts with the prescribed strokes, etc., but at least he should have a working knowledge of the Tantric techniques.

Purushâyata

Having clarified this, let's now consider the postures and start first with the inverted missionary's, where the shakti is on top. Tantric iconography shows Rati and Kâma, the god of love, in this posture beneath the goddess Chinnamastâ.

What are the benefits of it? First, the shakti controls the whole process. As for the shiva, he is not able to move much, but on the other hand, this posture allows him to relax fully.

For the shakti, it is not really the most comfortable of all positions and after some time she may wish to switch to another one, which would unfortunately disturb the experience. This is not really a fault on her part, especially while one is learning to control ejaculation, because to this end, switching to some other posture lowers the erotic tension.

By altering this posture slightly, the "reversed act" becomes possible as the shiva identifies himself with the shakti. To this end he should be positioned exactly like the woman's posture in the missionary posture. He should lie on his back with his legs apart while the shakti in turn plays the male's role with her legs taut. In this way shiva and shakti "swap" sexes, the male pretending to be female and vice versa.

Purushayâta is very popular in South India because it heightens the erotic experience to the utmost, particularly the shakti's. In fact, this posture grants the shakti total freedom to move as she likes. This inverted posture is not unknown in the West, and the female likes it because she can make the lingam penetrate deeply and she controls the rhythm. The male likes it too, but, alas, those ample to-and-fro motions are the very ones which cause the ejaculation.

In this âsana, the Indian Tantric couple Kale describe the corkscrew technique, which is very much in favor in South India, and for which Tamil women are famous: "A particularly effective coital movement...and one reputedly specialized in by the women of the southern states of India...is the hip rotation, much like the old-time stripper's 'grind.' This can be done by the man when he is lying on his back by the simple exercise of tightening his gluteus maximus muscles, the large muscles of the buttocks, and elevating his hips. After he has done this for a few times, he should then also impart a slight 'hula-hoop' movement of his hip on the upward and downward thrusts. The corkscrew-like movement of his penis during the upward thrust has a special delight all its own, because it lets the phallus touch every part of the vagina with a particularly demanding vigor. The female partner should watch this movement carefully; she will find it far easier to practice it than the male does because of the natural rotary movement of the heavier feminine hips.

"Later, when she assumes the Female Inferior Position, that is, when she is lying on her back, she should couple the downward corkscrew movement with a tightening and 'milking' action of her vaginal muscles. The combined effect of these three actions...the rotation, the in-and-out motion, and the 'milking' squeeze... provide a sexual stimulus that is quite indescribable" (KALE, Arvind & Shanta, *Tantra, the Secret Power of Sex*, Bombay, 1976, p. 71).

I am sure they are right, but, if you are like me, you will think that the shiva who agrees to perform to this test has to be in perfect control of himself in order not to succumb or ejaculate. In fact, the risk is less than if the shakti herself makes the usual long and ample pelvic motions. Thanks to the corkscrew technique, the shakti gets utmost erotic stimulation with a minimum of motions and this process can cause chain orgasms. The rotating motions of the male's pelvis over-excite both the shakti's clitoris and the walls of her yoni. If we add to this the suction from the contraction of her vaginal muscles, it becomes an explosive combination for the shakti! For the shiva, too, it is sexy but his lingam is not over-excited.

The Kale's say this all applies to the missionary's posture as well but with some changes. In fact, in the inverted act, the shiva, by squeezing and relaxing his buttocks, encourages the up-and-down motions of his pelvis. This is possible because his buttocks are firmly supported, which is not the case if he lies on top of the shakti. Then, she is the one who gets the benefits of the prop under her buttocks, and this is why she has to squeeze and release her muscles rhythmically. She can make these motions fuller with slight pelvic thrusts. Squeezing the buttocks makes it easier for her to contract the vaginal muscles and to "milk" the lingam. In this way there is almost an inversion of the roles by switching from the posture shiva-on-top to shiva-under. In both cases, both partners should take care to keep an intimate contact with the clitoris at all times.

Upavishta

Upavishta, meaning any seated posture, is not really the name of a specific âsana, but of a whole set of postures where the female is astride the seated male. The easiest position is called *Sukhâsana*, the "Happy Posture."

In this âsana, the Tantrist sitting on the floor with crossed legs welcomes his shakti on his lap and she puts her hands on his shoulders or on his neck.

This position remains comfortable even during a lengthy intercourse, provided the shakti is lightweight, and it applies to the Path of the Valley as well as to the "Abrupt Path." Because this is not a very erotic posture, controlling ejaculation is easy, and in this position "secret language" is advised.

Upavishta, the Asymmetric Variation

This asymmetric variation of the *Upavishta* posture is little known but interesting. To succeed with it, the shakti should sit with only her buttocks and coccyx touching the floor. This means she must lean a little backward, her hands resting on the floor to keep her balance. The shiva sits in front of her in the same position: therefore his lingam and her yoni are face to face. The shakti then puts her right thigh onto her partner's left thigh, and he in turn puts his right thigh onto the shakti's left. When lingam and yoni are so united, both partners are leaning somewhat backward and have to use their hands and arms to keep their balance.

This variation is very suitable for what is known as "melting through the gaze." Both partners gaze at each other and establish eye contact, which causes a powerful psychical attraction. They might even gaze at each other focusing on the spot between the eyebrows in the middle of the forehead, called the *Ajna Chakra*. In each case, their eyes remain wide open and don't blink. In the meantime both partners can practice their secret language, without moving, of course.

The above posture might also be called the Tantric rocking chair! Since their heels are touching the floor, if each partner pushes alternatively, a rocking motion is generated, and is in tune with their rhythmic breathing. Each partner inhales while reclining backward and exhales by coming forward. This means one partner inhales during the backward motions and exhales when coming forward: thus, the breathing is mutual—inhalation lasts as long as exhalation. The partners may also add a mantra to their rocking motion, *Om* or any mantra given by their guru—see the chapter about the power of the mantras.

I do admit that *Sukhâsana* is not a very erotic posture, but it does produce mutual fascination and could induce altered states of consciousness similar to hypnosis. An intense psychic relationship is created, especially if the partners keep gazing at each other without blinking for at least two minutes. As soon as one cannot keep his or her eyes open any longer and tears begin to flow, he or she should close the eyes, but still remain in close contact. In this way a very deep relationship is established within a very short period. Note, too, that this posture can be practiced without the lingam being inserted into the yoni.

Upavishta, a Variation

Although the above positions need no physical preparation, this variation requires that the shiva's knees and hips be very flexible. Sitting on the floor with his knees bent and the soles of his feet touching each other, the shiva pulls his heels rather close to his body: in this way, his feet provide a seat for the shakti. If his knees are stiff and remain too far from the floor, it would be uncomfortable for both partners, and it is best to forget it.

For Tantra, both variations have the same value and the choice is simply a matter of convenience. Another variation is the *Padmâsana*, the well known Lotus posture. With the shiva being seated in a not very tight Lotus posture, his shakti sits on his lap and inserts the lingam into her yoni. Of course, this practice does not allow much room for motion but this is not necessarily a drawback.

Uttana Bandha

This easy variation of the missionary's posture does not have the inconvenience of the ordinary one. Instead of lying on top of his shakti, who is on the floor with her legs spread out, the shiva, instead, squats between her legs, and then inserts his lingam. As his shakti is not able to move much, the shiva controls the motion and with no unexpected movement to fear, he is able to control himself quite easily.

Tiryakâsana

Tiryak, means "sideways." This asymmetric position, which is not practiced very much in India, is very useful in our countries, and we shall see why. Let me first describe it.

The starting position for the female is quite similar to the "missionary"—she lies on her back with only one leg bent, the other being stretched out on the mattress. The male lies on his left side but on *his partner's right side*, with his body approximately perpendicular to hers. Then he positions himself under the shakti's bent right leg and squeezes her left thigh between both his thighs. Now, the shakti's right leg rests on shiva's right flank. When the lingam is inserted the male's pubic bone is perpendicular to the woman's.

This posture looks rather difficult, but in fact, it is much easier to perform this âsana than to describe it! A quick glance at the picture will make it clearer. There is also a simpler variation: the woman lies on her back with both legs bent as in the missionary's posture. Instead of lying on top of her, the male lies on his side, perpendicular to the shakti's body, and positions his legs under the "bridge" made by the shakti's own bent legs. When the lingam is positioned in front of the yoni, it glides into it. In this position, the female's legs *rest* on the male's flank, while in the former âsana one of her legs was *squeezed* between the shiva's thighs.

Because this position can be performed in a bed, covered with blankets, it is easily practiced in our culture. In India, where Tantrists almost never have beds like ours, they have to practice on the floor on a thin mattress or a carpet, and this posture would soon become uncomfortable to the shiva. *Tiryakâsana* has other advantages: first, genital contact remains even if the erection subsides, and second, although the posture is asymmetric, in bed it can comfortably be kept for a long time. Both partners can even fall asleep, and although the "I"-consciousness fades away, both bodies know what's happening and their magnetic exchanges continue.

Tiryakâsana and this variation are well suited for the Path of the Valley. First, because movement is limited, and, second, because the lingam is much less stimulated than in the missionary's position. This lack of stimulation enables the ejaculatory spasm to be more easily controlled. Last but not least, in this position the shiva's arms and hands are free to caress the shakti's body or her clitoris.

Parshva Piditaka, the Retrolateral Posture

In this position, the shiva lies on his side with his knees bent. His shakti lies also on her side and against him with his lingam being inserted from behind into her yoni. From *Tiryakâsana*, the shakti has

Tibetan Tantric Buddhism usually shows this posture, i.e., the goddess astride, small, while the male god always shows this terrifying face.

only to turn onto her side to have the *Parshva Piditakâsana*. Many a Tantric couple selects this âsana at night before falling asleep because it can be held indefinitely. Of course, after a while, the lingam slides out of the yoni, although the bodies are still touching each other. This posture is very suitable for the Path of the Valley.

In active contact, however, because the shakti is taken from behind in this practice, it is very erotic and to control oneself can be difficult, especially if the shakti moves. If she remains totally motionless and leaves the initiative to the shiva, he can go up to the razor's edge, and stay there for a long time. For this reason this posture is very good training for the control of the ejaculatory spasm. At this point however, the shakti must control herself fully: a single movement on her part could cause ejaculation, thereby ending the experience, at least for the moment! When he feels he is approaching ejaculation, the shiva can, little by little, train himself to move slowly, and with perseverence he will be able to move more and still remain on the razor's edge without ejaculating. Staying indefinitely on the razor's edge is the shiva's way to achieve the ultimate male orgasm.

As this posture is so simple, it needs no illustration.

Janujugmâsana, the X Posture

Janujugmâsana, the X posture, is a typical maïthuna âsana. It is also impressive that this posture has been practiced in India since prehistoric times. We know this because archeologists in Daimabad, Maharashtra, discovered an earthen pot adorned with a crude drawing showing a couple in this position. Apparently, the prehistoric artist's foremost concern was not erotic nor was it simply ornamental: everything points to his purpose being rather ritualistic and therefore close to Tantrism.

In spite of its primitive aspect, this drawing is quite explicit. And, in this respect, it is interesting to keep in mind, first, that few prehistoric coital illustrations exist, and second, that the position drawn is a very unusual one. It is uncommon to the extent of not being found among the numerous erotic sculptures carved on the Khajuraho or Konarak temples. Nor do we find it on the Indian miniatures or in the well known erotic scriptures, like the *Kama Sutra* or the *Koka Shastra*, which do not exactly lack imagination in this field! Why did they not include this âsana? Is it not erotic enough? I don't know. In the West, too, this position seems to be almost unknown.

It appeals to Tantra because it permits prolonged sexual contact, with total relaxation, and promotes lengthy prânic, magnetic exchanges between the genital organs. If profane love does not like it much, is it because of the shallow penetration of the lingam, which

Representation of the X posture ornamenting a prehistoric pot discovered in Daimabad.

A Cabalistic mandala found on a medal from Pompei.

should not be fully erect? Whatever the answer, the Path of the Valley likes this practice, because sexual contact can be maintained with little or no erection.

As for the body movements, they are, of course, limited. Though perhaps not very erotic, in this posture one can experience Tantric sex fully, which does not exclude an orgasm, especially for the shakti.

The "X" posture is very simple to achieve. Often, the initial sexual contact begins with *Sukkhâsana*, the happy posture, with the shakti seated in the male's lap. Staying in this position, both partners then lean backward and stretch out their legs. Instead of lying completely flat on the carpet, the shiva and his shakti can prop their body up with cushions and recline at a 45° angle. In this way, all the benefits of the âsana are maintained, the lingam penetrates deeper into the vagina and a full erection is not a problem.

The ritualistic aspect of this posture reveals itself in another tradition, which is closer to the Western culture. Let's therefore have a look at the esoteric mandala with the ROTAS magical square. This cabalistic mandala appears on a medal from Pompei, from an Italian church, on a Latin Bible from A.D. 822, on a Greek manuscript and on a wall of a French castle, existing in the 12th century. Four centuries later, it reappears on an Austrian coin! This is strange, isn't it?

If one tries to decipher this mandala with the help of Tantric symbolism, at first one sees a nude shakti on an inverted triangle, the symbol of the yoni. She is black, like the goddess Kali, and this color symbolizes that she reigns over the powers of the night, the unconscious. On top of her head, we can see the crescent of the moon. The shiva lies on a triangle and is clad in white, the male's color in Tantra and the symbol of the conscious powers performing during the day. The two superimposed triangles indicate the union of the male and female cosmic principles. Hidden under the ROTAS square, the couple is united in the "X" posture. The N at the center of the ROTAS square hides the genitals. But where are their hands and what do they do? The sole discrepancy to the Tantric "X" posture is that the shiva's legs are on shakti's.

The mandala symbolizes the original cosmic act of creation and the creative forces involved in the manifestation of the universe. At the four cardinal points, we find symbolic figures making the whole mandala revolve: the bull, Shiva's mount, Nandi, the winged lion (one of the chief figures of Middle East esotericism). The eagle is Garuda, while the angel symbolizes the Spirit.

Is it not surprising to find in this mandala the essentials of Tantric tradition? Of course, this explanation of the symbolism of the mandala is not final. There is always more than meets the eye.

Ritualistic Maïthuna

The yonipûjâ is adoration "par excellence."
To ignore it is to take away the value of all other aspects of the cult.

(Yonitantra, I 5b; VI, 24cd and VIII.13)

This quotation indicates the importance given to the *yonipûjâ*, the adoration of the yoni in the Shakta cult—the cult of the creative power which is embodied in the female sex organ.

Among the few texts published about this ritual, I only know the *Yonitantra*—not to be confused with the *Yoginîtantra*—and the *Brihadyonitantra*, of which only parts are available. My description of this ritual stems from the *Yonitantra*, which can be practiced, with some slight changes, in the West. However, like many other Tantric texts, it is more of a summary than an instructive text: the guru himself has to teach the techniques. The *acharya* (instructor), who can be a woman or a man, plays an important part in the ritual, and special rules have been formulated in the event of a *pûjâ* being practiced in his or her absence.

Since we Westerners do not have the opportunity of being taught by a guru, it is necessary to supplement the few hints given in the original text. The unknown author first tells us which women are suitable for the ritual. According to him, the woman should be sensuous, even wanton (*pramâda*), beloved (*kânta*) and free of any false modesty. Often the *acharya*'s wife will be the acting *yoginî*, or the disciple's companion.

At the beginning of the adoration ritual, the shakti places herself in the middle of the *mandala*, usually a triangle, which symbolizes the cosmic yoni, included in a circle. Then the *sadhak*, or adept, will give her an aphrodisiac beverage, called *vijayâ*, whose ingredients are not given, probably because at the time the text was written everybody in India knew about it. J. A. Schoterman, who translated the scripture, thinks it was *bhang*, a mixture made of *indica cannabis*, or marijuana, but it is imperative that the shakti should not be drugged. In our culture, this beverage could just as well be champagne or a gin and tonic.

The aim is to excite the shakti to the utmost, to heighten her sexual energy and to bring her to the ecstasy.

The preparatory part of the ritual includes mantras, which the author does not mention. At the beginning of the *yonipûjâ*, the shakti will sit on the Tantrist's left thigh, and he in turn starts to adore her unshaved (*sakuntala*) yoni by anointing it with some perfumed sandal paste. Next the Tantrist gives the shakti one more cup of *vijayâ* and draws a red crescent on her forehead. This ritual should never become routine: the symbolism of each gesture should be intensely felt by both partners. While the adept draws the crescent on her forehead, he and she should both become conscious of the moon's energy as manifested in the shakti.

Then the shiva puts his hands on the shakti's breasts, becoming conscious of the motherly aspects of the cosmic Shakti, and repeating 108 times the *bhagabîja*, which should be *Hrîm*. Finally, the worshipper makes all the gestures and caresses possible to turn the shakti on and excite her to the utmost. First, he gently strokes her breasts, then her thighs and finally her yoni.

No doubt, those who scorn Tantra will say that the whole ridiculous thing is nothing more than ordinary petting. It's as if they are confusing the rite of baptism with taking a shower: in both cases, one gets wet! In the *yonipûjâ*, the arousal of the shakti spreads to the shiva and an abundant flow of *tattva uttama*, the "sublime essence," i.e., her vaginal fluid, is produced. Thus the worshipper has awakened the subtle, prânic energies which play a prominent role in the *pûjâ*.

Now comes the main part of the *yonipûjâ*. The shakti anoints the lingam with some perfumed sandal paste, colored with saffron. The guru, who is always watching, chants the appropriate mantras and makes sure the ritual is correctly followed. Next the lingam is inserted into the yoni. Tantric maïthuna should never become an ordinary sexual union, but should always remain controlled. Both partners should at all times be conscious of the sacredness of any sexual union. Of course, the rules for the Tantric maïthuna must, at all costs, be followed, especially the proper posture and the control of the ejaculatory spasm.

Regarding *yonipûjâ*, one of the most important things is the mutual absorption of the "sublime essence," or the mixed vaginal and penile fluids. The shakti, it is said, absorbs by osmosis the mixed fluids through the vaginal lining, whereas the shiva should suck the fluids up by performing the *vajroli* act (see this chapter). According to Tantric tradition this invigorates both partners. Even without this absorption of fluids, the intense erotic arousal increases the flow of gonadal hormones, which could just as well be the "sublime essence."

Why not? While united, the lovers meditate upon the cosmic creative power now fully awakened in the woman's body.

As soon as the ritualistic maïthuna is over, the shiva should pay respect to the shakti's yoni by inserting a finger and taking some of the vaginal fluid which he then puts in the middle of his and her forehead, at the very spot where Indian women have a red dot or *tilaka*. The guru does the same and both the shiva and shakti thank him respectfully for the help they received from his presence during the *pûjâ*. According to the *Yonitantra* (II, 6ab; IV, 30a), this *yonipûjâ* should be practiced daily (!) and it paves the way to the *chakra pûjâ*.

The fact that the *acharya* and his own shakti do practice these sexual rituals with their students may be shocking by Western standards, but since they do exist, why should we conceal them? And what about the Western Tantrists? Of course, it is most probably out of the question to practice *yonipûjâ* as it stands, without making any changes, but Tantric couples could practice a milder form of the ritual and still maintain the spirit involved, which is the most important aspect.

The Ritualistic Triangle

During the Tantric sexual union, Mr. X is not meeting Mrs. X, but the ultimate Shiva is becoming known to the Shakti. To this end, both have to disassociate themselves from their own insignificant ego in order to be able to perceive themselves as either the absolute male, Shiva, or as the cosmic female, Shakti. This altered way of perception has to be prepared.

This is why, long before the maïthuna takes place, the male Tantrist draws a red triangle with a dot at its center, the *bindu*. He then meditates on the symbolism of the inverted triangle and of the seed-dot, the *bindu*. Next, and still repeating the mantra his guru gave him, he projects Shakti's image on the triangle until he actually feels the *real* woman, his partner in the ritual, the truly cosmic Shakti incarnate, or cosmic feminine energy.

Next, he envisages her yoni and meditates deeply on its cosmic significance as the gateway to life. He then perceives the creative strength of her yoni, of her pole of the species. He feels the irresistible sex appeal with its power to make his lingam erect, to absorb it, and draw out the fertile sperm. Next, he envisages the Shiva's white triangle and projects it onto the Shakti's inverted red triangle. The *bindu*, or seed-dot at the center of the triangle, symbolizes the ultimate fusion of both cosmic principles, Shiva and Shakti. In this way, the Tantrist, still repeating his mantra, comes face to face with the unfathomable mystery, the significance and sacredness of the sexual union. Regarding the mantra, western Tantrists can actually use the *Om* mantra: cf. the chapter about this mantra's power. Only when he is able to superimpose perfectly both aspects of his partner—the individual and the cosmic—will she join him and will both unite sexually, after having of course performed all the ritualistic gestures. Only by constant recollection of the triangle and their suprapersonal dimension, will they be able to separate themselves from their own egos.

The Chakra Pûjâ

> "What is the use of speaking much?
> O Kalika, know this for certain that there is no other way
> except the Kula form of worship capable
> of conferring happiness here and in the next world.
> By concealing the Kuladharma
> during the sway supreme of the Kali Yuga
> —when all forms of religion will be abandoned—
> even a Kula is dragged into hell"
> Mahanirvana Tantra (VII, 202).

The *Chakra Pûjâ*, or worship practiced in a circle, is, along with the five Makaras, the foremost Tantric rite, but also the least understood and the least able to be practiced in the West. Thanks to its symbolical wealth, it includes the essentials of the Tantric cult and philosophy. He who does not know nor understand the chakra pûjâ and the five Makaras, knows nothing about Tantra.

What is it all about? In short, the "crude," "objectionable" facts are: in a secret place, eight men and eight women meet. "On the occasions of the performance of divine worship the women and girls deposit their julies, or bodices, in a box in charge of the Guru, or priest. At the close of the rites, the male worshippers each take a julie from the box, and the female to whom it belongs becomes his partner for the evening in these lascivious orgies" (Sellon quoted in Francis King, p. 27). Next, sitting together in a circle, they will perform complex symbolical rites including the five M's: drinking wine (*Madya*), eating meat (*Mâmsa*), fish (*Matsya*), cereals (*Mudrâ*) and, finally, what a scandal, they all will have ritualistic intercourse (*Maïthuna*) with their one night's partner.

The least understood part of the worship is, of course, the maïthuna. Some will smile at it and say it is nothing more than ordinary group sex. Others will see it only as a lewd, hedonistic sexual practice. Of course, they all are wrong. True, the facts are there, but we will try to unravel them to expose a deeper, more symbolic meaning.

Let's consider the facts starting from testimonies, the first stemming from a quite uncommon man by name Edward Sellon. "Born in 1818, the son of a gentleman of moderate fortune whom I lost when quite a child." Sellon adds, in his autobiography, *The Ups and Downs of Life*, that as a consequence of this early bereavement he was "designed from the first for the army" and, when still only sixteen years of age, he went to India where, on October 27th, 1834, he was gazetted as an Ensign in the 4th Madras Native Infantry. Sellon seems to have enjoyed his ten years in India, taking a more than average interest in native social, religious and sexual life—particularly the latter—"In his rather short life (less than half a century!), he has been not only a soldier, but a coach driver, a fencing-master and a pornographer" (Francis King, op. cit. p. 11).

He wrote in his autobiography, *The Ups and Downs of Life*:

I now commenced a regular course of fucking with native women. The usual charge for the general run of them is two rupees. For five, you may have the handsomest Mohammedan girls, and any of the high-caste women who follow the trade of a courtesan. The 'fivers' are a very different set of people from their frail sisterhood in European countries; they do not drink, they are scrupulously cleanly in their persons, they are sumptuously dressed, they wear the most costly jewels in profusion, they are well-educated and sing sweetly, accompanying their voices on the viol de gamba, a sort of guitar, they generally decorate their hair with clusters of clematis, or the sweet scented bilwa flowers entwined with pairs of diamonds. They understand in perfection all the arts and wiles of love, are capable of gratifying any tastes, and in face and figure they are unsurpassed by any women in the world.

It is impossible to describe the enjoyment I experienced in the arms of these syrens. I have had English, French, German and Polish women of all grades of society since, but never, never did they bear a comparison with those salacious, succulent houris of the far East (*Memoirs of the Anthropologican Society of London*, 1866, vol. II, p. 274).

Most Indian puritans will dismiss this entire subject and even deny the very existence of the chakra pûjâ, but nevertheless it still does occur nowadays. "In present-day Rajasthan, the religious cults which practice these secret esoteric rites are known by the generic title of Lâja-Dharma; in the Himalaya regions the cult is called Cholîmârg" (Devangana Desai in *Erotic Sculpture in India*, New Delhi, 1975, p. 118).

About Konarak, F. Yeats-Brown in *Lancer at Large*, Tauchnitz, Dresden, 1939, writes: "The Temple was built in honor of the Sun-God, perhaps in the twelfth, perhaps in the ninth century before Christ. It is Indo-Aryan style, and some of its carvings represent the conquest of aborigines by a northern race, but what race, and when, we shall probably never know. It stands, a pagan splendor, defying Time and criticism. Traditions of black magic haunt the place, and during the dark of the moon, Tantrik saddhus come here for their rites. Both sexes take part. Wine is drunk and seed is offered as at Eleusis. Circles are formed in which the female energies of the gods are invoked by various rituals that are never consummated, for the vital energies must be re-absorbed and re-manifested on the astral plane. By such means it is alleged that spirits may be summoned from the circum-ambiant ether." This text was written a few years before the Second World War.

As a warning to those who would like to travel to India, hoping to partake in a Chakra Pûjâ, let me tell you that it is practically impossible for Westerners to attend such a rite. Even to get first hand testimonies about it is very difficult because of the prejudice existing in India about Tantra and its practices, and the secrecy surrounding it. Or by the Tantrikas themselves as a protection against their enemies. Only very few handpicked initiates are being invited to this long, complex rite, and it is open only to those who have been especially trained for it by the guru.

Contrary to all appearances, the chakra pûjâ presupposes high moral standards on the part of all participants. Not only in its full blown form but even in abridged and simpler ones. It revolves around the guru, which can be a woman or a man, or around the couple guru-shakti, whose role is not solely to direct the pûjâ, but also to select and train the worshippers. He is well acquainted with all of them and thus knows they will be compatible.

On the appointed night, the worshippers gather at a secret spot, a cave or old temple, a lonely clearing in the jungle or even at someone's house. In the olden days, this ritual was also held on cremation grounds, first because sex is the antidote to death, and second, to make sure no Aryan Hindu will disturb their pûjâ, as they are horrified by anything linked to death and corpses.

What exactly happens in a chakra pûjâ is very difficult to discover. The secrecy is well kept, and one has to be very patient to glean here and there some pieces of the puzzle. In time, however, one is able to obtain a rather accurate picture of the whole process. Often the very existence of the chakra pûjâ is negated. According to Francis King (*Sexuality, Magic and Perversion*, London, 1971, p. 34), "On both sides of the Buddhist/Hindu fence claims have been made that members of their own faith do not indulge in sexual practices involving actual physical copulation. Certain Hindu pandits, for example, have claimed that *all* the *Tantras* dealing with physical intercourse are to be interpreted symbolically and that those who think otherwise are immoral, evil and 'dirty.' It is a pity that this sort of nonsense has received the support of some western scholars who should have known better; thus Evans-Wentz, who displayed an extremely puritanical attitude towards Tantricism—no doubt a hangover from his early years as a member of the Theosophical Society—so far forgot that moral detachment which is so integral a part of the equipment of Scholarship as to refer to 'those hypocrites who follow the left-hand path in Bengal and elsewhere.' Even Lama Anagarika Govinda has claimed that physical sexuality plays no part in Tibetan Tantricism—a statement that, in its literal meaning, is quite simply untrue."

With regard to sex and Buddhism, N. N. Bhattacharyya, in his scholarly *History of the Tantric Religion* (Delhi, 1982, p.225), writes: "In Buddhist Tantras, the Female and Male principles are known as Prajnâ and Upâya or as Shunyatâ and Karunâ respectively [...] One who can unite these two principles in oneself can have the highest knowledge and become free from the fetters of birth and death. This is real Buddahood. To have this spiritual experience, man and woman should first realize that they are representatives of Upâya and Prajnâ respectively and that their physical, mental and intellectual union alone can bring the experience of the highest truth. Accordingly, men and women should jointly strive for this secret knowledge and culture [...] Prajnâ denotes also the female organ as the seat of all happiness. Upâya, the Male Principle, is also known as Vajrâ, or the male generative organ. The union of man and woman, of Prajnâ and Upâya, brings the maximum pleasure in which all mental actions are lost and the world around forgotten; only a pleasing experience of non-duality prevails. This is known as Mahasukkha, the greatest pleasure, or Nirvana, the summum bonum, and the real manifestation of Bodhicitta." This clearly shows that, except for the vocabulary they use, Buddhist and Indian Tantra agree and partake in the same philosophy and practice.

With regard to Buddhism and Tantra in general, many books have been published, and among the few truly reliable and indisputable ones we find, for example, D. L. Snellgrove's translation of the *Hevajra Tantra*, a Buddhist scripture, and also an Indian Tantric scripture, the *Mahanirvana Tantra*, translated by Manmatha Nath Dutt, respectively quoted, in abbreviations, HEV or MAH. Another very important scripture is the *Sârada Tilaka Tantra*. Unfortunately it is not as yet translated.

Many other reliable authors and books confirm the actual practice of the Chakra Pûjâ. Horace Hayman Wilson (*Works*, London 1862, Vol. I p. 263) has written about the Kanchulias, a Tantric sect: "The Kanchiluas' worship much resembles that of the Caulas. They are, however, distinguished by a particular rite not practiced by the others, and throw into confusion all the ties of female relationship; natural restraints are wholly disregarded and a community of women among the votaries inculcated.

Monnier-Williams, in *Religious Thought and Life in India* (1883, p. 192), says: "It is well known that even in the present day, on particular occasions, the adherents of the sect go through the whole ceremonial in all its revolting entirety. When such occasions occur, a circle is formed, composed of men and women seated side by side without respect of caste or relationship. Males and females are held for the particular occasion to be forms of Siva and his wife respectively, in conformity with the doctrine propounded in one of the Tantras, where Siva addressing his wife says: 'All men have my form and all women thy form; anyone who recognizes any distinction of caste in the mystic circle (cakra) has a foolish soul.'"

Edward Sellon, previously quoted, and one of the first Westerners to describe the secret rite of the Chakra Pûjâ and the Five M writes: "Although any of the goddesses may be objects of the Shakta worship, and the term Shakti comprehends them all, yet the homage of the Shaktas is almost rectricted, in Bengal, to the consort of Shiva.

"According to the immediate object of the worshipper is the particular form of worship; but all the forms require the use of some or all of the five Makaras—Mâmsa, Matsya, Madya, Maïthuna, and Mudrâ—that is, flesh, fish, wine, women, and certain mystical gesticulations with the fingers. Suite muntrus (*sic!*), or incantations are also indispensable, according to the end proposed, consisting of various unmeaning monosyllabic combinations of letters, of great imaginary efficacy.

"All the principal ceremonies comprehend the worship of Shakti, or POWER, and require, for that purpose, the presence of a young and beautiful girl, as the living representative of the goddess. This worship is mostly celebrated in a mixed society; the men of which represent Bhairavas, or Viras, and the women, Bhairavis and Nayikas. The Shakti is personified by a naked girl, to whom meat and wine are offered, and then distributed among the assistants. Here follows the chanting of the Muntrus and sacred texts, and the performance of the Mudra, or gesticulations with the fingers. The whole terminates with orgies amongst the votaries of a very licentious description. This ceremony is entitled the SRI CHAKRA, or PURNABISHEKA, THE RING or full Initiation.

"This method of adoring the Shakti is unquestionably acknowl-
edged by the texts regarded by the Vanis as authorities for the impuri-
ties practiced.

"The members of the sect are sworn to secrecy, and will not therefore acknowledge any participation in Shakta-Puja. Some years ago,
however, they began to throw off this reserve, and at the present day
they trouble themselves very little to disguise their initiation into its
mysteries, but they do not divulge in what those mysteries consist."

False Initiates

In the *Kularnava Tantra* we read: "Wine to be drunk, flesh eaten and
the fair face to be seen—this indeed is the object, this the way to be followed," many wrongly think. Deluded in themselves, bereft of the
guidance of the Guru, they delude others, too.

> If by mere drinking of wine one were to attain fulfillment, all
> drunkards would reach perfection.

> If mere partaking of flesh were to lead to the high state, all flesh
> eaters in the world would come by immense merit.

> If liberation were to ensue by mere cohabitation with woman, all
> creatures would stand liberated by female companionship
> (*Kularnava Tantra*, translated by Shri M. P. Pandit, Madras, 1973,
> p. 36).

The numerous and vindictive enemies of Tantra, of course, misinter-
preted this. To them, this text clearly prohibits the use of wine, meat
and sex in the Tantric rite, which would contradict the Kularnava
Tantra itself. The real meaning is: "If *only* by mere drinking, etc. This
signifies that everything has to be performed according to and by following the rules and in the spirit of tantra."

In other words, the plain acts and facts are, by themselves, not
enough. They have to be performed according to the rules and the
spirit of Tantra.

Although the details of the rite vary from one guru and from one
area to the other, the fundamentals of the rite remain the same: the circle and its center, the chance meeting and matching of the couples, the
ritualistic intercourse and above all, the identification of each adept to
the cosmic Shakti or Shiva. One essential aim of the rite is the progres-
sive emergence of a strong collective Overmind (see the chapter titled
"The Overmind," p. 33) to temporarily dissolve the ego in each person
which prevents attaining a higher state of consciousness. As long as I

remain trapped in my little ego, I cannot transcend the ordinary state of wakeful consciousness. Last but not least, the chakra pûjâ makes those participating actually feel the power of sex as a cosmic creative urge, the ultimate vital power out of which the whole universe surges.

Before the onset of the chakra pûjâ, the new couples are being ritualistically wedded: "Saiva marriage is of two sorts ordained by Kula rites, one lasts till the completion of the Tantrik rite and the other for life. The Tantrik [...] should communicate his own desire unto the followers of Bhairavi, saying: 'Do ye grant us permission in this Shambhu (other name of Shiva) marriage.' Then O Shiva, in the presence of Kula worshippers he should address the woman saying 'with a guileless heart, do thou elect me as thy husband (for the duration of the rite). Thereupon electing him with fragrant flowers and unhusked rice (as her husband) according to the kula rites she should, O goddess, with great reverence place her hands on his. Then with the following mantra the pair should sprinkle the head of the Chakra with water. Thereafter all the Tantrik worshippers of the circle should welcome them with benediction" (Mah, IX, 268-274).

This ceremony is to be repeated for each pair partaking in the chakra pûjâ, and there is a reason for this. Remember, the partakers are, as a rule, either married or established couples; but for the duration of the pûjâ they will enjoy a very intimate relationship with a "new" partner. Of course, this is agreed to in advance, but the fact that this temporary relationship is solemnly proclaimed and accepted by the entire group as a "one-night" marriage, it is also confirmed that this should not become an affair to continue after the pûjâ: during the pûjâ, yes, but afterwards, no more!

An obvious question: why leave it to luck to match the couples? Why not let the guru do it? The aim is to put the ordinary man-woman relationship into question, a relationship that is usually held to be the most personal one possible. On doing this, possessiveness is non-existent. Sex becomes an impersonal force. Guenther, in *Yuganaddha: The Tantric View of Life* (Varanasi, 1979, p. 58), writes: "It is certainly correct to speak of an actual relation between a man and a woman, but this relation must not be thought of as a merely personal adjustment. Its roots lie deeper and transcend the frontiers of the limited personal world. [...] This is ample evidence for the fact that the union of maleness and femaleness is not just a passing love affair of two individuals."

The chakra pûjâ intends to make all participants realize this in practice, since simultaneously, in the same circle, his or her partner will be sexually united to somebody else. They know this union will not last beyond the pûjâ.

In an ordinary couple, both lovers think their relationship is unique, inevitable, and possible only between them. Without denying the existence of true and deep love, Tantra holds this relationship to be less personal and individual than they think it is: both are unaware of the fact that it extends far beyond them as a couple. Tantra knows that in and through the actual woman, the male loves and worships the eternal Shakti, his true beloved who is, here and now, embodied. The reverse is, of course, true for the woman.

Ordinary lovers do not realize the transcendental aspects of their relationship. What's more, Tantra knows that, more than any other factor, chance is what makes lovers meet, and their sexual drive is derived only from the libido which exists not only in the human race, but in all living beings. When a woman says to her husband: "My love, you are the man of my life and I never could love another man...," she is being 100 percent sincere and honest, and in this case, does luck come in? It is not far away! If this man had not been born, or if she had met another man, she would have sworn the same thing in another man's arms! In fact, every woman, every Shakti, not knowing it, can only be in love with the cosmic Shiva, of whom her beloved is a kind of perfect embodiment. The very intensity of her love depends on the somewhat faithful similarity between the ideal Shiva and her actual partner. Again, the reverse is, of course, true.

This is why, for the chakra pûjâ, Tantra leaves the matching of the couples to sheer luck. In the West, understandably, a question will immediately arise: "But, what about love?" In our society, it is assumed that love is a prerequisite to any intercourse. Without love, sex is considered to be vulgar, even primitive. Now, in the chakra pûjâ, because luck is the "wedding factor," obviously love is absent. Tantrists interpret the saying "to make love," practically. This ritualistic intercourse engenders a deep feeling that has nothing in common with the ordinary passionate, romantic love. It is, instead, a subtle adoration, a worship of what's "behind" the partner: his or her divine, incarnate aspects.

To understand what is meant by "supra-personal love," let's take the most "personal" love possible, that of a mother's love for her child. First, we should remember that this love does not always exist at birth: in many cases it comes only a few days later, when the newborn child begins to suck his mother's breasts. In fact, it is pure luck if this one baby is born at all. If, out of the hundreds of millions of spermatozoa, the ovum had been impregnated by another, this mother would have had quite another baby. Whichever sperm succeeds, the resulting baby is still loved by the mother in the same "personal" way. Life is the biggest lottery of all. It is sheer luck when "I," out the billion possible babies, have been born!

Back to the chakra pûjâ. Without romantic love, the Tantric couples partaking at a pûjâ become incredibly close to each other as they melt into a common collective mind. This Overmind excludes egotism or possessivity, and their relationship extends far beyond ordinary love. Nevertheless, once the pûjâ is over, the couples part and do not try to have a love affair. Moreover, at the next pûjâ, the same participants will not be invited and, because of chance, the same couples will not be formed.

Another question: "Why drink, eat, and copulate in common? Cannot the same be done by the couple alone?" Yes, it can, especially in the West, as we are not yet ready to practice these collective Tantric rites. My aim is certainly not to promote the chakra pûjâ in our society. Nevertheless, we should at least be able to understand it and discover its meaning. Ajit Mookerjee, in *Tantra Asana* (New Delhi, Basel, 1971), explains: "To practice in common acts powerfully on the partakers. The ritual's vibrations lead them all in the same direction, towards the same goal. This group-participation, suspends the identification to the ego as well as the self-assertion. It frees the adepts of their egocentrism, and triggers their latent energies" (p. 25, translation). This group-practice does not suppress the ego—this is impossible—but by melting the individual egos into one single Overmind, it fulfills their needs. The other dimension of this joint practice is the subtle bond it creates between the participants. For example, at an ordinary wedding, after the ceremony the families usually join each other for dinner. The reason for this is not to feed hungry guests, but to create a bond between them. Having enjoyed a meal together they become closer. It is also true that when nourishment is not the most important goal, what is served should be excellent. In short, sharing something in common intensifies everybody's enjoyment, and this can be true for sex as well, as the chakra pûjâ illustrates.

The other essential item of the pûjâ is the circle, the chakra. When eight couples sit together in a circle and share an intense common emotion, the group becomes a kind of a psychic cyclotron. In fact, it has always been very common for humans to join together in circles. Practically all tribal dances in India and elsewhere in the world are practiced in a circle. This is because the circle is a unique geometrical figure which permits the participants to touch and be joined together as well as to the center of the circle. During the chakra pûjâ at the center of the magic chakra or circle, there is usually a bhairavi, a naked, very beautiful young woman, the symbol of the Cosmic Shakti, with whom the guru will unite. As goddess of the prehistoric rites which are the basis of the chakra pûjâ, the Bairavi (shakti) receives offerings of wine, fish, meat, cereals and flowers which are then ritualistically shared with the other participants, after first being blessed by the guru.

The young woman, symbol of the cosmic womb, then lies on her back, her legs spread apart, showing her perfumed yoni, the narrow gate of life, where everybody, king or beggar, saint or murderer, has to pass to enter this world. The guru respectfully kisses the yoni and with some red paste, puts a red dot above it, and another between her eyebrows, followed by a row of smaller dots to link these first two. This dotted line marks the path of the ascending Kundalinî.

Then the male Tantrists respectfully kiss the various parts of their shakti, chanting: "Blessed are your knees who spread for this magic circle; blessed be thy yoni, the source of bliss, blessed be thy belly, the spring of life; blessed be thy breasts, the spring of milk; blessed be thy lips who utter magic and sacred words, blessed be thy forehead, behind which the awakened Kundalini dwells" (Colaabawala).

Then the guru and the shakti unite in the middle of the circle, symbolizing the union of the cosmic Male and Female principles, and this is the signal for the other couples to unite. At the start, they remain motionless, only "secret language" is permitted. Total control over ejaculation is, of course, required. In an ordinary Tantric maïthuna, to ejaculate is only a minor "technical incident," but in a chakra pûjâ, this would be something like a shortcut, and would ruin the pûjâ. This is why the acharya selects the participants with utmost care.

After some time, more motion is allowed, and the female partners may have orgasms provided they don't encourage the male Tantrist to ejaculate. Everybody in the group will feel these orgasms and this will heighten the sexual tension, producing extraordinary chain-reactions within the entire group. The chakra pûjâ has been exported to China, and R. van Gulik writes in his *Sexual Life in Ancient China* (Leiden, 1961, p. 260): "The dynastic history of the Mongol period, the Yüan-shih, gives in ch. 205 in the biography of the Emperor's favorite Hama a description of the Tantric rituals performed in the palace, which corroborates Chêng Szû-hsiao's remarks. There it is said: 'He (i.e., Hama) also presented to the Emperor (i.e., Hui-tsung, 1333-1367 A.D.) the Tibetan monk Ka-lin-chên, who was an expert in the secret (Tantric) ritual. That monk said to the Emperor: 'Your Majesty rules over all in the Empire, and owns all riches within the four seas. But Your Majesty should not think of this life only. Man's life is brief, therefore this secret method of the Supreme Joy (that ensures longevity) should be practiced.' The Emperor thereupon practiced this method, which is called 'Discipline in Pairs.' It is also called yen-t'ieh-érh, and 'secret.' All these practices refer to the Art of the Bedchamber. The Emperor then summoned Indian monks to direct those ceremonies, and conferred upon a Tibetan monk the title of Ta-yüan-kuo-shih 'Master of the Great Yüan Empire.' They all took girls of good families, some four, some three, for these disciplines and called that 'to sacrifice' (kung-yang). Then the Emperor daily engaged in these practices, assembling for this purpose great numbers of women and girls, and found his joy only in this dissolute pleasure."

This text confirms the historical authenticity of sexual rituals, but does not prove that the Emperor went beyond the level of pure physical enjoyment. It is not necessarily true that by importing the chakra pûjâ and practicing it according to the rules, that one will suddenly become a full blown Tantrist! The fact that the Emperor practiced this every day does at least prove that he had full control of the ejaculatory spasm!

Through the use of the circle, the chakra pûjâ becomes linked to the symbolism of the moon and to the time cycle. According to Tantra, 16 is the most sacred number because it divides the moon's cycle into 4 quarters, each in turn being divided in 4 more parts, equaling 16. The number 16 also includes all the other most sacred numbers: $3 \times 3 = 9$ and if we add 7 we get 16! These numbers, 16 and 8, are also used in Tantric Buddhism. In the following quotation (HEV. II, iii. 13) the number 16 is included, and at the same time it proves beyond doubt that ritualistic intercourse really did happen: "The *Prajnâ* (yogini) of sixteen years he clasps within his arms, and from the union of the *vajra* and the bell, the Master's consecration comes about."

And: "The *mandala*-ritual should be performed as it is given in the *Tattvasamgraha*. Into the *mandala* (circle) one should cause to enter the eight blissful Spells, twelve or sixteen years of age, and adorned with necklaces and bangles. They are called wife, sister, daughter, niece, maternal uncle's wife, maternal aunt, mother-in-law, and paternal aunt. These the yogin should honor with deep embraces and kisses. Then he should drink camphor and sprinkle the *mandala* with it. He should cause them to drink it and he should quickly gain *siddhi*. Wine is drunk and meat and herbs are eaten. Next he removes their garments and kisses them again and again. They honour him in return and sing and dance to their best, and they play there together in the union of *vajra* and lotus" (HEV. II. v. 57-63).

Obviously, 16 is only the symbolic age of the yoginîs. If this were to be taken literally, a girl could only participate for one year in the chakra pûjâ. Something else to remember: when the Tantrist calls these yoginîs "mother, sister" etc., this means he should see the Cosmic Shakti even in his own mother, sister, etc. According to N. N. Bhattacharyya, *History of Tantric Religion* (Delhi, 1982, p. 62), "Prajnâ (shakti) is called the Mother, because she gives birth to the world; and likewise the Sister (*bhaginî*) because she shows the apportionment (*vibhâga*). She is called Washerwoman (*rajakî*) because she tinges all beings (*ranjanât*); daughter (*duhitâ*) because she yields good qualities (*duhanât*); Dancer because of her tremulous nature. She is called Dombî (outcast) because she is untouchable" (*Hevajra Tantra* 16-18). In the Hevajra Tantra, Prajnâ is called *Jananî* (mother), *Bhaginî* (sister) *Rajakî* (washer-woman), *Nartakî* (dancing girl), *Duhitâ* (daughter), etc. She is also the female organ, which is the seat of great pleasure (*mahasukha*). Undoubtedly, this has all to be taken symbolically but, here again, Tantra's enemies take it literally and charge the Tantrists with systematic incest...uniting sexually with the whole family, etc.

In most cases a mystical diagram, or yantra (for example, a red triangle, or a black stone lingam), symbol of the cosmic embrace, is placed in the middle of the circle. The guru and the participants chant some mantras, like *Om Namo Shivaya*, or else they sing *kirtans* while the black lingam is sprinkled with a mixture of milk and honey, symbolizing sperm and universal fertility power. This part of the rite, which is also part of the "Right Hand's Path," can last all night, and is even performed in very puritanical ashrams (see the chapter "Symbols to be Experienced," p. 201).

At this stage of the pûjâ, erotic tension is already high, but no direct sexual caresses are allowed. Because the chakra pûjâ is held at night, only the dim light of oil lamps shines. When the erotic tension reaches its climax, the guru and his shakti unite and the other participants do the same. The roots of the chakra pûjâ may be found in the pre-Aryan collective sex rites, as they themselves are an extension of the ancient fertility rites when collective intercourse was performed in the fields and was thought to promote fertility, not only of human beings, but of animals and crops as well.

The chakra pûjâ temporarily abolishes the ego, obliterates the ordinary wakeful awareness and gives access to deeper levels of consciousness, magnified by the collective Overmind.

These orgiastic rites have deep roots in the collective human mind and they still survive sporadically today, despite two thousand years of repression. The chakra pûjâ is not group sex, but even the most corrupt group sex parties could be a kind of modern resurgence of these prehistoric orgiastic rites. Who knows? By describing the chakra pûjâ, my aim is to make us understand the underlying philosophy of this practice but in no way to promote its practice in our countries, at least not in the foreseeable future. Nevertheless, at some point, perhaps, some truly serious adepts will be able to have access to this experience. It is true that even in India, the chakra pûjâ has been abused, but this still does not breach the authentic rite's deep wisdom.

One can be an earnest follower of the Left Hand Path without ever attending a chakra pûjâ, but no Tantrika should ignore or condemn this aspect of the Shakta cult. I already mentioned how difficult it is to get first hand testimonies about the chakra pûjâ, but it is still more difficult to find people who have witnessed one without having taken part. Fortunately, this is what happened to Alexandra David-Neel, in collusion with an Indian gardener, and with the help of a good baksheesh! Here is what she says in her book *L'Inde que j'ai connue*, Paris, 1951 (pp. 190-191): "I met the gardener who told me his masters worshipped the Goddess on certain nights of the dark moon. Being himself a vaishnavite, he strongly disapproved of the ritualistic killing of a goat during the pûjâ which his masters and their guests performed in a lonely cottage in the garden.

"According to the gardener, it would be very easy to let me in through the back door next to his hut.... In a corner of the verandah there are stairs leading to the flat roof and from these stairs I would be able to peep inside the cottage."

On the night designated, Alexandra, clad in a dark blue sari, like those worn by low caste women, hid herself on the stairs. Through the small space existing above the door she could see the yantra drawn in a frame filled with earth. She also could see the plates with the food and a large container full of wine. From her hidden spot, she could follow the entire ritual. "I became tired. My uncomfortable position on the stairs, with my head stretching to peek through the space so as not to miss anything in the pûjâ became very tedious. The night was pitch black and packs of yelping jackals, the nocturnal scavengers of the Indian cities, roamed about.

"Then the poor little bleating goat was brought in to be sacrificed. Wine was poured over its head, and the celebrant whispered some mantra into its ear, then, with one blow of a sharp sword its head was severed, and, still bleeding, was put on the yantra. A little oil lamp was then placed onto its head between the horns. What a pitiful sight it was!

"The reciting of mantras began again, followed by the taking of communion which seemed to be done in a rather excessive way, especially as to the liquid element, as each mouthful of food was followed by a big gulp of wine. However, as far as I could see, no worshipper became drunk.

"A long time elapsed, and then each worshipper drew his shakti against his body. In the center of the gathering, I did not notice the presence of the *pûjâ shakti* being worshipped as an embodiment of the Goddess. Each Tantrist had only one shakti, either his spouse or his shakti chosen for one night only. Of course, it was impossible to guess what kind of relationship existed between the couples I saw.

"To me, the fifth part of the *pûjâ* or the ritualistic intercourse, appeared to be perfectly chaste. To the people of the Orient, the notion of what's decent or indecent is very different from our Westerners' ideas, and nothing regarding sex should be ridiculed or considered scandalous.

"The sadhakas remained silent and motionless like those sculptures of Hindu gods embracing their goddesses, performing a truly religious act, devoid of any obscenity. It is known that other shaktas in other similar gatherings wallow in drunken orgies, this is known and I have watched this in Nepal, but this was not the case in this particular unknown house."

"*True religious acts, devoid of any obscenity,*" to quote Alexandra David-Neel's own words, should *necessarily* be the hallmark of any authentic chakra pûjâ. This is also why it has to be ritualistic. Very different from group sex, don't you think?

Of course, the sacrifice of the goat is no doubt shocking, but in the chakra pûjâ the two ultimate powers—to take and to give life—are actually present. Death and sex. In our culture when we eat a steak, we kill by proxy! Having not seen the killing of the animal nor having killed it ourself, we do not give it another thought. Incidentally, the goat whose head is chopped off by a single stroke suffers much less than do the animals in our slaughterhouses.

To a Westerner who asked a Baul (the Bauls are wandering tantric mystics) why he ritualistically killed a goat, he answered candidly: "To eat!" This simple answer hides a basic truth: on our planet, since the beginning, Life proliferates by devouring itself! The rule of the game is: to live I have to sacrifice other lives, whether they are animals or plants.

Sure, not every chakra pûjâ includes the killing of an animal, but when a worshipper is eating the meat, the fish or the cereals, he is conscious of what he is doing and why he is doing it, and he does it with a feeling of thankfulness.

The Orgy and Me

Today, many Westerners are shocked when they hear about the chakra pûjâ, because sixteen people are involved. Seen through our eyes, the chakra pûjâ is no more than group sex, an orgy, and therefore it is lewd, immoral, and evil. As I said previously, I do not promote the chakra pûjâ in our countries, but I feel we should at least become aware of the fact that our vision of sex is very much conditioned by our religion and our laws. In our society, restrictions are often imposed on us and although we should not necessarily reject the mores of our education and culture, we should be aware of the customs of others. What we consider to be immodest or indecent behavior may be perfectly normal and decent in other countries or in time past. Half a century ago, a woman who sunbathed on the beach in public with bare breasts would have been called a whore. Today in Iran, for example, she would be stoned!

To be ashamed of one's genital organs or the idea that sex is a sin are not natural reactions, but acquired ones. To primitive people, sex was something quite natural, something to be enjoyed without shame and something that not only gave pleasure, but ensured the tribe's fertility and prosperity. During *Holi*, the most important Indian festival that celebrates plant life, nothing is forbidden. Until recently, it was nothing less than a huge collective orgy. The same is true for the feast of *Bah*. The Hoses living in the northwestern part of India have formidable orgies at the time of harvest, and, despite the strong opposition of the Church, this happened in many parts of Europe as well.

According to Mircea Eliade, an orgy is a necessity of collective living during which the individuals melt into one collective Overmind. In Europe take, for example, the custom of planting the maypole and the dances which follow. The staunch, puritanical Englishman, Philip Stubbes, in his book *Anatomy of Abuses* (London, 1583) condemns these customs indignantly because, according to him, when the young boys and girls spent the night in the woods, Satan became their god, and in the morning when they brought the maypole—"this stynking ydol"—to the village, only one girl out of three remained "undefiled." Let's also not forget the chapter about the witches: at night in a clearing in the forest they celebrated the Horned God, the European Shiva, who later became Satan and, to the Church, the very incarnation of evil. Did those boys and girls with their maypole not perpetuate some rites of the Old Religion? This was probably the main reason Philip Stubbes was so upset—nothing to do with the sexual aspect of the feast. Why does he call the maypole "this stynking ydol" if he did not see it as a symbol? And as a symbol, could it not be some sort of lingam or phallic symbol?

At any rate, there are many more examples of these customs, such as the Scandinavian feast of St. John and the Carnival festivities which exist all over Europe. Even the Semites, at some period in their history, worshipped the divine couple, the Hurricane god and the god of Fertility (Ba'al) as well as the goddess of plant fertility, Bêlit. These paleo-semitic rites which celebrated to the utmost the sacredness of sex and fertility, went on for ages, or at least for many centuries. The puritanical overreaction which came later was probably in proportion to the many excesses which were committed.

Is Tantra Promiscuity?

If, in the West, many equate Tantra to promiscuity, this prejudice stems partly from people like Rajneesh—the man with the 92 Rolls-Royces—called Bhagwan Shree Rajneesh, or Our Divine Lord Rajneesh. An Indian would translate Our Lord Jesus Christ as Bhagwan Shree Christ.

Rajneesh, who died in 1990, at the age of 58, was a charismatic person, a great orator and a utopian thinker. He has said some very interesting things and I have no quarrel with him nor with his followers and, occasionally, I even quote him. Perhaps he himself did not even know what really happened with the "sex-groups" in his own ashram in Poona. Suffering from the worst form of asthma (he was allergic to fragrant soaps and perfume) he surely never attended one.

In fact, what he himself and his disciples did, or did not do, is none of my business. But, it is a pity he called his doctrine "neo-Tantra" because, in fact, it really is "no-Tantra": in his teaching there is no place for rituals, yantras, mantras, not even as a means toward the awareness of the sacredness of sex and of the cosmic aspects of the union of Shiva and Shakti. Making love is not enough in itself to obtain Tantra! Could we call "neo-Christian" a doctrine which would leave no place for Christ, the Bible, the Gospel, and for Catholics, no Mass, etc.?

Because of Rajneesh and a few authors of books about Tantra, many people believe Tantra to be immoral. True, Tantra is amoral, which is not synonymous with immoral. Since Tantra is not a religion, nor an organization, it brings no dogma, no credo, no moral principles. Morality being a relative concept depending on one's country and time, Tantra leaves the choice to the Tantrists themselves. Nobody should adjure his faith for the sake of Tantra. Just because Tantra has no ready-made moral principles one should not reject automatically all moral laws!

For instance, when Tantra dissociates "marriage" from "sexual union," considering sex to be the union of the cosmic principles Shiva and Shakti on the human plane, this does not in any way mean that Tantra rejects marriage! Each Tantrist has to conform his or her own conduct to the moral and social laws *he or she* abides by, and Tantra has nothing to say in this respect. Yes, Tantra ignores the notion of sin in connection with intercourse, which is to be seen the closest possible exchange between two human beings and does not ask if the couple is married or not. Tantra, however, knows that religion and society somehow must regulate sex, and in our countries there seems to be no alternative to marriage.

Does Tantra endanger the married couples? First, let's be well aware of the fact that a high percentage of marriages end in divorce and not because of Tantra. On the other hand, I personally know many couples whose marriage was faltering and who, thanks to Tantra, found their way to a much better and more stable relationship. Tantric couples, married or unmarried, are not less firmly established than are non-Tantric ones.

The Symbolism
of the Five Makaras

Obviously the chakra pûjâ is unthinkable without the five Makaras, but the reverse is quite possible, and this is lucky for us who live in the Western world. Deeply symbolical but at the same time very concrete, the five Makaras enable us to perceive—here and now—the surging of ultimate cosmic forces, to give access to the sacredness, to the "significant" hidden behind the "insignificant," to the trivial, and to the profane.

Although the five Makaras include only such trivial acts as eating, drinking, and copulating, they nevertheless imply the two most important powers, i.e., to take or to give life, both inextricably linked. This is especially important for modern people, who are becoming incapable of feeling the sacramental aspects of food and sex. To primitive people, these are ceremonies through which they can communicate with the life force itself. Here I quote Mircea Eliade:

One of the main differences between archaic and modern man lies in the fact that the latter is unable to live his organic life fully, and first of all his sex life and the act of eating, as a sacred rite.

To modern man they are only physiological acts, whilst to archaic man, they are sacraments, ceremonies through which he can unite himself to the *power* of *Life* itself.

Power and *Life* being manifestations of the ultimate reality; these elementary acts become, to primitive people, rites helping them to come closer to the real.

The rite consists always in the repetition of archetypal gestures accomplished *in illo tempore* (at the onset of "History") by the ancestors or by the gods, in order to render holy the most common and trivial acts. The rite *coincides*, through the repetition, with its archetype, abolishing the profane time. One witnesses, so to say, the *same act* accomplished *in illo tempore* at a cosmogonic "dawning" moment...

By eating or by making love, primitive man inserts himself in another plane, which is not simply feeding or making love (*Histoire des Religions*, p. 40).

The 5 M and the chakra pûjâ both tend toward the expansion of consciousness, the transcendence of the ego, the suppression of all illusory borders between "you," "me," "the others," and between the "inner" and the "outer" world. Viewed by Tantra, our universe is a gigantic fabric in which each being, each object, each atom is a fiber. As an individual, I have the illusion that I am (almost) self-sufficient, which is a tragic mistake, because if I am unable to transcend my own little ego, it becomes my prison and the hidden root of all suffering. But to "transcend" does not mean to negate or destroy it. Although my ego, as a necessary structure of my being, has a limited but real existence, it is not my true Self, nor my ultimate Reality.

Here we have to remember the fact that for the Tantrist and the physicist alike, the infinite multiplicity of forms we perceive, veils the fundamental unity of matter and its essence, the pure cosmic energy, the Shakti. Likewise, the multiplicity of species and individuals veils the oneness of Life, the other modality of nature's creative cosmic energy.

However, instead of turning our back to life to reach some metaphysical, abstract Absolute, and therefore becoming a rigorous ascetic, the Tantrist integrates in the world and enjoys life fully. To the Tantrist, to enjoy (*bhoga, ananda*) is essential to life: everywhere and always, each living being pursues happiness and flees suffering.

Whether you like it or not, in order to live and survive, the most staunch egotist has to unite with other life-forms by eating or copulating. To eat is also an act of intimate fusion, much more intimate than to have intercourse because what I eat becomes my very being. On the other hand, to perpetuate ourselves, we must give up our ego, with which we identify ourselves: we have to meld our genes with those of a "stranger"!

Eternally, living matter recycles itself: what's my body today will be tomorrow another's and so on, endlessly. To eat, I must kill an animal or a vegetable, hence the sacrifice of the goat Alexandra David-Neel witnessed. When one eats a good steak with friends in a restaurant, one forgets the cow that has been killed and it becomes an abstraction. But, having watched the killing of the goat right before the pûjâ, Tantrists realize they cannot survive without killing other life-forms. Even eating a piece of cheese implies the killing of millions of bacteria, which are also conscious living beings. The same law applies to all that is living, from a bacterium to the whale. Only people try to escape being eaten by having their corpse sealed in a coffin or, "better," cremated.

Beyond this permanent drama, Life is one and sex is the universal vital drive, the antidote to death, the mysterious fabric of all species whose genes are permanently mixed. Eating and copulating are also the ultimate joys: far from feeling guilty about it, during the chakra pûjâ and while enjoying the five Makaras, the Tantrists try to intensify everything to the utmost.

If all living beings kill, eat, and beget, are they all Tantrists? No, because Tantra transforms crude biological urges into something sacred, into a rite to transcend them. Mircea Eliade (*L'épreuve du labyrinthe*, Paris, 1978, p. 87) wrote: "In Tantra, during the rites, carried out after a long preparation, human life becomes transfigured.... During the ritualistic embrace, love becomes more than eroticism or sex, it is some sort of sacrament; drinking wine during the pûjâ is not taking some alcoholic beverage but partaking in a sacrament..." To ritualize, to transfigure, is the very essence and meaning of the five Makaras.

The Hidden Meaning of the Elements

According to the *Mahanirvanam Tantra*: "The best worshippers, well-versed in Kula (Tantra) rites, adore the Prime Kâlikâ, the Queen of Kulas, with the five essential ingredients (tattwas). Enjoying all the objects of the universe they roam at large untouched by any danger or calamity.

"O dear, know energy (fire) as the first Tattwa, air as the second, water as the third, and earth as the fourth, O Shiva! Know the fifth, O thou of a beautiful countenance, as the root of the universe. Knowing these five Tattwas, and Kula rites, a man becomes liberated even when alive.

"The characteristic of the first Tattwa (fire, radiation) is that it is the great panacea of the creatures which gives them felicity and (by virtue of which) they forget their sorrows.

"The characteristic of the second Tattwa (meat) is that it should be produced either in villages, in the air, or in a forest, and should give nourishment and increase understanding, energy, and strength.

"The characteristic of the third (fish) is, O auspicious Lady, that it should be born in water, beautiful, delicious and such as to create generative power.

"The characteristic of the fourth (cereals) should be that it is cheap, produced from earth, gives life to creatures and is at the bottom of all life of the three worlds.

"The characteristic of the last Tattwa (intercourse) is, O Goddess, that it yields great joy, is the root of the origin of all creatures, is without beginning or end and is the root of the universe" (MAH., 101-110).

M. N. Dutt specifies the second Tattwa to be meat, either of goat or sheep reared in a village, or of partridges, or other birds that move about in the air, or of a deer, etc., that live in the forest. The third element is undoubtedly fish, and according to the text, this increases the progeny; in other words, strengthens the generative power of man. The fourth are cereals, the fifth, the maïthuna "being the support of all creation" (p. 111).

An interesting fact: the 5 Tantric and alchemist elements, i.e., Earth, Water, Air, Fire, and Ether are identical and their aims are the same, i.e., to regenerate ordinary, trifling human beings to reveal their higher reality and powers, hidden deep within. Nevertheless if alchemy's way and Tantra's overlap, the means used to reach this goal are totally distinct.

The five elements have been in use in our Western culture until the appearance of modern chemistry and physics, which seem to do pretty well without them. This means that one may understandably ask what's the point of wasting precious time on these five "outdated" elements? Out of curiosity? If this were the case, they would hardly be worth more than a few sentences, but we know otherwise.

Defining the Tattwas

It is no easy task to give a clear definition of the elements, or tattwas, which are very concrete though imponderable, subtle though material forces. An element is not some tangible object, but rather a set of laws and forces ruling a given state of matter and having specific properties.

The Element Earth (*Ksiti*): Suffice to look at the star-studded firmament to notice our universe above is all made of...void! However, in some peculiar spots, cosmic matter agglomerates instead of being evenly distributed all over the cosmic space, whose gigantic dimensions are inconceivable to our limited mind. All the universal laws and forces acting to densify the cosmic matter are the element Earth, and not the stars or the planets themselves, which are but the results of it. Our own planet is nothing more than a local manifestation of those laws and forces as are the sun, the stars, and the billions of galaxies. More: each atom in the agglomerated cosmic matter partakes in the element Earth. My own body is, really, cooled down "sun-matter." If these laws did not exist, there would be no planet Earth, and we would not be discussing it!

The Element Water (*Apa*): All the laws and forces which retain matter in a fluid state result in the element Water, and the actual water we drink is only a manifestation of this element. OK, you say, but what's the point? The importance is enormous because the essential property of all fluids is to pick up the cosmic rhythms, which, in turn, govern all our own biorhythms. On our planet, the most visible cosmic rhythm is the one which controls the tide, moving oceans day and night as they respond to the moon's and sun's attraction. In fact, the waters of our earth even respond to the rhythms of the remotest galaxies, to the rhythms of the entire universe.

These cosmic rhythms do not solely rule the oceans or the seas; there are tides in a glass of water or in a dew-drop! Because my own body is composed of 85 percent water, all my biorhythms are, day and night, influenced by the moon, the sun, the stars and the galaxies (see the chapter "A Tantric Meditation: Contemplating Our Mother, the Sea").

Humans and beasts, as well as trees, are influenced by the tides. The properties of the timber vary according, not only to the season, but also to the phase of the moon during which the tree has been felled. The timber that keeps the longest comes from trees felled during winter and at the new moon, a time of rest for all plant life, a time when they should be the least sensitive to any outside influences. Theodor Schwenk, in his book *Das Sensible Chaos*, notes that precious South American timber is still being marked by a seal indicating the phase of the moon during which the tree has been felled, and this fixes its value.

Thus, through the medium of all my body fluids, deep within my tissues and my cells, the moon and all celestial bodies attune the imperceptible ballet of all my vital rhythms. Remember: Life is rhythm, and rhythm is life.

The Element Air (*Vayu*): Of course, the element Air is gas. According to Tantra, and yoga as well, the gases are the vectors, the carriers of subtle cosmic forces. For thousands of years, the Tantric yogis knew air not to be a dead gas, but something which carried a very subtle life-force, called prâna, varying according to the season and the spot. They know our very vitality depends on prâna, whose nature, they say, "is the same as the lightning," which is an extraordinary intuition.

Until very recently, science (especially biology) was only concerned about the molecular composition of the air we breathe: nitrogen, oxygen, and rare gases, neglecting its ionization. Now, physicists know that, for instance, an oxygen atom can be "loaded" with an extra electron. Depending on the proportion of such ionized atoms of oxygen, air's vital properties vary widely. Knowing this, yogis and Tantrists alike discovered special techniques to increase our vitality. See my book *Pranayama: the Dynamics of Breath*.

This prânic theory of the element Air is of considerable practical importance because it is linked to our very vitality and health. Let's take for example, the office-sickness that strikes people working in buildings without proper ventilation. These offices are, it is true, air-conditioned, but according to the prânic theory, conditioned air is devoid of prâna and this is what causes the office-sickness. The ionized oxygen atoms lose their extra electron while traveling through the air-conditioning system. This fact, which was sadly ignored for so many years, has slowly gained recognition, but the proud skyscrapers with their sealed windows are still there! Since the people who work in these buildings cannot change this, they have to compensate for the lack of vital prânic energy by practicing, for a few minutes daily, pranayama-type breathing exercises.

The Element of Fire or Light (*Tejas*): The element "Fire" is matter in its radiant form, like, for instance, the light and warmth of the sunshine or of an ordinary candle. Without this element our planet would be frozen and barren because the sun would not be able to radiate its heat and light through the distance between our star and us. Living beings existing on Earth would not only be unable to see the sun, but they would never see the stars either.

But we, the inhabitants of our beautiful Earth, are immersed in an ocean of radiations of all kinds, from the lowest infra-red to the highest ultra-violet. Not only are we subject to these radiations, but we also "broadcast" many forms of radiation, known and unknown. Is not radiation the purest form of energy? And perhaps the closest to psychic energy? In this respect, the chapter about the Dancing Shiva shows us the Cosmic Shiva dancing in the midst of flames and holding fire in his hands.

The Element Ether (*Akasha*): Akasha, or ether, was the last of the five elements of the ancient alchemists to resist modern science, in fact, almost up to the end of the 19th century. Until then, it was considered to be self-evident that cosmic space was "filled" with a very subtle substance, having practically no resistance to the propagation of radiations of any kind. It seemed unthinkable that radiation could propagate in space devoid of a medium, in nothingness. Things have changed since 1881, when Albert Michelson tried, with his interferometer, to measure the motion of our planet within the ether: his world-famous experiences failed to prove the existence of ether, but he discovered that the velocity of light remained always constant and this lead to Einstein's theory of relativity. Thus science dropped the notion of ether, at least provisionally.

But to Tantra, the notion of Akasha is more complex than simply an ultra-subtle medium filling the cosmic void. To Tantra, Akasha is more than matter in its subtlest state. It is what could be called "dynamic space." Our ordinary common sense, conceives space as a huge, inert "hole," big enough to hold God's universe. To be sure, this is, of course, not the scientific view about the nature of space, which remains a mystery. If we imagine space as being pure void, it is, of course, totally passive.

Not so to Tantra, where Akasha is still more than dynamic space to become creative space. The worldly objects emerge out of Akasha; in fact, each object creates its own space, and space engenders the universe, which is too big a chunk for our solid commonsense and logic to swallow. Akasha is the indefinite border, everywhere present in our universe, where the unmanifest becomes manifested. Akasha is the omnipresent sustainer of our manifested world, symbolized by the cosmic embrace of Shiva and Shakti. This makes us understand why human intercourse, the replica of the cosmic creative urge, is symbolized by the Akasha.

This is all rather schematic, I agree, like so many topics in this book which try to give a panoramic rather than an academic view of Tantra—above all, a practical view of it.

How to integrate this symbolism within the five Makaras? Let's start with *Mudra*, i.e., grain or cereals. Eating grain with respect, the Tantrist knows this ingredient is "cheap, produced from the earth, gives life to creatures, and is at the bottom of the life of the three worlds." Through *Mudra*, the Tantrist goes back to our fertile Mother-Earth, sustainer of all animal life, for whom primitive people held orgiastic fertility rites. To eat cereals is to unite ourselves with our foster-mother Earth, to absorb parts of the material world with which we have incessant exchanges.

By eating fish (*Matsya*) "born in the water, delicious and able to create generative power," the Tantrist unites with the element of Water, without which no life on Earth would be possible, and with all living beings in the oceans, seas, lakes, rivers, ponds, etc. Water is the element where life first started on our planet. In the chapter "A Tantric Meditation: Contemplating our Mother, the Sea," I quoted Commandant Cousteau: "We are organized sea-water." This is really true: I am a walking aquarium! And that's why in almost all Tantric rites there is the *ghata*, an amphora (symbol of the uterus) filled with perfumed water representing the amniotic fluid, adorned, as a symbol of fecundity, with flowers, fruits and green branches. While in my mother's uterus I was like a fish and, mysteriously, somehow my body's wisdom remembers this.

By eating meat (*Mamsa*), the adept unites with all beings living on our planet, from mammals to birds. Above all, when he respectfully eats the goat's meat, the Tantrist knows he had to kill. Before severing the goat's head with one single stroke, the goat had been ritualistically "initiated" by the guru who whispered in its ear the saving mantra through which it would enjoy a higher reincarnation. I have a film of this ceremony and what's really remarkable is that the goat does not struggle, but remains very calm, even when its head is being tied to the Y-shaped sacrificial pole: it is as if it understood and accepted to sacrifice its life.

In the *Markandeya Purana* (XCI. 32) it is said:

OM, Blessed be the animal
with its horns and limbs
OM, fasten the animal to the dark pillar
who parts life and death

Just before striking the fatal blow:

OM, Hrim, Kâli, Kâli,
with thy awful teeth
devour, swallow, cut,
kill...

...and the scimitar swoops down on the goat's neck. This seems cruel to those who kill by proxy, but in our slaughterhouses do we protest the killing, do we respect the beasts?

In order not to forget the sacrifice, the head is put on a plate with an oil-lamp between the horns, a symbol of the goat's consciousness and of the immortal Self.

Wine (*Madhya*) is the element of Fire and *Mahanirvana Tantra* (VI, 185-191) gives us the following indications: "Then having placed his own shakti on a separate seat on his left or seated on the same seat with her, the worshipper should place a charming vessel. The drinking cup (*Pânâ Pâtra*) must be made either of gold, silver, glassware or a cocoanut. He should keep it on the right side of the vessel containing meat (*Shuddi Pâtra*). Then the intelligent worshipper should distribute wine in various cups in order of precedence. He should distribute wine in the cups and meat and fish in the dishes. He should eat and drink with all the persons assembled. First they should take most excellent meat dishes. Then with delighted hearts all worshippers should take up their respective cups filled with wine. Then meditating on the spiral tube (Kundalini), the seat of consciousness, extending from the tongue to the base of the body, reciting the principal mantras and obtaining each other's permission they should pour it into their mouth."

Wine often plays an important part in rites, especially in the Mediterranean: think of Communion, for instance. And then there is the beaker that symbolizes the yoni, i.e., the vagina, and the skull: during the pûjâ, the idea of death should always be present, not as something macabre or gruesome but with an idea to enjoy the two antidotes to death: food and sex. Traditionally and in days of old, wine was drunk out of a real skull, preferably a Brahmin's.... Later, Brahmin's skulls became scarce, and were replaced by a coconut shell, or by a beaker. Knowing this, we understand why at the funerals of an Aryan, the eldest son shatters his father's skull with a club. Officially, this is done to facilitate the Soul's departure, but in fact it is to prevent the skull from being used for some ritualistic practice!!!

In Tibet, such skulls are still in use. They are inlaid with silver plating and nicely carved with ritualistic signs. Once, in Geneva, in an antique shop, I saw such a skull but, because of the price, I did not buy it. The next day, I changed my mind and went back to the shop: too late. It had been sold a few minutes before. But, as feeling sorry is the most useless of all unpleasant feelings, I have no regrets!

Now, let's get back to the wine. The role of wine is to stir up sexual desire and awaken the fire of the Kundalinî at the pole of the species, at the lower part of the spine. The guru, as well as the other Tantrists, holding the beaker with both hands, presents it to his shakti, looking straight into her eyes. She takes the beaker with both hands, too, and drinks slowly a first sip, then hands him the cup, and he, too, sips some of the wine. The beaker, or the coconut shell, or the skull, goes back and forth from shiva to shakti till the beaker is empty. This is a very strong part of the pûjâ, especially because everybody knows the culminating point of the rite is near. We should not forget that it is pure luck if both are together and for one night only.

Next comes the ritualistic embrace (Maïthuna): "The characteristic of the last Tattwa is, O Goddess, that it yields great joy, is the root of the origin of creatures, is without beginning or end and is the root of the universe" (MAH, VII, 108).

Let's meditate upon this short sentence that includes the essence of the pûjâ. The entire rite aims at the Maïthuna to make this experience as intense as possible. I quote Colaabawala: "In Tantra, after having awakened the sexual power, it has to be put at work. To become pure energy, it has to leave its usual seat, the sex organs. Thus, the physical intimacy, stemming from sexual contact, runs into a psychic fusion; nothing is done, quite the opposite, to have an orgasm with genital contact, everything aims at building up a powerful current of spiritual exchange.... Orgasm is not denied, but it has to be at the cerebral level not at the genital level, as in profane sex.

The way the Tantric pairs are placed, is not the same in all rituals. Sometimes, the shaktis lie down on their back, arms and legs spread, each one drawing a pentacle, the symbolic flaring sword; the head, the fifth part of the diagram, is, most of times, turned to the inside of the circle, but the opposite happens too."

During the entire pûjâ, always, the incantatory magic of the mantras is used (see this chapter) along with their visual concretized in the form of yantras. If the chakra pûjâ is not to be practiced in the West, the five Makaras may well be used.

Part 5

Sexual Control

The Male Orgasm

According to modern psychology, most women never experience an orgasm. On the other hand, sexual literature has made the problem worse by making us believe that any sex act ending without an orgasm is a failure. Tantra is not obsessed with this "compulsory orgasm" that is supposed to be any modern couple's ideal. Nevertheless, Tantra agrees that the problem of female orgasm does exist, but adds to it the problem of the male orgasm. Rajneesh, a dubious reference, wrote in his *Book of Secrets* (Vol. 2., Poona, 1976, p. 397): "That is why women are so angry and irritated, and they will remain so. No meditation can help them to be peaceful and no philosophy, no religion, no ethics, will make them at ease with the men with whom they are living. They are in frustration, in anger, because modern science and old tantra both say that unless a woman is deeply fulfilled orgasmically, she will be a problem in the family. That which she is lacking will create irritations and she will be always in a fighting mood.

"So if your wife is always in a fighting mood, think again about the whole thing. It is not simply the wife: you may be the cause. And because women are not achieving orgasm, they become anti-sex. They are not willing to go into sex easily. They have to be bribed; they are not ready to go into sex. Why should they be ready if they never achieve any deep bliss through it? Rather, they feel after it that the man has been using them.

"Ninety percent of women have never reached a peak of such a blissful convulsion of the body that every fiber vibrates and every cell becomes alive. They have not reached it, and this is because of an anti-sexual attitude in the society. The fighting mind is there, and the woman is so repressed that she has become frigid."

And the *Hite Report* adds to it: "Yes, the woman often has to learn how to really enjoy the sex act *despite* her partner... "

Generally speaking, it is accepted that orgasm is a problem, but only to the woman: when the male ejaculates, he has an orgasm. This is not true! Ejaculation is one thing, and orgasm is quite another. Although some modern sexologists know this, the "average" citizen is quite astonished when somebody tells him that 90 percent of all males never experience orgasm. Since ejaculation and the few seconds before it are the climax of his sexual pleasure, the male takes it for granted that this is the only male orgasm to be enjoyed. On the contrary, Tantra has known for thousands of years that ejaculation is precisely what prevents the male from experiencing the real orgasm, or the sexual ecstasy which leads him to higher levels of consciousness, in fact, cosmic levels. Ejaculation puts a grinding halt to the sex act, to the man as well as the woman. To put it bluntly: if 90 percent of all females do not have orgasms, it is because 85 percent of the males are "premature ejaculators."

Premature ejaculation is any ejaculation that happens before the woman is fully satisfied, after she has had one or more orgasms. Remember: the mere fact that a man is able to withhold his ejaculation does not mean that he had a real orgasm, even if he had very intense sexual pleasure, but it's a good start!

Ejaculation not only stops the ascent toward a true male orgasm, but it also kills desire, whose enchanting magnetism should be permanent in the couple during intercourse and afterward. This magnetism and the magic of the union of Shiva and Shakti vanishes as soon as the lingam becomes limp: the lovers part and return to the dull reality of daily life. This is sad.

To the male, Tantra promises unlimited sexual power, erections as prolonged as his partner and he wants them, plus the possibility of having two, three, or more sexual unions a day and still be able to desire his shakti. No doubt, such a program is quite tempting to him and to his partner as well, but, as soon as the price tag is shown—to give up ejaculation—the smile disappears and the face becomes long and serious.

This is quite understandable: because of the age-old ejaculatory reflex which is so deeply ingrained in us, the common routine of kisses, love-play, intercourse, ejaculation, detumescence seems so natural, even intangible. The sex impulse has its roots in our irresistible will to survive, and this implies copulation followed by ejaculation. Such sexual behavior is deeply engraved within our genes and is reinforced by our education and culture. To Tantra, except, of course, for the sake of procreation, ejaculation is superfluous. Nevertheless, the male's reticence to avoid ejaculation is understandable. But, regarding harmony within the couple, and without even thinking of linking sex and spirituality, it is well worth trying.

Tao, which is a form of Chinese Tantra, agrees to it. Jolan Chang, in his book *The Tao of Love and Sex* writes:

"The Taoïsts of old taught that male orgasm and ejaculation were not the same thing. To the male, to ejaculate less frequently does not at all mean to be sexually diminished or to experience lesser degrees of joy. To say 'ejaculation is the culmination of sexual pleasure' is only a habit. And a bad one.

"People often ask me what is pleasure when I emit only once out of every hundred copulations. My usual answer is: 'I certainly will not exchange my joy for your kind of pleasure. To me, the twelve years during which I had this pleasure of ejaculation, are simply long wasted years.' If my interlocutor happens to be a male, he cannot doubt I am sincere; he can see how peaceful, happy and healthy I am, and unquestionably happy to make love. If a woman puts me the question, and if she at first regrets it —to me—as soon as we start a sexual relationship, my passion does not allow the slightest doubt regarding the intense pleasure I have with her. After only a few hours, she will soon find out she is discovering a totally new way to love and she probably will notice the fact she previously never experienced such an intense sexual delight. In fact, many women had the generosity to acknowledge that until then they had not known the sexual union could bring such an intense joy (p. 23).

"Thus, for twelve years I satisfied myself with ejaculation—or to masturbate inside a vagina, as I see things now—but today I can say a sex act without ejaculation represents also a relief of tension, but without an explosion. This pleasure ends with peace, not violence, and gives a sense of merging in something vaster and more transcendental than the little "I." It is a communion with a wholeness, not a separation, but a close union and not an individual and solitary spasm excluding the other partner. No words could express this" (pp. 31-32).

Before I approach the subject further, let us first be aware that what is asked of us is not to give up ejaculation all of a sudden, totally, once and for all. It should be a gradual practice and the following argument persuaded quite a few couples to make a stab at it.

First, if a male's sexual prowess varies from once a week (on Sunday morning at 8:15 A.M.?) to daily contacts, obviously it has its limits. On the other hand, a woman's sex potential is unlimited.

Second, as long as there is desire, physiology does not limit the number nor the duration of the erections. If there is no ejaculation, desire does not subside, the strength of the erection remains intact and makes it possible to have unlimited sexual intercourse of long duration. To conclude: every sexual act ending without ejaculation is a "net erotic profit" for the couple! The more the male saves his "ejaculatory ammunition" the more his sexual potency will match the female's, and this is definitely an important factor contributing to the couple's harmony. So, why not try?

Of course, this is just basic reasoning, but before attempting to go beyond "ordinary" sexual pleasure, let's first understand it! During

"normal" sexual intercourse, the *last few seconds* before the final movement which releases the ejaculatory spasm are the most gratifying to
the male. With the spasm, it's all over: what remains is disappoint-
ment. The pleasure the male gets from ejaculation is less than that
experienced when he is on the verge of it. Tantra's solution is as clever
as it is simple: making the most intense joy last as long as possible.
Therefore, we have to avoid the ejaculatory spasm, and Tantra provides us with the techniques needed to achieve this.

The supreme art, for a Tantric male, is to remain indefinitely on the
verge, and by doing so, he has access to the "sexual heaven" in the
brain, paving the way to the true male orgasm. A couple's experience
is no more limited, nor interrupted by the male's sexual breakdown.
Tantra offers this experience to all couples because no sexual acrobatics are involved and one can go from purely genital pleasure to erotic,
and finally to the spiritual.

In the beginning, when the shiva comes close to ejaculating, he still
will have to cease all movements, and his shakti as well, to avoid the
spasm. Only a very experienced Tantrist is able to stay on the razor's
edge or near ejaculation and still remain totally active, without sliding
into the spasm: even in India these who succeed are very few!
Nevertheless, any male is able, with a little practice and the help of his
shakti, to remain longer and longer on the verge of ejaculation. In the
beginning, he will have to avoid all movement, but after a short while,
he will be able to move his body lightly, and after some time, these
movements will become greater without unleashing an ejaculatory
spasm. It is all a matter of relaxation, breathing, concentration, plus a
few technical hints. For these, please refer to the chapters about how
to control ejaculation.

The Erection,
its Secrets, its Problems

Mankind's survival depends on erection! If the penis stayed limp, the ovum would be waiting in vain for the spermatozoon. Whether we like the idea or not, since Adam's time, at the very beginning of our life, there was an erect penis.

This most precious erection, about which the male only becomes concerned when he has lost it, looks as simple as inflating a tire but, in fact, with man—and the monkeys—the "hydraulics" of erection are most complex. With other animals, Nature often chooses the simplest and safest path. The penile bone, which nature provided some mammals with, automatically guarantees an unbending erection, but, with some drawbacks: a bone can break, an erect penis never. The male otter, because he is such a fiery lover, breaks his more than once in a lifetime! Luckily it mends itself. The squirrel's tiny penile bone is as sharp-pointed as a nail, but unquestionably, the champion penis is that of the whale: six feet long, as compared to the walrus' which measures "a mere" three inches. Dogs, wolves, and bears all have a penile bone.

Man would rather lose a limb than lose his penis but, paradoxically, he knows very little about its structure and how and why it becomes erect. Only recently did we unravel the very complexity of its mechanism. I wonder, too, why books on sexology go on at great length about the female sex organs, but say so little about the penis? Is it because we can see and readily touch it that we think there is no mystery in it?

To ignore the structure of the penis is a luxury which only men with no erection problems, or no desire to control it, can afford, but any Tantrist must know how it works. By "Tantrist," I mean not only the male adept, but the yoginî as well: how could she cleverly cooperate during the act if she does not know the rules of the game?

There is no need to go into full details about the lingam's physiology; nevertheless, we should have a clear idea of how it works. So many males do not even know that their penis is very much like an inflatable beach-mattress made of three separate inflatable cylinders. In an inflatable mattress, they're located side by side, while in the lingam they are like a package. The central cylinder (*corpus spongiosum*) contains the urinary passage, which, because it is also the ejaculatory tract, plays an important role in the ejaculatory process. Its head, also called the *glans penis*, is the most sensitive part of the lingam.

On both sides of this central cylinder are two more pressure cylinders (*corpus cavernosum*), the most important ones to do with an erection. The penis is firmly connected to the pubic bone and the ischium, and its root is the bulb, next to the anal aperture: without this strong base the erect penis would wobble.

And the penis is muscular! The muscles surrounding its base are powerful ones (cf. the chapter about "How to Control Ejaculation") and their spasmodic contractions generate the too short ejaculatory pleasure. Now, if we cover the three cylinders with a tough sheet of skin, we get our beloved penis!

Exposed, it looks vulnerable and fragile but, in fact, it can withstand the worst maltreatment and is seldom injured. I guess nobody would want to try to prove the surgeon's word when he tells us that even with the help of a sharp knife it is very difficult to cut it off: it escapes the blade the way a slippery eel would. If a penis is only partially cut, one needs only to put the pieces together, then make a few stitches and Mr. Penis will heal all on his own!

Three inflatable cylinders plus some muscles wrapped up in a thick sheet: not that complicated! As for the erection, not difficult either: just inflate the cylinders, and you have a stiff lingam ready for use! Simple!

But nature seems to like to make things more complicated, until by sheer sophistication it becomes simple again. The hydraulics of erection involves millions (!) of tiny valves to regulate the flow and the pressure of the blood in the penis. The regulation by the nervous system is so wonderfully programmed and computerized, that no man-made irrigation system could ever match it.

Concerning blood pressure, one would think that in its limp state, the pressure inside the lingam is the same as in the rest of the body, but this is not true: only in full erection is the pressure inside the penis the same as in all the other arteries of the body! To know this is important: because they ignored it, those who attempted to cure impotence by "strangling" the lingam at its base with rings to trap the blood inside the erection chambers, failed to get the result: the penis swelled a little, turned bluish, even black but stayed woefully limp.

While at rest, the rush of the blood into the lingam has to be checked but, quite on the contrary, to get an erection those millions of valves should be opened wide. Here we come to a very important fact: an erection is produced by the relaxation of those valves which regulate the bloodstream within the lingam. All stress, nervous tension and anxiety—for example, the fear of not being able to have an erection—will make the erection impossible, and this is the *most common* cause of male impotence. *Relaxation* is the only thing which will allow the bloodstream to rush into the lingam and to stiffen it, and this state of relaxation should last as long as the erection itself. As a rule, all impotent men are somewhat prone to anxiety. To solve this problem, the best way is to relax, to take it easy and to breathe slowly, deeply.

To get an erection is one thing, to maintain it is something else, and because this depends on double control, things become complicated. As soon as the correct pressure of a tire is attained, we trap the air inside and to control it a single valve is enough. But let's imagine a tire with two valves, one allowing air to enter the tire, the other one letting the air escape. The correct pressure will only be maintained if there is a precise balance between the working of those valves; if not, the pressure in the tire would become too high or, on the contrary, the tire would deflate. During an erection this most precise balance is achieved by the greater wisdom of the body which controls not only two but *millions* of those tiny valves, and this is done without the happy owner of the erect penis knowing it! Inside a tire, no harm is done if the air remains there for months on end, but in a living penis the intake of rich arterial blood into the spongy tissues of the lingam has to occur at the same time as when the used blood is to be drained off. As soon as we get the correct pressure in all three cylinders, this precise balance between in- and outflow of blood in the penis should be maintained. In real life situations, due to mental or physiological changes, the degree of stiffness of the penis often varies, and this is quite normal and still incredible.

During Tantric Maïthuna

Tantric intercourse, first, requires a strong and lasting erection, which implies great erotic stimulation, but not so intense that it causes premature ejaculation.

To control this, we should keep in mind that sex depends on the working of totally distinct sets of nerves in our bodies:

—a first set maintains the sensory and motor connection between the genitals and the brain, our most important sex organ;

—a second one, the *parasympathetic*, which has to first induce the erection and then keep it intact;

—third, the *sympathetic* nervous system which is in charge of the ejaculation.

Before drawing Tantric conclusions for our practice, let's differentiate a) erections occurring during the night (or early morning, the
"piss-horn"!) whose origin is purely reflexory, occurring *without* any
erotic stimulation; b) the nightly ones generated by erotic dreams; c)
the ordinary ones during a real or imagined sexual situation, with or
without direct manipulation of the penis.

Erections of the a) kind are much in favor with older couples when
the man's sexual prowess is diminishing, but are also very welcomed
by the so-called "false" impotent men who, usually and wrongly,
blame their problem on some unknown physiological fault.

In fact, except for exceedingly rare cases, every man, every night,
even he who believes he is impotent, has at least five full blown erections lasting for at least half an hour, and this occurs almost from the
womb to the tomb!

Dr. Sherman J. Silber, in his book *Understanding Male Sexuality*
(London, 1983), quotes German scientists who watched numerous
male sleepers and, according to them, their penis (the sleeper's, not
the doctor's) had a hard-on for 25 minutes every 84 (sic) minutes,
always during a REM (Rapid Eye Movements) phase, thus while
dreaming. If the sleeper is awakened during such a dream episode, he
remembers his dream very well, and thus we know that the erections
have nothing to do with the kind of dream, which is usually not at all
erotic. Mathematically speaking, this means that a 75-year-old gentleman's penis will have raised bedsheets for some 33,000 hours, or 4
years, 4 months and 4 weeks!

Because we know that erections are controlled by the *para*sympathetic nervous system, the very one that makes the breathing and the
heartbeat slow down, widens the blood vessels, and causes erection,
we understand how and why impotence and premature ejaculation
have a common origin: anxiety, which overstimulates the *sympathetic*
nervous system, the antagonist to the *para*sympathetic.

When I was in Melbourne in a bookstore, I noticed a pile of one
bestselling book called: *It's Up to You* with the subtitle: *Self-help for
Men with Erection Problems*. My conclusion: many Australians have
this problem! Australian men only? Now let me quote what the
author, William Warwick, writes: "The single most important psychological factor contributing to impotence is anxiety, which is a very
powerful inhibitor of the erection mechanism. Anxiety of almost any
cause can do the trick! Once a man has experienced an episode of
impotence, he will very often be anxious about it happening again.
This anxiety about possibly being impotent, is sometimes called 'performance anxiety.' Performance anxiety is enormously important, and
grossly destructive" (p. 41). The author is 110 percent right!

A classical situation: a man meets for the first time a new and much desired partner. Apprehensive, he thinks: "What if I don't get a hard-on?" The fear of failure overexcites his sympathetic nervous system, his heart beats fast, his breath is short and shallow, and this is the best way not to get a hard-on! The worst error would be to try to *make* the erection occur, for example, by manipulating the penis itself or by his partner doing so, because this is bound to fail and make the problem worse.

If his partner happens to be an experienced woman, she will have him relax, breathe slowly and deeply and allow some time for the sympathetic nerve to calm down. Soon the parasympathetic will take over and, after a few minutes, an erect penis will become the key to the door to the sexual heaven!

Let's consider the process of ejaculation. Premature or not, as we have seen, ejaculation is controlled by the sympathetic nervous system. When closing in to the point of no return, the seminal glands which secrete the seminal fluid (but not the spermatozoon) and are located behind the prostate gland, are ready to eject the sperm gathered in the prostate during sexual excitement. On the razor's edge, a single movement would release the ejaculation, which nothing in the world could stop: the muscles at the base of the penis constrict powerfully and the semen gushes out.

The Tantric tactic to inhibit ejaculation is to calm the sympathetic system and, on the contrary, to *stimulate* the parasympathetic. This explains why Tantra advocates breathing slowly, deep down in the abdomen, not only before the intercourse but all the time. The exhalation should mimic sighing, especially when one is on the razor's edge. During the maïthuna, the shiva remains always calm and unruffled. His reward is unbending erection and a fully satisfied shakti.

During the sex act, he should be careful his coital motions follow the shakti's, his body should remain supple and relaxed, with no jerks! And why not smile at each other?

When they age, Tantrists do not become less sex-efficient, but quite the opposite is true! The 40-year-old non-Tantrist already worries because he notices the instant-erections he had in his 20s are no longer, and he sees his potency slowly fading away. He also notices the fact that the space of time between two erections, the refractory period, now takes hours as compared to minutes for young boys.

In fact, being more mature does not make him a less interesting partner. It takes a little more time for the graying partner to get an erection, but he holds it much longer, even if he is not a Tantrist. Many a passionate young woman will prefer him to a clumsy, overexcited young cock who is finished when it should really be starting!

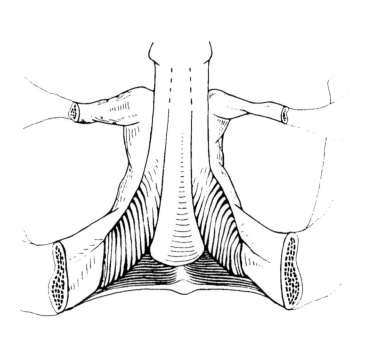

This picture shows the powerful muscles at the base of the lingam. Like any other muscle, they can be trained and grow stronger with exercise. It is these muscles which are used for the "secret language" where the constriction of the yoni and of the lingam alternate. On the other hand, since anatomically the male and female organs, though looking very dissimilar, in fact have the same muscles bearing the same names, the exercises described in the chapter "How to Get a Strong Yoni" and in "Erection, the Backbone of Tantra" apply to both sexes.

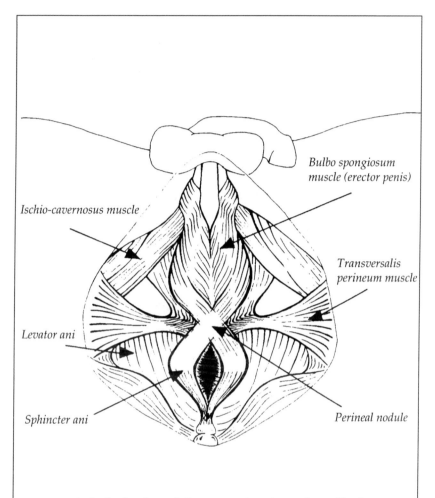

Bulbo spongiosum muscle (erector penis)

Ischio-cavernosus muscle

Transversalis perineum muscle

Levator ani

Sphincter ani

Perineal nodule

As in the female genitalia, anus and erector penis are like the two loops of an 8, the junction between the two being the perineal nodule.

Nevertheless it is a fact that ordinary men, as they grow older, progressively lose their sex power. For Tantra, the cause is not hard to understand: the inconsiderate wastage of semen because of too frequent ejaculations. Inhibiting ejaculation allows sexual prowess to be unaffected by age. In order not to have one's sexual power decline with age, there is only one remedy: Tantric sex that saves the semen but not the sex. Nature did not plan such a wastage of semen. Sure, man is not an ordinary mammal but still, if we observe the wild animals we see, they copulate only at certain periods of the year. Outside the rut, they are sexually calm, whereas the "ordinary," non-Tantrist human males ejaculate "normally" at least once a week, and sometimes daily. This is much too much! Tantra and Tao maintain that the draining off of one's sperm is draining off one's vitality and that this causes premature senility. The retention of semen, quite on the contrary, ensures a richer sexual life, up to several encounters a day and explains the astonishing lasting biological youthfulness of their adepts.

In fact, if a man takes the trouble not to ejaculate for one or two weeks, his willpower rapidly fully restores his sexual power, even if he experiences a slow-down.

Some will raise an objection and say that since the testicles are continuously producing sperm cells, it does not matter if a man ejaculates or not. This is not quite up-to-date. If we ejaculate too often, the testicles try to catch up and become overworked. The sperm cells become less numerous and are expelled before being really mature.

At any rate, Tantrists and Taoists can boast over thousands of years of experience in seminal retention. To comfort everybody, let's keep in mind that even to abstain totally from ejaculating is not harmful: if necessary, the body always finds a way to expel the excess semen. One example of this is wet dreams!

The Erection
is the Pillar of Tantra

Strong and long lasting erections are a gauge of a man's virility: any man unable to have an erection is labeled "impotent," no matter how broad his chest or how muscular his biceps. As to his endurance, Tantra categorizes a premature ejaculator as any male unable to refrain from ejaculating until his partner has had one or more orgasms. If a man is able to control ejaculation until his partner is satisfied, he is said to be virile, but to a Tantrist this is not enough: he should have complete mastery over ejaculation and not ejaculate at all, because in doing so he kills desire, loses a force of life and prevents the shiva from having a true male orgasm.

The practice of Tantric sex exercises will enable any male to enjoy much stronger erections, sometimes lasting for hours on a stretch. Thanks to these exercises, male virility has no limits, and instead of being a leakage of life force, his powerful erections will enhance his vitality.

Thus, erection is the backbone of the Tantric maïthuna and the pillar supporting the entire sex life of men and women, whether profane or Tantric. Premature ejaculation or, worse, impotence, prevents the transformation of ordinary sex into a spiritual experience. Luckily, both problems are easily solved thanks to the Tantric exercises described in this chapter.

The previous chapter has made us realize what a biological feat an erection is. Now let's summarize. As soon as the desire for sex arises, sex-nerves open millions of penile valves, the bloodstream rushes into the penis, inflates its spongy tissues and the lingam raises its head. Remember: erection starts with relaxation. Since desire for sex happens to be a psychological fact, the causes for impotence are mostly in the mind.

And so, the lingam remains erect because the valves don't let the blood flow out, and also because powerful muscles constrict the base of the penis, thus helping to keep the erection intact. Knowing this, Tantra wants to strengthen the penile muscles, and the only way to do this is to train them by having frequent and prolonged Tantric intercourses.

This means already a good training, and a pleasant one, too! It then explains why the male Tantrists, instead of becoming sexually and physiologically weaker with age, remain very active and surprisingly youthful when they are old. What's more, the rich sex life they enjoy stimulates the gonads to secrete more rejuvenating hormones.

Another interesting, almost unbelievable result of Tantric sex: the penis grows larger. Although the size of the penis is quite irrelevant to sexual ability or performance, for centuries men all over the world have tried and try to contrive gadgets and methods to enlarge the penis. Most, if not all of these gadgets, are either useless or dangerous. Physiologists maintain that it is impossible to develop an adult's penis beyond the size it has reached. This statement is true and false at the same time. Let's consider it for a moment. The cylinders of the penis are not simply hollow tubes, but they are made of spongy tissue, containing countless tiny arteries and veins which are elastic. During a moderately powerful erection and a rather short intercourse, which is often the case in ordinary sex, these capillaries do not have the possibility to expand fully. This means that the majority of the men do not give their penis the opportunity to reach its true size. Very powerful and long-lasting erections enlarge the tiny elastic blood vessels, and by switching from ordinary to Tantric sex, the male will see his penis "grow," to in fact reach its full size. Now, if we have another quick look at the figure on p. 306, we notice the powerful erector muscles at the base of the lingam, and these as well can grow stronger and, of course, thicker.

With regard to the size of the penis, some Tantric scriptures quote fantastic lengths varying anywhere from 25 to 30 cm, i.e., almost twelve inches! Western physiologists would no doubt raise their eyebrows at these figures and bring the size back to between 15 and 18 cm (6 to 8 inches). Are the Tantrists boasters or liars? It all depends on how we measure. If we measure the erect penis from the pubis up to the tip, we will get 15 to 18 cm, but if we start from the base of the lingam, at the perineum, the length will be greater.

Question: Why should we waste our time about this? The answer is: if, during intercourse, Tantra asks one to relax the penile muscles when nearing the point of no return, it is better to be conscious of the entire length of the lingam, from its very base to its very tip. Since the proof of the pudding lies in the eating, try it and see for yourself!

Exercises

Most Tantric exercises given in this book apply to both men and women. In this chapter, however, only Mula Bandha is for both sexes.

For the full technique about Mula Bandha, see the chapter "How to Get a Strong Yoni."

Mula Bandha

Mula Bandha is one of the foremost Tantric practices. Easy to perform, we only have to contract both anal sphincters and the levator ani, the "anal lifter." In this chapter we will learn how to strengthen the penile muscles, and to this end, Mula Bandha is of great help.

If one contracts the anal sphincters, one can feel the muscles of the lingam reacting and even the coccyx bone moving at the base of the sacrum. With the lingam half-erect, let's do Mula Bandha: the anal muscles contract at the same time followed by the contraction of the muscles at the base of the lingam. The aim is, first, to become conscious of these muscles, and second, to be able to contract them separately, without Mula Bandha, and even while relaxing the anal sphincters. To be able to dissociate the penile muscles from the sphincters is very important and is the aim of this exercise. With the lingam still half-erect, contract the penile muscles, and you can actually see the penis move and come closer to the abdomen. If you really put your mind to it, you should be able to contract and relax these muscles in rapid succession, say 20 times. Then rest for a while, and repeat.

By doing this, the half-erection will most probably become a full one. By the way, Mula Bandha and this exercise can be practiced in any posture, at any time and almost anywhere. Nobody will know. In the beginning, the most important thing is to be able to contract the penile muscles separately while relaxing the anal sphincters. Later on, the most important item will be the speed with which you do this. We should be able to tense and relax these muscles very rapidly. During intercourse, being on the razor's edge, to repress ejaculation, among other things (see the chapter "How to Control the Ejaculation"), it is essential to relax the muscles at the base of the penis quickly.

Now, let's try another exercise to enable us to dissociate anus and penis. Normally, when having a bowel movement, we pass the feces and urinate simultaneously. Tantrists will not do this. They will pass the stool and urinate afterward. This exercise is not time consuming and helps to gain full control of the ejaculatory tract.

Ever heard of the Cremaster?

This part of the chapter is devoted to the muscles of the scrotum. It is surprising to see how little most men know about this part of their body. The testicles, of course, they know, but the scrotum is thought to be simply a bag to contain them. In fact, the scrotum has two distinct sets of muscles, one being particularly important in order not to ejaculate. This muscle is the cremaster, from the Greek *Kremastêr* = suspensor. It acts as a living suspensory bandage, but its task goes far beyond that. Logically, the testicles would be better off if they remained inside the abdomen, where they would be much less exposed than outside the body. But, the abdomen is too hot a place for the testicles which would then be unable to produce the millions of sperm cells a day needed to keep the human species alive. The cremaster is a thermoregulatory device. If the testicles feel cold, the cremaster draws them close to the warm body. If too warm, the cremaster relaxes and the testicles move from the body.

Now, what's the link between the cremaster and Tantric sex?

When one is close to the point of no return—to ejaculation—the scrotum as a whole shrinks, and the cremaster brings the testicles close to both sides of the lingam's base, thus in a way "cocking" the penis, setting it ready to fire, ready to ejaculate. This happens automatically, and we don't even notice it. On the razor's edge, if the Tantrist relaxes the cremaster, it "de-cocks" the penis, if I may say so, and the testicles leave their ejaculatory position, making it much easier to control oneself.

To train oneself to relax the cremaster one must first concentrate on the scrotum, then try to contract whatever one feels inside it. Little by little, one becomes aware of what's happening. This can be done during the day, even in our car while waiting for the traffic lights to turn green! If we have some leisure time, we can sit, close our eyes and imagine the cremaster contracting, then relaxing. After some time, one will actually feel and be able to control the cremaster. With more practice, one will be able to lift or to lower the scrotum at will. In the beginning, one feels little and it takes some patience to get the desired result.

Now, regarding the testicles and the Tantric maïthuna, one thing has to be known: it is quite normal for beginners, after a long intercourse, say one hour or more, to feel that the testicles are a bit swollen, or congested, and even aching a little, something that does not occur if one ejaculates. Some people worry about this, but they should not, and, on the contrary, this a rather good sign of progress! It is quite normal, and to relieve the congestion, it suffices to bathe the scrotum in or with warm (not hot) water. If left alone, the congestion will subside by itself after half an hour or so. After a few days, the scrotum's blood vessels become more permeable to the bloodstream, and this congestion will never occur again.

More About the Scrotum

The mere aspect of the scrotum may indicate a man's biological age. If the scrotum's skin looks wrinkled like bark, if the testicles are firmly held, one can safely say that the owner is youthful and healthy whatever his real age may be. If, on the contrary, the scrotum is a flabby, drooping bag, if the skin is too smooth and the testicles enlarged, no doubt, this man is weak or senile, or both.

Now, who is responsible? The cremaster, yes, but above all the dartos. Excepting physicians and physiologists, how many men know this name? We need no picture to locate it: this thin muscle is the lining of the scrotum's skin, and it is responsible for the tonicity of the scrotum's content. Something cold makes it shrink, and this is why, after a swim in very cold water, the testicles are squeezed by the constricted dartos and shrink almost to the size of small plums. This is excellent for the general health of the body: the testicles are like sponges and while they are compressed, they release rejuvenating hormones into the bloodstream. The testicles are squeezed and drawn close to the body and this, we know, is the cremaster's work. To compress the testicles permanently and artificially is harmful. For example, young men who continually wear tight jeans could eventually become sterile.

For the spermatogenesis, the temperature of the scrotum should be 3° Celsius less than the body's. In conclusion, keeping the testicles too warm has an adverse effect on the production of sperm cells. That's why men should wear skirts, and not women: the Scottish people have it right and if it becomes fashionable for men to wear skirts, I certainly would be the first to follow! Why not start the fashion? But the Scots are not the only ones to keep the bottom side of their body cool or even cold. All year round in the olden days, the Bavarians wore short leather pants where the cold winter wind could freely blow in. Remembering that our testicles need a cold atmosphere, an excellent habit is to give the scrotum daily a cold shower, and the colder, the better! I advocated this practice outside the scope of Tantra, for the general tonicity of the body. Many older men, who did this regularly, told me that, to their happy surprise they were again able to have sex, which they had had no more, and in some cases, for years. Instead of a shower, we can also sit in a cold bath until the dartos constricts and makes the scrotum shrink. So—to stay young and virile, keep your scrotum cold!

How to Control Ejaculation

In pre-Communist Tibet a strange story was told about the fifth Dalai Lama. The "Fifth," who died *circa* 1680, was unique among Dalai Lamas in that he was a libertine, a rake and a notorious womanizer. Until recently the love-songs he wrote were still popular with the common people of Tibet and, in Lhasa, certain houses, where tradition averred that he had held assignations with one or other of his mistresses, were marked with a mysterious red sign and were the subject of a furtive and unofficial veneration.

The story runs that the Dalai Lama was on one of the upper terraces of his palace. He was being subjected to the reproaches of his advisers who found his sexual immorality little to their taste.

"Yes, it is true that I have women," he admitted, "but you who find fault with me also have them, and copulation for me is not the same thing as it is for you."

He then walked to the edge of the terrace and urinated over it. With the force of gravity the stream of urine flowed down from terrace to terrace, finally reaching the base of the palace. Then, miraculously, it re-ascended the terraces, approached the Dalai Lama, and re-entered the bladder from whence it had come.

Triumphantly he turned to those who had been abusing him: "Unless you can do the same," he said, "you must realize that my sexual relations are different from yours."

This tale precedes the classic gag from silent films when the actual film is run backward and the diver is brought back up onto the diving-board; and it is also typical of the Tantric mentality: all these fabulous, unbelievable tales hide the true meaning from the non-Tantrics, which, in this case, describes a secret Tantric practice.

When the Dalai Lama says that the way he has sex is not like the sex act of the average man—or a counselor of the Dalai Lama—that is, to make love, enjoy it and follow the drive of mankind to survive and reproduce; whereas, the Tantrists transcend the sex act and raise it to a cosmic level.

You may well ask, what can we get from this cock-and-bull story of the re-absorbed urine? What secret process, common to both the

Indian and Tibetan Tantrists, lies hidden behind this tale? Let's see. Tantric Buddhism and Chinese Tao both require absolute control over ejaculation which, in principle, should never occur, although some Indian gurus occasionally accept it.

Retention of the semen allows the male to prolong the sex act indefinitely, to intensify the enjoyment until it becomes ecstasy, or the true male orgasm. The door is also opened to higher levels of consciousness which are unattainable with ejaculation. To achieve this retention, absolute control over the ejaculatory tract, especially through the control of the sphincters, is needed. A very effective method of achieving this is by urinating in spurts rather than in a single stream, as most people do.

This is very easy to do: let a small stream of urine trickle for about two seconds, then stop, and after about five seconds, let the urine flow again for two more seconds, and so on until the bladder is totally empty. During the retention, one imagines reversing the process of passing the water while making a powerful *Mula Bandha*, i.e., forcibly contracting both anal sphincters. This technique often produces a peculiar feeling, difficult to describe, a kind of shiver up the spine. In other words, it is like controlling an urgent need to urinate.

The number of spurts depends on how much urine there is, and one should make as many as possible, generally 5 - 10. With regular practice, it will become a habit and will help everyone achieve full control of ejaculation.

Practice

Up to now, we have emphasized the *contraction* of those muscles we can see or feel easily while contracting them. For example, during an erection we can see the lingam move and come closer to the belly. These muscles are the same ones used for the "secret language" because if they are contracted when the lingam is inserted in the yoni, the female partner then answers with her own vaginal contractions.

But, in order not to ejaculate, one should relax these muscles deliberately when approaching the "point of no return." To train for this, the male should take advantage of his erection and contract the muscles as tightly as possible, until he feels that shiver up his spine, and by doing this, the lingam comes closer to the body. Next comes the most important part of the exercise, i.e., *relaxing* those muscles. As soon as they start to relax, the tightness diminishes and the lingam moves a little off of the body. As soon as one feels this happening, one should alternatively for a few seconds *contract* and *relax* the muscles as much as possible. When the relaxation deepens and lasts longer, the erection slowly subsides and eventually disappears altogether.

Why not try this method the next time you have sexual intercourse? To achieve this control is not difficult, although at first one should try it while remaining motionless. With a little practice, this relaxation will be possible even during coital movements and is very effective in avoiding the "point of no return," and ejaculation.

When the shiva is aware of his own reflex actions as he approaches the urge to ejaculate, he will note how the rhythm and the depth of his breathing changes and the tension increases in the muscles of his buttocks, his abdomen, the small of his back and, most importantly, in the lingam. If he lets go, as he usually does, the irrepressible ejaculatory reflex will be unleashed with the help of all the above-mentioned muscles.

To delay or to avoid this, when on the verge of ejaculating, the male should slow down and deepen his breathing, especially in the abdomen, and at the same time concentrate on his muscles and relax them. Thanks to this relaxation, his coital movements will become smoother, more harmonious, and the rhythm will be more pleasurable for the shakti. It is the relaxation of the muscles at the base of the lingam that helps one most to gain control over oneself. True, the erection subsides a little, but, as we are out of the "danger" zone, sexual intercourse can continue.

With some practice, the Tantrist will be able to give his shakti the freedom to enjoy the highest form of ecstasy, at least in the beginning. By identifying himself with her, he can participate in her enjoyment, and his own bliss will also be much more intense than the short-lived pleasure he usually experiences with ejaculation. This level of sensual experience is already much higher than what the ordinary male experiences although it is not the absolute climax.

From Pleasure to Ecstasy

Bhagwan Shree Rajneesh, although he himself a somewhat questionable individual, writes: "When there is no anxiety, ejaculation can be postponed for hours—even for days. And there is no need of it. If the love is deep, both parties can invigorate each other. The ejaculation completely ceases, and for years two lovers can meet with each other without any ejaculation, without any wastage of energy. They can just relax with each other. Their bodies meet and relax; they enter sex and relax. And eventually, sex will not be an excitement. It is an excitement right now. Then it is not an excitement: it is a relaxation—a deep let go.

"But that can happen only if you have first surrendered inside to the life energy—the life force. Only then can you surrender to your lover or beloved. Tantra says this happens, and it arranges how it can happen" (*The Book of Secrets*, Poona, 1976, Vol. 1, p. 398).

In this case, Rajneesh is right: anxiety and the tensions related to it are major obstacles to sex in general, since they often lead to impotence or premature ejaculation. Moreover, anxiety prevents the control of ejaculation, but suppressing the anxiety is not in itself enough. Sure, with the Path of the Valley, when one remains motionless and free from anxiety, ejaculation is inhibited, but such is not the case with the Path of the Razor's Edge. In this case, the proper Tantric techniques are necessary: the very fact they exist and are taught is proof of this.

But before elaborating on this subject, let's listen to S. B. Dasgupta in his book *Introduction to Tantric Buddhism* (Calcutta, 1976, p. 142): "The advocates of Vajra-yâna hold that the pleasure that is realized through the discharge of matter is much lower, in respect of degree as well as in intensity, than the bliss that can be realized through the control of this matter, i.e., by checking its downward flow through subtle yogic processes and by giving it an upward flow as well to make it reach the lotus situated in the cerebrum region...and to make it steady there: the bliss resulting from the steadiness of the matter is the *Mahâsukha* (from *Maha* = great, *sukha* = happiness, bliss)."

What exactly is behind this somewhat esoteric text? Let's have a closer look. To understand this Tantric method, we should remember that, according to subtle yogic and Tantric physiology, our life force is divided into five main *vayus*, or specialized forms of vital energy, and controls various organs of the body. With regard to the control of ejaculation, we will limit our scope to the two most essential ones, *prâna vayu* and *apâna vayu*. The first one, *prâna vayu*, is in charge of absorbing energy and matter from the outside world, whereas *apâna vayu* controls the exodus of matter out of the body. In short, like a balance sheet of our body, *prâna vayu* provides the receipts, *apâna vayu* the expenses, and our overall health depends on the exact balance between the two. Too little *prâna* means reduced vitality, but if *apâna* does not excrete whatever has to go out of the body, i.e., waste matter, our body becomes clogged and our health is at risk. This excreting energy is responsible for eliminating stools, urine, sweat, menstrual blood, etc., but it is responsible also for childbirth and ejaculation, as semen too flows out of the body. *Apâna* flows to the lower parts of the body and towards all its exits.

Keeping this in mind, the Tantric way to inhibit ejaculation is very logical: we have to *reverse* the flow of the excreting energy which leads to ejaculation. And this clarifies Dasgupta's rather esoteric text: "Checking its downward flow through subtle yogic processes and to give it an upward flow to make it reach the lotus situated in the cerebrum region." Obviously, this does not mean that the actual sperm should flow to the brain, but rather the subtle *apâna* energy that controls the ejaculatory process. We can now better understand the Dalai Lama's tale: by reversing the flow of his urine, *apâna*, the excretory energy, is brought under control, as is ejaculation. By controlling this energy, and practicing Tantric sex meditation, the Tantrist is able to indefinitely postpone or totally inhibit ejaculation.

With this knowledge we are also provided with an extra "anti-ejaculation" weapon! Among the different forms of excretion, an important, and perhaps the most important function of apâna has been omitted, namely *expiration* or exhaling. Expelled poisonous gases are at least as harmful as, for example, urine. The Tantrist, as well as the Indian yogis, did not fail to notice that our breathing is the *only double-sided* bodily process: it relies on *prâna vayu* when inhaling, but on *apâna* for exhaling. Now, everything becomes very clear: to control *apâna*, which includes the control of ejaculation, lets learn to control our exhalation. Our breathing is linked to our vegetative or unconscious vital functions as well as to our conscious functions. Normally, day and night, breathing is automatic and controlled by the unconscious vegetative system, but at any time, if I wish, I can change it. In other words, I can control *prâna* and *apâna*, which is the key to the control of ejaculation. Controlling one's breathing is an easy way to inhibit ejaculation: sounds interesting, doesn't it?

How do we achieve this? First, while sexually joined to the shakti, at all times, and especially when approaching ejaculation, one should remain very calm, totally conscious of what's going on and *totally aware of one's breathing*. During normal intercourse, the rhythm of breathing and coital movements are synchronized spontaneously: when pushing in, one exhales, when withdrawing, one inhales. As long as we remain calm and not too close to the point of no return, we can continue like this. If, however, we come too close to the razor's edge, there are two options:

1. To *reverse* the spontaneous rhythm of coital movements—this means one *exhales* on the backward movements and inhales while pushing forward.

2. Or to desynchronize breathing and motion by continually taking very long, very deep, and above all very slow abdominal breaths.

We can also alternate both processes during the same sexual intercourse: slow, deep breathing most of the time, and reversed breathing when nearing the point of no return. If the shiva comes too close to ejaculation and has to stop moving for a while, it is safer to switch to the second choice. As soon as the "danger" is over and he can move again, he should continue for a while with this slow breathing. In fact, each couple should progressively come to know each other's reactions and act accordingly.

Another effective technique: *inhale by steps* through the nose, and *exhale all of a sudden* through the mouth. "By steps" means: taking some air in while pushing, holding the breath while pulling the lingam back, taking some air again while pushing, and so on, until the lungs are full. This could take from five to nine forward and backward movements. The man should hold his breath for a few seconds and then expel all the air, with a "ha" sound *through the mouth*. When reading this, it seems a bit complex, but it is, in fact, very simple.

At the very last second, when a single movement would irresistibly trigger off ejaculation, still breathing as described above, he should imagine he is holding back his urine, better still, reabsorbing it as did the Dalai Lama. His breathing should be very deep, and slow, as if the air is reaching the very lowest part of his abdomen. Do not forget to relax the buttocks and the stomach muscles: on the razor's edge, if one stops breathing and tightens his buttocks and abdominal muscles, one risks losing control and ejaculating.

One more point. At any time, the Tantrist could also practice *jiva bandha*, that is, folding his tongue back and pressing it against the palate. The pressure on the palate should be as strong as possible. Jiva bandha is a replacement for *kechari mudra*, which is the ultimate practice but which is practically unattainable by Westerners. To attain *kechari mudra*, Indian yogis daily cut a minute portion of the frenum of the tongue and then, by pulling ("milking") the tongue, they stretch it so as to be able to "swallow" it and thus block the glottis (the opening to the larynx). During this practice, the yogi should stop breathing. This tongue-cutting is done gradually, takes weeks, and should be done only under the strict guidance of an experienced guru. Should the frenum be cut too far, one would be unable to control his tongue, and to speak normally. My first Tantric master's tongue was so long that he could push it far out of his mouth and, with the tip of it, he could reach the space between his eyebrows! Amazing!

Kechari mudra contradicts the rule not to hold one's breath on the razor's edge, but what is true to us is not the same for expert Indian Tantrists.

Taoists have another "trick" to inhibit the discharge of semen: just before the urge to ejaculate, they grind their teeth and squeeze their eyelids tightly shut, until a vibrating sound is felt in their ears.

By using some or all of these methods, the risk of losing control is greatly reduced. The shiva will gradually become able to stay longer and longer, closer and closer to the point of no return, his mind centered on his breathing and on the inside of his stomach. Tantra says: "One should check the semen deep inside the abdomen."

What does this mean? When ejaculating, the male feels as if his sperm is rushing out of his testicles, whereas it starts flowing from the prostate gland, next to the bladder, and is expelled through the ejaculatory tract. It is during this journey, from the prostate to the tip of the penis, that we have to act, and this is the aim of the Dalai Lama's exercise. On the razor's edge, one's awareness should not be concentrated at the head of the penis, but centered inside the lower part of the abdomen; and here, Mula Bandha is very effective.

Nevertheless, despite all these methods and tricks, in the beginning, one will often be unable to control himself, and ejaculation will take place. This is quite normal, but by persevering, one will progress quickly.

Tantra says also: "He who controls his mind, controls his breath and his semen as well." This is true, but the shiva is not alone. His shakti should also play the game according to the rules! The experienced shakti feels and knows very well when and if the shiva is close to the point of no return. She helps by not moving and by remaining centered on the event. In fact, much depends on her: few are the males who are able to withstand the "attack" of a passionate woman wanting his semen! It is true that, in the beginning, the sexual union without emission of semen is less pleasurable; but soon, both partners will discover new dimensions of sexual bliss, and they will know they have everything to gain by following the Tantra practice. Only a shakti who has the exceptional luck of meeting a shiva able to perform kechari mudra can let her passion express itself fully without releasing an unwanted ejaculation.

Nevertheless, by practicing the Tantric maïthuna, even in the beginning, we are not forced to stay motionless. While performing the normal instinctive pelvic motions, one should become aware of the muscles involved. If an ejaculation occurs, the Tantrist should try to observe how his lumbar muscles are reacting and what really is happening while he is expelling his semen. The better we are able to feel these muscles, the easier it will become to control them. We should be aware of which muscles act while ejaculating and we should know how to relax them when we are in danger of losing control. Especially important are the muscles at the base of the penis, at the bulb, which should be tensed during the whole act, but fully relaxed when coming close to the point of no return, still more on the razor's edge.

With regard to the coital movements, Taoists advocate, in the beginning, "Three shallow thrusts, one deep, for 81 strokes." Later on, nine shallow thrusts for one deep one. If, being on the razor's edge, the Taoist fears ejaculation, he should withdraw his penis almost entirely, leaving only the tip inside the vagina. After a period of 20 to 30 seconds, he may again start moving. At the last moment, Taoists hold their breath, filling their lungs with air, and lifting their midriff by widening the chest and contracting the muscles of the lower part of the abdomen. According to the Tao, no male should eject his king (semen) unless he has given 5,000 thrusts!

Jolan Chang, in his book, *The Tao of Love and Sex*, adds that, in time, it becomes less and less necessary to pull the penis back, and eventually, never.

In ancient China, at the very edge of ejaculation, the Taoist firmly pressed the bulb at the base of the penis, between the anus and the scrotum, with his fore-finger and second finger, taking a deep breath at the same time. If ejaculation occurs, this method does prevent the semen from flowing out of the penis and makes it flow back, not, of course, into the prostate gland, but into the bladder. Unlike the Taoist, if an ejaculation occurs, the Tantrist will accept it and let the sperm flow into the yoni. The only thing he regrets is that this interrupts the Tantric sex-meditation and, for some time extinguishes his desire for sex.

Premature Ejaculation

To prevent premature ejaculation, the shakti sits astride the male who is lying on his back, but she does not take the lingam into her yoni. With her fingers, she spreads the labia and puts her vulva against his lingam, taking care not to touch the glans. In doing so she establishes a genital contact without penetration. While the male relaxes (his buttocks and his abdomen above all) the shakti lets her moist vulva glide alongside his penis, and sometimes has an orgasm. If this "test" becomes too difficult for the shiva, without changing her posture, the shakti will then remain motionless for a few minutes, to let things cool down.

Then comes the long awaited moment of actual penetration. During ordinary intercourse, the male "does things" to the woman: it's he who penetrates, whereas, in the Tantric maïthuna, the yoni engulfs the lingam, but without any haste. At first, only the glans is being seized by the muscles of the yoni's opening. All senses are wide awake, and the partners stay motionless and remain totally aware of what's happening between them, within them. No more stroking, no gesture is made that could intensify sexual excitement: they are fully open to the process of melting one into the other. No motions of the lingam, or thrusts forward inside the yoni are permitted: only the secret language of reciprocal contractions of the genital muscles is allowed.

When approaching the point of no return, the shiva relaxes all the above-mentioned genital muscles, particularly the scrotal ones. As soon as the erotic tension is stabilized, subtle, harmonious motions are allowed. The shakti should remain fully aware of her own reactions so that her own spontaneous pelvic motions will not begin. She can— and should— have an orgasm solely with the almost unnoticeable motions of her own rhythm.

In ordinary intercourse, the thrusts from the lower back follow one after another, becoming stronger and faster; at each thrust the pubic bones meet and spread wider each time the lingam retreats. The unavoidable result is well known: almost always, after twenty or more long, deep movements of the lingam inside the yoni, the semen bursts forth, leaving the man empty and exhausted, and the woman frustrated.

Just as the jockey follows his horse's gait without bumping against the saddle, so the shiva has to follow his shakti's rhythm, with all its subtle changes. By keeping very close to her pubic bone and reducing the reciprocal motions between lingam and yoni, he reduces the risk of ejaculation.

Some Tantric gurus advocate penetration step-by-step: first, the shakti takes the glans inside her, next about one third of the lingam's length, then gradually up to two-thirds, and finally the whole penis. Or, they advise a change of position and choose the "scissors" technique (see chapter "The Maïthuna Âsanas," the posture named Tiryakâsana) where the pelvic motions can be ample but, since the shiva clasps one thigh of the shakti between his, the movements of the lingam in the yoni are not very broad. Moreover, the male's pubic arch is perpendicular to the shakti's and, when he moves, it excites her clitoris, intensifying her enjoyment, without being too "risky" to the shiva!

Calm, relaxed, without any haste, both shiva and shakti will be able to stay united, eventually for hours at a stretch without any difficulty.

Vajroli, the Absolute Weapon

Among the various anti-ejaculatory methods, Vajroli is the most successful and has turned many premature ejaculators into experts in the control of the ejaculation!

Of all the numerous esoteric Tantric techniques, Vajroli remained a well-kept secret for thousands of years: you will look in vain for precise and detailed instructions as to how to achieve this practice in the numerous available texts on Tantra. At the most, one gets only a brief description of the method, which is never taught in the West, and rarely in India.

From the start, let me say that this method is not required to have full control over ejaculation (*bindhusiddhi*). Still, Vajroli is a very easy, very effective method and concerns only the male Tantrists. In short, to perform Vajroli one must insert a catheter into the urinary tract, as far as the bladder. Once you have achieved this, you can train yourself to suck up fluids into the bladder, first with the help of the catheter, and eventually without it. This technique sounds terrible, but in fact, it is neither difficult nor really painful.

For centuries Vajroli has always been passed from teacher to student, because if practiced without proper guidance, it could be risky; but, if we take a few precautions, it is not dangerous. Before talking about how to practice it, let me say that the capability to suck up liquids is not at all required, and, in our Western culture, it is best to forget it.

Now let us come to the actual practice of Vajroli. The first thing is to get a catheter and a lubricating jelly! Modern Tantrists and yogis use a rubber or a plastic one, the kind used to drain off urine. A nasal catheter can also be used and is easier to get at the drugstore. One should buy three catheters, each with a different diameter. The one printed at the end of this chapter is medium-sized and okay for our purpose. In India, before rubber ones were available, Tantrists used rigid tubes, made mostly of silver, which did not exactly enhance the procedure!

Now, let's proceed! I just bought a brand new catheter, and I am going to start practicing. First, I put some gynecological jelly, bought at the drugstore, onto the catheter to lubricate and at the same time keep it sterile. With one hand I hold the lingam vertically (never when an erection or semi-erection is present) and with the other I slowly glide the catheter into the aperture at the tip of the penis. For the first half inch there is no pain, no problem! Further on, since the delicate mucous lining of the urinary tract (which is also the ejaculatory tract) is very sensitive, I have to be very careful and proceed very slowly. On the first day, one half an inch is enough. Tomorrow, I can go a little further. This should not be really painful. While the catheter is inserted, I make a few short movements backwards and forwards inside the penis, to gradually desensitize the lining of the urethra. I am not in a hurry, since I have plenty of time! The whole procedure takes only about one minute, and as soon as the catheter is out, I immediately pass water to rinse the urethra with the sterile urine. Before starting the process, one should urinate without totally emptying the

bladder: some urine should remain in the bladder. In fact, the least pleasant part of the whole process is passing urine, because this is a bit painful. With a little patience, after a short time this pain will subside. Now, the process is over, and I have to wash the catheter with water and store it in a glass with some mild antiseptic solution so that it will remain sterile.

The next day—and not before!—I will do it again and proceed a little further inside the urethra. Remember, the aim of the whole thing is to desensitize the urethra. It may take two or three weeks before I get the catheter into the bladder: in a hospital, if the nurse has to drain a patient's bladder, because it is urgent, she has to insert the whole catheter at once! One day, the catheter will reach the bladder. How shall I know when this happens? Since I kept some urine in my bladder, as soon as the catheter is in the bladder, this urine flows, and it is impossible not to notice it! Immediately, I withdraw the catheter a bit, in order not to empty the bladder, make some backwards and forwards motions with the catheter and pull it out. Now I totally empty the bladder. Nothing is to be feared since I proceed cautiously and above all very slowly.

I must reach the bladder, and then retreat a few millimeters, because this is the strategic zone where the sperm duct from the prostate gland runs into the urethra, and it is from here that ejaculation really starts. With practice, after some time, the catheter will easily glide into the urinary tract without causing any irritation or even discomfort. In India this would only be the beginning of the technique! The catheter being inserted till it gets inside the bladder, the yogi puts the loose end of it into a bowl filled with water and performs Uddiyana Bandha (refer to my book *Yoga Self Taught*) or, still better, Nauli, the manipulation of the muscles of the abdominal wall. This will cause a depression inside the abdomen and enable water, milk, milk with honey or even mercury to be sucked up. Needless to say, this is not to be played with, and in the West it is best to avoid this technique as it is not required to control ejaculation, which is our main concern.

Let's go back now to the aim of Vajroli, the inhibition of ejaculation. How does Vajroli do the trick? Let's remember the fact that during the ejaculation, spasmodic, uncontrollable waves of contractions go all along the ejaculatory tract to eject the seminal fluid out of the body. By desensitizing the nerves of the ejaculatory tract, the ejaculatory reflexes will be dulled without making the sensual bliss less intense. Once we get to this point, it is no longer necessary to perform Vajroli daily. We can do it only twice a week and, later on, only once a week, or once a month. Vajroli has another advantage: it makes us aware of the entire ejaculatory tract from the aperture at the tip of the penis up to the prostate gland.

But the Tantrists have a further, secret goal. They use catheters with increasing diameters to considerably enlarge the urethra. When the aperture of the penis is large enough, it resembles a little mouth and is able to engulf the clitoris and suck it, the ultimate version of the "reversed act," which is often mentioned in the Tantric literature but without explaining in what it consists. Not only does the shakti sit astride the shiva, in the inverted union, but with this reversed act, her clitoris, which is in fact a mini-penis, is sucked into the lingam that in turn becomes a mini-vagina. A Tantric guru, Shri Bapuji, told me that by stimulating the shakti's "secret nerve," in this way, the Tantrists give her the highest, supreme joy: divine bliss without any risk of ejaculation.

Finally, Vajroli invigorates the scrotum as well as the testicles, increasing the strength, vigor and vitality, while the increased secretion of gonadal hormones rejuvenates the body.

Let's have a look now at the *Hatharatnavali*, a Tantric scripture that has only been recently (1982) translated by Mr. Venkata Reddy (Secundarabad, India) and which gives some information about Vajroli, but not enough for us to start practicing it. About the catheter, he writes: "It should be of gold, silver, copper, or of iron" (II-78).

The technical "description" which is given is not very precise, to say the least: "One should insert the tube for a moment in the urethra without fear. This will give stability and strength of penis as well as increase the semen" (II-84).

"The tube should be inserted in the urethra in an effort to enlarge (the hole of the penis); in this way, the penis will become stronger" (II-85).

Our comment is: knowing about the "inverted act," we understand why the text lays emphasis on the enlargement of the hole of the penis.

Then the scripture proceeds to the actual sexual practice: "In a secret place, a beautiful naked woman lies on her back while the man, naked too, lies on top of her and both should practice a little Kumbhaka (holding the breath in)" (II-86,87).

"Embracing each other deeply, the man inserts his penis into the woman's vagina. Then both kiss each other (drink the lips) and also make little sounds" (II-88).

"They scratch each other with their nails and hit each other till they perspire. Then, with constant practice, the bindu (fluid) coming out of the female organ of the woman should be drawn up (into the penis)" (II-89).

"Thus, if the bindu or semen has been ejected, it will be reabsorbed by the man's penis, thanks to Vajroli; and in this way, by saving his own bindu (semen), the yogi conquers death" (II-90).

This explains why they train themselves to absorb fluids: they want to suck in the female's genital secretions while, on the other hand, they want to keep their own! The scripture is interesting, especially from the point of view of yogic practice. Most modern Indian yoga teachers preach celibacy and, according to them, the ideal yogi should be a sort of naked, ascetic eunuch. About the references made in the scriptures regarding sex, they tell us we should take these symbolically. It is difficult to believe this when reading II-86, 90 above.

The same practical details about sexual practices are to be found in another, well-known yogic scripture, the *Hathayogapradipikâ*, but have been censored as the translator bluntly told us he omitted them because he considered the sentences to be "lewd."

Rai Bahadur Shri Chandra Vasu, translator of the another classical yogic scripture, the *Siva Samhita*, puts this footnote: "Vajroli, described in the original text, is omitted because this is a very obscene practice in which only low class Tantrists indulge" (p. 51).

Now back to us and the present: If, at first, Vajroli does not appeal to you, so be it. This technique is not at all essential to practice Tantra, but without the description of Vajroli, my book would be incomplete.

How to
Strengthen Your Yoni

I once upset a woman saying that, with a few exceptions, the vagina of Western women is as muscular as a worn-out slipper! I agree, that to say this is neither romantic nor flattering but, alas, relevant, although it is not their fault. Nobody told Western women how to have a strong yoni.

As I organized the writing of this book, I also subscribed to a sex magazine. In one of the issues a reader boasted about his numerous female partners but, only one stood out because she had strong vaginal muscles and was an expert at manipulating them. He couldn't get over it! OK, but why the hell didn't the magazine tell its readers how to train those muscles? No wonder that vaginal control is exceedingly rare in our culture.

For a couple to have a harmonious relationship and a perfect sexual rapport—even without aiming at Tantric practices—this muscular control gives any woman a decisive asset, and no one should renounce it. Sure, not every woman can have Liz Taylor or Raquel Welch's dazzling beauty, but a male will prefer a less beautiful woman who has such a control to a very attractive woman who lacks this power. (I am not insinuating that Liz or Raquel does—or does not—have this control. I simply don't know!)

On the other hand, if a woman takes the trouble to train her vaginal muscles, is it not fair enough that she and her partner(s) take advantage of it? Strong muscles are also an asset in other circumstances as, for example, in childbirth.

Because of a woman's control of her vagina, the "secret language" during maïthuna becomes possible, and also helps the shiva to inhibit his ejaculation. Any woman could—and should—strengthen and train her vagina. Obviously, a young South Indian girl who has been trained since puberty by her own mother will have much better control than any American or European woman who starts this training later in life, nevertheless, any amount of control is welcome and gratifying.

Sahajolî, or Vaginal Control

Alex Comfort, in his book *The Joy of Sex* (New York, 1974, p. 219), quotes Richard Burton: "This is the most sought-after feminine response of all.... She must close and constrict the Yoni until it holds the Lingam as with a finger, opening and shutting at her pleasure, and finally acting as the hand of the (Indian) Gopala-girl who milks the cow. This can be learned only by long practice, and especially by throwing the will into the part affected, even as men endeavor to sharpen their hearing.... Her husband will then value her above all women nor would he exchange her for the most beautiful queen in the Three Worlds.... This superlative knack can be learned because girls in South India learn it. How exactly they learn has never been written down, unfortunately."

I do not know if I am the first one to write it down, but what I know for sure is that the exercises I am going to explain are very effective, and with them any women can have the right "knack." All that's required is a little practice.

In India, these exercises, called *Sahajolî*, are taught from childhood on, first by the mother, and later on by the Tantric guru if the girl is to be trained as a full blown shakti, suitable for the Tantric Sadhana. Of course, the sooner one starts, the better, but it's never too late!

Sahajolî is part of the secret training of the Devadâsis, the Indian temple dancers, as it was for the hetaira of the past. To test the vaginal strength of these Greek courtesans, they had to split a clay phallus with their vaginal muscles and this was a kind of exam!

Of course, no modern Western woman will aim at such a feat, but anyone can get quite satisfactory results: after all, vaginal muscles *are* muscles, and like all other muscles they can be trained and become stronger. Whatever the age of the woman, when she starts practicing, she will be surprised how effective these exercises are. The first and the best exercises are called Mula Bandha.

How to Perform Mula Bandha

Before explaining in full how to perform Mula Bandha, please note that these exercises apply to male Tantrists as well as to the shaktis. Both sexes should practice these exercises, although they are described here as if they were solely intended for women.

In short, to do Mula Bandha, constrict both anal sphincters and the *levator ani*. Mula Bandha can be practiced in almost any position, but for training purposes it is better done while sitting. The most important thing, as Richard Burton says, is to "throw the will into the affected part." This is not at all difficult: just think of your anus, breathe calmly, and then start constricting—lightly to begin with—the most external sphincter, then by constricting a bit more, the second one and finally the *levator ani*. To do this, we should act as if we had to refrain a really urgent need to have a bowel movement.

Or else one should try to suck the anus up into the body, to *lift* it, and this is the true meaning of the Latin name: *levator* = lifter; *ani*, of course = anus. If the constriction is done slowly, one can readily feel those muscles separately, even on the first try. Gradually, one has to constrict the whole set of muscles as much as one can, until a strong vibration is felt in the area and a shiver runs up the spine. Then, one should hold one's breath in for, say, five to ten seconds. While exhaling, relax all the muscles involved in the process, still keeping the awareness centered in this part of the body. If you don't let your mind run astray, a pleasant feeling of warmth is felt at the base of the body and to the lumbar region. Keep breathing normally, if you wish, while you practice Mula Bandha. It's up to you!

The whole process should be repeated five times.

Thanks to this strong Mula Bandha, one will feel reactions not only in the anus but spreading throughout the whole region: between the anus and vulva or scrotum (perineum), vulva, clitoris, even the uterus. This is quite understandable since the anal and vaginal sphincters are like the two loops of an 8: by squeezing one, the second automatically follows.

Let's try it again: first constrict one loop of the 8 while centering the mind at the junction of both loops, the perineum, and try to feel them separately. With some practice, one will have a very good awareness of the entire vagina and experience previously unknown sensations. Thanks to Mula Bandha, the whole set of muscles will get stronger and the sensations will become more acute.

Acquiring a Strong Vagina

The function of all sphincters and hollow organs is constriction. During orgasm, the rhythmic, undulating waves of contractions in the vagina produce the ultimate sensual bliss, and the stronger the muscles, the greater this bliss!

The purpose of the following Tantric practice is to selectively strengthen the vaginal muscles and should not be done while having sex. To constrict a sphincter more effectively, the best way is first to *widen* it. To achieve this, the shakti will use any cylindrical object: the more it resembles a lingam, the better the yoni will be able to grip it. This cylinder need not have the same size as a real penis:

some use a finger, which is a bit too small. Some women buy one of those vibrating devices sold in sex shops and this is okay, but *never* let it vibrate in the yoni. After some time the vibration would progressively dull the very sensitive nerves of the vagina and make sex much less pleasurable. Of course, before being inserted in the yoni, the object should first be coated with some lubricating jelly to be found in sex shops, or some gynecological jelly sold at the drugstore. *Never* use a fatty cream, and if nothing else is available, saliva will do the trick.

Do the actual exercise while lying on the back with the legs wide apart. When the cylinder is inserted in the vagina, it becomes easy to keep the awareness there. Inhale, hold the breath in, constrict the vagina with Mula Bandha thus grasping the cylinder as firmly as you can and hold for a few seconds. Meanwhile be aware of whatever sensations can be felt in the genital region, particularly in the vagina, of course! Exhale, relax. Repeat five times.

The exercise may also be done like this: inhale, do Mula Bandha for three seconds while holding the breath in, exhale, relax, inhale again and so on. It should be practiced for three minutes. Regular practice is essential and daily short sessions are much more effective than long, irregular ones.

Soon, your vaginal muscles will grow stronger and you will be able to try this while having sex: a pleasant surprise to your partner! It is true that without any exercise at all, some few lucky women are naturally endowed with this grasping power; nevertheless, they too should practice because these muscles can never become too strong.

How to Manipulate the Cylinder

Strengthening the vaginal muscles is one thing, manipulating the cylinder is another and a very essential one. Shakti's yoni should have fantastically well-developed muscles. Anyone can learn to do this.

To have total control over the yoni, the cylinder should be long enough to be seen, for example in a mirror. In the beginning, the cylinder will move vertically only, but with practice, it will be possible to have it make circling motions. It is worth doing as it can radically improve a couple's sex life, even long after the menopause.

Question: Is it possible to do these exercises *without* a cylinder?

Answer: Up to a certain point, yes, but *with* an object the exercises are a lot more effective. The cylinder is to the yoni what dumb-bells are to the body-builder. In short, to get maximum results, it is necessary: a) to widen the vagina, b) to give it something to grasp, and this is achieved by using the cylindrical object.

Constricting the muscles, plus concentrating the mind, ensures an increased flow of rich arterial blood and life force (prâna) in the genital organs and this is very beneficial to them, and, also, increases production of sex hormones which rejuvenate the body as a whole.

While practicing these exercises, pleasurable sensations could eventually arise. Though this is not the aim of the exercise, it is no sin and does no harm.

One more advantage to Mula Bandha, and up to a certain point to Sahajolî (obviously without the object), is that it can be practiced, even in a crowd.

Perfecting Vaginal Control

Thanks to the above-described exercises the shakti is able to constrict and relax the muscles of the ano-genital region altogether. Now she has to train herself to be able to constrict separately, one by one, each muscle of the anus, the vagina and, eventually, the uterus.

Performing Mula Bandha already affects the *erector clitoridis*, which is attached to the pubic bone and whose fibers run along both sides of the vulva, up to the clitoris, which could become erect, very much like the mini-penis it is. One more point, and a very important one. By doing Mula Bandha, one can feel the *coccyx* being pulled upward. We should be aware of the fact that the *coccyx*, of which we are rarely conscious, except when we fall on it, has very sensitive nerve-endings. Thanks to *Mula Bandha* we act on the very root of our spinal cord. This is the place where Tantra locates the *Muladhara Chakra*, the root-chakra that is, together with the *Swadisthana Chakra* (vagina plus clitoris, or penis) the seat of the mysterious *Kundalinî*, the Cosmic Life Force acting within our body. To awaken the *Kundalinî* is one of the foremost aims of Tantra and yoga practices.

It should be added that the muscles of the lower part of the abdominal wall also help in performing Mula Bandha.

The Hand of the Gopi

Now, the shakti trains herself to be able to contract *separately* every muscle of the ano-genital region. When one constricts the anal sphincters, automatically the anal and vaginal muscles contract together. The shakti's first aim is to dissociate these muscles, and to be able to constrict the anal sphincters while, at the same time, relaxing the vagina. With a little practice and a good deal of concentration, this can be achieved without too much difficulty. Even if it is not possible, at least

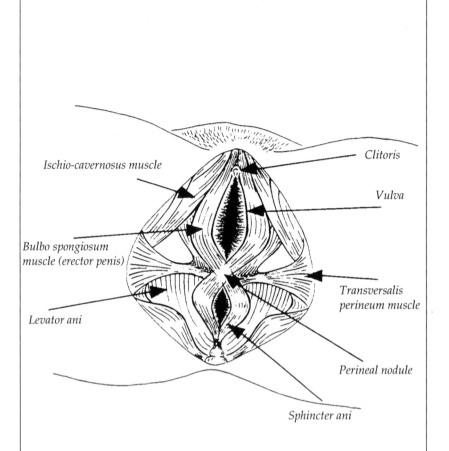

Ischio-cavernosus muscle

Clitoris

Vulva

Bulbo spongiosum
muscle (erector penis)

Levator ani

Transversalis
perineum muscle

Perineal nodule

Sphincter ani

The muscles surrounding the vagina form a "figure 8," and must be developed in order to have vaginal control.

right from the beginning, don't worry; you are training all the muscles involved, and this is important.

With the object still inserted in the yoni, try first to constrict the sphincter at the "mouth" of the vagina, but not it's "lifter." Afterwards, do the same with the "lifter" of the vagina only. To know if this is correctly done, put one finger in the vagina: constricting the vaginal sphincter will cause the finger to be grasped; when you contract the "lifter," your finger will be pulled inside.

Here is another practice, and a very pleasant, but not very easy one! Remember, the vagina is muscular. From the opening of the vagina to the cervix—the mouth of the uterus—there are separate sets of muscles, as if rings were piled one on top of the other. When one is able to contract and relax these in succession, the sensation will be like the fingers of the cow-girl on an udder's teat. Even without having ever actually milked a cow, everybody knows how the fingers work to make the warm milk gush out into the bucket. The vaginal muscles should be able to do the same thing to the lingam, and if practiced during intercourse, both shiva and shakti experience fantastic sensations.

To achieve it, the cylinder is inserted and the shakti first constricts the entire vagina. Then, slowly, cautiously, and consciously, she has to relax, step by step, level by level, the muscles of the yoni, starting from the cervix, down to the outward sphincter. When she is able to do this, again starting with the vagina constricted as a whole, she can relax step by step, the muscles from the opening of the vagina up to the uterus.

In the beginning this must be done very slowly. At the end, it will become easy and generate a wave-like motion inside the yoni. At first, it requires a good deal of concentration, but after some time it all becomes automatic, though still conscious. In actual maïthuna, at any time the shakti can start this undulating motion. In fact, she deliberately mimics the spontaneous undulating motions which occur during an orgasm.

By exploring new sexual sensations, which the experienced shakti shares with her shiva, she really helps him to inhibit ejaculation. It is well known that pelvic motions make it very difficult for the shiva to restrain from ejaculating. Few men are able to control themselves, but with this "secret language," done without movement, this control becomes much easier without lessening any of the enjoyable sensations.

Practicing Mula Bandha in an Upright Position

This way of doing Mula Bandha involves the buttocks and the muscles connected to the clitoris and can be done unnoticed almost anywhere.

Posture: Upright, legs about one foot apart, both hands touching the buttocks: to feel what will happen.

First, be aware of your knee-caps facing forward. Then, without moving the feet, exhale and make them "squint" on both sides, tighten the buttocks forcibly, as well as the muscles of the lower part of the abdomen. The upper part of the body, from the waist on, is relaxed. While tightening the buttocks, Mula Bandha happens almost by itself. Now, constrict the sphincter of the vagina and feel how the clitoris is being pulled downward. It doesn't matter if the clitoris becomes erect while you do this.

Now try to feel the muscles connected to the clitoris, and contract them as much as you can for one minute, approximately. Relax and take note of what is happening in the vagina.

This exercise is very important, because it strengthens the whole pelvic diaphragm. It should be done several times a day.

The "Hoola Hoop"

In our Western culture, the pelvis is not very mobile, to say the least, when it is compared to the Hawaiian belly dancers. Yet, this pelvic mobility is very important for our sexual efficiency. Therefore, we should practice the following exercise.

Posture: The same as above, except that the toes are pointed to the sides, the way Charlie Chaplin walked in his movies. Both hands rest at the waist. The aim of this exercise is to make the pelvis circle around. To do this, first bend your knees a little and tilt the pelvis backward by contracting the muscles of the abdomen. How to make the pelvis circle:

1. Thrust the pubic bone forward by tilting the pelvis up and contracting the muscles at the small of your back;

2. Push the left hip as far out as you can;

3. Thrust the bottom backward;

4. Push the right hip as far out as can be.

Done in succession, these four movements make the pelvis rotate clockwise. After three or four circles, do the same movement anti-clockwise.

This can be done any time during the day.

Apart from endowing one with a very mobile pelvis, this exercise restores the normal suppleness of the lumbar part of the spine and important nerves are being stimulated. Since these nerves command, among others, the sex organs, this exercise is highly beneficial to the health of the feminine genital organs—and the male's as well!

No Woman is Truly Frigid

Mary Cool—a true case study with a fake name —42, U.S. citizen, considered herself truly frigid, and with good reasons: married for twenty years she had *never* experienced an orgasm, and her sex life was restricted to a few times a year. Yes, a year! She usually felt nothing and, because her vagina stayed almost as dry as beach sand in summer, sex became almost painful. In short, she seemed to have a case of frigidity beyond hope.

Worse still, she had another problem which later became a lucky one: she suffered incontinence. Any excessive abdominal pressure, for example a sneeze, cough or lifting a weight, would cause her to wet her underwear. Not funny at all! It didn't comfort her to know that one woman out of two would have this problem at some time in her life, mostly when growing old.

One day, after suffering from this problem for seven years, and as she intended to have an operation, a friend of hers told her that a Dr. Arnold Kegel cured such cases *without* surgery, simply by rehabilitating the muscle connecting the coccyx to the pubis. Arnold Kegel had contrived something called a perineometer, a device made of a rubber cylinder coupled to a manometer. When this cylinder was inserted in a woman's vagina, she was asked to constrict her vaginal muscles as much as she could: the manometer instantly showed the amount of pressure and, later on, what progress, if any, was made.

The first consultation with Dr. Kegel established that there was atrophy and distention of Mary Cool's vaginal muscles: the manometer showed zero pressure. Mary Cool did not know it was possible to train these muscles, but after only six weeks of training, the pressure on the perineometer rose to 12mm/Hg. After six months she was cured and did not wet her underwear any more. On her last visit to Dr. Kegel, the pressure measured by the perineometer reached 22 mm/Hg, and her vaginal muscles had become much thicker and stronger.

Smiling, Mary Cool told Dr. Kegel, that she regretted not knowing twenty years earlier that it was possible to train these muscles. Blushing, she also told Dr. Kegel she and her husband were now having sex several times a week, more than they previously had in a whole year! For the first time in her life, she even had an orgasm!

To conclude: a) it is never too late; b) a so-called frigid woman is, in fact, a sensuous one who doesn't know it. Alas, there will be many

Mary Cools who stay icy not knowing they can so easily be cured. Sad.

As for Dr. Kegel himself, in 1951, on the basis of the positive results he had with his treatment of incontinence, he published an article about sexual functions and advised other doctors to always check the vaginal muscles of the so-called frigid woman, particularly the pubo-coccygeal one. In hundreds of cases, he could establish a direct link between the lack of sexual response and the atrophy of this muscle and *vice versa*, he found that very sexually responsive women had, as a rule, a vagina with strong, elastic muscles. He also noted they never suffered from incontinence and had very few gynecological problems.

This is understandable: whereas the mucous membrane of the vagina has comparatively very few nerve endings and is consequently almost insensitive, the vaginal *muscles* are *very sensitive* because they are very richly innervated. Atrophy and distention of these muscles render them almost insensitive sexually. Moreover, after menopause, the vaginal muscles of most woman become thinner and dryer. The Tantric shaktis, thanks to their rich sex life, do not have this problem.

Even after menopause, women need not despair: practicing these exercises and having Tantric sex, they can definitely restore the functions of the vaginal glands which secrete lubricating fluid and the glands producing female hormones as well. I would not be surprised if this practice would prove a preventive against osteoporosis that is not unavoidable, since two thirds of all women do not get this even without taking hormones.

The previous exercises were for the ano-genital sphincters. The following ones are aimed at the pubo-coccygeal muscle. This muscle is much like a hammock, fills almost the entire pelvic diaphragm and has three apertures: anus, vagina, urethra. This most important sex muscle has to be trained separately with the help of the following exercises.

Training the Pubo-Coccygeal Muscle

Take a blanket, roll it up tightly, put it on the floor and sit with it between your legs. Make sure the anus and the vulva press against the blanket to feel the action of the exercises.

Since we have no perineometer, our hands take its place. The left hand, placed between the blanket and the body, covers the vulva. And, if one practices this naked, one inserts the middle finger in the vagina. The right hand goes behind the back to put the middle finger against the anus and the coccyx. In other words, the left hand's finger is in the vagina, the right hand's middle finger presses the coccyx and the anus.

Close your eyes to concentrate better. Take a deep breath, exhale and, while checking your breath, constrict the pubo-coccygeal muscle as forcibly as you can, until the whole perineum vibrates. The right finger should feel the coccyx slightly moving forward. The left hand's finger will feel how the vaginal muscles react. At this stage, the entire genital region (anus, vulva, vagina) and the whole set of muscles connected to it, buttocks included, is constricted. Remember, we are still holding the breath out, but as soon as this ceases to be comfortable, we breathe in and relax. This has to be repeated for two or three minutes.

If it is not possible to practice on a rolled-up blanket, one can do it simply while sitting on a chair, provided there is good contact between anus, vulva and the seat.

Firming up the Buttocks

For sex, muscular buttocks are an important asset. Training the buttock's muscles can be done anywhere, any time, while sitting on a chair. Empty the lungs, hold the breath out, constrict the muscles of the buttocks. Automatically a spontaneous Mula Bandha comes. Let it be. Hold on as long as you can, then release the constriction and inhale. Relax the buttocks for a while, then repeat the exercise. By the way, relax for twice as long as the time you devoted to the constriction. Repeat five times.

This same exercise can be done in a slightly different manner. Instead of holding the constriction during the whole duration of the breath retention, one constricts and relaxes the buttocks rapidly, while holding the breath out.

Another practice to do while standing: just imagine you are holding a postcard between your buttocks and somebody tries to take it, but because you don't want to let it go, you squeeze it very firmly. While doing this, the abdominal wall, too, is strongly constricted.

The Perineum, a Strategic Point

Let's have a closer look at the figure on p. 335 and particularly at the nodule of the perineum. Located at the junction of all the important muscles of the ano-genital region, it is like a Gibraltar to our body. During childbirth, it is often partially torn and has to be surgically repaired. If not, it will produce a hernia in the vagina.

From the Tantric point of view, it is an all-important part. While sitting on a chair or on the floor, with eyes closed, concentrate only on this point. Forgetting, for a while, the anal and vaginal sphincters, starting from the nodule, slowly and gradually, constrict concentrically all the *muscles* of the pelvic floor, until a vibration is felt. The buttocks should be excluded from the constriction, but the lower part of the abdominal wall participates. Breathe normally. This is the first part of the exercise.

As for the second part, one slowly and gradually relaxes all these muscles one by one, starting from the periphery and ending at the center, the nodule, until the whole region is relaxed. This requires a good deal of concentration on this specific point.

Three to four times = one round. Do five rounds.

Most of the above described exercises are intended for both male and female Tantrists, since they have the same sets of muscles.

Part 6

Tantra
for Our World

Getting Initiated in the West

In the West, being exposed to a reliable Tantric initiation is quite a problem which is expressed in the following letter: "Being a woman, I am very much interested in Tantra and have read a good deal about it. But I never tried to get initiation because of the bad name Tantra has in the West, where it is believed to be sex acrobatics or a lewd sect, and I feared this would attract doubtful individuals.

"Do you know where and with whom I could start practicing under a safe guidance?"

My answer was that I did not know such a place—except in her own home—nor such a person—except her own partner. In fact, if Tantra is to become popular, this problem will grow even worse. Inevitably, fake gurus will pop up and some already have, and they pose as high initiates. Even in India true Tantric gurus are very few and they don't advertise. "Doubtful individuals," to quote this lady's words, not only will be attracted by Tantra but will take advantage of it and claim to be great gurus. Be aware and... beware!

Is there no scope nor hope? In the foreseeable future I do not see an answer to this question, but I think it is possible to grasp the essential part of the Tantric view of life through good books and there are quite a few. But, alas, most of them remain dead silent about the actual practices—that is better than publishing rubbish—and to fill this gap, at least partly, did I write this book. With the help of the techniques described and some common sense, one can safely practice and progress a good deal, in fact as far as it is possible to go in the West. To tell the truth, for many years I wondered if it would be a good idea to go public with these things, many of them being well-kept secrets for many centuries. But now I think the time has come to make them readily available to enable sincere seekers to practice without the help a guru, not because gurus are of no value, but because they are not available. Publishing them is, in a sense, undercutting the fake gurus who won't like this because they no longer can tell or do any nonsense under the cover of Tantra.

As for the true and full Tantric initiation, we should be well-aware of the fact that this is no joke. It takes many years of preparation and practice before getting ready. First, the body has to undergo a strict discipline implying the practice of Hatha Yoga, which is a branch of Tantra. There is also a long spiritual and mental preparation under the guidance of the guru before he (or she) is ready for initiation.

Guru and Chela

Since time immemorial, Tantra revolves around the guru-chela relationship, especially for the Path of the Left, and this relationship is of the closest intimacy and highest intensity that only those who actually experience it can understand. What's the use of talking much about cherries: tasting one is much better than reading hundreds of books and the same is true about gurus. The aim of this chapter is not to describe the experience in itself, but to help to differentiate a true guru from a fake one.

Tantra says "when the chela is ready, the guru appears," and this is really true. Meeting the guru is an unpredictable event, but when it occurs, it changes life for both, and is as indelible as a tattoo: one can divorce one's wife, never one's guru. In Tantra, the guru can be a woman as well as a man.

The chela does not go in search of a guru, and the reverse is also true. One just waits until "it" happens. But a meeting is not by pure chance, but destined to happen: as soon as they meet, they "know"; and it is very much like falling in love at first sight. How do they know? There is no logical answer to this question, but the fact is they do know. Strangely, it is as if they had already met before. A permanent bond is created between them: "after," nothing is as it was "before."

A Tantric guru is altogether a tutor, a master who hands over techniques, a guide who dispels doubts, but above all a trustee and an incarnation of the ancient Tantric tradition. Usually, before the meeting the chela has had some serious preparation with several instructors in yogic or Tantric techniques.

The rapport in their relationship produces a psychic catalysis or reaction. What happens between them cannot be experienced individually. It happens because they have met each other. But theirs is not a relationship where one is superior to the other; the guru is not an all-knowing master teaching a submissive student. The true guru never exploits the chela, neither financially, morally, nor on any level whatsoever. Exploitation is a trait of the fake gurus. On the other hand, it is also not a one way relationship, where only one gives and the other receives. The guru gets at least as much as he gives and, in this case, age, sex, and years of practice are irrelevant.

Their relationship relies on a very essential thing: the guru and the chela must *practice together* and, by so doing, unexpected reactions are triggered, sometimes from the very beginning, and an awakening of a new type of vital energy (Kundalinî) is created. With the shakti, this reaction could be called a cosmic orgasm. Through the magic of a reciprocal catalysis, other states of consciousness are obtained, which otherwise would take years of ascetic or self-denial practice to achieve.

The guru-chela relationship involving a man and a woman often implies actual sexual practices whose intensity goes far beyond what is ordinarily experienced. Most of the time, however, they do not live together and do not have many occasions to meet. They can lead a distinct sex life with their "normal" partner without becoming jealous. The guru-chela relationship, far from destroying the relationship of a settled couple, can on the contrary, make it stronger and more lasting. Is this paradoxical or contradictable? Impossible? According to our Western religions, our laws and ethics, perhaps, but what are they worth? Do they have absolute and universal value? Whatever the answer, no one is forced to accept these ideas.

Whatever is characteristic of a normal love relationship (possessiveness, jealousy, etc.) does not exist in theirs, and their bond is similar to that which exists between twins. This is probably what makes theirs a stable, lasting relationship. Even if the guru and chela remain for a long period without having the opportunity to meet physically, there is no sadness, because their relationship transcends time and space: mysteriously, they are always in contact with each other on a subtle, spiritual plane, just as twins are. During their daily meditation, they contact each other, sometimes even without being conscious of it. Their beings remain linked forever, maybe even beyond death. Who knows?

This kind of encounter between guru and chela is rare, but it exists. Sometimes guru and chela live for years near each other without knowing it. What I have written in this chapter seems to make it clear that a guru cannot have very many chelas, and that his relationship to each one will be different. A true Tantric guru will not have a big ashram and many followers. He often is not even recognized as a guru. In some cases, however, he may have a large following, but few true chelas, and these very few keep the relationship strictly secret. This is true in India and so, too, in the West. So, you may ask, is there no hope for the serious guru seeker? It is hard to say. On the Tantric path, any true seeker will always find a way to progress. True, a guru is irreplaceable, but if one does not find his own guru, the genuine seeker can always rely on his inner guru, his own Self, which is the supreme guru and can be reached through meditation and serious practice.

Beware of Fake Tantric Gurus

Fake Tantric gurus have already played havoc in the West, and in India as well. Why are they able to fool us so easily? The simple answer is: because we are incredibly gullible. Most fakes are Indians and they always promise us the earth, plus the moon and the stars! Fake Hatha Yoga gurus are never or seldom seen. The reason is not difficult to guess. Should a Hatha Yoga guru promise to straighten out the spine of all those who are hunchbacked in just a weekend seminar, of course, nobody would believe him. But, if some fake guru promises to awaken the Kundalinî in a matter of hours, people believe it and readily open wide their mouths and their wallets. To awaken the Kundalinî is much more difficult than to straighten a hump. To master and adjust one's body takes years of stubborn practice; to tame the Kundalinî, even more.

The infallible recipe for being believed is readily explained: to a fancy Indian dress, add an ounce of charisma, a few old tricks—known by all stage hypnotists—some advertising, and you will impress gullible people and get a huge following.

These old tricks are not only of no value, specifically of no Tantric value, but they can—and often do—damage unstable minds, and here I am not joking. It is rather easy to produce bizarre phenomena in people's minds, and this is always dangerous. The man who promises the "earth" stays only a short time in one place, then moves on to charm a new group of fools. After he has left, if something goes wrong, there is no one to help. My conclusion: beware of the wandering gurus who triumph in India as well as in the West. A famous (non-Tantric) Indian guru's specialty is to perform miracles: he "materializes" or publicly produces *small* objects of all kinds, such as rings, watches, coins, etc., and by so doing becomes godlike to his followers, not necessarily all Indians. I myself would be very much more impressed if he produced, for example, a locomotive, or a cruise ship! A genuine Tantric guru would never do such things. He doesn't need to. His work is done in silence and he remains unseen.

Another very important point. We should be well-aware of the fact that Tantra is not merely to do with sex, and especially sexual promiscuity. Some so-called Tantric initiations consist of getting a few people, most of them quite naïve, and making them have group sex. I am afraid to say that this is bound to happen and has already happened.

I might add that a fake guru doesn't have to worry that he will have no more customers. The supply of suckers in the world is inexhaustible.

And, by the way, did I give you my favorite guru's name? It is His Holiness Maharishi Yogiraj Commonsensananda-ji whose advice I often take, whereas most people don't. Why? Is it because he does not promise miracles? Or because his advice costs nothing? You answer!

A Ritual for the West

At the core of all great religions and traditions, Western or Oriental, there is a ritual, which is a set of symbolical acts to be performed in a fixed succession and with the help of ritualistic objects and symbols. Symbols and symbolical acts are the most efficient way to intuitively grasp what the intellect cannot understand, what no words can express, the foremost thing being the *regular repetition* of the ritual. Tantra is no religion, not even a sect, but it surely is a tradition. In India, each *Gurukula*, which literally means a guru's family, has its own ritual. The Chakra Pûjâ is the highest of all Tantric rituals, but for obvious reasons not really suited for us Westerners.

What we need is an acceptable, simplified ritual, but one which is genuine and in tune with the great Tantric Tradition, without interfering with our own religion or philosophy. The symbols should therefore be universal and neutral. And here again stress should be put upon the fact that Tantra is no religion, and a Tantric ritual is not some kind of pagan mass, but rather a succession of *significant* acts.

First, a ritual requires ritualistic objects. In any Tantric ritual the *human body* is the foremost significant "object," since it truly is the living Temple where the Cosmic Wisdom expresses itself. To ordinary people, the body consists only of flesh and bones, but to the Tantrist it manifests subtle cosmic energies. Whatever our religion or philosophy, the body is unquestionably a privileged place or space in the cosmos where "I" (not my ego) draws energy and particles from the outside world to shape a living, conscious entity. No doubt, within the body all aspects of the individual, from the grossest to the subtlest, meet. May I say that the body is divine? I quote Arthur Avalon who says: "The body is Shakti. Its life and all its activities are conceived as parts of the Divine action in nature—Shakti manifesting and operating in the form of man. The Tantrist realizes in the pulsing beat of his heart the rhythm which throbs through and is the sign of the Universal Life....Governed by such a concept, even the lowest physical needs take on a cosmic significance." Finally, Tantra wants me to awaken all my potential, to unfold my personality as a whole, and this cannot be in contradiction to any religion. With regard to the body and its powers, let's remember the chapter "An Unknown Universe, My Body."

First, the ritual is a way to become aware of the cosmic forces acting in my body as in my partner's. Next, one has to awaken these subtle forces by practicing pranayama and, finally, comes the maïthuna, the climax of the ritual. The easiest way to solve the problem of the ritual would be to describe some Indian rituals, but it would be quite a task to adapt it to our Western culture, because they are complicated, sophisticated, and require a daily discipline in suitable surroundings and circumstances, and, above all, plenty of time, a rather scarce commodity in our modern world! The other choice would be to devise a simplified ritual without losing its significance. I therefore have tried to rediscover the simple rituals of the original Tantra.

Let's make a comparison here. The Catholic mass is a sophisticated ritual and sometimes a very complex one; for example, Christ's Last Supper. Jesus did a very simple thing: he shared wine and bread with his disciples and told them to do the same thing in memory of Him. Starting from this simple, but essential core, the Church developed a ceremony which became the present day mass which endures. Although it is far removed from that Last Supper, without it the mass loses its meaning.

Tantra did the same. Starting from very simple beginnings, the rituals became intricate: for example, the Chakra Pûjâ, is the result of the original fertility rites of prehistoric times. But, as we are lacking any written or other reliable historical records, how can we hope to rediscover these simple beginnings? The only option was to extract the essentials and leave it at that.

These essentials are enclosed in this excerpt from the *Kulârnava Tantra* (VI.56): "The worshipper enters the ritual as soon as he reaches that state of consciousness where he is able to perceive the divinity, where he is connected with the Divine and, to this end, he should become conscious of his own divinity." Our very body *is* divine and this is a fact; but I am unable to realize this divinity as long as my little ego is in its ordinary state of consciousness. To transcend this state of being, one needs the ritual.

Theoretically, nothing more should be needed. It should be enough to sit in an easy yogic posture, or simply on the floor, with an erect spine, to be aware of one's breathing process, and to meditate on Life. This leads one to realize that this very life that throbs in my arteries and veins, is really the Life of the origin. Since the very remote moment it first appeared on earth, Life has been transmitted, without any break, through innumerable generations up to my own, and to know *I verily am*, this Universal Life Force is a foremost Tantric experience. In short, I really *am* this Life Force that transcends my own little ego. To quote Arthur Avalon: "It is not merely the separate individual who acts and enjoys....His life and the play of all its activities are not a thing apart to be held and pursued egoistically, but part of a much greater Life" (op.cit. p. 414). This is, of course, true.

To be able to *actually* experience this, however, one has to put together a few favorable circumstances. First, the "where" is important. If we practice at home, which should be the rule in the West, we should have a place or, if possible, a room specially reserved for the ritual or else simply a corner in the bedroom where we should keep a small, private "altar." I know, the word "altar" may irritate both religious people and atheists. To the former, this word would evoke some kind of heretical cult, while to the latter, the atheists, it would appear as some kind of religious trick. In fact, I could have written "a small table," instead, which would not get on anybody's nerves, but "altar" implies sacredness, and we know "sacred" and "religious" are not synonymous: life is "sacred," our earth is "sacred."

This simple altar, on which we keep a few significant, symbolical objects, should be kept secret not to be noticed by those who might ridicule it. So, how should it look? Very simply! On a small table, we put, for example, a yantra, a red triangle, and in the center of it a candle in a candlestick. The candle symbolizes the lingam or Shiva, and the candlestick is the yoni or Shakti, the Primeval Womb of the Universe. Better still, of course, would be a real lingam if one could bring one home from India. Or else, also from India, a small cast statue of the Dancing Shiva.

To you and your partner, the chosen object should symbolize the cosmic maïthuna, the union of the Male and Female Principles, or the origin of our universe. If some other symbol appeals to you, this is your choice. And even if we don't have anything to use as a symbol, we could imitate the poor South Indian people and take an oval pebble, put it into a cup filled with sand and raise it: it then becomes the symbol of the cosmic Maïthuna.

Another symbol could be an earthen jar filled with reddish water, representing the (cosmic) uterus as well as our mother's womb where we lived for nine months. The water is the amniotic fluid. We could use a hollow shell symbolizing the ocean, the source of life on our planet. Above all, the small altar should be adorned with flowers—even the simplest will do—for no pûjâ should be done without some flowers, some living expression of the creative dynamism of our universe, and symbols of our world's divine beauty.

In India, nobody other than the participants of the pûjâ are allowed to touch the symbolic objects, and they themselves dress the altar: this already contributes and puts them in the right mood for the pûjâ.

As soon as the altar is dressed, the pûjâ can start. Of course, the participants first take a bath, or better a shower, and rub perfumed oil on their bodies. In India, this can be a lengthy process and become part of the *nyasa*. As soon as everything is ready, the right mood must be established.

It is important that the rite takes place in dim light. In our countries, the candle will replace the traditional castor-oil lamp used in India. If you have Indian incense, you can light three or four of the sticks. If not available, your favorite perfume will do. A suitable musical background is also very helpful. This need not necessarily be Indian music, but if one likes it, it is perfect and very erotic. Everything should be beautiful and peaceful.

The worshippers should be clad in light garments, for instance in silk bathrobes and should sit, side by side, in front of the altar with knees and hands touching to establish a first physical contact. Meanwhile, both should gaze at the candle's flame, without blinking (*tratak*), breathe slowly, and be aware of the symbolic objects on the altar and of their meaning, though this should not be expressed in words. One should simply open his mind to their significance: the unconscious mind will "decode" it.

After some time with their minds very calm and serene, they should sit face to face, knees and hands both touching, aware of the presence of their partner and of his or her body's divinity. No need to hurry! After a while, the female shares some dried fruit, nuts, or biscuits with her partner. There is no need to have the five "M" but, of course, this is not forbidden! While eating, the two shall become very conscious of the fact that this food will become their very blood, flesh, and bones, and that their life depends on the outer world and is not separated from it.

Next comes a very intense part of the pûjâ. The shakti will pour some red wine in a bowl, and, still gazing at her partner's eyes, she will take one or two sips. Then she will hand the bowl over to her partner and he will have a few sips as well. The bowl will thus go back and forth between shakti and shiva. Traditionally, the shakti should empty it.

They should then again sit face to face and meditate for a while. The first to start the caresses should be the shakti, and then they should fondle each other until desire is awakened. At a given moment, the shakti will undress and stay naked in front of the shiva, who will do the same. What follows is left to them but, most importantly, they should meet slowly and respectfully. Maïthuna is, needless to say, the most intense, the most symbolical part of the pûjâ, and this book tells you how to make the experience "Tantric." The embrace should be a feast, not only to the individual minds, but to every cell of the bodies: it should become a communion. This is the feast of the return to the primeval unity, to the primeval androgynous state and, thus by reenacting the cosmic creative surge, both partners will experience the highest ananda, or supreme bliss.

At this point, all speaking should stop; what remains is what they themselves experience.

The Future
of Tantra in the West

Is there any scope for Tantra in the West? This question has been answered by Wendell Charles Beane in his excellent book *Myth, Cult and Symbols in Shakta Hinduism* (Leiden, 1977, p. 268):

"A final significance of our study resides in its theoretical and practical implications for *others* outside of India as a *new possibility* for reevaluating the theological symbolization of Ultimate Reality and the role of human reproductive capacities (i.e., sexuality). It is not necessary to regard this as a romantic summons to encourage an antinomian perspective of religious freedom; although it is doubtful that even the more radical aspects of the Left-handed Tantric tradition are completely gone in India.

"The important thing is that the worship of the goddess allows for the integration of aspects of human life into a whole, which includes the achievement of a type of *balance* in view of the oft-stated generalization that religious pantheonic structures tend to mirror the sociopolitical structures of civilizations. In a civilization outside India this possibility may still become of wholesome consequence. Furthermore, there is some significance to the modern movements toward the liberalization of sexual practices, as much as it has import for the liberation of women themselves from being regarded solely as sexual 'objects' instead of persons of value.

"Individuals might therefore learn from the testimony of the worshippers of the goddess that, even if certain ideas and forms of the Tantric Vogue may be found unsuitable to certain modern milieux, it is essentially the vision of what both man *and* woman can become to one another in mutual respect of another's identity, influence and activity *in* the world that matters finally."

W. C. Beane's academic style notwithstanding, his conclusion is very important. He expresses my own firm belief that the Tantric outlook on life is not only suited to Western people, but it progressively will have a great effect on our modern society. This will happen through a new awareness and a change in the values on which our society is based, and without having to renounce our own religions, beliefs, or cults.

Appendix

The Tantric Philosophy

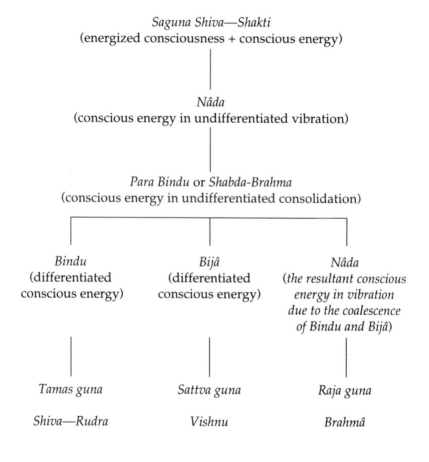

Saguna Shiva—Shakti
(energized consciousness + conscious energy)

Nâda
(conscious energy in undifferentiated vibration)

Para Bindu or *Shabda-Brahma*
(conscious energy in undifferentiated consolidation)

Bindu (differentiated conscious energy)	*Bijâ* (differentiated conscious energy)	*Nâda* (*the resultant conscious energy in vibration due to the coalescence of Bindu and Bijâ*)
Tamas guna	*Sattva guna*	*Raja guna*
Shiva—Rudra	*Vishnu*	*Brahmâ*

Para-Bindu or *Shabda-Brahma*

Mahat
Cosmic intelligence

Ahangkâra
(Egoism—I-sense)

The 10 senses—5 senses of perception and 5 senses of action—are considered as conscious energies, their consciousness aspects being the presiding deities of their unconscious energy aspects, the sense or nerve powers which are the karanas or instruments of their presiding deities.	The Tanmâtras, 5 in number, which are the subtle principles of solidity, fluidity, luminosity, vitality and spatiality;

Akâsha (space)	Shabda Tanmâtra (sound or spatiality)
Vâyu (life or vital air)	Sparsha Tanmâtra (touch or vitality)
Tejas (fire or light)	Rûpa Tanmâtra (form or luminosity)
Apa (the waters, liquid and gaseous fluids)	Rasa Tanmâtra (taste or fluidity)
Kshiti (earth)	Gandha Tanmâtra (smell or solidity)

Glossary

Abhayamudrâ: gesture to protect.

Abhichâra: "magic," incantations, spells (especially black magic).

Abhinavagupta: famous Shâkta tantric (seventh century). Wrote numerous works, including commentaries on the Shaivâgamas.

Abhisheka: brahmanical consecration rite of the king by anointment.

Achâryâ: a spiritual guide or teacher, guru.

Adhikâra: someone qualified for the tantric initiation.

Adyâ-Sakti: primal, divinized energy.

Agama: "That which has come down," i.e., traditional non-vedic texts; i.e., 77.

Aghora: "non-terrifying." Term applied to Siva, to propitiate him.

Agni: vedic god of fire.

Agnihotra: vedic sacrifice of fire.

Ahamkâra: the samkhya principle of the ego.

Akasha: "All-pervading," space; vacuity, the most subtle of the five elements.

Akula: aspect if Siva within Sakti.

Ambâ: "Mother," a name of Durgâ.

Ambikâ: a nature goddess formed from the energies of all the gods to destroy the enemies of the gods.

Ananda: highest bliss.

Anjali mudrâ: gesture to honor, done with both hands joined together.

Amrita: immortality (from "*a*" privative, and *mrita*, death).

Apâna: an aspect of the vital energy (prâna) especially excretion.

Apsara: seductive celestial nymphs, "essence of the waters." In the Hindu mythology equivalent of the nordic Walkyries.

Âsana: "seat or throne," yogic posture; tantric maïthuna posture.

Ashrama: hermitage; stage of life.

Ashvamedha: the Aryan horse-sacrifice.

Asura: demon, enemy of the Devas (Aryans).

Atharvaveda: the Veda of magical spells.

Atman: "Essence or principle of life," spirit.

Ayurveda: from *âyus*, life, and *ved*, knowledge. India's traditional medical science.

Bhaga: vulva.

Bhairavi: "Terror," power of death which goes on throughout life; one aspect of Rudra-Siva.

Bhakti: from *bhaj* devotion, adoration, affection; a path of yoga.

Bhang(â): Indian name for hashisch.

Bhâvinî: another name for the Devadâsîs.

Bhoga: enjoying.

Bhuta: material elements.

Bija: mantra-seed, monosyballic; sperm.

Bindu: subtle energy, located at the Mûlâdhara cakra, which the yogi guides upward along the Sushumna; perceived as light at Ajna; a dot.

Brahmâ: the Creator, an aspect of Brahman.

Brahmacârin: A religious student, living in the house of his guru; one of the ashramas, or stages of life.

Brahman: "All-pervading, self existent Cause." Hindu priest.

Buddha: "Enlightened" title given to someone having achieved full wisdom; name given to Gautama, "the" Buddha.

Buddhi: in Samkhya philosophy, the intellect.

Chakra: "wheel," "disk," "circle." Subtle psycho-physiological center in the body.

Chakra pûjâ: tantric ritual where the adepts are seated in a circle.

Chandâla: outcaste; untouchable; the Aryans do not consider them as human beings.

Chandra: the moon; the Moon-goddess.

Chandrakâla: crescent of the Moon in the crown of Candra.

Chinnamastâ: "beheaded"; one of Durgâ's forms, without her head.

Chit Sakti: principle of consciousness.

Dâkinî: demoniac, quasi-divine beings in Hindu and Buddhist tantrism; they eat raw flesh.

Dakshina-marga: Tantric right-hand path, without actual sex.

Damaru: drum-shaped, like an hourglass. The upward and downward triangles symbolize the union of lingam and yoni.

Dâsa: name given by the Aryans to the indigenous tribes hostile to the invading Aryans.

Dasyu: synonymous to dâsa.

Dyana: meditation on a chosen deity, while controlling the sense-organs.

Deva: "luminous being." Vedic god; personified natural forces.

Deva-dâsî: "slave-servants of the gods." Dancing girls and temple-prostitutes, especially in southern India, for the gratification of the priests and of anyone willing to pay the price. Some were rich. Could read, sing, dance, and entertain princes and priests, and provided the temple with cash.

Devî: feminine of deva.

Dharma: law, duty, custom.

Dhyânayoga: in Tantra, process of concentrating the mind on the ascent of Kundalinî.

Dîkshâ: "initiation," "consecration," "dedication." The student had to undergo the *diksa*, in order to be accepted as a pupil by the guru.

Drâvida: Brown-skinned, long-head people, living in India before the invasion by the Aryans. The proto-Dravidians appear to have been the originators of the Indus civilization, and later they mixed with tribes coming from the northwest. They traded with Western Asia, Egypt, the Greek and Roman empires.

Durgâ: A tantric goddess from the Shakta-cult; a form of the Mother-Goddess. To the Aryans, she was a frightful War-Goddess, to be feared.

Dûtî: female partner in the tantric rites.

Ganapati: cf. Ganesha.

Ganesha: God with an elephant-head. Propitious.

Garuda: mythic eagle.

Gopî: lit. "cowgirls." Herds-maiden in love with Krishna.

Grihâvadhuta: tantric adept living as an ordinary householder.

Guru: Religious guide or teacher who gives initiation to the pupil.

Hamsa: mantra combining *hang* on the inhalation and *sa* on the exhalation.

Idâ: Moon-nadî. Left nostril.

Indra: tutelary god of the Aryans, chief of the gods; destroys enemy fortresses and kills the Dasyu. His favorite weapon is the lightning.

Jâti: Birth and social status based on lineage and the color of the skin. Determines one's status within the caste system.

Jîvasakti: another name for Kundalinî, the body's vital energy.

Jîvatmâ: individual soul.

Jnâna yoga or Jnâna marga: "knowing," intellectual or philosophical yoga.

Kâla: time.

Kalânyâsa: perception of the goddesses located in the various parts of the tantric female partner.

Kalasa: water pot, pitcher, ewer, filled with water and the symbol for the universe. An item of the tantric ritual. Archetype of femininity.

Kâlî: a goddess, a spouse of Siva, ugly, four-armed, having fang-like teeth, she destroys everything, Time included.

Kâma: (from *kam*, longing for) the god of love, the Indian Cupid.

Kâmakalâ: sex act. In tantra, form of maïthuna where the static and dynamic aspects of Siva are balanced.

Kanda: starting point (egg-shaped) of all the nâdîs, located at the perineum.

Karman: Any act.

Karma yoga: practical yoga.

Khecharî: yogic practice where the frenum of the tongue is gradually cut, in order to be able to swallow the tongue, thus witholding the breath for a very long time.

Krishna: dark, blue-skinned god. Lover of all the gopîs and of Radha as well. Krishna's cult is a very popular erotico-religious cult.

Kula: "Family, lineage." The tantric guru and his followers form a single *kula* or family.

Kumârîpûjâ: tantric ritual in which a virgin is being worshipped.

Kumbha: pot (used in a ritual). When a yogi seals air in his lungs like water in a pot, this practice is named *Kumbhaka*.

Kundalinî: mysterious latent (sleeping) energy, located at the Mûlâdhâra cakra. Kundalinî is likened to a female serpent lying coiled eight times. It is the supreme sakti, the original source of everything. The yogi works to awaken this dormant energy and attain the highest bliss.

Latâ: female partner in the tantric cult.

Lingam: "sign," "symbol," "mark." Any sign of Siva's creative energy united to a Sakti is a linga. The highest symbol of this energy being an erect male organ inserted in a yoni.

Lingam: also an erect penis.

Madhya: used in the 5-M ritual.

Mahâdeva: *Mahâ*, great. The great god = Siva.

Mahâdevî: the great goddess = Sakti.

Mahat: in the samkhya-philosophy, the cosmic intelligence, stemming from Prakriti.

Maïthuna: copulation, sex act.

Makara: a goddess. The sanskrit *m*, pronounced *ma*. Indicates the five Makârâs (the 5-M) of the tantric rite.

Mamsa: meat: one of the 5-M.

Manas: mind (perception, intellect, understanding, etc.).

Mandala: circle formed by the tantrics during a Chakra Pûjâ, with, at the center, the pair directing the pûjâ. Symbolizes the unfolding cosmos. Complex circular diagrams.

Mantra: a sound, magical formula, incantation endowed with a secret power.

Manu: the Aryan's "Adam." Mythical compilator of the *Manu-smriti*, Manu's law, the *Mânava Dharma-Sastra*.

Mârga: way, path. Example: *Bhakti-Mârga*, the way of devotion to God.

Mâtâ: "Mother;" "Moon."

Matsya: "Fish," one of the 5-M.

Maya: cosmic power to project forms, material cause of the creation. Power to veil reality, hence "illusion."

Mithuna: a pair (human or animal).

Mleccha: "foreigner," any non-Aryan regarded as a barbarian.

Mudra: a sign made by the hand. Partner of the tantric rite; in the 5-M—grain and aphrodisiac plants.

Mukhalinga: lingam related to several heads of Siva.

Mûla: root of a plant.

Mûladhara: root-cakra, located at the perineum.

Nâbhi: "navel," "center."

Nâda: "Sound or tone-vibration." Important aspect of tantra, combined with the science of mantras.

Nadî: "river," "flow," In tantrism a *nadi* is a channel through which energies flow through the human subtle body.

Nâga: "snake." Phallic symbol.

Nanda: "the happy one." The bull, symbol of strength, fertility; Siva's vehicle. Doorkeeper of the temples and sanctuaries.

Natarâja: "Lord of the Dance," Siva.

Natî: dancing girl.

Nâtya: dance.

Nirvâna: lit. "extinction"; in Buddhism, extinction of all (wordly) desires; mental emptiness.

Nyâsa: an aspect of tantric rite in which various parts of the body are assigned to tutelary deities.

OM: The absolute sound, the seed (bija) of all mantras, the root syllable of origination and dissolution.

Padma: lotus.

Padmâsana: lotus posture. A maïthuna asana.

Pancamakârâ: *panca*=five. The 5-M: cf. *makârâ*.

Panca Sakti: one of the five great Saktis: the mother, the sister, the daughter, the daughter-in-law, the mother-in-law.

Parakîyâ: partner for the rite, other than the adept's own wife.

Pârvâti: Siva's spouse.

Pâsupati: "Lord of Animals," a title of Siva.

Patanjali: author of the *Yogasutra*.

Pingala: Solar nadi, beginning at the right nostril.

Prakshâ: Static aspect of the ultimate reality.

Praktriti: primal material nature, personified as the active female principle of manifestation.

Pralaya: "dissolution," "melting." *Mahâpralaya* = the great dissolution, in which all forms disappear, disintegrate.

Prana: Vital, cosmic energy.

Pranava: another name for "OM" (ONG).

Prânâyâma: yogic techniques to control the pranic (vital) energies in the human body, through sophisticated breathing processes.

Pûjâ: "Homage," "worship" with flowers. Word not to be found in any Indo-European language, appears to be of Dravidian and Tantric origin.

Purâna: collection of ancient (post-vedic) tales.

Purusha: "man," "mankind."

Purushamedha: human sacrifice.

Râdhâ: Krishna's beautiful spouse, tantric symbol of sensual love.

Râga: A musical mode or melody in the Indian music.

Râja Yoga: psychic yoga according to the *sutras* of Patanjali.

Râjayoga: according to tantra union of *retas* (male energy, sperm) with *rajas* (female energy, vaginal moisture).

Rasa: elixir, mood. Intense emotional link between Siva and Sakti.

Rati: desire, passion, love; also a tantric goddess. Name given to the female erotic energy (sexual arousal). When Sakti sees Siva, her *rati* becomes active.

Retas: flow, sperm. Mixed with rajas during copulation.

Rigveda: the oldest of the four Vedas.

Rishi: "Seer," sage.

Rudra: "The howler," vedic god of the tempest, later identified to Siva in the Vedic pantheon.

Sâdhak(a): adept of yogic or tantric discipline.

Sâdhanâ: discipline, yogic practice. In tantrism, ritualistic sex.

Sahajoli: female counterpart of Vajrolî. Control of the vaginal muscles.

Samâdhi: final goal of Raja Yoga.

Samarasa: shared bliss. Maïthuna, witholding ejaculation with breath control.

Sâmkhya or Sânkhya: one of the six orthodox Indian philosophical systems stemming from tantra.

Samsâra: the endless cycle of birth and rebirth, dictated by the inexorable law of *karma*.

Samskara: subtle seeds of action.

Sannyâsin: monk having relinquished all wordly attachments; one of the ashramas.

Sati: "real, true, virtuous woman," according to patriarchial rules. As a widow, on the death of her husband, proves her devotion by being burned with her dead husband on the funeral pyre.

Shaiva: pertaining to Siva.

Shakta: cult of the female energy. "Saktism" = cult to Sakti.

Shâktâgamas: tantric texts.

Shakti: cosmic aspect of the female energy. She makes Siva alive, and without whom Siva would only be a Sava (a corpse).

Shakti: woman, female partner in the tantric maïthuna.

Shavasâdhana: tantric rite with a human corpse.

Shishna: lit. penis. "Shishnadeva" = phallus, divinized penis. The Aryans despised the Dravidians as being "penis worshippers."

Shishya: follower of a guru.

Siddhi: "successful achievement." Supranormal powers obtained through yogic practice.

Shri chakra: foremost yantra in tantrism; represents the yoni.

Shruti: "hearing" orally transmitted knowledge.

Shûdra or Sudra: one of the four classes; had to serve the Aryans.

Shukra: sperm.

Shiva: "the red one," "the auspicious one." Shiva's true name is holy to the point of never being uttered (also Siva).

Soma: mythical plant whose juice, after having been filtered, had strong intoxicating and probably hallucinogenic properties. Essential libation of the Aryan gods.

Sukhâ: happiness, pleasure.

Sukhâsana: a maïthuna-posture.

Sutra: lit. "thread," "aphorism."

Tamas: "darkness," ignorance, inertia.

Tândava: Siva's cosmic dance.

Târâ: aboriginal Mother goddess whose name lit. means "star." Tantric goddess, synonymous to Sakti.

Tattwa: "primary subtle elements;" used in tantric rite.

Trikona: triangle, yoni.

Trishûla: Siva's trident. Symbolizes Ida-Pingala-Sushumna.

Upanishads: treatises of esoteric wisdom, in the form of tales.

Vaishnava: cult of Vishnu.

Vajra: "thunderbolt, lightning," male organ.

Vajroli: tantric and yogic practice by which fluids can be sucked in the penis, in order to have a greater witholding power during the maïthuna.

Vâmâcâri: tantric follower of the Left-Hand Path, in which ritual copulation is really performed.

Varna: "color" name used to denote groups having different skin colorations.

Veda: lit. "knowledge," sacred texts of the Aryans. Rigveda, sacred hymns; Sâmaveda, hymns for the sacrifices; Yajurveda, magical sacrificial spells, with archaic indigenous magic, stemming from tantrism.

Vedanta: "end of the veda," non-dualistic philosophical system.

Vïra: "hero, leader," name for some Aryan gods, but of Siva as well. In tantra, a vîra is someone who no more belongs to the pashu (animal), or the herd.

Virya: energy, male sexual arousal, sperm. Same as rati to the female.

Vishnu: lit. "Pervader," the second part in the Hindu triad. Brahma creates the universe, but Vishnu preserves it.

Vritra: Dravidian military leader protecting an important dam; important barrage. Indra having killed Vritra, became the hero "who frees the waters," thus opening the dam—destroying Dravidian villages and towns.

Yogi: male yoga adept.

Yoginî: a class of goddesses. Female adept of yoga.

Yoni: The female generative organ associated with the lingam.

Yuga: The four periods or ages. Our age is the Iron Age, the Age of Kâlî, whose end is destruction or dissolution.

Yuganaddha: male principle united to the female principle. Very common in Buddhist Tantric art. The Tibetan yab-yum.

Bibliography

Abhedananda, Swami. *The Yoga Psychology*. Calcutta: 1967; and Los Angeles: Vedanta Press, n.d.

Agehananda (Bharati). *The Light at the Center*. Santa Barbara, CA: 1976.

———. *The Tantric Tradition*. London, 1969.

Aguilar, Enric. *Vers une sexologie de la religion*. Barcelona, 1982.

Albarn, Keith. *Diagram*. London, 1977.

Amiet, Pierre. *L'Art antique du Proche-Orient*. Paris, 1977.

———. *The Art of the Ancient Near-East*. New York: Abrams, 1980.

Anshan, Sinh. *Hatha-Yoga Pradîpikâ*. Delhi, 1975.

Argüelles, Miriam & José. *The Feminine*. London, 1977.

Avalon, Arthur (John George Woodroffe). *Garland of Letters*. London: Theosophical, 1922.

———. *Shakti and Shakta*. 1918. New York: Dover, 1978.

———. *The Serpent Power*. 1924. Madras: Ganesh, 1965; and New York: Dover, 1974.

———. *Tantrarâja Tantra*. 1956. Madras: Ganesh, 1971; and Deli: Motilal Banarsidass, 1981.

———. *The World as Power*. Madras: Ganesh, 1966.

Banerjea, J. N. *Paurânic and Tântric Religion*. Calcutta, 1966.

Banerjee, P. *Early Indian Religions*. Delhi, 1973.

Basham, Arthur L. *La Civilisation de l'Inde ancienne*. Paris, 1976.

Basu, Manoranjan. *Tantras: a General Study*. Calcutta: Mrs. Mira Basu, 1976.

Beane, Wendel Charles. *Myth, Cult and Symbols in Sakta Hinduism*. Leyden, 1977.

Beyer, Stephan. *The Cult of Tärä: Magic and Ritual in Tibet*. Berkeley: University of California Press, 1974.

Bhattacharya, Benoytosh. *An Introduction to Buddhist Esoterism.* Motilal Banarsidass, 1931; Delhi, 1980.

———. *Guhyasamaja Tantra.* Baroda, 1967.

———. *Saivism and the Phallic World.* New Delhi: Oxford, IBH, 1975.

Bhattacharya, D. K. *Prehistoric Archeology.* Delhi, 1972.

Bhattacharya, Dr. Hari Satya. *An Introduction to Buddhist Esoterism.*

Bhattacharyya, Narendra Nath. *Ancient Indian Rituals.* Delhi, 1970.

———. *History of the Tantric Religion.* Delhi: Munshiram Manoharlarl, 1982.

Bhavnani, Menakshi. *The Dance in India.* Bombay: Taraporevala, 1984.

Bittel, Kurt. *Les Hittites.* Paris, 1976.

Blofeld, John. *Le Bouddhisme Tantrique du Tibet.* Paris, 1976.

———. *Mantras, Secret Words of Power.* London, 1976.

———. *The Tantric Mysticism of Tibet.* New York, 1970.

———. *Taoist Mysteries and Magic.* London, 1973.

———. *The Way of Power.* London, 1970.

Bord, Janet & Colin. *Mysterious Britain.* London: Granuda, 1978.

Bose, D. N. *Tantras, their Philosophy & Occult Secrets.* Calcutta: Mukhopadhyay, 1981.

Boudet, P. *La jouissance de Dieu—ou le roman courtois de Thérèse d'Avila.* Paris: Hallier, 1979.

Briggs, George Weston. *Goraknath and the Kanphatha Yogîs.* Delhi: Motilal Banarsidass, 1973.

Budhananda, Chela. *Moola Bandha, The Master Key.* Monghyr, 1978.

Capra, Fritjof. *The Tao of Physics.* Boston: Shambhala, 1975.

Cardin, Alberto. *Guerreros, Chamanes y Travestis.* Barcelona, 1985.

Casal, Jean-Marie. *La Civilisation de l'Indus et ses énigmes.* Paris, 1969.

Chakravarti, Chintarahan. *Tantras, Studies on their Religion and Literature.* Calcutta, 1972.

Chanda, Ram P. *The Indo Aryan Races.* Rajsahi: Cosmo Publications, 1916.

Chander, Ramesh. *Tantric Yoga Techniques.* Delhi, 1979; and Flushing, NY: Asia Book Corporation, n.d.

Chandra, Vasu. *The Gheranda Samhita.* Allahabad, 1975.

Chang, Jolan. *Le Tao de l'art d'aimer.* Paris and New York, 1977; also available as *The Tao of Love and Sex.* London and New York: Arkana Penguin, 1991.

Chanson, Paul. *L'accord charnel*. Paris, 1963.

Chatterji, J.C. *La philosophie ésotérique de l'Inde*. Paris, 1917.

Chattopadhyaya, Sudhakar. *Reflections of Tantras*. Delhi, 1978; San Jose, CA: Asia Books, 1979.

Chintaran, Chakravarti. *Tantras, Studies on Religion and Literature*. Calcutta, 1972.

Chunder, Pratap Chandra. *Kautilya on Love and Morals*. Delhi: Gian, 1987.

Chung-Yuan, Chang. *Le monde du Tao*. Paris, 1971.

Colaabawala, F. D. *Tantra: The Erotic Cult*. New Delhi: Orient Paperbacks, 1976.

Comfort, Dr. Alex. *Das Koka Shastra*. Stuttgart, 1968.

————. *Joy of Sex*. New York: Simon & Schuster, 1974.

————. *More Joy of Sex*. New York: Simon & Schuster, 1975.

Coomaraswamy, Ananda. *La Danse de Civa*. Rennes, 1979; also published as *The Dance of Siva*. New York: Dover, 1985.

Cooper, J-C. *La philosophie du Tao*. Paris, 1977.

Cowell, E. B. & A. E. Gough. *Sarvâ-Darsana-Samgraha*. Varanasi: Chowkhamaba, 1961.

Cox, Sir George W. *The Mythology of the Aryans*. Varanasi, 1973.

Dallapiccola, A.L. *Princesses et courtisanes*. Paris, 1978.

Danielou, Alain. *The Gods of India*. Rochester, VT: Inner Traditions International, 1988; *Le polythéisme hindou*. Paris, 1960.

————. *L'histoire de l'Inde*. Paris, 1971.

————. *Les quatre sens de la vie*. Paris, 1976.

————. *La sculpture érotique hindoue*. Paris, 1973.

————. *Shiva and Dionysos*. Rochester, VT: Inner Traditions International, 1984.

————. *Le temple hindou, centre magique du monde*. Paris, 1972.

Dasgupta, Kalyan Kumar. *A Tribal History of Ancient India*. Calcutta: Navabharat, 1977.

Dasgupta, Shashi Bhusan. *An Introduction to Tantric Buddhism*. Calcutta: University, 1974.

————. *Obscure Religious Cults*. Calcutta: Mukhopadhyay, 1969.

Dasgupta, S. N. *Yoga as Philosophy and Religion*. 1924. Delhi: Motilal Banarsidass, 1987.

————. *Yoga Philosophy*. Calcutta: University, 1976.

David-Neel, Alexandra. *L'Inde où j'ai vécu*. Paris, 1951.

Desai, Devangana. *Erotic Sculpture of India*. New Delhi, 1975; Philadelphia: Coronet, 1984.

De Smedt, Marc. *L'Erotisme chinois*. Freibourg-Geneva, 1981.

————. *L'Europe païenne*. Paris, 1980.

Deshpande, Mahdev M. *Aryan & Non-Aryan in India*. Ann Arbor: Michigan Papers on South and South-East Asia, No. 14, 1979.

Dossey, Larry. *Space, Time and Beyond*. Boston: Shambhala, 1982.

Douglas, Nik. *Tantra Yoga*. New Delhi: Manoharlarl, 1971.

Douglas, Nik & Penny Slinger. *Sexual Secrets*. Rochester, VT: Inner Traditions International, 1979.

Dröscher, Vitus B. *Ils se déchirent et ils s'aiment*. Paris, 1975.

————. *Les sens mystérieux des animaux*. Paris, 1965.

Dupé, Gilbert. *La sexualité et l'érotisme dans les religions*. Paris, 1980.

Dutt, Manmatha Nath. *Mahanirvana Tantram*. Varanasi, 1979.

Duval, Paul-Marie. *Les Celtes*. Paris, 1977.

Edwards, Allen. *The Jewel in the Lotus*. New York, 1976.

Eliade, Mircea. *Le chamanisme et les techniques archaïques de l'extase*. Paris, 1968; also published as *Shamanism: Archaic Techniques of Ecstasy*. New York: Penguin, 1989.

————. *L'épreuve du labyrinthe*. Paris, 1978.

————. *Histoire de Religions*. Paris, 1964.

————. *Le Yoga, immortalité et liberté*. Paris, 1954; also published as *Yoga, Immortality and Freedom*. New York: Penguin, 1989.

Elmore, W. T. *Dravidian Gods of Modern Hinduism*. New Delhi: Manohar, 1984.

Esnoul, Anne Marie. *L'Hindouisme*. Paris, 1972.

Evola, J. *Eros and the Mysteries of Love*. Rochester, VT: Inner Traditions International, 1991.

————. *Metaphysique du sexe*. Paris, 1959; also published as *Metaphysics of Sex*. Rochester, VT: Inner Traditions International, 1991.

————. *Le Yoga Tantrique*. Paris, 1961.

Feldenkrais, Moshe. *Body and Mature Behavior*. London, 1949; Independence, MO: International University Press, 1970.

Feurstein, Georg. *The Essence of Yoga*. London, 1974.

Fisher, Helen E. *The Sex Contact*. London, 1983; New York: Morrow, 1983.

Foote, Bruce Robert. *Prehistoric and Protohistoric Antiquities of India*. 1916. Delhi: Leeladevi, 1979.

Fouchet, Max-Paul. *L'art amoureux des Indes*. Lausanne, 1957.

Fremantle, Fr. & Ch. Trungpa. *The Tibetan Book of the Dead*. Boston: Shambhala, 1975.

Gangadharan, N. *Lingapurâna: A Study*. Delhi: Ajanta, 1980.

Gaudio, A. & Pelletier, R. *Femmes d'Islam, le sexe interdit*. Paris, 1980.

Glasenapp, H. de. *Les littératures de l'Inde*. Paris, 1963.

Godved, Helle. *Beckenboden & Sexualität*. Stuttgart, 1983.

Gonda, J. *Les religions de l'Inde*. Paris, 1962.

Gopal, Ram. *Classical Dances of India*. London, 1965.

Goswami, Shyam Sundar. *Hatha Yoga*. London, 1963.

———. *Laya Yoga, An Advanced Method of Concentration*. London: RKP, 1980.

Goudriaan, Teun. *The Vînâshikhatantra*. Delhi, 1985.

Govinda, Lama Anagarika. *Foundations of Tibetan Mysticism*. York Beach, ME: Samuel Weiser, 1969.

———. *Mandala, der Heilige Kreis*. Zurich, 1973.

Greer, Germaine. *The Female Eunuch*. London: Paladin, 1970.

Gregersen, Edgar. *Sexual Practices*. London, 1982.

Guénon, René. *Les états multiples de l'être*. Paris, 1957.

———. *Etudes sur l'hindouisme*. Paris, 1968; also published as *Studies in Hinduism*. Columbia, MO: South Asia Books, 1987.

———. *Orient et Occident*. Paris, 1948.

Guenther, Herbert V. *Yuganaddha: The Tantric View of Life*. Varanasi: Chowkhamba, 1979.

Guenther, Herbert & C. Trungpa. *The Dawn of Tantra*. Boston: Shambhala, 1975.

Gulik (van), R. H. *La vie sexuelle en Chine ancienne*. Leiden, 1961.

Gupta, Beni. *Magical Beliefs and Superstitions*. Delhi: Sundeep, 1979.

Harasimhaiah, B. *Neolithic and Megalithic Cultures in Tamil Nadu*. Delhi: Sundeep, 1980.

Herbert, Jean. *Introduction à l'Asie*. Paris, 1960.

————. *Spiritualité hindoue*. Paris, 1947.

Hesnard, Dr. A. *La sexologie*. Paris, 1959.

Hinze, Oscar Marcel. *Symbolon*. Bâle, 1968.

————. *Tantra Vidya*. Delhi: Motilal Banarsidass, 1979.

Hite, Shere. *Le rapport Hite*. Paris, 1977; also published as *The Hite Report*. New York: Dell, 1987.

Hoyle, Fred. *The Intelligent Universe*. London, 1983.

Idries Shah, Sayed. *La magie orientale*. Paris, 1957.

Ijima, Rev. Kanjitsu. *Buddhist Yoga*. Tokyo, 1975.

Ion, Véronica. *Mythologie Indienne*. Paris, 1970.

————. *Mythologies du monde entier*. Paris, 1984.

Iyengar, T. R. Sesha. *Dravidian India*. New Delhi: Asian Educational Services, 1982.

Jadunath, Sinha. *Shakti Sadhana*. Calcutta, 1977.

Jaggi, O. P. *Scientists of ancient India and their acheivements*. Delhi: Atma Ram, 1966.

————. *Yogic and Tantric Medicine*. Delhi, 1973.

Jaideva, Singh. *Siva Sutras*. Delhi: Motilal Banarsidass, 1979.

————. *Vijnânabhairava*. Delhi: Motilal Banarsidass, 1979.

Jansen, Michael. *Die Indus-Zivilisation*. Köln, 1986.

Jayadeva. Gita Govinda, *Les amours de Krishna*. Paris, 1957.

Jelinek, Dr. Jan. *L'homme préhistorique*. Paris, 1975; also published as *Homo Erectus and His Time*. London: Collets, 1980.

Jha, Akhileshwar. *Sexual Designs in Indian Culture*. New Delhi: Vikas, 1981.

Jnanaprakasha. *Shivayogaratna* (tran. T. Michael). Pondicherry, 1975.

John, Bubba Free. *Love of the Two-Armed Form*. Lower Lake, CA: Dawn Horse, 1978.

Joshi, Ramchandra Vinayak. *Stone Age Cultures of Central India*. Poona: Deccan College, 1978.

Jung, C.G. *L'inconscient collectif*, text published in the *Cahiers de psychologie Jungienne*. Paris 1978, compiled by Lise Fourniol and Joan Clausse.

————. *Mandala Symbolism*. Princeton, NJ: Princeton University Press, 1973.

Kale, Arvind & Shanta. *Tantra: The Secret Power of Sex*. Bombay: Jaico, 1976.

Kalyanaraman, A. *Aryatarangini: The Saga of the Indo-Aryans*. Madras, 1961.

Karanjia, R. K. *Kundalini Yoga*. Delhi, 1977.

Kellman, Stanley. *Living your Dying*. New York, 1975.

Kessler, Herbert. *Das offenbare Geheimnis*. Freiburg, 1977.

Khanna Madha. *Yantra: The Tantric Symbol of Cosmic Unity*. London: Thames Hudson, 1979.

Khokar, Mohan. *Traditions of Indian Classical Dance*. New Delhi: Clarion Books, 1979.

King, Francis X. *Sexuality, Magic and Perversion*. London, 1971; New York: Citadel, 1972.

De Kleen, Tyra. *Mudras, Ritual Hand-Poses of the Buddha Priests and the Shiva Priests of Bali*. New York: Carol Publishing, 1970.

Kothari, Sunil. *Bharata Natyam*. Bombay: Oriental Book Dist., 1979.

Kramricseh, Stella. *Drâvida and Kerala in the Art of Travancore*. Ascona, 1961.

Kumar, Teg Bahadur. *Dhyâna Mandala*. Delhi: Shiksha Bharati, 1978.

Kumara, Swami. *The Mirror of Gesture*. New Delhi: Manoharlal, 1970.

Lal, Kanwar. *Kanya and the Yogi*. Delhi: Arts and Letters, 1970.

———. *The Religion of Love*. Delhi: Arts and Letters, 1971.

Landry, Dr. M. *Les déficiences sexuelles masculines et la frigidité*. Paris, 1966.

Lannoy, Richard. *The Eye of Love: Temple Sculpture of India*. London, 1963.

Le Bon, Gustave. *Psychologie des foules*. Paris, 1895 and 1947.

Lévy, V. *Les mystères du cerveau*. Moscow: Editions Mir, 1979.

L'Heureux, Christiane. *L'orgasme au féminin*. Montreal, 1979.

Lloyd, J. William. *Karezza Praxis*. Zielbrücke-Thielle, 1966; also published as *The Karezza Method*. New York: Revisionist Press, 1971.

Lommel, Hermann. *Les Anciens Aryens*. Paris, 1943.

Luk, Charles. *Taoist Yoga: Alchemy and Immortality*. London, 1970; York Beach, ME: Samuel Weiser, Inc., 1970.

Macdonnell, Arthur A. *A History of Sanscrit Literature*. Delhi, 1961; Philadelphia: Coronet, n.d.

MacKellar, J. *Le Viol*. Paris, 1975.

Madanjeet, Singh. *L'art de l'Himalaya*. New York: Unesco, 1968.

Maetcrlinck, Maurice. *La vie des abeilles*. Bruxelles, 1943.

Maillant, Dr. Charles. *Les aphrodisiaques.* Paris, 1969.

Mair, Lucy. *Le marriage.* Paris, 1971.

Manou, Lois de. *Manava-Dharma-Shastra.* (tran. by A. Loiseleur).

Marcadé, Jean. *Étrurie et Rome — L'art et l'amour.* Geneva, 1975.

Mariel, Pierre. *Sectes et Sexe.* Paris, 1978.

Markale, Jean. *Les femmes celtes.* Paris, 1972; also published as *Women of the Celts.* Rochester, VT: Inner Traditions International, 1986.

Marques-Rivere. *Le yoga tantrique hindou et thibétain.* Paris, 1939.

———. *Rituel de magie tantrique hindoue.* Paris, 1939.

Maspero, Henri. *Le Taoisme et les religions chinoises.* Paris, 1971.

Masters, W. H. & V. E. Johnson *Les réactins sexuelles.* Paris, 1966; also published as *Human Sexual Response.* New York: Bantam, 1981.

Maupertuis, Alexandre. *Masterpieces of the Female Form in Indian Art.* Bombay: Taraporavala, 1981.

———. *Le sexe et le plaisir avant le christianisme.* Paris, 1977.

Mehta, Rustam J. *Scientific Curiosities of Love-Life and Marriage.* Bombay, 1950.

Merton, Thomas. *Zen, Tao et Nirvana.* Paris, 1970.

Messing, Marcel. *Symboliek, Sleutel tot zelfkennis.* Amsterdam, 1977.

Michael, Tara. *Hatha-Yoga Pradîpikâ.* Paris, 1974.

Miles, Arthur. *Le Culte de Civa.* Paris, 1935.

Miller, David L. *Le nouveau polythéisme.* Paris, 1979.

Mookerjee, Ajit. *Kundalini: The Arousal of the Inner Energy.* Delhi, 1982; Rochester, VT: Destiny, 1983.

———. *Tantra Art.* New Delhi: Kumar Gallery, 1966.

———. *Tantra Asana.* New Delhi, Bale, 1971.

Mookerjee, Ajit & Anand, M. R. *Tantra Magic.* New Delhi: Heinemann, 1977.

Mookerjee, Ajit. & Khanna, M. *La voie du Tantra.* Paris, 1978. Also published as *The Tantric Way.* London: Thames Hudson, 1989.

Moor, E. *The Hindu Pantheon.* New Delhi: Asian Educational Services, 1981.

Mukerji, P. N. *Yoga Philosophy of Patanjali.* Calcutta, 1963.

Mukherjee, S. K. *The Science of Mantra Japa.* Puri, 1974.

Muktananda, Swami. *L'Epouse idéale, la Satî Gîtâ.* Paris, 1973.

———. *Nawa Yogînî Tantra.* Monghyr: Bihar School of Yoga, 1975.

————. *Chitshakti Vilas*. Pondicherry, 1974.

Muller, Max. *The Six Systems of Indian Philosophy*. London, 1928.

Mumford, Jonn. *Sexual Occultism*. St. Paul: Llewellyn, 1975.

Nagaswami, R. *Art & Culture of Tamil Nadu*. Delhi: Sundeep, 1980.

————. *Tantric Cult of South India*. Delhi: Agam Kala Prakashan, 1982.

Naglowska, Maria de. *Le rite sacré de l'amour magique*. Paris, 1932.

Nandimath, S. C. A *Handbook of Virasaivism*. Delhi: Motilal Banarsidass, 1979.

Nataraja, Guru. *The Word of the Guru*. Cochin, 1968.

Navijivan, Rastogi. *The Karma Tantricism of Kashmir*. Delhi, 1979.

Neumann, Erich. *The Great Mother*. Bollingen Series 47. Princeton, NJ: Princeton University Press, 1964.

O'Flaherty, Wendy D. *Siva: The Erotic Ascetic*. London: Oxford University Press, 1973.

Padoux, André. *Recherches sur la symbolique et l'energie de la parole*. Paris, 1967.

Panniker, Raimundo. *The Vedic Experience*. London, 1977; Wilmont, WI: Lotus Light Auromere, 1983.

Paramjyoti, V. *Saiva Siddhanta*. London, 1954.

Pastori, Jean-Pierre. *L'homme et la danse*. Freiburg, 1980.

Pathar, S. Veeraswamy. *Temple and its Significance*. Tiruchirapalli, 1974.

Pauwels, Louis. *Planète Magazine*. Paris, 1964.

Pilay, A. P. *The Art of Love and Sane Sex Living*. Bombay: Taraporevala, 1968.

Piotrovski, Boris. *Avant les Scythes, préhistoire de l'art en URSS*. Paris, 1979.

Possehl, Gregory L. *Indus Civilisation in Saurashtra*. New Delhi: B.R. Pub., 1980.

Prasad, Lalan (Singh). *Tantra, its Mystic and Scientific Basis*. Delhi: Concept Publishing, 1985.

Prasad, Rama. *Nature's Finer Forces*. Madras: Theosophical, 1947.

Prasad, Ramchandra. *Rajneesh: The Mystic of Feeling*. Delhi: Motilal Banarsidass, 1978.

Pratapaditya. *The Sensual Immortals*. Los Angeles, 1977.

Projesh, Banerjee. *Erotica in Indian Dance*. New Delhi: Cosmo, 1983.

Radhakrishnan, Sarvepalli. *History of Philosophy Eastern and Western*. London, 1967.

Rajan, K. V. *Indian Culture, Architecture, Art & Religion*. Delhi, 1981.

Rajmohon, Nath. *Rig-Veda Summary*. Shillong, 1966.

Rajneesh, Bhagwan Shree. *The Book of the Secrets*. Poona, 1976; Boulder, CO: Chidvilas, 1982.

———. *Returning to the Source*. Poona, 1976; Boulder, CO: Chidvilas, 1976.

Ram Kumar, Rai. *Encyclopedia of Yoga*. Varanasi, 1975.

———. *Mantra-Yoga Samhita*. Varanasi, 1976.

Rambach, Pierre. *Le Bouddha secret du tantrisme japonais*. Geneva, 1978.

Randolph, P. B. *Magia Sexualis*. Paris, 1931. Also published as *Sexual Magic*. New York: Magickal Childe, 1989.

Rao, S. K. Ramachandra. *Tantra, Mantra, Yantra*. New Delhi, Heinemann, 1979.

———. *Tibetan Tantrik Tradition*. New Delhi: Heinemann, 1977.

Rao, S. R. *Lothal and the Indus Civilization*. Bombay, Asia, 1973.

Rastogi, Navjivan. *The Karma Tantricism of Kashmir*. Delhi: Motilal Banarsidass, 1978.

Rawson, Phillip. *L'art érotique de l'Inde*. Paris, 1978.

———. *Tantra Art*. London, 1978. Also published as *Art of Tantra*. London: Thames Hudson, 1985.

———. *Tantra, le culte indien de l'extase*. Paris, 1973. Also published as *Tantra: The Indian Cult of Ecstasy*. London: Thames Hudson, 1984.

Rawson, Phillip and Legeza, and Laszlo. *Tao, la philosophie chinoise du temps et du changement*. Paris, 1965. Also published as *Tao: The Chinese Philosohy of Time and Change*. London: Thames Hudson, 1984.

Reich, Wilhelm. *La fonction de l'orgasme*. Paris, 1952: also published as *The Function of the Orgasm*. New York: Farrar, Straus & Giroux, 1986.

Renou, Louis. *Hymnes speculatifs du Véda*. Paris, 1956.

———. *L'Inde fondamentale*. Paris, 1978.

Rome, Lucienne and Jesus. *L'érotisme primitif*. Freiburg, 1982.

Rostand, Jean. *Ce que je crois*. Paris, 1953.

Salomon, Paule. *Les nouveaux aventuriers de l'esprit*. Paris, 1979.

Sankalla, H. D. *Prehistoric Art in India*. New Delhi: Vikas, 1978.

Sastri, Nilakanta. *A History of South India*. Calcutta, 1976.

Satyananda, Paramahamsa. *Prâna Vidya*. Sydney, 1976.

———. *Tantra Yoga Panorama*. Rajanandgaon, 1970.

Sayan, Lus de. *Magie des Sexus, Pan-Amrita-Toga*. Freiburg, 1966.

Schoterman, J. A. *The Yonitantra*. Delhi: Manoharlarl, 1980.

Schwenk, Theodore. *Das Sensible Chaos*. Germany: Verlag Freies Geistesleben, 1962.

Scott, George Ryley. *Phallic Worship in the World*. New Delhi: Ameriko Book Agency, 1975.

Serbranesco, Gérard. *Les Celtes et les Druides*. Paris, 1968.

Shankaranarayan. *Sri Chakra*. Pondicherry and Wilmont, WI: Lotus Light, 1970.

Sharma, Chandradhar. *A Critical Survey of Indian Philosophy*. Delhi, 1964; Livingston, NJ: Orient Book Dist., 1971.

Sharma, R. S. *Sûdras in Ancient India*. Delhi: Motilal Banarsidass, 1980.

Shastri, J. L. *Linga purana*. Delhi: Motilal Banarsidass, 1973.

Shendge, Malati J. *The Civilized Demons: The Harappans in Rigveda*. New Delhi: Abhinav, 1977.

Silber, Sherman J. *Understanding Male Sexuality*. London, 1983.

Silburn, Lilian. *Hymnes aux Kâlî*. Paris, 1975.

———. *Le Vijnana Bhaïrava*. Paris, 1976.

Sinha, A. K. *Science and Tantra Yoga*. Kurukshetra, 1981.

Sivara, Mamurti. *L'Arte en Inde*. Paris, 1974.

Slater, Gilbert. *The Dravidian Element in Indian Culture*. New Delhi: Manoharlarl, 1986.

Snellgrove, D. L. *The Hevajra Tantra*. London: Oxford University Press, 1959.

Sparks, John. *La Vie amoureuse et érotique des animaux*. Paris, 1979.

Srinivasa Bhatta. *Hatharatnavali*. Secunderabad: Vemana Yoga Institute, 1982.

Starhawk. *The Spiral Dance*. New York: HarperCollins, 1979, 1989.

Story, Francis. *Rebirth as Doctrine and Experience*. Kandy: Buddhist Publication Society, 1975.

Stutley, Margaret and James. *A Dictionary of Hinduism*. London, Aquarian, 1977.

———. *Ancient Indian Magic and Folklore*. Delhi, 1980.

Suarès, Carlo. *Le cantique des cantiques selon la Cabbale*. Geneva, 1969.

Subramanian, V. K. *Saundaryalahiri of Sankaracharya*. Delhi: Motilal Banarsidass, 1977.

Sundara, Dr. A. *The Early Chamber Tombs of South India*. Delhi: 1975.

Svatmarama, Swami. *Hatha-Yoga-Pradîpikâ*. Madras, 1933; New York: AMS Press, n.d.

Tart, Charles T. *Altered States of Consciousness*. San Francisco: Harper San Francisco, 1990.

Taylor, Gordon R. *The Great Evolution Mystery*. London, 1983.

Thieuloy, Jack. *L'Inde des grands chemins*. Paris, 1971.

Thirleby, Ashley. *Das Tantra der Liebe*. Scherz, 1979.

Thomas, Louis-Vincent. *Mort et Pouvoir*. Paris, 1978.

Thomas, P. *Epics, Myths and Legends of India*. Bombay: Taraporevala, 1980.

Tsong-Ka-Pa. *Tantra in Tibet*. London, 1977; New York: State Mutual Books, 1977.

Tucci, Guiseppe. *The Theory and Practice of the Mandala*. London: Unwin Hyman, 1961.

Upadhaya, S. C. *Kama Sutra of Vatsyayana*. Bombay: Taraporevala, 1990.

Urban, Dr. Rudolf von. *La perfection sexuelle*. Paris, 1960.

Ushte, Tahca and Erdoes, Richard. *De mémoire indienne*. Paris, 1977.

Vajpeyi, Kailash. *The Science of Mantras*. New Delhi: Heinemann, 1979.

Van der Veer & Moerman. *Nieuwe sporen naar het verleden*. Deventer, 1972.

Van Gulik, Robert. *Sexual Life in Ancient China*. Leiden, 1961.

Varenne, Jean. *Le Tantrisme*. Paris, 1977.

Velde, Th. van de. *Le Mariage parfait*. Bruxelles, 1930.

Venkata Reddy (trans.) *Hatharatnavali*. Arthamuru, India, 1982.

Verrier, Elwin. *Une vie tribale*. Paris, 1973.

Vidyarti, L. P. & B. K. Rai. *The Tribal Culture of India*. New Delhi: Concept, 1976.

Wakankar, Vishnu S. & Robert R. R. Brooks. *Stone Age Painting in India*. Bombay, 1976.

Watts, Alan. *Amour et connaissance*. Paris, 1966.

———. *Nature, Man, and Woman*. New York: Pantheon, 1958.

———. *The Temple of Konarak*. Delhi, 1957.

Watts, Alan & Liang-Huang Al Chung. *Tao: The Watercourse Way*. New York: Pantheon, 1975.

Wayman, Alex. *The Buddhist Tantras*. York Beach, ME: Samuel Weiser, 1973; Delhi: Motilal Banarsidass, 1990.

———. *Yoga of the Guhyasamajatantra*. Delhi: Motilal Banarsidass, 1977.

Werner, Karel. *Yoga & Indian Philosophy*. Delhi: Motilaa Banarsidass, 1977.

Wheeler, Sir Mortimer. *The Indus Civilization*. Cambridge, 1968.

Wilkins, W. J. *Hindu Mythology: Vedic and Puranic*. Varanasi, 1972; Flushing, NY: Asia Book Corp., 1989.

Windengren, G. *Les religions de l'Iran*. Paris, 1968.

Wosien, Maria-Gabriele. *La danse sacrée*. Paris, 1974; also published as *The Sacred Dance*. London: Thames Hudson, 1986.

Yocum, Glenn E. *Hymns to the Dancing Siva*. Delhi: South Asia Books, 1982.

Zabern, Philippe von. *Vergessene Städte am Indus*. Mainz am Rhein, 1987.

Zahner, R. C. *Hindu Scriptures*. London, 1968.

Zimmer, Hienrich. *Myths & Symbols in Indian Art & Civilization*. Bollingen Series, Vol. 6. Princeton, NJ: Princeton University Press, 1971.

———. *Les philosophies de l'Inde*. Paris, 1953; Also published as *The Philosophies of India*. Bollingen Series, Vol. 29. Edited by Jos. Campbell. Princeton, NJ: Princeton University Press, 1969.

Index